The Galaxy's Greatest

STAR WARS ®

collectibles price guide
1999 edition

The Galaxy's Greatest
STAR WARS ®
collectibles price guide
1999 edition

by Stuart W. Wells III

ANTIQUE TRADER BOOKS
A Division of Landmark Specialty Publications
Norfolk, Virginia

ISBN: 0–930625–97–8

Library of Congress Card Catalog Number: 98-71064

Written, photographed, and designed by Stuart W. Wells III

Editor:	Tony Lillis
Copy Editor:	Sandra Holcombe
Design Coordinator and Cover Design:	Chris Decker

Printed in the United States of America

To order additional copies of this book, or to obtain a free catalog, please contact:

Antique Trader Books
P.O. Box 1050
Dubuque, Iowa 52004

or call 1-800-334-7165

CONTENTS

ACKNOWLEDGMENTS

A number of avid Star Wars collectors were kind enough to let me photograph their collections. Thanks especially to: Rob Rintoul, Rob Johnson, Wats Wacker, Morgan McClain and Harry Rinker Jr. Thanks also to Chris Decker for supplying the items for the cover, and to Sam Pagano for letting me photograph his sticker books.

Many manufacturers of Star Wars items supplied information, catalogs or photographs. Thanks to: Don Post Studios, Alan Payne at Icons, Don Schmidt at Tiger Electronics, Tracy at Illusive Originals, Chaz Fitzhugh at Applause, Jim Schneider at Star Jars, Joshua Izzo at Topps, and Matt Mariani at Decipher, Inc. Thanks also to Kenner, Galoob, JusToys for all the trips through their showrooms during Toyfair for many years.

Several local retailers were kind enough to let me photograph inventory in their stores. Thanks to:

Todd Testa and Larry Russo at Castle Comics, Milford, Conn.
    (Comics, Toys, Model Kits and Statues) (203) 877-3610, Website: www.castlecomics.com

David Kruseski and Steven Bryant at Heroes Comics & Cards, Norwalk, Conn.
    (Comics and CCGs) (203) 750-0505

Jeff Kubarych at Route 7 Comics & Collectibles, Ridgefield, Conn.
    (Comics, Action Figures and Star Wars collectibles) (203) 894-1499

Rich Casiglio, Jack Simon and John Stambraugh at Area 51 Comics, Trumbull Mall, Trumbull, Conn.
    (Comics and Magazines) (203) 371-6197, Email: Area51cmx@aol.com

THIS BOOK COVERS

Star Wars Collectibles
Made Between 1976 and 1998

This book covers *Star Wars* collectibles from their beginning in 1976, through the end of May 1998, with additional information on forthcoming items for the rest of 1998. This covers from the very beginning of the first, or classic age of *Star Wars*, to just about the end of the second age of *Star Wars* collectibles, perhaps destined to be known someday as the "Silver Age." Many manufacturers have slowed or completely stopped the introduction of new *Star Wars* collectibles based on the original trilogy while they save their creative energy, and budgets, for the veritable flood of items beginning in 1999 based on the new movies. Collectors hope that this new era will be a new "Golden Age," but that can't happen unless the new movies are at least as good as the original trilogy.

Distribution in the United States

This book covers *Star Wars* collectibles distributed in the United States. While just about every foreign item makes its way to a few collectors in the United States, the only items listed here are ones which were distributed in enough quantity to be generally available. The most significant of these are the "Tri-Logo" action figures. These figures came on header cards with logos for *"Return of the Jedi"* in three languages (thus the name) and were intended for foreign markets. However, they were widely distributed in the United States as the *Star Wars* phenomenon was winding down in 1984–86. A few foreign figures, such as the Power of the Force Yak Face, are listed for completeness. Although never distributed in the United States, it is a necessary and expensive figure for collectors who want to complete their collections. Other figures on foreign header cards are worth less than their U. S. counterparts, and are more likely to be bought by a collector as a temporary measure, until the more desirable American figure can be acquired. A more recent example is the Pizza Hut PVC figures which came out as in-store premiums in 1995 in Australia, but were distributed in quantity to comic shops in the United States in 1997, in sets of four.

Categories

The book is divided into sections based on the categories which collectors most frequently use in organizing their collections. The amount of coverage given to any category depends on its popularity. Action figures are the most popular *Star Wars* collectible and so they are given the most coverage — 64 pages, with additional sections on the vehicles, accessories, and the 12 inch dolls. Actually, many of the less popular categories could just as well have been grouped in a section called "Other Stuff," because that is how most collectors view the items. However, this would have made it hard to use the book.

Grading

Most *Star Wars* items are graded on a 10-point scale from C-10 (the best) down to C-1. Hardly anything old qualifies as a C-10 and nobody admits that anything they are trying to sell is a C-1, so the actual number of categories is probably less than 10. Prices in this book are for items in their original packaging in "near mint" condition, which corresponds to about C-9 or C-9.5. The occasional extraordinary item that is actually "mint" (i.e. C-10) commands a slightly higher price. How much higher depends on how much better than an ordinary near mint copy it actually is. Mint means the same thing, regardless of age and type of product. It is not the same thing as "new." Many, probably most, new action figure header cards are not mint. They have been handled when they were put in the shipping box, taken out of the box and hung on a rack, maybe dropped on the floor, handled by the checkout clerk, etc. This leaves an item which is a defect-free collectible acceptable anywhere at the near-mint price. The figure inside is most likely mint, but rarely the package. "Near mint" does vary somewhat with the type of product. Some kinds of things are simply more durable than others and do not normally show any wear from normal handling. For those things, there is very little difference between the ordinary, (i.e. near mint) and the extraordinary, (i.e. mint) and probably very little difference in price.

Prices

A single price is given for each listed item. This represents the full retail price or asking price. Prices vary from one dealer to another and from one location to another, so prices may actually fall into a range. But even though no single price can be perfect for all situations, a price range of, for example, $40 to $100 is no more meaningful than a single price, and even less satisfying. The single price given in this book should be used as a guideline or baseline. If you can find the item that you want to buy for 10% to 25% less than this price, you are getting a good deal. If you are paying more, but you really want the item, that's okay too. Just shop around a little first to see if you can do better.

This book is based on the author's research. The author is not a dealer in *Star Wars* collectibles and not associated with any dealer or manufacturer nor with Lucasfilms or any of its licensees.

INTRODUCTION

The *Star Wars* Phenomenon

The *Star Wars* phenomenon started in 1977, and, after a little slump in the late 1980s, it is still going strong, fueled by great expectations for the new movie scheduled for summer 1999. Collectibles from the original movie were available beginning in late 1976 — first a poster and a book, then the comics in early 1977, and finally, after the movie opened, a few games and puzzles. The real flood didn't start until 1978 when the action figures actually arrived.

It's tempting to say that everybody was "asleep at the switch" or almost "missed the boat," or some other similar euphemism, but the truth is that before *Star Wars* came along there was no boat to miss nor any switch to throw.

A movie, then and now, doesn't stay in the theaters long enough to support a toy line all by itself unless the movie is incredibly successful. A lot of huge movies, which everyone thought could support action figure toy lines, have come out in the 1990s, and most have been duds. TV shows and comic books do a much better job because the support continues over months or years. Before *Star Wars* came along, no new movie had ever been made into a successful toy line. The closest the toy industry had ever come was the *Planet of the Apes* action figures made by Mego. However, these were based on a series of five movies, plus a TV show.

Before *Star Wars,* action figures (really dolls) were either 8" or 12" tall, but Kenner made their figures 3¾" tall so that they could fit in vehicles of a reasonable size. The idea was so successful that most action figures became small and most action movies had action figure lines thereafter. It took the toy industry almost a decade to grow action figures back up to 5" to 6" tall, the current standard, and almost two decades to bring out any significant number of new 8" to 12" action dolls for boys. And, in a sense, the toy industry has never recovered from basing action figures on the summer's hot new movie.

What Might Have Been

In *Star Wars* collecting, Kenner is King. Almost anything made by Kenner is collected more intensely than anything, however attractive, made by anyone else. Was this inevitable? It didn't seem to be so at the time.

The first *Star Wars* collectible available to the general public was the original paperback book. I call it "*Star Wars* collectible #1." There was also a poster, which was available at the San Diego Comics Convention, held earlier that fall, but it was available only at the convention. The book appeared in November 1976, a full 7 months before the movie opened, and it was available at bookstores everywhere. Later book editions had a different cover and can easily be distinguished by the date on the copyright page. Unlike some of the most valuable action figures, the original paperback cannot be faked. Nevertheless, this paperback is not as valuable as any of the early action figures. A hardcover version of the book which came out in the fall is worth a lot more.

"*Star Wars* collectible #2" are the first issues of the comic book series from Marvel. They're worth a lot more than the paperback book, and the 35¢ test issue of this comic is more valuable than many of the early action figures. A couple of issues of the comic came out before the movie opened. Other pre-opening collectibles include articles in movie magazines about the forthcoming movie. The week the movie opened, *Time* magazine ran a two page spread calling it the best movie of the year. Then there are ticket stubs to the movie. Stubs from opening day would be the most valuable, with stubs from the first anniversary being a strong contender.

Movie photos, autographed by the stars, could be prime collectibles. Other significant movie anniversary events also yielded some items to collect. After the movie was finally out of the theaters, Lucas and company sent a high quality studio copy of the film to Noreascon II, the 1980 World Science Fiction convention in Boston, for a free showing. The movie was accompanied by the world premiere of *The Making of The Empire Strikes Back*. There is sure to have been something to collect at the convention. (I was there collecting autographs in the science fiction books from my collection.)

Star Wars opened May 25, 1977. By November 19 it was the largest grossing picture of all time, doing $200 million domestic and $400 million worldwide. It received a special Hugo award in 1977 at the World Science Fiction Convention. *The Empire Strikes Back* grossed $23 million in the first 3 weeks.

These were huge numbers for pictures that cost $10 million to $20 million to make, not $100 million to $200 million like today.

Ten-year-olds were not the only people who saw the movie 10 times in the theater. A lot of older kids and adults did too. Fans and potential collectors who liked movies of this type were the people who read the cinema magazines about forthcoming science fiction, fantasy, horror and action pictures.

They were more likely to read the comics and the books and less likely to play with action figures. These were the people Lucas was thanking when he sent the movie to the World Science Fiction Convention, a convention primarily of authors and book readers, who also happen to like science fiction movies.

During all of this, *Locus*, the "Newspaper of the Science Fiction Field" had a *Star Wars* picture on its first page exactly one time. The movie was mentioned from time to time. Once was to report that Leigh Brackett, a respected science fiction writer, would do the screenplay for the sequel, and another time was to indicate that the success of *Star Wars* had convinced Paramount that they shouldn't do a *Star Trek* movie.

Fans had been begging Paramount to make a *Star Trek* for years, but they didn't figure there was any money in it. Now they concluded that George Lucas had captured all the money, so there still wouldn't be any money in it. Of course, they eventually did make one, but talk about being "clueless!" I estimate that they could have had about a billion dollars in revenue if they had made a *Star Trek* movie every couple of years in the 1970s, with a budget and schedule similar to the James Bond movies. On the other hand, they probably would have farmed the project out to someone who would have destroyed the entire *Star Trek* franchise by the mid 1970s. With all this on their minds, perhaps it's not surprising that science fiction fans didn't become today's *Star Wars* collectors.

Many of today's *Star Wars* collectors were kids filled with wonder when they first saw the movie. They saw the movie 10 times in the theater and now they are grown up, have some money and want to collect the neat toys that they played with in their youth. Even these fans might have collected the comic books and the earliest toys, by Kenner and others, who hastily scrambled to get licenses. Many of these items came out before the first action figures, which did not appear until 1978. Nevertheless, it's the action figures that everyone

collects and that have the highest prices. Every tiny variation in the figures is noticed, found, analyzed, evaluated and collected.

Prices of most other *Star Wars* items are fairly reasonable, especially by comparison to the action figures. This has little to do with scarcity. Millions of action figures were produced, while only tens of thousands of most other items were ever made. When many other classic *Star Wars* collectibles were completely gone, action figures, especially those from the *Return of the Jedi*, were still available.

What Happens to *Star Wars* Things?

Did you ever wonder what happens to leftover *Star Wars* stuff after the stores can't sell it anymore? You probably assumed that the stores just leave it hanging around until the last one is sold and then they are all gone. This may even be true for the items that have been unpacked from their boxes. But what about the boxes still in the storeroom, not to mention the ones back in some warehouse somewhere?

What stuff? Unsold action figures, and toys of all kinds; leftover fast food and other promotional figures. Just about everything yields leftovers.

Excess stuff back at the factory can be repackaged for overseas. The Orient is a great place for this, because that is where a lot of the factories are. In the case of *Star Wars*, some excess action figures became the cheap (then, not now) three packs.

One place excess stuff goes is KayBee. KayBee Toys has made a business of buying the tail-end of action figure series and selling them at discount. They have only been doing this for the last few years, so the original *Star Wars* merchandise didn't get there and the new stuff hasn't had a chance to get there yet.

Second, there are surplus dealers who buy up toys at pennies on the dollar and sell them to variety stores and other surplus merchandise outlets. You can get extraordinary bargains at these stores, but it all depends on what happens to show up.

One other place merchandise can show up is a lot closer to home — your local comic shop. Enterprising dealers who have acquired enough warehouse stock can sell it to comic shops through Diamond Distribution Company, by offering it in *Previews Magazine*. In the early and mid 1990s, leftover Mego figures such as the 8" Kirk, Spock and the Klingon *Star Trek* figures, and the 12" Batman, Spider-Man and Wonder Woman figures were advertised periodically. The price reflected the collector market, so no shop bought a huge supply, but these figures were still available, in the original package.

Quite a number of leftover *Star Wars* figures were also advertised in *Previews Magazine* in the early 1990s. Most were on *Return of the Jedi* header cards, which is hardly surprising, but a few were even from *The Empire Strikes Back*. Typically, the figures carried a $15.00 retail price tag and the comic shop would have paid about $9.00 to $10.00.

While writing this book, I looked through most of the back issues of *Previews Magazine,* starting in 1991. I found all of the following action figures listed for sale on the original header cards. I have only listed the ones which had their first appearance in the *Return of the Jedi* series (and Lobot from *The Empire Strikes Back).* There were also a number of reissue figures offered.

In addition, there were assorted Droids figures and assorted Ewoks figures, including Dulok Scout, Urgah Lady Gorneesh, Dulok Shaman and King Gorneesh. You could also buy a group of ten 1" metal, hand-painted micro figures from 1983 for $30.00.

What does this all mean? For one thing, if you are operating on the assumption that all of the action figures, vehicles and other items being sold by dealers are from private collections and that there can't be too many of them around, you might be mistaken. There was enough leftover stock from 1983 and 1984 for it to

be distributed in quantity to comic shops just a few years ago. That's probably why the prices are still somewhat reasonable for many of these figures.

What to Look For

There haven't been too many *Star Wars* red tag specials for the new toys so far, but keep in mind how much merchandise Kenner is making today. Someday there will be a lot of it sitting around in a warehouse. That day may not be too far off, either. You may not care if the classic characters are still being sold, but most toy stores are going to want action figures, vehicles and everything else from the new movie on their shelves, starting in early 1999. This could easily mean that a lot of the current merchandise will be available at bargain prices starting after Christmas 1998, and possibly for some years after that. If the new movie is as big a hit as the previous movies, new toys will fill the action figure aisles and the current crop will be shoved into the bargain bins. If the new movie is a dud, both new and current toys will be in the bargain bins.

There won't be as many collector dollars chasing these leftover figures either. Most collectors will be pushing the kids aside to grab the week's hot new item off the toy store shelves, just as they usually do.

Savvy collectors will be looking in the bargain bins for vehicles and ships, both common and deluxe action figures, carry cases, and role play weapons. Deluxe creatures, 12" dolls and store exclusives shouldn't last long enough to get there, but you never know.

Partial Checklist	
Admiral Ackbar	$15.00
Bib Fortuna	15.00
Biker Scout	15.00
C-3PO, removable arms and legs	30.00
bagged (*still available in 1997!*)	10.00
Chief Chirpa	15.00
Emperor's Royal Guard	15.00
General Madine	15.00
Klaatu	15.00
Lando Calrissian, Skiff Guard	20.00
Lobot (*The Empire Strikes Back*)	18.00
Logray	15.00
Nikto	15.00
Nien Nunb	15.00
Rancor Keeper	15.00
R2-D2 with pop-up sensorscope	30.00
Ree-Yees	15.00
Squid Head	15.00
Weequay	15.00
Many reissue figures, each	15.00

Classic Star Wars *figures distributed to comic shops in the early '90s*

ACTION FIGURES
CHRONOLOGICAL

ACTION FIGURES: CHRONOLOGICAL

STAR WARS (ORIGINAL)
Kenner (1977–1986)

Time magazine picked *Star Wars* as the best picture of the year in a two-page feature when it opened in early summer 1977 (*Time*, May 30, 1977). It played to packed houses for about a year, but it has been off the big screen since 1980. The special edition, with added scenes and improved special effects, opened on January 31, 1997, and the other two films followed a few weeks later.

All *Star Wars* action figure prices are volatile and generally increasing. This will almost certainly continue with the forthcoming release of another movie in the series.

The very first *Star Wars* action figures arrived in 1978, in the mail. Of course, they only did so if you bought the famous Early Bird Package. The figures came in a white plastic tray in a white mailer box. There were four figures — R2-D2, Luke Skywalker, Princess Leia and Chewbacca — all individually bagged, along with a bag of plastic pegs for the display stand which was included in the Early Bird Package. Already there were variations. In the very earliest packages, Chewbacca has a dark green plastic rifle instead of the later black plastic and Luke has a telescoping lightsaber. Some people call it a double telescoping lightsaber, but I call it a telescoping lightsaber. Umhummm. Anyway, it not only extends out of his arm, it telescopes out of the middle of the blade and almost reaches the floor. This version lightsaber can occasionally be found on carded Luke Skywalker and sometimes even on Darth Vader and Ben (Obi-Wan) Kenobi

Early Bird Certificate Package, front (Kenner 1977)

figures. It adds about $1,000 to the value of the Luke Skywalker figure and $2,000 to the value of the other two! It also increases the value of the loose figure, but it can be faked, even on a carded figure. For that kind of money, anything can be faked, and some experts believe that there are more fakes on the market than genuine items.

Early Bird "Figures" (Early 1978)
Early Bird figures R2-D2, Luke Skywalker (telescoping lightsaber, Princess Leia and Chewbacca (green blaster rifle), in tray and box $500.00
See under Carry Cases and Display Stands for listing of the Early Bird Package.

Packaging Variations — Header Cards

Star Wars action figures are heavily collected, both on their original header cards and loose. Every tiny variation in the figure or the packaging makes a difference in the price and *Star Wars* figures have many of both kinds of variations. The chief variation comes about because Kenner continued to produce the original figures for many years, but changed the movie logo to "*The Empire Strikes Back*" and then to "*Return of the Jedi*" as each of those new movies premiered. After the movies, figures were issued on *Power of the Force* header cards with a collectible coin as a premium.

In addition, most of the figures were available in the United States on foreign "Tri-Logo" header cards which had *Return of the Jedi* movie logos in three languages. There are variations among Tri-Logo header cards as well, but all are lumped together for pricing purposes. This means that there are four or five different packages for most figures, before you even consider the normal variations that occur in any action figure line, such as hair color or other changes to the figure and photo or text changes to the card.

Packaging Variations — Card Backs

The most significant of the header card changes involves the first group of figures to be produced, which includes all of the major characters. The cards for these figures have a picture and list on the back which shows just the original 12 figures. Consequently, these figures are called 12-backs and command the highest prices, as befits the earliest figures. Nine of the figures were released in the initial assortment and the other three — Death Squad Commander, Jawa and Sand People — were added fairly quickly. All these figures appeared on 12-back cards. Original figures on 12-back cards are scarce and desirable, so they are worth a lot more money — $75.00 to $100.00 more at current prices.

The second figure release added eight new figures and the card back was changed to reflect this, becoming 20-backs. The original 12 figures also appeared on these cards. After all, Kenner wanted you to buy all 20! The earliest of these cards are lacking the Boba Fett mail-in offer, while later issues contain the offer.

The 21st figure was the regular Boba-Fett figure and it got a 21-back card. Most collectors treat 20 and 21-back figures as part of the same series, without distinction or price difference. They are listed as 20/21-backs in this book.

The first of *The Empire Strikes Back* figures appeared on 31-back cards, but the earlier 21 figures were re-released on 21-back cards with *The Empire Strikes Back* logo. There are also figures on so-called 32-backs which are 12-back cards with a sticker listing the other 20 figures. When 10 more figures were added in the second release, the cards were changed to 41-backs.

Six more figures were added in the third *The Empire Strikes Back* release, but R2-D2 with Sensorscope and C-3PO with removable limbs replace the earlier versions of these figures and consequently all of them were released on 45-backs. 47-back cards came later, when two of the final figures (TIE Fighter Pilot and Zuckuss) of the third release were added. The very last figure was 4-LOM, making 48-back cards. Zuckuss actually appeared on this card, and not on the 47-back card which first listed him.

The pattern continued with the *Return of the Jedi*. The first use of this logo was on 48-backs, but prior to that, some 48-back cards contained a *Revenge of the Jedi* offer. These later cards command a premium, as does anything that mentions this title.

New *Return of the Jedi* figures appeared first on 65-back cards. With the second figure release came 77-backs and finally, with the addition of Lumat and Paploo, 79-backs.

Power of the Force figures only come on 92-back cards, but they do come with coins. *Droids* and *Ewoks* figures had their own cards, one per series and only the A-Wing pilot and Boba Fett figure crossed over. Otherwise they have their own group of cartooney looking figures.

Collectors, however, had Tri-Logo cards to worry about. There are a lot of variations in these cards; so many that collectors just ignore them. All tri-logo cards for a given figure sell for the same price, subject, of course, to condition.

Within each group of 12-backs, 20-backs, etc., there are variations. There are two slightly different 12-backs, eight different 20-backs, and two or more versions of most of the others, for a total of 45 different U.S. header cards.

Figure Variations

The most significant of the figure variations was with the Jawa, where the original version had a vinyl cape. This was quickly changed to cloth, which was used for all the rest of the figures. The few vinyl-caped Jawas are the most valuable of all the *Star Wars* figures and currently sell in the $1,500.00 range, with loose figures going for $250.00 to $300.00. Care in buying is essential, because a loose Jawa in cloth cape is only worth $15.00 and a fake vinyl cape is not hard to make.

All of the figures are listed below in the chronological order in which the various batches or groups were released. This is a shortened list, with variations only briefly noted. A much more detailed list of the figures, in alphabetical order and with all variations described, is given in a subsequent section of this book. Prices in each section are the same. The purpose of this chronological list is to allow you to compare the value of a given figure with the values of all the others that appeared in the same series. The alphabetical list lets you compare a figures value with all other versions of the same figure.

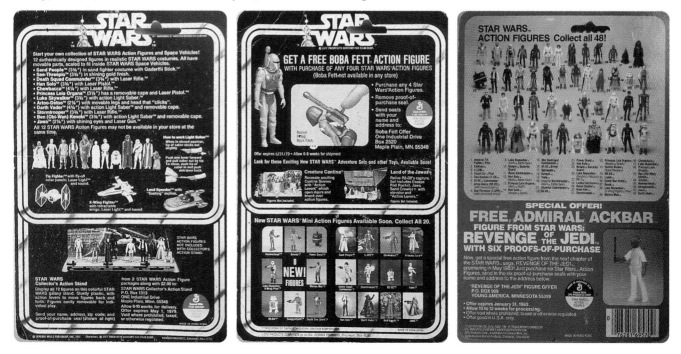

Package Backs: 12-Back; 20-Back with Boba Fett offer; 48-Back with Revenge of the Jedi figure offer (Kenner 1978–82)

STAR WARS SERIES
Kenner (1978–79)

First series, 12-back cards (1978)
Artoo-Detoo (R2-D2) (#38200)	$150.00
Ben (Obi-Wan) Kenobi (#38250) **gray hair**	225.00
Ben (Obi-Wan) Kenobi (#38250) **white hair**	225.00
Chewbacca (#38210) **black blaster rifle**	200.00
Chewbacca (#38210) **green blaster rifle**	225.00
Darth Vader (#38230)	200.00
Death Squad Commander (#38290)	200.00
Han Solo (#38260) **large head**, dark brown hair . . .	575.00
Han Solo (#38260)**small head**, brown hair	500.00
Jawa (#38270) **vinyl cape**.	2,500.00
Jawa (#38270) **cloth cape**	200.00
Luke Skywalker (#38180) **blond hair**	325.00
Princess Leia Organa (#38190).	300.00
Sand People (#38280)	225.00
See-Threepio (C-3PO) (#38220).	150.00
Stormtrooper (#38240)	225.00

Second Series, New Figures on 20/21-back cards
Boba Fett (#39250).	850.00
Death Star Droid (#39080)	150.00
Greedo (#39020)	150.00
Hammerhead (#39030)	130.00
Luke Skywalker X-Wing Pilot (#39060)	150.00
Power Droid (#39090).	135.00
R5-D4 (#39070)	135.00
Snaggletooth (#39040) **red**	125.00
Walrus Man (#39050)	135.00

Reissue Figures on 20/21-back cards
Artoo-Detoo (R2-D2) (#38200)	100.00
Ben (Obi-Wan) Kenobi (#38250) **gray hair**	125.00
Ben (Obi-Wan) Kenobi (#38250) **white hair**	125.00
Chewbacca (#38210)	100.00
Darth Vader (#38230)	100.00
Death Squad Commander (#38290)	100.00
Han Solo (#38260) **large head**, dark brown hair	400.00
Han Solo (#38260) **small head**, brown hair.	400.00
Jawa (#38270) **cloth cape**	90.00
Luke Skywalker (#38180) **blond hair**	250.00
Princess Leia Organa (#38190).	250.00
Sand People (#38280)	150.00
See-Threepio (C-3PO) (#38220)	100.00
Stormtrooper (#38240)	150.00

THE EMPIRE STRIKES BACK

In the second movie of the series we learn the secret of Luke's parentage and meet Yoda, played by a puppet, and Lando Calrissian played by Billy Dee Williams. There are lots of new figures. Luke looses his hand, C-3PO gets chopped into pieces, Han Solo gets to cool off on the way to Jabba's palace and Lando gets his ship and favorite Wookiee back. Not to worry, though, because before the movie is over Luke gets a new hand, C-3PO gets put back together and Lando turns out to be a good guy and not a traitor.

Lots of neat figures and vehicles got produced. They are cheap by the standards of the first series, but valuable by any other standard.

Star Wars Series Figures: Chewbacca and Stormtrooper (Kenner 1978)

THE EMPIRE STRIKES BACK SERIES
Kenner (1980–82)

Third Series, New Figures (1980)
Bespin Security Guard (#39810) **white** $65.00
Bossk (Bounty Hunter) (#39760) 100.00
FX-7 (Medical Droid) (#39730) 50.00
Han Solo (Hoth Outfit) (#39790) 75.00
IG-88 (Bounty Hunter) (#39770) 95.00
Imperial Stormtrooper (Hoth Battle Gear) (#39740) . . . 60.00
Lando Calrissian (#39800) **no teeth** 60.00
Lando Calrissian (#39800) **white teeth** 65.00
Leia Organa (Bespin Gown) (#39720) **crew neck** . . . 175.00
Leia Organa (Bespin Gown) (#39720) **crew neck,
    new package** 150.00
Leia Organa (Bespin Gown) (#39720) **turtle neck** . . 175.00
Leia Organa (Bespin Gown) (#39720) **turtle neck,
    new package** 150.00
Luke Skywalker (Bespin Fatigues) (#39780) 185.00
Luke Skywalker (Bespin) (#39780) new package . . . 145.00
Rebel Soldier (Hoth Battle Gear) (#39750) 50.00

Fourth Series, New Figures (1981)
AT-AT Driver (#39379) 50.00
Dengar (#39329) 50.00
Han Solo (Bespin Outfit) (#39339) 125.00
Imperial Commander (#39389) 45.00
Leia Organa (Hoth Outfit) (#39359) 125.00
Lobot (#39349) 45.00
Rebel Commander (#39369) 40.00
2-1B (#39399) 50.00
Ugnaught (#39319) blue smock 45.00
Yoda (#38310) **brown snake** 90.00

Yoda (#38310) **orange snake** 75.00
Fifth Series, New Figures (1982)
Artoo-Detoo (R2-D2) (with Sensorscope) (#69590) . . 50.00
AT-AT Commander (#69620) 40.00
Bespin Security Guard (#69640) **black** 50.00
Cloud Car Pilot (Twin Pod) (#69630) 60.00
C-3PO (Removable Limbs) (#69600) 60.00
4-LOM (#70010) 150.00
Imperial TIE Fighter Pilot (#70030) 100.00
Luke Skywalker (Hoth Battle Gear) (#69610) 75.00
Zuckuss (#70020) 75.00

Reissue Figures on The Empire Strikes Back header cards
Artoo-Detoo (R2-D2) (#38200) 50.00
Ben (Obi-Wan) Kenobi (#38250) **gray hair** 90.00
Ben (Obi-Wan) Kenobi (#38250) **white hair** 90.00
Boba Fett (#39250) 275.00
Chewbacca (#38210) 85.00
Darth Vader (#38230) 75.00
Death Star Droid (#39080) 130.00
Greedo (#39020) 125.00
Hammerhead (#39030) 115.00
Han Solo (#38260) **large head**, dark brown hair 250.00
Han Solo (#38260) **small head**, brown hair 300.00
Jawa (#38270) **cloth cape** 75.00
Luke Skywalker (#38180) **blond hair** 200.00
Luke Skywalker (#38180) **brown hair** 225.00
Luke Skywalker (X-Wing Pilot) (#39060) 115.00
Power Droid (#39090) 125.00
Princess Leia Organa (#38190) 295.00
R5-D4 (#39070) 125.00
Sandpeople (#38280) 125.00
See-Threepio (C-3PO) (#38220) 60.00

The Empire Strikes Back Series Figures: Greedo and Lando Calrissian (Kenner 1980)

Snaggletooth (#39040) **red**	100.00
Star Destroyer Commander (#38290)	100.00
Stormtrooper (#38240)	80.00
Walrus Man (#39050)	125.00

RETURN OF THE JEDI

The third movie in the series had the distinct advantage of being able to tie up all the loose ends and have the Rebels win. Solo is rescued, Jabba gets his just deserts, the new, improved, even bigger Death Star is blown up and the Ewoks steal the show. Everybody went home happy.

Collectors were happy too, with plenty of figures and vehicles to collect. They were even happier a couple of years later when the series had finally run its course with kids and the figures finally became red tag specials. Super Powers figures were red tag specials around the same time. You just couldn't go wrong, no matter what you bought.

There were a lot of *Return of the Jedi* figures produced and a number of them, particularly figures from the sixth series, were still available wholesale to comic shops and similar outlets in the early 1990s.

RETURN OF THE JEDI SERIES
Kenner (1983–84)

Sixth Series, New Figures (1983)

Admiral Ackbar (#70310).	$30.00
Bib Fortuna (#70790)	30.00

Biker Scout (#70820)	35.00
Chief Chirpa (#70690).	30.00
Emperor's Royal Guard (#70680)	40.00
Gamorrean Guard (#70670)	25.00
General Madine (#70780)	30.00
Klaatu (#70730) **tan arms** or **gray arms**	30.00
Lando Calrissian (Skiff Guard) (#70830)	45.00
Logray (Ewok Medicine Man) (#70710)	30.00
Luke Skywalker (Jedi Knight) (#70650) with **green** lightsaber	100.00
Luke Skywalker (Jedi Knight) (#70650) with **blue** lightsaber	175.00
Nien Nunb (#70840)	35.00
Princess Leia Organa (Boushh Disguise) (#70660) . . .	50.00
Rebel Commando (#70740)	30.00
Ree-Yees (#70800).	30.00
Squid Head (#70770)	30.00
Weequay (#70760)	30.00

Seventh Series, New Figures (1984)

AT-ST Driver (#71330)	30.00
B-Wing Pilot (#71280).	30.00
8D8 (#71210)	30.00
The Emperor (#71240)	35.00
Han Solo (Trench Coat) (#71300)	50.00
Klaatu (Skiff Guard) (#71290)	30.00
Lumat (#93670)	40.00
Nikto (#71190)	30.00
Paploo (#93680).	40.00
Princess Leia Organa (Combat Poncho) (#71220) . . .	60.00
Prune Face (#71320)	30.00
Rancor Keeper (#71350)	30.00

Return of the Jedi *Series Figures: Darth Vader and Chewbacca (Kenner 1983)*

Teebo (#71310) 40.00
Wicket W. Warrick (#71230) 50.00

Reissue Figures on Return of the Jedi header cards
Artoo-Detoo (R2-D2) (with Sensorscope) (#69420) . . . 35.00
AT-AT Commander (#69620) 35.00
AT-AT Driver (#39379) 35.00
Ben (Obi-Wan) Kenobi (#38250) **gray hair** 50.00
Ben (Obi-Wan) Kenobi (#38250) **gray hair** new
    package. 50.00
Ben (Obi-Wan) Kenobi (#38250) **white hair** 50.00
Bespin Security Guard (#39810) **white** 30.00
Bespin Security Guard (#69640) **black** 45.00
Boba Fett (#39250). 300.00
Boba Fett (#39250) new package 275.00
Bossk (Bounty Hunter) (#39760). 75.00
Chewbacca (#38210) 50.00
Chewbacca (#38210) new package 45.00
Cloud Car Pilot (Twin Pod) (#69630) 40.00
Darth Vader (#38230) 50.00
Darth Vader (#38230) new package 45.00
Death Squad Commander (#38290) 65.00
Death Star Droid (#39080) 70.00
Dengar (#39329) 35.00
4-LOM (#70010) 30.00
FX-7 (Medical Droid) (#39730) 40.00
Greedo (#39020) 55.00
Hammerhead (#39030). 75.00
Han Solo (#38260) **large head**, dark brown hair,
    new package 200.00
Han Solo (#38260) **large head**, brown hair 175.00
Han Solo (#38260) **small head**, brown hair new
    package. 200.00
Han Solo (Bespin Outfit) (#39339) 75.00
Han Solo (Hoth Outfit) (#39790) 75.00
IG-88 (Bounty Hunter) (#39770) 75.00
Imperial Commander (#39389) 35.00
Imperial Stormtrooper (Hoth Battle Gear) (#39740) . . . 50.00
Imperial TIE Fighter Pilot (#70030) 55.00
Jawa (#38270) **cloth cape** 45.00
Lando Calrissian (#39800) **white teeth** 45.00
Leia Organa (Bespin Gown) (#39720) **turtle neck** . . 150.00
Leia Organa (Bespin Gown) (#39720) **crew neck** . . . 125.00
Lobot (#39349) 35.00
Luke Skywalker (#38180) **blond hair** 175.00
Luke Skywalker (#38180) **blond hair** new package. . 165.00
Luke Skywalker (#38180) **brown hair** 160.00
Luke Skywalker (#38180) **brown hair** new package . 150.00
Luke Skywalker (Bespin Fatigues) (#39780) new
    package, **yellow hair** 140.00
Luke Skywalker (Bespin Fatigues) (#39780) new
    package, **brown hair** 90.00
Luke Skywalker (Hoth Battle Gear) (#69610) 40.00
Luke Skywalker (X-Wing Fighter Pilot) (#39060) 50.00
Power Droid (#39090). 55.00
Princess Leia Organa (#38190). 400.00
Princess Leia Organa (Hoth Outfit) (#39359) 100.00
Princess Leia Organa (Hoth Outfit) (#39359) new
    package. 75.00
R5-D4 (Arfive-Defour) (#39070) 60.00
Rebel Commander (#39369) 30.00
Rebel Soldier (Hoth Battle Gear) (#39750) 35.00
See-Threepio (C-3PO) (Removable Limbs) (#69430) . 35.00
Snaggletooth (#39040) **red** 55.00
Stormtrooper (#38240) 50.00
Too-Onebee (2-1B) (#71600) 40.00
Tusken Raider (Sand People) (#38280) 75.00
Ugnaught (#39319) 35.00

Walrus Man (#39050) 60.00
Yoda (#38310) **brown snake** 65.00
Yoda **The Jedi Master**, (#38310) **brown snake** 60.00
Zuckuss (#70020) 35.00

THE POWER OF THE FORCE
Kenner (1985)

The Power of the Force figures were produced after all three movies had come and gone. Kenner wanted to keep the figure series alive and so they changed the name of the series and added silver colored aluminum coins as an in-package premium.

Without a new movie to pump-up sales, less of these figures were ordered and many that were scheduled were never made. As sales slowed, collector interest waned and the figures became red tag specials. When the collectors finally realized that they didn't have these figures, it was too late and so now they are among the most valuable of *Star Wars* figures. Several were released only overseas.

There were 15 new figures and 22 figures which were reissued in this series. All of them came with coins, making a total of 37 figures that came with coins. However, two of the foreign release figures (AT-AT Driver and Nikto) came with coins from other figures, so only 35 different coins came with these 37 figures. Two other foreign Power of the Force figures (Imperial TIE-Fighter Pilot and FX-7) are claimed to exist in some publications and denied in others.

Power of the Force Figure: Emperor (Kenner 1985)

However, coins were also available as a mail-in premium with a proof of purchase from some prior *The Empire Strikes Back* and *Return of the Jedi* figures and so there are actually 62 coins in the series to collect. See the COINS section of this book.

THE POWER OF THE FORCE SERIES
Kenner (1985)

Eighth Series, New Figures (1985) with silver coin
A-Wing Pilot (#93830)	$100.00
Amanaman (#93740)	200.00
Anakin Skywalker (#93790) foreign release	1,600.00
Artoo-Detoo (R2-D2) Pop-up Lightsaber (#93720)	150.00
Barada (#93750)	100.00
EV-9D9 (#93800)	150.00
Han Solo (Carbonite Chamber) (#93770)	225.00
Imperial Dignitary (#93850)	75.00
Imperial Gunner (#93760)	150.00
Lando Calrissian (General Pilot) (#93820)	110.00
Luke Skywalker (Battle Poncho) (#93710)	100.00
Luke Skywalker, Stormtrooper Outfit (#93780)	400.00
Romba (#93730)	50.00
Warok (#93810)	50.00
Yak Face (#93840) foreign release	1,500.00

Reissue Figures on Power of the Force header cards
AT-AT Driver (#39379) foreign release only	325.00
AT-ST Driver (#71330)	60.00
B-Wing Pilot (#71280)	30.00

Power of the Force Figure: R2-D2 with Pop-Up Lightsaber (Kenner 1985)

Ben (Obi-Wan) Kenobi (#38250) **white hair**	100.00
Ben (Obi-Wan) Kenobi (#38250) **gray hair**	125.00
Biker Scout (#70820)	80.00
Chewbacca (#38210)	100.00
Darth Vader (#38230)	90.00
The Emperor (#71240)	75.00
Gamorrean Guard (#70670) foreign release only	150.00
Han Solo (Trench Coat) (#71300)	500.00
Imperial Stormtrooper (#38240)	150.00
Jawa (#38270) **cloth cape**	75.00
Luke Skywalker (Jedi Knight) (#70650) with **green lightsaber**	175.00
Luke Skywalker (X-Wing Fighter Pilot) (#39060)	100.00
Lumat (#93670)	50.00
Nikto (#71190) foreign release only	300.00
Paploo (#93680)	45.00
Princess Leia Organa (Combat Poncho) (#71220)	100.00
See-Threepio (C-3PO) Removable Limbs (#69430)	75.00
Teebo (#71310)	200.00
Wicket W. Warrick (#71230)	200.00
Yoda (with **brown snake**) (#38310)	350.00

TRI-LOGO (RETURN OF THE JEDI)

There is no series of figures which has the words "Tri-Logo" on it. Tri-Logo is just the universally used collector's shorthand name for figures on header cards with *Return of the Jedi* logos in three languages. It is not even really a single series, as there are differences among Tri-Logo header cards depending on the countries that were the intended market for these figures. Collectors generally ignore such differences and all such cards for a given figure have the same value. Generally, a figure on a Tri-Logo card has a lower value than the same figure on any other type of card from the 1970s and 1980s.

There are foreign versions of *Star Wars* figures from many countries and some of them always end up in the United States, in the hands of some collectors. What makes Tri-Logo carded figures into a "domestic series" in the eyes of collectors and dealers, even though they were manufactured for foreign markets, is that they were distributed in quantity in this country at many stores. As the least desirable version of *Star Wars* figures and the last ones distributed, they often spent the longest time at toy stores. They were knocked onto the floor by collectors looking for scarce figures and plastered with red tag stickers. Consequently, Tri-Logo figures are often in lesser condition than those from other series, which further reduces their value. Figures on beat-up cards are often worth little more than the corresponding loose figure.

TRI-LOGO "SERIES"
Kenner (1984–86)

Reissue Figures on Tri-Logo header card
Admiral Ackbar (#70310)	$15.00
Amanaman (#93740)	150.00
Anakin Skywalker (#93790) foreign release	125.00
Artoo-Detoo (R2-D2) (#38200)	35.00
Artoo-Detoo (R2-D2) (Sensorscope) (#69590)	28.00
Artoo-Detoo (R2-D2) (Pop-up Lightsaber) (#93720)	100.00
AT-AT Commander (#69620)	25.00
AT-AT Driver (#39379)	25.00
AT-ST Driver (#71330)	14.00
A-Wing Pilot (#93830)	60.00

Tri-Logo Series Figures: AT-ST Driver, Lumat and Biker Scout (Kenner 1985)

B-Wing Pilot (#71280) 12.00	Jawa (#38270) **cloth cape** 65.00
Barada (#93750) 60.00	Klaatu (#70730) with **tan arms** or **gray arms** 15.00
Ben (Obi-Wan) Kenobi (#38250) **gray hair** 50.00	Klaatu (in Skiff Guard Outfit) (#71290) 15.00
Ben (Obi-Wan) Kenobi (#38250) **white hair** 50.00	Lando Calrissian (#39800) **white teeth** 45.00
Bespin Security Guard (#39810) **white** 25.00	Lando Calrissian (General Pilot) (#93820) 70.00
Bespin Security Guard (#69640) **black** 25.00	Lando Calrissian (Skiff Guard Disguise) (#70830) 20.00
Bib Fortuna (#70790) 15.00	Leia Organa (Bespin Gown) (#39720) **turtle neck** . . 125.00
Biker Scout (#70820) 15.00	Leia Organa (Hoth Outfit) (#39359) 60.00
Boba Fett (#39250) 150.00	Lobot (#39349) 25.00
Bossk (Bounty Hunter) (#39760) 55.00	Logray (Ewok Medicine Man) (#70710) 15.00
C-3PO (Removable Limbs) (#69600) 25.00	Luke Skywalker (#38180) **blond hair** 125.00
Chewbacca (#38210) 35.00	Luke Skywalker (#38180) **brown hair** 135.00
Chief Chirpa (#70690) 17.00	Luke Skywalker (Bespin) (#39780) yellow hair 125.00
Cloud Car Pilot (Twin Pod) (#69630) 30.00	Luke Skywalker (Bespin) (#39780) brown hair 125.00
Darth Vader (#38230) 40.00	Luke Skywalker (Hoth Battle Gear) (#69610) 35.00
Death Squad Commander (#38290) 65.00	Luke Skywalker (in Battle Poncho) (#93710) 60.00
Death Star Droid (#39080) 60.00	Luke Skywalker (Jedi Knight) (#70650) **blue**
Dengar (#39329) 25.00	**lightsaber** (#70650) 90.00
8D8 (#71210) 15.00	Luke Skywalker (Jedi Knight) (#70650) **green**
Emperor (#71240) 15.00	**lightsaber** (#70650) 60.00
Emperor's Royal Guard (#70680) 20.00	Luke Skywalker (X-Wing Fighter Pilot) (#39060) 80.00
EV-9D9 (#93800) 100.00	Luke Skywalker (Stormtrooper Outfit) (#93780) 225.00
4-LOM (#70010) 25.00	Lumat (#93670) 25.00
FX-7 (Medical Droid) (#39730) 50.00	Nien Nunb (#70840) 20.00
Gamorrean Guard (#70670) 18.00	Nikto (#71190) 15.00
General Madine (#70780) 15.00	Paploo (#93680) 25.00
Greedo (#39020) 60.00	Power Droid (#39090) 60.00
Hammerhead (#39030) 60.00	Princess Leia Organa (#38190) 150.00
Han Solo (#38260) **large head**, dark brown hair 125.00	Princess Leia Organa (Boushh Disguise) (#70660) . . . 25.00
Han Solo (#38260) **small head**, brown hair 150.00	Princess Leia Organa (Combat Poncho) (#71220) . . . 25.00
Han Solo (Bespin Outfit) (#39339) 40.00	Prune Face (#71320) 15.00
Han Solo (Hoth Outfit) (#39790) 40.00	R5-D4 (#39070) 60.00
Han Solo (in Carbonite Chamber) (#93770) 175.00	Rancor Keeper (#71350) 15.00
Han Solo (in Trench Coat) (#71300) 25.00	Rebel Commander (#39369) 25.00
IG-88 . . . . 75.00	Rebel Commando (#70740) 15.00
Imperial Commander (#39389) 25.00	Rebel Soldier (Hoth Battle Gear) (#39750) 25.00
Imperial Dignitary (#93850) 45.00	Ree-Yees (#70800) 15.00
Imperial Gunner (#93760) 125.00	Romba (#93730) 30.00
Imperial Stormtrooper (Hoth Battle Gear) (#39740) . . . 50.00	See-Threepio (C-3PO) (#38220) 45.00
Imperial Stormtrooper (#38240) new package 60.00	Snaggletooth (**red**) (#39040) 60.00
Imperial TIE Fighter Pilot (#70030) 55.00	Squid Head (#70770) 15.00

Teebo (#71310) 20.00
Tusken Raider (Sand People) (#38280) 65.00
2-1B (#39399) 40.00
Ugnaught (#39319). 25.00
Walrus Man (#39050) 60.00
Warok (#93810) 30.00
Weequay (#70760) 15.00
Wicket W. Warrick (#71230) 25.00
Yak Face (#93840) foreign release 325.00
Yoda (with **brown snake**) (#38310) 50.00
Zuckuss (#70020). 25.00

LOOSE FIGURES

A lot of *Star Wars* figures are collected as loose figures. This is a popular type of collecting for persons whose mothers did not throw away all their *Star Wars* figures when they left home. There's nothing like finding half the figures for your collection in a box in your own attic. The condition of the figure and finding the correct weapons and accessories is usually the challenge. The prices below are for near mint figures complete with original weapons and accessories. The list of recently available replacement weapons given at the end is to remind collectors that not all available weapons are "originals."

Loose figures
Admiral Ackbar, with staff $10.00
Amanaman, with skull staff 100.00
Anakin Skywalker, no accessories, foreign release . . . 30.00
Artoo-Detoo (R2-D2) no accessories. 12.50
Artoo-Detoo (R2-D2) (with Sensorscope) 12.50
Artoo-Detoo (R2-D2) with Pop-up Lightsaber 75.00
AT-AT Commander, with pistol 10.00
AT-AT Driver, with rifle. 10.00
AT-ST Driver, with pistol 10.00
A-Wing Pilot, with pistol 45.00
Barada, with staff 40.00
Ben (Obi-Wan) Kenobi **gray hair**, with lightsaber 15.00
Ben (Obi-Wan) Kenobi **white hair**, with lightsaber. . . . 15.00
Bespin Security Guard **black**, with pistol. 10.00
Bespin Security Guard **white**, with pistol. 10.00
Bib Fortuna, with brown cloak and staff. 10.00
Biker Scout, with pistol 12.50

Boba Fett, with pistol 60.00
Bossk (Bounty Hunter) with rifle 10.00
B-Wing Pilot, with pistol 10.00
Chewbacca, with black rifle. 12.50
Chewbacca, with green rifle, (Early Bird Figure) 35.00
Chief Chirpa, with long club 10.00
Cloud Car Pilot (Twin Pod) with pistol and light 15.00
Darth Vader, with lightsaber 10.00
Death Squad Commander, with pistol 15.00
Death Star Droid, no accessories 10.00
Dengar, with rifle. 10.00
8D8, no accessories 10.00
Emperor, with cane. 10.00
Emperor's Royal Guard, with staff. 10.00
EV-9D9, no accessories 75.00
4-LOM, with weapon. 10.00
FX-7 (Medical Droid) no accessories. 10.00
Gamorrean Guard, with axe 10.00
General Madine, with staff 10.00
Greedo, with pistol 10.00
Hammerhead, with pistol. 12.50
Han Solo with **large head**, with pistol 25.00
Han Solo with **small head**, with pistol. 35.00
Han Solo (Bespin Outfit) with pistol. 12.50
Han Solo (Carbonite Chamber) with carbonite sheet . 100.00
Han Solo (Hoth Outfit) with pistol 15.00
Han Solo (in Trench Coat) with pistol 15.00
IG-88 (Bounty Hunter) with rifle and pistol. 15.00
Imperial Commander, with pistol 10.00
Imperial Dignitary, no accessories 30.00
Imperial Gunner, with pistol. 75.00
Imperial Stormtrooper, with weapon 15.00
Imperial Stormtrooper (Hoth Gear) with rifle 10.00
Imperial Tie Fighter Pilot, with pistol 15.00
Jawa **vinyl cape**, with weapon 300.00
Jawa **cloth cape**, with weapon. 13.00
Klaatu, with **tan arms** or **gray arms**, with apron and
    spear. 10.00
Klaatu (in Skiff Guard Outfit) with weapon. 10.00
Lando Calrissian **no teeth** version, with pistol. 12.50
Lando Calrissian **white teeth** version, with pistol 12.50
Lando Calrissian (Skiff Guard Disguise) with spear . . 15.00
Lando Calrissian (General Pilot) with cape and pistol . 50.00
Leia Organa (Bespin Gown) **crew neck**, in cloak
    with pistol 20.00

Loose Figures: R2-D2 and C-3PO, Yoda, LograY and Wicket (Kenner 1978–85)

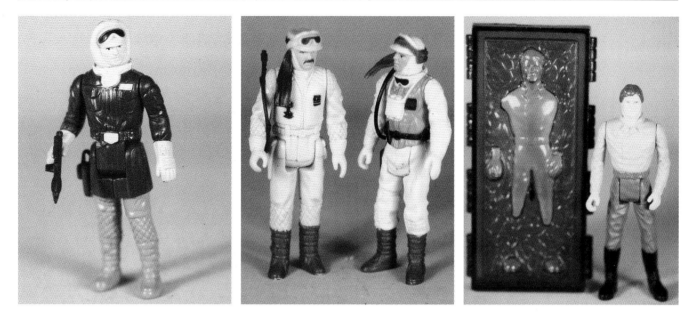

Loose Figures: Han Solo (Hoth), Rebel Commander and Luke Skywalker (Hoth), Han Solo (Carbonite) (Kenner 1980–85)

Leia Organa (Bespin Gown) **turtle neck**, in cloak
   with pistol 20.00
Leia Organa (Hoth Outfit) with pistol 20.00
Lobot, with pistol. 8.00
Logray (Ewok Medicine Man) with mask, staff and
   pouch 10.00
Luke Skywalker **blond hair**, with lightsaber. 35.00
Luke Skywalker **brown hair**, with lightsaber 35.00
Luke Skywalker (in Battle Poncho) with poncho and
   pistol 50.00
Luke Skywalker (Bespin Fatigues) **brown hair**, with
   pistol and lightsaber. 20.00
Luke Skywalker (Bespin Fatigues) **yellow hair**,
   with pistol and lightsaber 20.00
Luke Skywalker (Hoth Gear) with rifle 15.00
Luke Skywalker, Imperial Stormtrooper Outfit, with
   removable helmet and pistol 150.00
Luke Skywalker (Jedi Knight) with **green light-
saber**, cloak and pistol. 40.00
Luke Skywalker (Jedi Knight) with **blue light-
saber**, cloak and pistol. 60.00
Luke Skywalker (X-Wing Pilot) with pistol 15.00
Lumat, with bow 15.00

Nien Nunb, with pistol. 10.00
Nikto, with staff. 10.00
Paploo, with staff 15.00
Power Droid, no accessories. 10.00
Princess Leia Organa, with pistol 40.00
Princess Leia Organa (Boushh Disguise) with
   helmet and weapon 20.00
Princess Leia Organa (Combat Poncho) with pistol . . . 20.00
Prune Face, with cloak and rifle 10.00
R5-D4, no accessories 10.00
Rancor Keeper, with prod 10.00
Rebel Commander, with rifle. 10.00
Rebel Commando, with rifle 10.00
Rebel Soldier (Hoth Gear) with pistol 10.00
Ree-Yees, with weapon 10.00
Romba, with spear 20.00
See-Threepio (C-3PO) no accessories 10.00
C-3PO (Removable Limbs) with back pack 10.00
Snaggletooth (**blue**) from Cantina Adventure Set . . . 150.00
Snaggletooth (**red**) with pistol 10.00
Squid Head, with pistol and cloak 10.00
Teebo, with club, mask and pouch 12.50
Tusken Raider (Sand People) with cloak and weapon. . . 15.00

Loose Figures: Dengar, three Tusken Raiders and Princess Leia (Boushh Disguise) (Kenner 1978–85)

2-1B, with weapon 10.00
Ugnaught, in blue smock with case 10.00
Ugnaught, in lavender smock with case 12.50
Walrus Man, with pistol 12.50
Warok, with bow and pouch 20.00
Weequay, with spear 12.50
Wicket W. Warrick, with spear 12.50
Yak Face, with staff, foreign release 150.00
Yoda, with **brown snake** and stick 20.00
Yoda, with **orange snake** and stick 20.00
Zuckuss, with rifle 10.00

Replica Equipment (1997)
Set #1: 25 different weapons $19.00
Set #2: 16 different weapons 12.00
Replica Stormtrooper helmet 5.00

These are **not** by Kenner. They are advertised in such places as *Previews* magazine for sale in comic shops. They include lightsabers of various colors, telescoping and regular, and just about anything else needed to complete your loose figure, if you don't have the authentic weapon. Of course, it makes it easy to fool the unsuspecting, as well. Be careful so that you do not fall into this category yourself!

(THE TV ANIMATED SERIES)
DROIDS
"The Adventures of R2-D2 and C-3PO"
Kenner (1985)

The real movies were gone from the theaters, but there was still money to be made, so a couple of Ewok movies (*The Ewok Adventure* and *Ewoks: The Battle For Endor*) were produced, along with both an Ewoks and a Droids animated ABC

television series. I didn't see any of them when they came out and they put me to sleep when I try to watch them on television now. They must do the same to just about everybody, because the figures haven't attained much of a collector following. This may be undeserved, because, judged on their own, the figures are not too bad. So far, anyway, these figures haven't gotten much of a boost in value from the incredible popularity of the *Star Wars* series and the current re-releases and hype. Maybe they will, or maybe all the money will chase the huge pile of new figures and other collectibles, and these will be completely overlooked.

Two of the Droids figures are collected — the A-Wing Pilot and Boba Fett — but only because they are popular figures from the previous lines. In fact, the greatest collector interest in the rest of the Droids and Ewoks may well be in the coins, rather than the figures. Although the coins are not part of the 62-coin regular set, they do form their own sets and sell for between $5.00 and $8.00 each. This is a significant fraction of the value of the carded figures, and it may mean that coin collectors are affecting the market more than figure collectors.

Another area of interest in these figures centers on the unproduced 1986 figures. There were six new Ewoks and eight new Droids advertised in Kenner's 1986 catalog, but they never appeared. Collectors are looking for prototypes, packaging proofs and similar items for these unreleased figures. The catalog itself is also highly collectible.

3¾" Figures (1985) with copper or gold colored coin
A-Wing Pilot (#93830) reissue $145.00
    Loose . . . . see Loose Figures listing

Produced and unproduced Droids figures and Ewoks figures (Kenner 1986 Catalog)

Artoo-Detoo R2-D2 (#71780) with pop-up lightsaber . . 45.00
    Loose 15.00
Boba Fett (#39260). 250.00
    Loose 50.00
Jann Tosh (#71840) 20.00
    Loose 10.00
Jord Dusat (#71810) 20.00
    Loose 10.00
Kea Moll (#71800) 20.00
    Loose 10.00
Kez-Iban (#71850) 20.00
    Loose 10.00
See-Threepio C-3PO (#71770) 45.00
    Loose 15.00
Sise Fromm (#71820) 45.00
    Loose 20.00
Thall Joben (#71790) 20.00
    Loose 10.00
Tig Fromm (#71830) 50.00
    Loose 20.00
Uncle Gundy (#71880) 15.00
    Loose 9.00

EWOKS
Kenner (1985)

3¾" Figures (1985) with copper or gold colored coin
Dulok Shaman (#71150) $15.00
    Loose 9.00
Dulok Scout (#71160) 15.00
    Loose 9.00

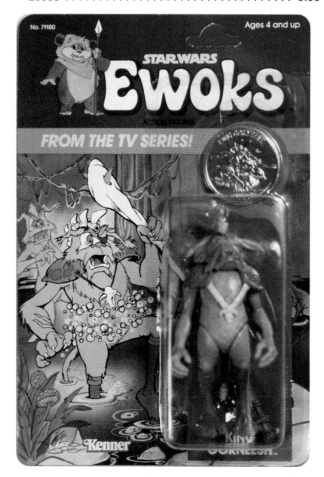

Ewok Figure: King Gorneesh (Kenner 1985)

Urgah Lady Gorneesh (#71170) 15.00
    Loose 9.00
King Gorneesh (#71180) 15.00
    Loose 9.00
Wicket W. Warrick (#71250) 20.00
    Loose 10.00
Logray (Ewok medicine man) (#71260) 15.00
    Loose 9.00

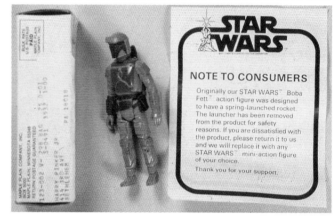

Mail-In Boba Fett figure (Kenner 1980)

MAIL-INS

Mail-Ins
Boba Fett with Rocket Launcher (mail-in offer)
    unpainted blue/gray with red missile, with
    mailer box and letter $200.00
Bossk, Boba Fett, Darth Vader, IG-88, in plastic
    bags with Kenner logo, plus white mailer box
    listing the figures (#38871, 1980) 200.00
Bossk (1980) 25.00
4-LOM (1982) 25.00
Admiral Ackbar (1983) 20.00
Nien Nunb (1983) 20.00
The Emperor (1984) 20.00
Anakin Skywalker (1985) 40.00

ORIGINAL SERIES — MULTI-PACKS

In addition to all the different versions of the figures previously listed, Kenner also produced various multi-packs from time to time. "Action Figure Sets" of three figures were issued for each of the three movies. They were subtitled "Hero Set," "Villain Set," "Rebel Set," etc. They are quite scarce and there is some uncertainty as to their precise value.

Two six-pack sets of figures were issued for *The Empire Strikes Back* movie. These are not as valuable as the three packs. Last, and least, *Return of the Jedi* two-packs were issued with leftover figures. They are worth the price of the two loose figures contained in the pack (if they have their weapons) and maybe an additional dollar or two for oddity.

Star Wars Action Figure Sets — Three-Packs
Villain Set: Darth Vader, Stormtrooper and Death
    Squad Commander (#38650) $1,000.00
Hero Set: Han Solo, Princess Leia Organa and Ben
    (Obi-Wan) Kenobi (#38660) 1,000.00
Android Set: C-3PO, R2-D2 & Chewbacca (#38640) 1,000.00

Star Wars Three Packs with backdrops
Hero Set: Luke X-Wing Pilot, Ben Kenobi & Han
    Solo (#39450) 1,250.00

Droid Set: R5-D4, Death Star Droid, Power Droid
(#39460) 1,250.00
Villain Set: Sand People, Boba Fett, Snaggle Tooth
(#39470) 1,250.00
Creature Set: Hammerhead, Walrus Man, Greedo
(#39480) 1,250.00

The Empire Strikes Back — Three Packs
Rebel Set: 2-1B, Princess Leia Organa (Hoth
Outfit) and Rebel Commander (#69650) 900.00
Bespin Set: Han Solo (Bespin Outfit) Ugnaught and
Lobot (#69660) 900.00
Imperial Set: Imperial Commander, Dengar and
AT-AT Driver (#69670) 900.00
Rebel Set: Princess Leia Organa (Hoth Outfit),
Artoo-Detoo (R2-D2) with sensorscope and
Luke Skywalker (Hoth Battle Gear) (#70040) . . . 900.00
Bespin Set: See-Threepio (C-3PO) with Removable
Limbs, Ugnaught and Cloud Car Pilot (#70070) . . 900.00
Imperial Set: Zuckuss, AT-AT Driver and Imperial
TIE Fighter Pilot (#70080) 900.00
Hoth Rebels: Han (Hoth), Rebel Soldier (FX-7) 900.00
Bespin Alliance: Bespin Security Guard (white),
Lando, Luke (Bespin) 900.00
Imperial Forces: Bossk, Imperial Stormtrooper
(Hoth Battle Gear), IG-88 . . . . 900.00

The Empire Strikes Back — Six-Packs
Rebel Soldier, C-3PO, R2-D2, Han Solo (Hoth),
Darth Vader and Stormtrooper (Hoth) (#39320) . 750.00
Darth Vader, Stormtrooper (Hoth Battle Gear), AT-AT
Driver, Rebel Soldier, IG-88 & Yoda (#93390) . . . 750.00

Return of the Jedi — Three Packs
Admiral Ackbar, General Madine and Rebel
Commando (#93550) 750.00
Gamorrean Guard, Squid Head and Bib Fortuna
(#93570) 750.00
Rebel Set: Admiral Ackbar, Leia (Boushh), Chief
Chirpa 750.00
Imperial Set: Biker Scout, Emperor's Royal Guard,
Bib Fortuna 750.00

Sy Snootles and the Rebo Band (Kenner 1985)

SY SNOOTLES AND THE REBO BAND

Sy Snootles and the Rebo Band (#71360, 1984)
Original *Return of the Jedi* header card $150.00
Reissue on Tri-Logo header card 95.00
Loose: Sy Snootles, Droopy McCool or Max
Rebo, each 15.00

Classic Edition 4-Pack (Kenner 1995)

STAR WARS (NEW):

THE POWER OF THE FORCE
Kenner (1995–98)

Kenner reintroduced the *Star Wars* figures starting in 1995. The first item to appear was the Classic Edition 4-Pack and, in some ways, it is the functional equivalent of the Early Bird Figures from the original series — an initial four figures which are not on their own header cards.

The Classic Edition 4-Pack caused quite a bit of controversy when it first appeared because the figures were very close to being identical to the original Luke Skywalker, Han Solo, Darth Vader and Chewbacca from 1978. These original loose figures sell for over $25.00 each and there was some fear that collectors could be duped. Just enough difference between new and old was discovered so that these fears proved groundless. Now the 4-pack has risen considerably in value, so it is even less likely that someone will open one and try to pass off the new figures as the old ones.

If you find one of these 4-packs in below average condition and buy it to obtain the loose figures, don't ignore the trading cards. The cards form a distinct group of promo cards for the *Star Wars* Widevision trading cards series and are worth about $8.00 each or about $25.00 for the set.

Star Wars Power of the Force Classic Edition
4-Pack, including Luke Skywalker, Han Solo,
Darth Vader and Chewbacca with 4 Topps
"Star Wars Widevision" special promo cards
K01–K04 (#69595, July 1995) $60.00

The reintroduction of *Star Wars* action figures was a resounding success and hooked many collectors who had played with *Star Wars* figures as kids when they first came out. Collector interest in the original figures — always strong — got even stronger.

Packaging Variations

The most significant packaging changes in the new series is in the color of the header card. The 1995 and 1996 header cards have a red or orange laser blast running diagonally across them, while the 1997 cards have a green laser blast. Shadows of the Empire figures, from late 1996, are on purple laser blast cards. In 1998, the cards remain green, but all figures have a "Freeze Frame Action Slide." Most 1997 green cards have a holographic picture sticker, but limited quantities of many of the figures were issued without this sticker. All green cards, and late 1996 red cards for some figures, have collection numbers at the top. In 1998, the collection numbers are at the bottom and the cards are color coded by collection. Hopefully, the following information will help you sort all of these changes out.

Package Printing Numbers

All of Kenner's 1995–98 action figures have a small printed number on the back, at the bottom, which can be used to distinguish earlier packages from later ones. The first six digits of the number are unique to the particular figure and do not change even if the UPC code or the figure's name are changed. It's no doubt used at the factory to see that the figures are matched up with the correct header cards. However, it's the two digits after the decimal point that collectors look at. These are package revision numbers. The first version of each package is numbered ".00" and each time there is a printing change this number is increased, so that if there have been three changes, the number will read ".03" and so on. Many of the figures have had printing changes on their header cards. These range from name changes for the figure or his weapons, "Collection number" changes, and photo changes, down to correction of tiny typographical errors. All of these changes affect the value of the figure, and the earlier version is almost always the more valuable. If you are at a store or a show, and can't remember whether the "Han Solo in Carbonite Freezing Chamber" or "Han Solo in Carbonite Block" is the scarce figure, or whether the "Collection 2" or the "Collection 3" Grand Moff Tarkin figure is the first version, just look at this code. The one you want is the one with

the lower revision code, usually ".00". However, this number only works for *printing* changes, not for variations in the figure itself.

Throughout this book, these numbers are reported in [brackets] so as to distinguish them from UPC codes, which are listed in (parentheses).

Collection Numbers

Some collectors think that the idea of having "collection numbers" was primarily to drive them crazy and to change the number so as to force them to buy different versions of each figure. After all, the average kid throws away the header card and couldn't care less what collection it was from. However, in fairness to Kenner/Hasbro, this was not its purpose.

The idea of the "collection number" was to sort the action figures into groups so that "Collection 1" would be the Rebel Alliance, "Collection 3" would be the Galactic Empire and "Collection 2" would be the various non-aligned aliens. The point of all this, and the real idea, was that the boxes shipped to the stores would indicate which collection was in the box and so the store would have to devote space for all three collections and there would always be a wide variety for sale — plenty of Rebels, plenty of Aliens and plenty of Imperial forces.

Unfortunately, there weren't equal numbers of each type, and new figures were not added at uniform rates in each group, but all boxes have to contain 16 figures. Except for the occasional "Block Case" of all one figure, Kenner doesn't ship more than three of any one figure in any assortment, and usually it's no more than two.

Suppose Kenner wants to introduce eight new figures. The best way to get them out in equal quantities would be to put two of each in a single assortment. Of course, if Kenner

R2-D2, red card; Princess Leia (Boushh Disguise) purple card; and Momaw Nadon, red "Collection" card (Kenner 1995–96)

did this, stores would only want the new assortment and sales of the old figures would grind to a virtual halt. So Kenner puts them into the various collections. But if five new figures should fall into Collection 2, but only two into Collection 3 and one into Collection 1, there is no way to make it work out for the store. To meet demand for equal numbers of new figures, they will have to open equal numbers of boxes in each collection and old figures will accumulate in Collections 1 and 2. The best way to fix this is to put some of the new figures into the "wrong" collection and then fix it later.

Of course, it isn't even this simple, since Kenner has to worry about distribution of recent figures, as well as new figures, and the fickle (i.e. uneven buying habits of kids and collectors) plus the occasional plain ordinary snafu.

The result has been that a lot of figures came out in the "wrong" collection and later in the "right" collection. The five most important (i.e. valuable) collection "errors" are Grand Moff Tarkin, Ponda Baba, Weequay Skiff Guard, Yoda and Rebel Fleet Trooper, all of whom came out first in Collection 2, but were soon switched to other collections (Yoda and Rebel Fleet Trooper, Collection 1; other three to Collection 3). All of these are quite difficult to find in the error collection and are worth about three to four times as much as they are with the correct number.

The next most valuable errors are: Luke in Hoth Gear, Luke in Ceremonial, Luke Jedi Knight, and Yoda, all from Collection 2, plus Boba Fett from Collection 1. All of these command about a 50% premium. The other collection errors: Hoth Rebel Soldier, AT-ST driver, Han Solo Carbonite and TIE-Fighter Pilot, all from Collection 2 together with Emperor Palpatine, Darth Vader and Bib Fortuna from Collection 1 have proven to be fairly easy to find.

Overall, that's 17 collection error figures to look for. Even if you found them all at retail, they probably cost you over $100.00.

Peg Holes and Stand Up Bubbles

There are two other packaging variations that you can see on the 1995–97 figure line by looking at the peg holes used for hanging the figures and at the plastic bubbles on the card.

Around June 1997, or so, figures started showing up with a slightly wider hook-shaped hanging slot cut out at the top of the package. This lets that scarce figure at the back of the store's hanging peg easily fall off right into your hands (and the figures next to it fall off onto the floor). The part of the slot where the figure hangs is rounder, and not quite so deep, while the part of the slot where it slips on or off the peg is wider. However, the easiest place to notice this difference is to look at the horizontal length of the slot, and particularly at the downward hanging part of the header card that remains. It's about 25% wider than the original.

Around the same time, figures began being shipped with an altered plastic bubble. The original plastic bubble used on all red and purple cards and on early green cards is a simple rectangular box with slightly tapered sides so that the box is slightly smaller at the top, than at the base. The new plastic bubble has a more pronounced slant at the top, but the big change is at the bottom. An outward slanting secondary bubble has been added to the shape, so that the carded figure will stand up if placed on a flat surface.

These two changes went largely unnoticed both by collectors and the collector magazines, magazines that normally report every minute change in *Star Wars* action figures or packaging. Part of the reason for this is that there was already plenty of action in the various "collection" changes. As of this writing, no differences in price have been noticed because of these two changes. Nevertheless, they are faithfully reported here for your reading pleasure, and in the event some difference in price shows up in the future.

Bossk, green card with holo picture; 2-1B, green card with plain picture; Luke (Stormtrooper) freeze frame card (Kenner 1997–98)

Holo Stickers or Plain Picture

A holo sticker picture was added to the header cards about the time that they switched from red/orange to green. The very earliest green cards were for the three "Collection 1" and five "Collection 2" figures that appeared briefly on red header cards. The first boxes of these green-carded figures had plain pictures of the characters on the front, similar to the ones used on all the red cards. Soon, these green-carded figures and all the subsequent ones had holographic picture stickers over the plain picture. Even though the plain picture green cards were scarce, collectors paid little attention to this change because the holographic stickers could be removed (carefully) to reveal the plain picture underneath. Plain picture green cards didn't seem to be a valuable variation. The best figures to get were the truly scarce red carded Collection 1 and Collection 2 figures.

During 1997, an occasional green card would show up without the holo sticker, but this made it just an error, like an upside down figure or a figure with the wrong card. Worth an extra buck as an oddity, but nothing else. No one noticed that the holo stickers had different glue starting in about July 1997 and could no longer be removed without leaving a residue and making a few bubbles in the cardboard underneath.

In early 1998, when the green cards were about to be phased out in favor of the Freeze Frame cards, a number of tail-end green cards showed up without holo pictures. The ones seen to date are mostly the original rebel characters which have been available for a long time plus a few new good guys such as Luke in Ceremonial Outfit and Princess Leia as Jabba's Prisoner. This may be an intentional change or it may be that Kenner ran out of the holo pictures and didn't want to print more. Either way, this makes these legitimate packaging variations and not errors. In addition, these figures without hologram will remain scarce, because the holograms on the more common version cannot be removed without leaving residue or bubbling the picture underneath or both. Knowledgeable collectors are looking for this variation and it may well turn out to be more valuable than the collection number change variation for many figures. There is not too much overlap so far. It is certain to be more interesting than the changes in peg hook (long vs. short) and bubble (square vs. stand-up). As of this writing it is not certain how many of the green card figures will be issued without holo pictures.

Summary

With so many variations, what do you look for? To date, collectors are looking for the three figures on Collection 1 and five figures on Collection 2 transition red cards, figures on green cards with plain pictures, and the scarce figures on cards with the "wrong" collection numbers. Basically, you can never go wrong with a package having printing number ".00."

Collectors are paying little or no attention to changes in the peg hooks and bubbles and to any card variation after ".01." Many of the card printing changes from the original ".00" card to the corrected ".01" are quite trivial and where both cards are generally available, there is little difference in price. This variation seems most likely to mirror the variation between 20-back to 21-back cards from the original series.

Luke Skywalker (X-wing Fighter Pilot)
short lightsaber in long tray (Kenner 1996)

Figure Variations

In addition to the packaging variations, there are several important variations in the figures. The one that affects the most figures is the change from the ridiculously long early lightsabers to shorter lightsabers. This yielded variations for Darth Vader, Luke Skywalker and Ben (Obi-Wan) Kenobi. The later figure also had a packaging change with his original head photo being replaced by a full-figure photo. If short lightsabers were not enough, some figures were found with short lightsabers in the plastic slots designed for long sabers. Luke Skywalker (Jedi Knight) originally came with a brown vest, but this was switched to black, matching the rest of his costume. Boba Fett now comes with a black circle on the back of each hand. Originally he had a bar across this circle, forming two "half-circles." These variations have had the most significant effect on price. Late in 1997, a variation occurred in Han Solo in Endor Gear. His pants changed color from Navy blue (almost black) to brown. This should have a very significant effect on price, but it is too soon to know how scarce this figure really is. These variations are covered more thoroughly in the Action Figure — Alphabetical section.

(NEW) POWER OF THE FORCE

Princess Leia was the hot early figure. She did not appear on the back of the header cards and many collectors thought she had not been released. Actually, she had been part of the original shipments and the only reason she was scarce was that every collector bought her as soon as she was spotted. Then she was not shipped for a while and prices increased still further. In the fall of 1996 she appeared again, along with Lando Calrissian from the second batch, who had also been scarce, and prices fell. Some collectors must have taken this personally, because we have seen these figures in stores with their header cards broken intentionally. We only hope that these irate collectors don't turn to gun collecting. Some of those paranoids really take things personally.

The last two figures, Jedi Knight Luke and Han Solo in Carbonite, shipped with the Shadows of the Empire figures. A wording variation was detected on the Han Solo in Carbonite package, providing some collector interest.

Except for a few popular variations, all of the figures were shipped (and purchased) in enormous quantity, keeping the price for most figures at or near the retail level.

RED CARD SERIES
Kenner (1995–96)

3¾" Figures (Asst. #69570, 1995)
Ben (Obi-Wan) Kenobi (#69576) head photo,
  long lightsaber [.00] $50.00
Ben (Obi-Wan) Kenobi (#69576) full-figure photo,
  long lightsaber [.01] 50.00
Ben (Obi-Wan) Kenobi (#69576) full-figure photo,
  short lightsaber 10.00
Chewbacca (#69578) [.00] 10.00
C-3PO (#69573) [.00] 10.00
Darth Vader (#69572) with long lightsaber [.00] 25.00
Darth Vader (#69572) short lightsaber, long slot 20.00

Darth Vader (#69572) short lightsaber 10.00
Han Solo (#69577) [.00] 12.50
Luke Skywalker (#69571) long lightsaber [.00] 30.00
Luke Skywalker (#69571) short lightsaber, long slot . . 75.00
Luke Skywalker (#69571) short lightsaber 15.00
Princess Leia Organa (#69579) 3 bands on belt 20.00
Princess Leia Organa (#69579) 2 bands on belt [.00] . 10.00
R2-D2 (#69574) [.00] 10.00
Stormtrooper (#69575) [.00] 10.00

Second Batch (Asst. #69570, March 1996)
Boba Fett (#69582) half circles on hand [.00] 50.00
Boba Fett (#69582) half circle one hand, full circle
  other hand, scarce 50.00
Boba Fett (#69582) with full circle on hand [.01] 10.00
Han Solo in Hoth Gear (#69587) open hand [.00] 25.00
Han Solo in Hoth Gear (#69587) closed hand 15.00
Lando Calrissian (#69583) [.00] 7.50
Luke Skywalker in Dagobah Fatigues (#69588)
  long lightsaber [.00] 25.00
Luke Skywalker in Dagobah Fatigues (#69588)
  short lightsaber in long slot 15.00
Luke Skywalker in Dagobah Fatigues (#69588)
  short lightsaber [.01] 15.00
Luke Skywalker in X-wing Fighter Pilot Gear
  (#69581) long lightsaber [.00] 25.00
Luke Skywalker in X-wing Fighter Pilot Gear
  (#69581) short lightsaber in long slot 20.00
Luke Skywalker in X-wing Fighter Pilot Gear
  (#69581) short lightsaber 10.00
TIE Fighter Pilot (#69584) warning on sticker [.00] . . . 25.00
TIE Fighter Pilot (#69584) warning on card [.01] 6.00
TIE Fighter Pilot (#69673) [.02] 6.00
Yoda (#69586) [.00] 7.50
Yoda (#69672) [.01] 6.00

Third Batch (Sept. 1996 with Shadows of the Empire figures)
Han Solo in "Carbonite Freezing Chamber"
  (#69613) [.00] 20.00
Han Solo in "Carbonite Block" (#69613) [.01] 7.50
Jedi Knight Luke Skywalker (#69596) brown vest [.00] . . 75.00
Jedi Knight Luke Skywalker (#69596) black vest [.00] . . . 8.00

Red Card Figures: Han Solo, 1st Batch; Boba Fett, 2nd Batch; and Han Solo (Carbonite) 3rd Batch (Kenner 1995–96)

Boba Fett vs. IG-88 (Kenner 1996)

SHADOWS OF THE EMPIRE

Shadows of the Empire figures appeared in September 1996 and were very popular. All the collectors bought them and then looked at every minute detail in an effort to spot some valuable variation. Unfortunately, none were found and none of the figures seemed to be scarce. They are based on the book series, not any of the movies.

One package variation did show up in the two-packs. Boba Fett vs. IG-88 packages with printing code ".01" stated on the back that Boba Fett's "Vehicle of Choice:" was the *Slave I*." This was the final line in his description, after "Weapon of Choice" Earlier packages, with printing code ".00" omitted the phrase "Vehicle of Choice:" but did include the words *"Slave I*."

All of the Shadows of the Empire figures were available at a few Kay-Bee stores in Dec. 1997. There were only a handful of each figure, but they stayed on the racks for several weeks. This indicated that most collectors were already well supplied and that price increases would be modest, at best. With no one looking for these figures, everyone was surprised when it was recently reported that Princess Leia in Boushh Disguise had been reissued on a purple header card that said "Collection 1." This seems to be extremely scarce.

PURPLE CARD SERIES
Kenner (1996)

3¾" Figures (Sept. 1996)
Chewbacca (Bounty Hunter) (#69562) [.00]. $7.00
Dash Rendar (#69561) [.00] 7.00
Luke Skywalker (Imperial Guard) (#69566) [.00] 7.00
Prince Xizor (#69594) [.00] 7.00
Princess Leia (Boushh Disguise) (#69602) [.00] 8.00
Princess Leia (Boushh) Collection 1 (#69818) [.01] . . . 50.00

Two-Packs, with special comic book
Darth Vader vs. Prince Xizor (#69567, 1996) 15.00
Boba Fett vs. IG-88 (#69568, Sept. 1996) [532459.00]
    without "Vehicle of Choice" on data card 15.00
    with "Vehicle of Choice: Slave I" [.01] 12.00

POWER OF THE FORCE 1996–97

The fourth batch of Power of the Force figures appeared in December 1996 with the captions "Collection 1" or "Collection 2" at the top. The two collections appeared at the same time, and the earliest versions came on a header card with an orange laser blast, the same color used on the other new "Power of the Force" figures from 1995–96.

These proved to be quite scarce, as the header cards were all quickly changed to a green laser blast design. Just as collectors were digesting these changes, holographic sticker pictures were added to the cards.

The Tatooine Stormtrooper (orange-carded) and the Sandtrooper (green-carded) are identical — only the name had been changed to confuse the weary collector. That figure, and most of the other initial figures in Collections 1 and 2, also had changes in the name of their weapon.

As the packaging changes occurred, collectors started to notice changes in the eight-digit number codes on the package back. The code for the first issue of any figure ended in ".00" and as the package changed, the code changed to ".01" and ".02" while the first six digits stayed the same, even when

Greedo, Collection 1 red transition card (Kenner 1996)

the figure got a new UPC code. Actually these codes appeared on the packages from 1995 on, but collectors had not payed any attention to them until 1997 when the large number of packaging changes made their function, and usefulness, clear. These printing/packaging codes are noted in this book in [brackets] to distinguish them from UPC codes, which are noted in (parentheses).

Jawas, Collection 2 red transition card (Kenner 1996)

TRANSITION — RED "COLLECTION" CARDS
Kenner (1996)

Fourth Batch (Dec. 1996)
Collection 1 Figures (Asst. #69570, Dec. 1996)
Death Star Gunner (#69608) [.00] $25.00
Greedo (#69606) [.00] 25.00
Tatooine Stormtrooper (#69601) [.00] 25.00

Collection 2 Figures (Asst. #69605, Dec. 1996)
Jawas (#69607) on red header card 20.00
Luke Skywalker in "Stormtrooper Disguise"
 (#69604) on red header card [.00] 25.00
Momaw Nadon "Hammerhead" (#69629) on red
 header card [.00] 20.00
R5-D4 (#69598) on red header card, no small parts
 warning and straight latch [.00] 20.00
R5-D4 (#69598) on red card, with small parts
 warning and straight latch 15.00
Tusken Raider (#69603) On red header card [.00] 25.00

As 1997 began, the three Collection 1 and and five Collection 2 figures were appearing on green header cards with holo pictures. New figures appeared in both Collection 1 and Collection 2, and figures for Collection 3 started to arrive. Some of these early 1997 figures were shipped in staggering quantities and figures such as Bib Fortuna, Emperor Palpatine, Lando Calrissian Skiff Guard, Bossk, 2-1B, Admiral Ackbar, 4-LOM and Grand Moff Tarkin were mind-numbingly common.

A few had their collection number changed, which made for some continuing collector interest. All of the hanging hooks were widened in mid-summer and the plastic bubbles were all changed to be "stand-up" bubbles, but this generated essentially no collector interest whatever.

All of the interest focused on the year's most popular figure, Princess Leia as Jabba's Prisoner. This scantily-clad number initially sold for $15.00 to $20.00 as all of the early ones were grabbed by eager collectors or dealers. However, more appeared and the price started to fall. As still more arrived and the figure became common, the price fell to be the same as the other figures. Other figures which appeared later in the year, such as Saelt-Marae (Yak Face), Malikili (Rancor Keeper), Emperor's Royal Guard and the Gamorrean Guard, all turned out to be common as well. Luke Skywalker in Ceremonial Outfit was the last figure to arrive, but it was not hard to find. Still, these later figures were never around in the same quantities as the early 1997 figures and, since all have now been replaced by the 1998 "Freeze Frame Action Slide" versions, there is some hope for future scarcity.

One really interesting development came just at the end of 1997 and the beginning of 1998, when a limited number of these figures arrived without their holo pictures. The earliest holo pictures can be removed without residue or damage to the picture underneath, but those from about July 1997 on cannot. There was always an occasional error figure which lacked a hologram, but now plain picture versions were an actual legitimate variation. In many cases, the underneath plain picture is more attractive than the holo sticker. You should look for plain picture versions of Luke Skywalker in Ceremonial Outfit and Princess Leia as Jabba's Prisoner to add to your collection, if you have not already done so.

GREEN CARD SERIES
Kenner (1997)

Reissue of Collection 1 Transition Figures
Death Star Gunner (#69608) [.01] $8.00
Death Star Gunner (#69608) [.01] with holo picture 6.00
Greedo (#69606) [.01] 8.00
Greedo (#69606) [.01] with holo picture 6.00
Sandtrooper (prev. Tatooine Stormtrooper) (#69601) [.01] 8.00
Sandtrooper (#69601) [.01] with holo picture 6.00

Collection 1, Second Batch (Asst. #69570, April 1997)
Bib Fortuna (#69634) [.00] 10.00
Emperor Palpatine (#69633) [.00] 10.00
Han Solo in Endor Gear (#69621) [.00] **blue pants** 5.00
Lando Calrissian as Skiff Guard (#69622) [.00] 5.00

Collection 1, Reissues (Asst. #69570, April–Aug. 1997)
Ben (Obi-Wan) Kenobi (#69576) [.02] 5.00
Boba Fett (#69582) [.02] 15.00

Luke Skywalker (X-wing Fighter Pilot) Collection 1, Nien Nunb, Collection 2 and Sandtrooper, Collection 3 (Kenner 1997)

Chewbacca (#69578) [.01] 5.00
C-3PO (#69573) [.01] 5.00
Han Solo (#69577) [.01] 5.00
Jedi Knight Luke Skywalker (#69816) [.02] 5.00
Luke Skywalker (Stormtrooper Disguise) (#69819) [.02] . . 5.00
Luke Skywalker (X-wing Fighter Pilot) (#69581) [.02] . . 5.00
Princess Leia Organa (#69579) [.01]. 5.00
Princess Leia (Boushh Disguise) (#69818) [.01 & .02]] . . 7.00
R2-D2 (#69574) [.01] 5.00
Yoda (#69586) [.03] 5.00

Collection 1, Third Batch (Asst. #69570, July 1997)
Bespin Han Solo (#69719) [.00] 5.00
Darth Vader (#69572) [.01] 10.00
Hoth Rebel Soldier (#69821) [.01] 5.00
Luke Skywalker (Hoth Gear) (#69822) [.01] 5.00
Rebel Fleet Trooper (#69696) [.01] 5.00

Collection 1, Fourth Batch (Asst. #69570, Oct. 1997)
Han Solo (Endor Gear) (#69621) **brown pants** 20.00
Han Solo in Carbonite (#69613) [.03] 5.00
Luke Skywalker (Ceremonial Outfit) (#69691) [.01] 5.00
Princess Leia Organa (Jabba's Prisoner) (#69683) [.00]. . 6.00

Reissue of Collection 2 Transition Figures (Early 1997)
Jawas (#69607) [.01] 6.00
Jawas (#69607) with holo picture [.02] 6.00
Luke Skywalker (Stormtrooper Disguise) (#69819)[.01] 12.00
Luke Skywalker (Stormtrooper Disguise) with holo
    picture [.01] 10.00
Momaw Nadon "Hammerhead" (#69629) [.01]. 6.00
Momaw Nadon (#69629) [.01] with holo picture. 6.00
R5-D4 (#69598) [.01] with warning 6.00
R5-D4 (#69598) [.01] with holo picture, with warning. . . 6.00
Tusken Raider (#69603) closed hand 25.00
Tusken Raider (#69603) [.01] open hand 6.00
Tusken Raider (#69603) [.01] with holo picture 6.00

Collection 2, Second Batch (Asst. #69605, March 1997)
AT-ST Driver (#69623) [.00] 7.50
Bossk (#69617) [.00 & .01] 5.00

Hoth Rebel Soldier (#69631) [.00]. 10.00
Luke Skywalker in Hoth Gear (#69619) [.00] 10.00
2-1B Medic Droid (#69618) [.00] 5.00

Collection 2, Third Batch (Asst. #69605, July-Aug. 1997)
Bib Fortuna (#69812) [.01] 5.00
Jedi Knight Luke Skywalker (#69816) [.01] 10.00
Ponda Baba (#69708) [.00]. 20.00
Rebel Fleet Trooper (#69696) [.00] 20.00
TIE Fighter Pilot (#69673) [.03] 10.00
Weequay Skiff Guard (#69707) [.00] 20.00
Yoda (#69672) [.02] 10.00

Collection 2, Fourth Batch (Asst. #69605, Sept. 1997)
Admiral Ackbar (#69686) [.00]. 5.00
ASP-7 Droid (#69704) [.00]. 6.00
Dengar (#69687) [.00]. 5.00
4-Lom (#69688) [.00] 5.00
Grand Moff Tarkin (#69702) [.00]. 20.00
Luke Skywalker (Ceremonial Outfit) (#69691) [.00] . . . 10.00

Collection 2, Fifth Batch (Asst. #69605, Nov. 1997)
EV-9D9 (#69722) [.00] 5.00
Gamorrean Guard (#69693) [.00] 5.00
Han Solo in Carbonite (#69613) [.02] 7.00
Malakili (Rancor Keeper) (#69723) [.00] 5.00
Nien Nunb (#69694) [.00] 5.00
Saelt-Marae (Yak Face) (#69721) [.00] 5.00

Collection 3 (Asst. #69705, July 1997)
Darth Vader (#69802) [.02] 5.00
Death Star Gunner (#69809) [.02]. 5.00
Emperor Palpatine (#69811) [.01] 5.00
Ponda Baba (#69708) [.01] 5.00
Sandtrooper (#69808) [.02] 5.00
Stormtrooper (#69803) [.01] 5.00
TIE Fighter Pilot (#69806) [.04] 5.00
Weequay Skiff Guard (#69707) [.01] 5.00

Collection 3, 2nd Batch (Asst. #69705, 1997)
AT-ST Driver (#69823) [.02] 5.00

Princess Leia (Jabba's Prisoner) Collection 1, Gamorrean Guard, Collection 2 and Emperor's Royal Guard, Collection 3 (Kenner 1998)

Boba Fett (#69804) [.03] 5.00
Emperor's Royal Guard (#69717) [.00] 5.00
Garindan (Long Snout) (#69706) [.00] 5.00
Grand Moff Tarkin (#69702) [.01] 5.00
Snowtrooper (#69632) [.00] 5.00

Specials
Four figure set of Han Solo in Endor Gear, Lando
    Calrissian as Skiff Guard, AT-ST driver and
    Darth Vader (J.C. Penney catalog 1997) 20.00

POWER OF THE FORCE 1998

The new header card packaging for 1998 adds a 35mm Freeze Frame Action Slide as an in-package premium and color codes the "Collection Number" (Red for Collection 1, Yellow for Collection 2 and Blue for Collection 3) on a strip at the bottom of the package. The color code stripes have been a great help in separating new packages from old ones so far, but this should diminish when the old figures have sold out and all retail figures have stripes. Even so, it will still be a help. Loose figures do **not** include the 35mm slide. In-package premiums are a separate collectible once they are removed from the package.

There are at least 33 new figures scheduled for delivery in 1998, eight of which have already appeared. This does not count the Princess Leia Collection, the Epic Force figures, nor the Gunner Station assortment. In addition, most or all of the previously issued figures will also reappear. There should be well over 100 different slides to collect by the end of the year.

Just about every beast, accessory and vehicle will have an exclusive figure packed with it. This will help strain the wallet of collectors looking for complete collections. Some of you may want to pay down your credit cards in anticipation of all the new figures coming in 1999 (and beyond) with the opening of the new movie.

The high points of this years new figures include the first Biggs Darklighter figure, Darth Vader in removable helmet, with his finely sculpted head revealed, Captain Piett and Expanded Universe figures Mara Jade and Grand Admiral Thrawn (from Heir to the Empire) and Kyle Katarn (from the Dark Forces Video Game and Comic).

The first batch of Freeze Frame Action Slide Collection 1 figures arrived on schedule in February 1998. Happily or unhappily, they all had a printing error and so corrected versions, with new printing numbers arrived quickly as well. The error is on the back of the header card, under the picture of Jabba and Han, where weary collectors are advised to "Collect all these *Star Wars* Action Figures." In the list that follows, "Saelt-Marae" is misspelled as "Sealt-Marie" — two errors in just 10 letters. The error is the same on all packages and the corrected version has the higher printing number: ".01" versus ".00" for the new figures and other numbers on the reissues (not ".01" as reported in some publications).

GREEN CARD — FREEZE FRAME SERIES
Kenner (1998)

1998 Figures With Freeze Frame Action Slide
Collection 1 (Feb. 1998) with spelling error on back
Bespin Luke (Detachable Hand) (#69713) [.00] $7.00
Endor Rebel Soldier with "Survival Backpack and
    Blaster Rifle" (#69716) [.00] 7.50
Lando Calrissian (General's Gear) (#69756) [.00] 7.00
Princess Leia Organa (Ewok Celebration Outfit)
    (#69714) [.00] 7.00
Above Figures, with spelling error corrected [.01] each . 6.00

Reissues (Feb. 1998) with spelling error on back
Ben (Obi Wan) Kenobi (#69576) [.03] 7.00
Bespin Han Solo (#69719) [.01] 7.00
Han Solo in Carbonite (#69817) [.04] 7.00
Han Solo in Endor Gear (#69621) [.01] 7.00
Hoth Rebel Soldier (#69821) [.02] 7.00

Lando Calrissian (Skiff Guard) (#69622) [.01] 7.00
Luke Skywalker (Stormtrooper) (#69819) [.03] 7.00
Princess Leia (Jabba's Prisoner) (#69683) [.01] 7.00
Rebel Fleet Trooper (#69696) [.02 sticker] 7.00
Reissue figures, spelling corrected [code +.01] each. . . 6.00

Collection 2 (Feb. 1998)
Biggs Darklighter (#69758) [.00] 7.00
Ewoks: Wicket & Logray (#69711) [.00]. 7.00
Lak Sivrak (#69753) [.00] 7.00
Reissues
Admiral Ackbar (#69696) [.01]. 6.50
EV-9D9 (#69722) [.01] 6.50
Gamorrean Guard (#69693) [.01] 6.50
Malakili (#69723) [.01] 6.50
Nien Nunb (#69694) [.01] 6.50
Yak Face (#69721) [.01] 6.50

Collection 3 (March 1998)
Captain Piett (#69757) [.00] 7.00
Darth Vader with removable helmet (#69836) [.00] 7.00
Ishi Tib (#69754) [.00]. 7.00
Zuckuss (#69747) [.00]. 7.00
Reissues
Boba Fett (#69803) [.04]. 6.50
Darth Vader (#69802) [.03]. 6.50
Emperor Palpatine (#69811) [.02] 6.50
Emperor's Royal Guard (#69717) [.01] 6.50
Garindan (#69706) [.01] 6.50
Grand Moff Tarkin (#69702) [.02]. 6.50
Snowtrooper (#69632) [.02] 6.50
Stormtrooper (#69803) [.02] 6.50
TIE Fighter Pilot (#69806) [.05]. 6.50

ADDITIONAL NEW 1998 FIGURES
Per Kenner Announcements

Collection 1, estimated prices
C-3PO with Cargo Net (June). $7.00
Luke Skywalker with Blast Shield Helmet (June) 7.00
Princess Leia (Classic) all new likeness (June) 7.00
R2-D2 with Periscope (June) 7.00
Chewbacca (Re-sculpt) (3rd Quarter) 7.00
Lobot (3rd Quarter). 7.00
Mon Mothma (3rd Quarter) 7.50
Prune Face (Orrimaarko) (3rd Quarter). 7.00

Expanded Universe (comic, video game and novel figures)
Clone Emperor (3rd Quarter) *Dark Empire* 7.50
Grand Admiral Thrawn (3rd Quarter) *Heir to the Empire* 7.50
Imperial Sentinel (3rd Quarter) *Dark Empire* 7.50
Mara Jade (3rd Quarter) *Heir to the Empire* 7.50
Luke in Black Cloak (3rd Quarter) *Dark Empire*. 7.50
Princess Leia in Black Cloak (3rd Quarter) *Dark Empire* 7.50
Kyle Katarn (3rd Quarter) *Dark Forces* 7.50
Darktrooper (4th Quarter) *Dark Forces* 7.50
Spacetrooper (4th Quarter) *Heir to the Empire* 7.50

Collection 2, estimated prices
8-D8 Droid (June). 7.00
Ugnaught 2-pack (June). 7.00

Collection 3, estimated prices
Death Star Trooper (June) 7.00
Ree-Yees (June). 7.00
AT-AT Driver (Sept). 7.00
Death Star Droid with Mouse Droid (Sept). 7.00
Pote Snitkin (Sept.). 7.00

(NEW) POWER OF THE FORCE

Only scarce variations of the new figures have attained any collector value as loose figures. They are listed below. All others are worth about $3.00. The only reason that they cost that much is that a dealer has to transport them to the show or advertise, take your order, and ship them to you, and needs some compensation for his time. If you are trying to sell your loose common figures you better not expect to get much for them.

LOOSE FIGURES
Kenner (1995–98)

Loose Figures, scarce
Boba Fett, with half circle on hand $10.00
Ben (Obi-Wan) Kenobi, with long lightsaber 12.50
Darth Vader, with long lightsaber. 10.00
Han Solo in Hoth Gear, with open hand 8.00
Luke Skywalker, with long lightsaber. 12.50
Luke Skywalker in X-wing Fighter Pilot Gear, with
    long lightsaber. 8.00
Luke Skywalker in Dagobah Fatigues, with long
    lightsaber. 6.00
Jedi Knight Luke Skywalker, with brown vest. 12.00
All others, common, each 3.00

MAIL-IN AND EXCLUSIVE FIGURES

There have been quite a few mail-in and exclusive figures in the new series. The first to be offered was the Froot Loops mail-in Han Solo in Stormtrooper disguise. Both the cereal box and the figure are collectible. Since this offer was not tied to any *Star Wars* event or product, many collectors

Han Solo (Stormtrooper Disguise) mail-in (Kenner 1995)

missed it. By contrast, the Spirit of Obi-Wan Kenobi mail-in from Frito Lay was tied to the theater release of the Special Editions of the movies in early 1997. Hardly anyone was unaware of it. The figure can not truly be said to be an action figure as it is not articulated, but Kenner treats it as one on its website and collectors have generally considered it so, as well.

The theater edition Jedi Knight Luke Skywalker is the most valuable of the exclusive figures. It was given away during the first showing of the Special Edition of *Star Wars, A New Hope* on January 31, 1997. There was no prior announcement, not all theaters got the figure and there was no sign of any such figure when I saw the picture at 7:00 p.m. that day. A number of alert movie theater ushers and ticket takers did quite well for themselves by taking home a supply. The figure is identical to the common version sold in stores — only the header card is different.

Many of the *Star Wars* vehicles came with exclusive figures. This practice will continue in 1998, when it will be hard to find a vehicle without an exclusive figure. If you want all the figures you will have to collect vehicles too. The most interesting of these exclusives is the Wedge Antilles error figure. The first batches of the *Millennium Falcon* carry case came with a Wedge Antilles with a white stripe down each arm. This was clearly visible as the figure can be seen in the gun turret of the ship. Later batches of these carry cases corrected the figure. Locally, the original carry case with the error figure was available for quite a while after news of the error appeared in collector magazines. While the error figure

is still the more desirable version, the price difference is not particularly large. New shipments of the carry case, with the correct figure, appeared in local Toys "R" Us stores in March 1998. This new supply will keep the overall price of the figure within reason, but may lead to a greater price differential between the error and corrected versions.

Mail-in Figures

Mail-in Han Solo in Stormtrooper disguise, in plastic bag, (Froot Loops offer) with mailer box	$30.00
Spirit of Obi-Wan Kenobi, with box (Frito Lay offer, 1997)	10.00
Cantina Band Member, Official Star Wars Fan Club exclusive, in plastic bag, with five musical instruments (#69734, 1997) in white mailer box	15.00
Cantina Band Set, five figures: (All five figures are the same as above. Only the instruments are different.) Official Star Wars Fan Club	50.00
Loose: Doikk N'ats with Fizzz Instrument	10.00
Loose: Figrin D'an with Kloo Horn Instrument	10.00
Loose: Ickabel with Fanfars Instrument	10.00
Loose: Nalan with Bandfill Instrument	10.00
Loose: Techn with Omnibox Instrument	10.00
B'Omarr Monk, Hasbro Internet Website offer, in plastic bag, with instruction sheet (#69718, 1997–98) in white mailer box	15.00
Oola and Salacious Crumb, Official Star Wars Fan Club exclusive (May 1998) in window box	15.00

Give-away figure

Jedi Knight Luke Skywalker, Exclusive Star Wars Trilogy Edition, carded, movie theater give-away (1997)	100.00

Exclusive Figures, loose

Wedge Antilles, from *Millennium Falcon* carry case, with white stripes down arms, error figure	10.00
Correct figure, no white stripes	4.00
AT-AT Commander, from Electronic Imperial AT-AT Walker vehicle	5.00
AT-AT Driver, from Electronic Imperial AT-AT Walker vehicle	5.00
A-Wing Pilot, from A-Wing Fighter vehicle	5.00
Han Solo in Carbonite, from Boba Fett's Slave I vehicle	5.00
Biker Scout Stormtrooper, from Imperial Speeder Bike vehicle	5.00
Swoop Trooper, from Swoop vehicle	5.00
Luke Skywalker in Endor Gear, from Speeder Bike vehicle	5.00
Princess Leia Organa in Endor Gear, from Speeder Bike vehicle	5.00

DELUXE FIGURES

Deluxe figures have met with a decidedly mixed review among collectors and in collector publications. None of the weapons/accessories in these packages appeared in the movie. When the first deluxe figure featured a "Capture Claw," many purists feared that Kenner would start issuing figures with every manner of absurd gear, as they have done with Batman. Fortunately, no Deluxe Ninja Luke Skywalker was planned. Only a few of the deluxe figures have been created, and they follow the basic concept behind the Mini-Rigs from the original series which was to sell weapons and accessories that fit in with the ones featured in the film and could be envisioned as "just off camera."

Jedi Knight Luke Skywalker, movie give-away (Kenner 1997)

Deluxe Crowd Control Stormtrooper (Kenner 1996)

Deluxe Probe Droid (Kenner 1997)

The next three deluxe figures featured popular characters with somewhat unmovie-like devices, but the last three (Probe Droid, Snowtrooper and Hoth Rebel Soldier) came much closer to the basic concept and were much more popular with collectors. Other one- and two-man weapons, radar and communication stations, loading dock, cargo handling, refueling and repair droids and equipment would also fit the concept and these could have included soldiers for each side as well. However, the kids probably prefer weapons and accessories associated with the major characters. Anyway, the deluxe figures have turned out to be among the few *Star Wars* items that I have seen discounted, so both Kenner and collectors may be lucky that only seven different ones were made.

For 1998, Kenner has added to, or replaced this line-up with, Gunner Station figures. So far we have two major characters (Han and Luke) plus the guns from the *Millennium Falcon* which they used in the first movie. These appeared in May and it is too soon to tell whether they will have more appeal than the previous offerings, but my guess is that they will be lumped together with the previous deluxe figures.

DELUXE FIGURES
Kenner (1995–98)

First Wave (Asst. #69610, 1996)
Deluxe Crowd Control Stormtrooper with "Flight-Action Thruster Pack and Capture Claw" (#69609,1996) on red *Power of the Force* header card, with 2 warning stickers [533029.00] .. $30.00
Variation, with 1 warning sticker? 15.00
Reissue, printed warnings [.01] 7.00
Loose, with complete Thruster Pack. 4.00
Deluxe Luke Skywalker's Desert Sport Skiff with "Blasting Rocket Launcher and Rapid-Deploy Wings" (#69611, 1996) on red *Power of the Force* header card [533032.00] 10.00
Loose, with complete Sport Skiff 4.00

Deluxe Han Solo with Smuggler Flight Pack plus "Battle-Pivoting Blaster Cannons and Cargo Claw" (#69612, 1996) on red *Power of the Force* header card [533035.00] 10.00
Loose, with complete Flight Pack. 4.00

Second Wave
Deluxe Boba Fett with "Wing-Blast Rocketpack and Overhead Cannon" (#69638, 1997) on green *Power of the Force* header card [536817.00] card says "Weaponry: Photon Torpedo" 10.00
Variation [.01] says "Weaponry: Proton Torpedo" 8.00
Loose, with complete Rocketpack 4.00
Deluxe Probe Droid with "Proton Torpedo and Self-Destruct Exploding Head" (#69677, 1997) on green *Power of the Force* header card [536814.00] with red color scheme back picturing Shadows of the Empire figures. 25.00
Variation [.01] 7.00
Variation [.02] green color scheme 6.00
Loose, complete 4.00

Third Wave
Deluxe Hoth Rebel Soldier with "Anti-Vehicle Laser Cannon" (#69744, 1997) on green *Power of the Force* header card [540061.00] 9.00
Loose, with complete Laser Cannon 4.00
Deluxe Snowtrooper with "E-Web Heavy Repeating Blaster" (#69724, 1997) on green *Power of the Force* header card [540058.00] 9.00
Loose, with complete Blaster 4.00

Gunner Stations (Asst. #69655, May 1998)
Millennium Falcon with Luke Skywalker (#69848) on green *Power of the Force* header card [551811.00] with warning sticker. 10.00
Millennium Falcon with Han Solo (#69766) on green *Power of the Force* header card [551809.00] with warning sticker 10.00

Electronic Power F/X R2-D2 (Kenner 1997)

ELECTRONIC POWER F/X

There are five Electronic Power F/X figures and all of them come with a light-up feature and an action feature controlled by hidden buttons and levers. The packages have diorama scenes which can be cut out and the first two figures, Ben and Darth, interconnect to allow a simulated duel. Luke can also connect with Darth for a duel, but not with the Emperor, who is facing the wrong way. The first version of the Emperor's package pictures his energy bolts shooting up, but the corrected version pictures them shooting down. In the movie scene, Luke was taking his punishment lying on the deck, not flying around the room like Peter Pan.

ELECTRONIC POWER F/X
Kenner (1997)

Electronic Power F/X (Asst. #69615) green header cards
Ben (Obi-Wan) Kenobi with "Glowing Lightsaber
   and Remote Dueling Action" (#69643, 1997) on
   green *Power of the Force* header card [536820.00] . $9.00
   Loose on stand, with backdrop cut-out 4.00
Darth Vader with "Glowing Lightsaber and Remote
   Dueling Action" (#69644, 1997) on green
   Power of the Force header card [536823.00] 9.00
   Loose on stand, with backdrop cut-out 4.00
Luke Skywalker with "Glowing Lightsaber and
   Remote Dueling Action" (#69746, 1997) on
   green *Power of the Force* header card [541867.00] . . 9.00
   Loose on stand, with backdrop cut-out 4.00

R2-D2 (Artoo-Detoo) with "Light-Up Radar Eye,
   Authentic Sounds and Remote Action"
   (#69646, 1997) on green *Power of the Force*
   header card [536826.00] 9.00
   Variation [.01] blue UPC code bars 8.00
   Variation [.02] black UPC code bars 7.00
   Loose on stand, with backdrop cut-out 4.00
Emperor Palpatine with "Dark Side Energy Bolts
   and Remote Action" (#69726, 1997) on green
   Power of the Force header card [541864.00]
   energy bolts pictured pointing up 12.00
   Variation [.01] energy bolts pointing down 8.00
   Loose on stand, with backdrop cut-out 4.00

EPIC FORCE

These 5" figures were introduced at the 1998 Toy Fair. Other than the size, the gimmick is the rotating base, which lets the collector see all sides of the figure without removing it from the package. Three figures appeared at first, and Boba Fett is the most desirable figure of the three, but it is not scarce. C-3PO arrived in late May. Each package back pictures three figures — C-3PO plus the other two from the initial batch of three. However, there were five figures announced for the initial batch and there is no sign of Han Solo Stormtrooper which was supposed to be the fifth figure. A second wave was also scheduled for May 1998.

5" Epic Force Figures with in-package rotating base.
Darth Vader (#69761) [548761.00] $15.00
Bespin Luke Skywalker (#69762) [548763.00] 15.00
Boba Fett (#69763) [548765.00] 15.00
C-3PO (#69764) [548767.00] 15.00

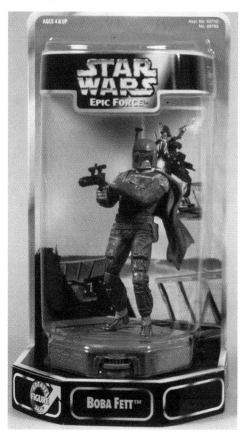

Boba Fett, Epic Force (Kenner 1998)

MILLENNIUM MINTED COIN COLLECTION

The original Power of the Force coins are a popular collectible and Kenner is bringing them back in 1998 in the Millennium Minted Coin Collection series. Each figure in the series comes with a gold-colored coin mounted on a display pedestal. Figures and coins are packaged in a window box which has a back window so you can see the back of the coin. The back of the coin is different from the back of the original coins, so even someone who doesn't notice that the original coins are silver-colored should still be able to tell them apart. The initial boxes appeared in early April and included just three different figures. The combination costs about $10.00, which is about $3.00 to $4.00 more than the figure alone. This seems about right, but a lot of collectors are reluctant to buy still another version of a character that they already own.

4" Figures with Gold Coin (Asst. #69675, April 1998)
    in window box (Toys "R" Us exclusive)
Bespin Han Solo (#84022) [551371.00] $10.00
Chewbacca (#84023) [551375.00] 10.00
Snowtrooper (#84028) [551379.00] 10.00
Emperor Palpatine (2nd Quarter) 10.00
Luke Skywalker in Endor Gear (2nd Quarter) 10.00
Princess Leia in Endor Gear (2nd Quarter) 10.00
C-3PO (3rd Quarter) 10.00

MULTI-PACKS

The Cinema Scenes three-packs first appeared in June 1997 with the Death Star Escape group. Although Kenner calls them Cinema Scenes packs, this phrase doesn't appear anywhere on the package, but the back of the package contains a scene from the movie, with sprocket holes down each side to look like a piece of 70mm film. They are collected, in part, because each one contains at least one figure that is not otherwise available.

The Death Star Escape was a Toys "R" Us exclusive and included a Han Solo Stormtrooper figure which had only been released as the Froot Loops mail-in. The Cantina Showdown was a WalMart exclusive, at least at first, and included the never-before released Dr. Evazan. At the beginning of 1998, two more appeared. The Purchase of the Droids featured Uncle Owen Lars and the Final Jedi Duel had the Emperor seated on his throne/chair. Another pair is scheduled for later in the year. This third group will include the first-ever versions of Jabba's Dancers and collectors are already

Cantina Showdown, out of box (Kenner 1997)

drooling. There's just nothing quite like a sexy alien female to get a collector's blood boiling.

Three-packs are produced in much smaller quantities than carded figures, contain at least one exclusive figure and retail for the same price as three figures, making them a pretty good deal.

"CINEMA SCENES"
Kenner (1997–98)

Cinema Scenes Three-Packs in green *New Power of the Force* window boxes
Death Star Escape with Chewbacca captured
    flanked by Han Solo and Luke Skywalker
    dressed as Stormtroopers, with removable
    helmets (#69737) [542704.00] $15.00
    Loose, 3 figures with backdrop. 8.00
Cantina Showdown with Dr. Evazan, Ponda Baba
    and Obi-Wan Kenobi (#69738, 1997)
    [544550.00] no assortment number 15.00
    Variation [.01] box lists assortment #69650. . . . . . 13.00
    Loose, 3 figures with backdrop. 8.00

Second Batch
Final Jedi Duel with Emperor Palpatine, Darth
    Vader and Luke Skywalker (#69783, 1998)
    [548078.00] 20.00
    Variation [.01] box 18.00
    Loose, 3 figures with backdrop. 8.00
Purchase of the Droids with Uncle Owen Lars,
    C-3PO and Luke Skywalker (#69778, 1998)
    [549672.00] 20.00
    Variation [.01] box 18.00
    Loose, 3 figures with backdrop. 8.00

Scheduled Third Batch, estimated prices
Jabba's Dancers with Rustall, Greeta and Lyn Me
    (1998) [.00] 17.00
    Loose, 3 figures with backdrop. 10.00
Mynock Hunt with Princess Leia in Hoth Gear, Han
    Solo in Bespin Gear and Chewbacca, all with
    respirators (#, 1998) [.00]. 16.00
    Loose, 3 figures with backdrop. 9.00

THREE PACKS

These are three figures, in original packages, with an outer corrugated cardboard package with holes so the the original packages show through. They are sold to various "wholesale club" stores, where they generally sell to members (customers) at a small discount from the prevailing toy store price for three figures. So far there have been two groups of three sets of these three-packs. There does not seem to be a lot of collector interest in them to date, with one exception, probably because the included figures are all common and the packs appeared much later than the original release of the figures. The one exception is the group two pack which contains a reissue Lando Calrissian on a green header card. This scarce version was never sold separately.

Wholesale Club Three-Packs
Group One (1996) all figures are on red header cards
Set One: Han Solo, Chewbacca and Lando Calrissian . $30.00
Set Two: R2-D2, Stormtrooper and C-3PO 30.00
Set Three: Luke Skywalker, Obi-Wan Kenobi and
    Darth Vader. 30.00

Wholesale Club Collector Pack, Set Three (Kenner 1996)

Group Two (1997)
Star Wars: Luke Skywalker in Stormtrooper
Disguise, Tusken Raider and Obi-Wan
Kenobi [547448.00] (#69851) 15.00
The Empire Strikes Back: Lando Calrissian, Luke
Skywalker in Dagobah Fatigues and TIE
Fighter Pilot [547449.00] (69852) 50.00
Return of the Jedi: Jedi Knight Luke Skywalker,
AT-ST Driver and Princess Leia in Boushh
Disguise [547450.00] (69853) 15.00

TWO-PACKS
PRINCESS LEIA COLLECTION

With four new outfits and four new hairstyles, the
Princess could launch her own signature clothing collection
for women who are well proportioned, but a little shorter than

Princess Leia and Luke Skywalker,
Princess Leia Collection (Kenner 1998)

the average super-model. The white outfit she is wearing with
R2-D2 is a little austere, but the same material looks quite
handsome in the low-cut version with see-through cape
shown with Luke Skywalker and it is nicely accessorized
with belt and silver necklace. Her hair includes a single braid
that hangs down a little below her derriere. The Endor outfit,
shown with Wicket, is a casual number, with designer tears up
the front which show a little thigh in combat. She also sports
two long, below-waist length braids (on her head) and long
hair from the Ewok Celebration Outfit figure. With Han Solo
she is wearing a maroon dress, with a floor-length lace top
attached to white shoulder pads which extend all the way up
to her chin. These elements, plus the knee-length boots seem
to be designed to tell Han to keep his "hans" off her.

Princess Leia Collection (Asst. #66935, Feb. 1998)
on green header card
Princess Leia and R2-D2 (#66936) [549367.00] $11.00
Princess Leia (Medal Ceremony) and Luke
Skywalker (#66937, 1998) [549370.00]. 11.00
Princess Leia (Bespin) and Han Solo (#66938)
[549373.00] 11.00
Princess Leia (Endor Celebration) and Wicket
the Ewok (#66939) [549376.00] 11.00

CARRY CASES AND DISPLAY
STANDS

The first display stand for Kenner's *Star Wars* action
figures was available well before the first figures appeared. It
was the one included in the Early Bird Certificate Package.
Actually, the package only held the backdrop. The pegs to
hold the figures came in the package with the Early Bird figures.

The *Star Wars* Action Display Stand was the first of
many mail-away premiums. It was offered on *Star Wars*
action figure cardbacks for two proofs of purchase plus $2.00.
The stand has a plastic base and a cardboard backdrop, plus
levers that rotate groups of figures. It originally came in a
plain mailer box. Later the stand was offered in *Star Wars*
packaging, and finally, in *The Empire Strikes Back* packaging, with six figures, as the Special Action Display Stand.

The *Star Wars* Display Arena also a mail-away premium
and consisted of four L-shaped plastic stands and four
reversible cardboard backdrops, with pegs for display of up to
14 action figures.

DISPLAY STANDS
Kenner (1977–83)

Early Bird Package, 19" x 9½" flat envelope with
certificate to purchase soon-to-be released
figures and cardboard backdrop (#38140)
Star Wars logo $300.00
See under Action Figures for listing of the Early Bird Figures.
Action Display Stand for Star Wars Figures, gray
plastic first offered as a mail-in premium, and
later in stores
Loose, with original plain box 50.00
Original *Star Wars* box (#38990) 350.00
Reissue as Special Action Display Stand in
The Empire Strikes Back box, with six figures. . 550.00
Loose, no box 40.00

Early Bird Certificate Package, back (Kenner 1977)

Display Arena, mail-order premium (1981)
    Original *The Empire Strikes Back* box 40.00
    Reissue in *Return of the Jedi* box 35.00
    Loose 15.00

COLLECTOR CASES

Vinyl Collector's Cases were offered in packaging for each of the movies in turn. The cases each have two storage trays designed to hold 12 figures each. The backsides had foot pegs and could be used to display your figures. There were stickers for the figures so each one would know where it lived. Later, the Darth Vader and C-3PO head-shaped cases along with the Laser Rifle carry case and even the Chewbacca Bandolier Strap proved to be more popular designs, making the rather plain Collector's Case much more common in *Star Wars* packaging than in packaging for the later two films.

CARRY CASES
Kenner (1979–84)

Carry Cases
Collector's Case, black vinyl with illustrated cover,
    holds 24 figures (1979–83)
    Star Wars package $30.00
    The Empire Strikes Back package, *Star Wars*
        Pictures (#39190, 1980). 50.00
    Variation, with *The Empire Strikes Back* pictures . 50.00
    Variation, with logo centered 50.00
    Return of the Jedi package 100.00

Darth Vader Collector's Case, black plastic bust of
    Darth Vader, holds 31 figures (#93630, 1980)
    illustrated wrapper around base
    Original *The Empire Strikes Back* package,
        no figures. 40.00
    With **IG-88**, **Bossk** and **Boba Fett** figures in
        original *The Empire Strikes Back* package
        (#39330) 350.00
    Loose, without figures 15.00
See-Threepio Collector's Case, gold plastic bust of
    C-3PO, hold 40 figures (#70440, 1983)
    illustrated wrapper around base
    Original *Return of the Jedi* package 35.00
    Loose, without figures 15.00
Chewbacca Bandolier Strap, holds 10 figures and
    has two containers for accessories (#70480,
    1983) in 16¼"x9¼x1½" box
    Original *Return of the Jedi* box. 10.00
    Loose, without figures 4.00
Laser Rifle Case, rifle-shaped, holds 19 figures
    (#71530, 1984) cardboard base with color
    illustrations
    Original *Return of the Jedi* box. 40.00
    Loose, without figures 20.00

New carry cases appeared along with the return of the figures in 1995. Generally they have a gimmick. The *Millennium Falcon*-shaped carry case came with a Wedge Antilles figure which was visible in the gun turret. At first the figure had white arm decorations, which did not match the uniform in the movie. Collectors and Kenner seemed to have noticed this about the same time and when later shipments corrected the error, collectors searched for the original figures. However, a lot of the originals are in circulation, which has moderated the dealer price.

CARRY CASES
Kenner (1995–98)

Carry Cases (1995–97)
Electronic Talking C-3PO carry case, head and
    shoulders (#27609, Oct. 1996) $20.00
Millennium Falcon Carry Case with exclusive
    Wedge Antilles figure (#27728, Sept. 1997)
    with white arm stripes (error) 35.00
    Reissue, corrected figure with no stripe on
        arm (#27728, 1998). 25.00
Darth Vader box shaped carry case 20.00

Star Wars *and* The Empire Strikes Back *collector cases (Kenner 1978 and 1980)*

ACTION FIGURES
ALPHABETICAL

ACTION FIGURES: ALPHABETICAL
Kenner (1978–98)

This section lists every *Star Wars* action figure which has appeared on a header card from 1978 through the first quarter of 1998. The listing is alphabetical by the characters current name and all versions of the same character are listed together. This means that characters which appeared in the original series under names such as "Yak Face" and "Hammerhead" are now listed under their new names, "Saelt-Marae" and "Momaw Nadon" and that "Jedi Knight Luke Skywalker" is listed under "Luke Skywalker." Cross references are given under the original names.

Figure and packaging variations which are specific to a given figure are described below, under that figure's listing. Major packaging changes and packaging variations which are common to many figures in a given series were described above in the chronological listings section.

ADMIRAL ACKBAR

Admiral Ackbar of the Rebel Alliance Fleet is a Mon Calamari and stands 1.88 meters tall. He was captured when the Empire invaded his home planet and served as a slave to Grand Moff Tarkin. He escaped during a Rebel attack and joined the Rebel Alliance, where he was instrumental in the design of the B-Wing Fighter. Promoted to Admiral, he first appears in Return of the Jedi.

His figure carried a staff in the classic series and was initially available as a mail-in. The new figure carries a wrist blaster.

Classic:
Admiral Ackbar (#70310, 1983)
    Original *Return of the Jedi* header card $30.00
    Reissue on Tri-Logo header card 15.00
    Loose, with staff. 10.00

New:
Admiral Ackbar with "Comlink Wrist Blaster" on *New Power of the Force* green holo header card (Collection 2, #69686, July 1997) [542901.00] with 2nd hook, in stand-up bubble. . . . 5.00
    Variation, without holo sticker. 5.00
    Reissue, on Freeze Frame header card (#69696) [.01] 6.50
    Loose, with black wrist blaster 3.00

AMANAMAN

This yellow and green reptile carries a skull staff. He was originally available in the Jabba the Hutt Dungeon playset from Sears.

No equivalent figure has appeared in the new series and none seems to be scheduled.

Classic:
Amanaman (#93740, 1985) 5"
    Original *Power of the Force* header card $200.00

Admiral Ackbar (Kenner 1985 and 1997)   *Amanaman and Anakin Skywalker (Kenner 1985)*

Reissue on Tri-Logo header card 150.00
Loose, with skull staff. 100.00

New:
None

ANAKIN SKYWALKER

The Anakin Skywalker figure has the gray and tan robes and benevolent face from the days before he was seduced by the dark side of the Force. His character reverted to this form after his death in *Return of the Jedi*. He is treated as a separate character from Darth Vader. Loose figures were available as a mail-in, but packaged figures are all foreign, which accounts for the large disparity in price.

Classic:
Anakin Skywalker (#93790, 1985) foreign release
    Original *Power of the Force* header card $1,600.00
    Reissue on Tri-Logo header card 125.00
    Loose, no accessories 30.00

New:
None

ASP-7

The ASP-7 droid is a domestic and industrial laborer. It is 1.6 meters tall. The figure comes with a small bundle of supply rods. This droid is from the new Special Edition footage and was not produced in the original figure line.

Classic:
None

New
ASP-7 Droid with "Spaceport Supply Rods" "Newly-Created Footage" sticker, on *New Power of the Force* green holo header card (Collection 2, #69704, July 1997) [540899.00] with 2nd hook, in stand-up bubble $6.00
    Loose, with olive drab supply rod bundle 3.00

AT-AT COMMANDER

The AT-AT (All Terrain Armored Transport) Walker is both a weapons platform and a troop transport. Each takes two pilots, with the Commander acting as navigator and gunner.

In the new series, an exclusive AT-AT Commander and AT-AT Driver are included with the Electronic AT-AT vehicle, and a 12" doll was released in 1997. The first 4" carded version is scheduled for 1998.

Classic:
AT-AT Commander (#69620, 1982)
    Original *The Empire Strikes Back* header card . . . $40.00
    Reissue on *Return of the Jedi* header card 35.00
    Reissue on Tri-Logo header card 25.00
    Loose, with pistol 10.00

New:
None, but see AT-AT Walker vehicle

AT-AT DRIVER

The AT-AT (All Terrain Armored Transport) Walker takes two pilots, with the second acting as navigator and gunner.

The AT-AT driver from the classic series was also included with the MTV-7 vehicle. In the new series, an exclusive AT-AT Commander and AT-AT Driver are included with the Electronic AT-AT vehicle, and a 12" doll was released in 1997. The first 4" carded version is scheduled for 1998.

Classic:
AT-AT Driver (#39379, 1981)
    Original *The Empire Strikes Back* header card . . . $50.00
    Reissue on *Return of the Jedi* header card 35.00
    Reissue on *Power of the Force* header card,
        foreign release only 325.00
    Reissue on Tri-Logo header card 25.00
    Loose, with rifle 10.00

New:
Scheduled for 1998 and see AT-AT Walker vehicle

ASP-7 Droid and AT-AT Commander (Kenner 1997 and 1985)   *AT-AT Driver and AT-ST Driver (Kenner 1981 and 1985)*

AT-ST DRIVER

The AT-ST (All Terrain Scout Transport) Driver is a human Imperial Ground-Assault pilot. He averages 1.8 meters tall.

The first AT-ST Driver issued in the new series came on a Collection 2 header card. This was corrected to Collection 3. There is only a slight premium for the original header card.

Classic:
AT-ST Driver (#71330, 1984)
  Original *Return of the Jedi* header card $30.00
  Reissue on *Power of the Force* header card. 60.00
  Reissue on Tri-Logo header card 14.00
  Loose, with pistol 10.00

New:
AT-ST Driver with "Blaster Rifle and Pistol" on *New Power of the Force* green holo header card (**Collection 2**, #69623, Feb. 1997) [538001.00] with 1st hook, in original bubble 7.50
  Variation, without holo sticker. 8.00
  Reissue [.01] with 2nd hook?, in stand-up bubble. 6.00
AT-ST Driver with "Blaster Rifle and Pistol" on *New Power of the Force* green holo header card (Collection 3, #69823) [.02] with 2nd hook, in stand-up bubble. 5.00
  Loose, with black blaster pistol and rifle 3.00

A-WING PILOT

When the A-Wing Pilot figure was reissued in the Droids series, there were no changes in the figure and the only change in the coin was in the color. Both versions are scarce and valuable.

Classic:
A-Wing Pilot (#93830, 1985)
  Original *Power of the Force* header card $100.00
  Reissue on *DROIDS* header card. 145.00
  Reissue on Tri-Logo header card 60.00
  Loose, with pistol 45.00

New:
  None, but see A-Wing Fighter vehicle

BARADA

Barada was a Klatoonian slave of Jabba the Hutt. He was the first one killed in the battle at the Sarlacc's pit.

Barada also came with the Jabba the Hutt Dungeon playset from Sears. He has not yet appeared in the new series of figures.

Classic:
Barada (#93750, 1985)
  Original *Power of the Force* header card $100.00
  Reissue on Tri-Logo header card 60.00
  Loose, with staff. 40.00

New:
  None

BEN (OBI-WAN) KENOBI

Two versions of Obi-Wan's head were made in the classic figure series, one with gray hair and one with white hair. They are about equally scarce (or equally common) and there is little or no difference in price between the two versions.

The really scarce figure variation is the telescoping lightsaber which came with just a few of the earliest versions of Luke Skywalker, Darth Vader and this figure . It adds about $2,000 to Obi-Wan's value, but beware of fakes, even on carded figures.

The header card photo was changed during the *Return of the Jedi* figure series. The original photo shows a bare-headed Obi-Wan facing left and holding a yellow lightsaber, which is pointing to the upper left. The new photo shows a hooded Obi-Wan facing forward and holding a blue lightsaber which is pointing to the upper right.

In the new figure series, Obi-Wan's photo on the back of the header card ".00" was changed from from a head and shoulders photo to a full figure photo on the ".01" card. In addition, a spelling error was corrected when "an" was changed to "and". More significantly, his lightsaber was shortened, along with Luke's and Darth's, resulting in two different versions of his figure.

A-Wing Pilot and Barada (Kenner 1985)   *Ben (Obi-Wan) Kenobi (Kenner 1978 and 1983)*

Ben (Obi-Wan) Kenobi, long lightsaber and bust photo back (Kenner 1995)

Bespin Security Guards, white and black (Kenner 1980 and 1982)

Classic:
Ben (Obi-Wan) Kenobi (#38250, 1978) **white** or **gray hair**
   Original *Star Wars* "12 back" header card. $225.00
   Variation, with telescoping lightsaber, scarce . . 2,250.00
   Loose, with telescoping lightsaber 400.00
   Reissue on *Star Wars* "20/21 back" header card . 125.00
   Reissue on *The Empire Strikes Back* header card . . 90.00
   Reissue on *Return of the Jedi* header card 50.00
   Reissue on *Return of the Jedi* header card
     new package, hooded, holding lightsaber
     in front. 50.00
   Reissue on *Power of the Force* header card. . . . 125.00
   Reissue on Tri-Logo header card 50.00
   Loose, with lightsaber 15.00

New:
Ben (Obi-Wan) Kenobi with "Lightsaber and
   Removable Cloak" on *New Power of the
   Force* red header card (#69576, July 1995)
   bust photo, long lightsaber [521791.00] 50.00
   Full-figure photo on package back, long
     lightsaber [.01]. 50.00
   Loose, with long lightsaber. 12.50
   Full-figure photo, short lightsaber [.01] 10.00
   Reissue, with holo sticker. 10.00
Ben (Obi-Wan) Kenobi with "Light Saber and
   Removable Cloak" on *New Power of the
   Force* green holo header card (Collection 1,
   #69576) [.02] with 2nd hook, in stand-up bubble . . 5.00
   Reissue, without holo sticker 5.00
   Reissue, on Freeze Frame header card [.03] 7.00
   Reissue, Saelt Marae spelling corrected [.04]. . . . 6.00
   Loose, with blue lightsaber (short) with silver
     handle 3.00

Bespin Han Solo: *See Han Solo (Bespin Outfit)*

BESPIN SECURITY GUARDS

The 1980 version of the Bespin Security Guard had white skin and the 1982 version (same name, different UPC code) had black skin. They are meant to be different figures and the packages have different photos, but neither package uses the words "black" or "white." These names have been added by collectors and dealers to distinguish between the figures. No doubt someone will eventually suggest politically correct names for these figures. In the mean time I am going to call them "white" and "black" like everybody else does. The white figure can also be found with slightly yellowish skin and a slightly longer, but not quite Fu Manchu-style mustache. He doesn't have oriental features, but then neither does Christopher Lee, who played Fu Manchu in several movies. The price is the same in either case. The white Bespin Security Guard also came with the Cloud Car vehicle.

Classic:
Bespin Security Guard (#39810, 1980) **white**
   Original *The Empire Strikes Back* header card. . . $65.00
   Reissue on *Return of the Jedi* header card 30.00
   Reissue on Tri-Logo header card 25.00
   Loose, with pistol. 10.00

Black:
Bespin Security Guard (#69640, 1982) **black**
   Original *The Empire Strikes Back* header card. . . . 50.00
   Reissue on *Return of the Jedi* header card 45.00
   Reissue on Tri-Logo header card 25.00
   Loose, with pistol. 10.00

New:
   None

BIB FORTUNA

Bib Fortuna is a Twi'lek from the planet Ryloth and serves as Jabba the Hutt's majordomo.

He first appears in the new series of figures on a Collection 1 header card, but this was changed to Collection 2. The original Collection 1 card is not especially scarce and carries only a slight premium over the more common Collection 2.

Classic:
Bib Fortuna (#70790, 1983)
   Original *Return of the Jedi* header card $30.00
   Reissue on Tri-Logo header card 15.00
   Loose, with brown cloak and staff 10.00

Bib Fortuna (Kenner 1983 and 1997)

New:
Bib Fortuna with "Hold-Out Blaster" on *New Power of the Force* green holo header card (**Collection 1**, #69634, April 1997) [538955.00] with 1st hook, in original bubble 10.00
Bib Fortuna with "Hold-Out Blaster" on *New Power of the Force* green holo header card (Collection 2, #69812) [.01] with 2nd hook, in original or stand-up bubble. 5.00
Variation, without holo sticker. 6.00
Loose, with black hold-out blaster 3.00

BIGGS DARKLIGHTER

Biggs Darklighter is a Tatooine native and childhood friend of Luke. He is the famous missing character of the original *Star Wars* movie because his scenes with Luke at the beginning of the movie were cut and all you saw was his death at the hands of Darth Vader. The Special Edition restored a brief reunion scene with Luke, just before they both took off in their X-wing fighters to attack the Death Star.

He did not appear among the classic figures, but he was a popular character with figure customizers. His figure was finally issued in early 1998.

Biggs Darklighter and Biker Scout (Kenner 1998 and 1983)

Classic:
None, but many custom figures exist.

New:
Biggs Darklighter with "Blaster Pistol" on *New Power of the Force* green Freeze Frame header card (Collection 2, #69758, 1998) [550387.00] $7.00
Loose, with black blaster pistol and rifle 3.00

BIKER SCOUT

One of several types of Imperial pilots which appeared in the classic series, but has only been sold with a vehicle in the new series. He is not a highly sought figure in either of these series.

Classic:
Biker Scout (#70820, 1983)
Original *Return of the Jedi* header card $35.00
Reissue on *Power of the Force* header card. 80.00
Reissue on Tri-Logo header card 15.00
Loose, with pistol. 12.50

New:
None, but see the Imperial Speeder Bike vehicle

BOBA FETT

Boba Fett is a notorious bounty hunter. Darth Vader hired him to track down Han Solo's ship in order to lure Luke Skywalker out into the open. Han Solo was his reward and Jabba the Hutt paid handsomely for Solo.

In the original series, Boba Fett also came an early mail-in figure. It was advertised with a spring-loaded rocket back pack missile, but this was a child safety hazard and was never shipped. A few prototypes exist and are extremely valuable. See "Mail-Ins" in the previous section for a listing of this, and other classic mail-in figures.

Boba Fett (Kenner 1983)

The front header card photo was changed during the *Return of the Jedi* figure series. The original photo shows your favorite bounty hunter facing forward in front of a starry background. The new photo shows him facing to the left, armed to the teeth in front of a blue sky.

The Tri-Logo version of Boba Fett is somewhat different from the versions on other header cards. The plastic is lighter in weight, the comb below the right knee is unpainted and the rocket is shorter and in a matte finish. In the domestic version of Boba Fett he is heavier, has the comb on his right knee painted the same color as the knee band and has a

*Boba Fett, front view, and close-up showing hand variations
(Kenner 1996)*

rocket with a glossy finish. Also, the Tri-Logo figures chest plate is a darker green and the shoulder and knee highlights are darker brown than those on the domestic figure.

In the new series of figures, Boba Fett initially came with a black disk painted on the back of each hand that was bisected by a bar that is the same color as the rest of the hand. This appears as two half-moons or half-circles. Later versions of the figure have a complete black disk or full-circle. The half-circle version is scarce and valuable. A comma after the word "Empire" on the ".00" header card was corrected to a period on the ".01" header card. It returned to a comma on the ".02" and ".03" cards.

Classic:
Boba Fett (#39250, 1978–79)
 Original *Star Wars* header card $850.00
 Reissue on *The Empire Strikes Back* header card . 275.00
 Reissue on *Return of the Jedi* header card. 300.00
 Reissue on *Return of the Jedi* header card
  new package. 275.00
 Reissue on Tri-Logo header card 150.00
 Loose, with pistol. 60.00
 Loose, Tri-Logo version, with pistol 60.00
Boba Fett (#39260, 1985)
 On *Droids* header card. 250.00
 Loose, cartoon version. 50.00

New:
Boba Fett with "Sawed-Off Blaster Rifle and Jet
 Pack" on *New Power of the Force* red header
 card (#69582, Feb. 1996) with half circles on
 back of hand [526520.00] "," 50.00
 Variation [.01] "." half circles. 45.00
 Variation, one half circle and one full circle. 50.00
 Loose, with half circles on hand 10.00
 With full circle on hand [.01]. 10.00
Boba Fett with "Sawed-off Blaster Rifle and Jet
 Pack" on *New Power of the Force* green holo
 header card (**Collection 1**, #69582) [.02] with
 2nd hook, in original bubble. 15.00
Boba Fett with "Sawed-Off Blaster Rifle and Jet
 Pack" on *New Power of the Force* green holo
 header card (Collection 3, #69804) [.03] with
 2nd hook, in stand-up bubble. 5.00

Reissue, on Freeze Frame header card
 (#69804) [.04] 6.50
Loose, with black sawed-off blaster and
 beat-up jet pack. 3.00

BOSSK

Bossk is a freelance Trandoshan bounty hunter. His specialty is catching Wookiees and he first appears in *The Empire Strikes Back*.

His was the famous "secret figure" offered as a mail-in at the end of the original *Star Wars* figure series.

Classic:
Bossk (Bounty Hunter) (#39760, 1980)
 Original *The Empire Strikes Back* header card . . $100.00
 Reissue on *Return of the Jedi* header card 75.00
 Reissue on Tri-Logo header card 55.00
 Loose, with rifle 10.00

New:
Bossk with "Blaster Rifle and Pistol" on *New Power
of the Force* green header card (Collection 2,
#69617, Feb. 1997) [537991.00] with 1st hook
 and original bubble 5.00
Variation, without holo sticker. 5.00
With holo picture [.01] and 2nd hook, with
 stand-up bubble. 5.00
Loose, with light gray rifle and pistol. 3.00

Bossk and B-Wing Pilot (Kenner 1997 and 1983)

B-WING PILOT

This has never been a highly sought figure. He comes in a nifty red jumpsuit.

Classic:
B-Wing Pilot (#71280, 1984)
 Original *Return of the Jedi* header card $30.00
 Reissue on *Power of the Force* header card. 30.00
 Reissue on Tri-Logo header card 12.00
 Loose, with pistol. 10.00

New:
 None

*Captain Piett and Chewbacca Bounty Hunter
(Kenner 1998 and 1996)*

Chewbacca (Kenner 1983 and 1985)

CAPTAIN PIETT

Captain Piett was promoted to Admiral during the assault on Hoth and commanded Darth Vader's ship *Executor* until its destruction during the Battle of Endor.

Classic:
None

New:
Captain Piett with "Blaster Rifle and Pistol" on *New Power of the Force* Freeze Frame header card
(Collection 3, #69757, 1998) [550624.00] $7.00

CHEWBACCA

Chewbacca is from the planet Kashyyyk and owes a life debt to Han Solo for releasing him from an Empire prison.

The original figure was included in the Early Bird Package and many of these had a green blaster rifle. All other original series versions of the figure had a black blaster rifle. The front photo was changed during the *Return of the Jedi* series. The original photo shows Chewbacca with slicked-back hair and carrying his weapon. In the new photo Chewie has frizzy hair and no visible weapon.

Classic:
Chewbacca (#38210, 1978) 4¼" figure
  Original *Star Wars* "12 back" header card with
    green blaster rifle $225.00
  Original *Star Wars* "12 back" header card with
    black blaster rifle 200.00
  Reissue on *Star Wars* "20/21 back" header
    card. 100.00
  Reissue on *The Empire Strikes Back* header card . . 85.00
  Reissue on *Return of the Jedi* header card 50.00
  Reissue on *Return of the Jedi* header card
    with new frizzy head and shoulders photo 45.00
  Reissue on *Power of the Force* header card. . . . 100.00
  Reissue on Tri-Logo header card 35.00
  Loose, with black blaster rifle 10.00
  Loose, with green blaster rifle 35.00

New:
Chewbacca with "Bowcaster and Heavy Blaster
  Rifle" 4¼" on *New Power of the Force* red
  header card (#69578, July 1995) [521795.00] . . . 10.00
Chewbacca with "Bowcaster and Heavy Blaster
  Rifle" on *New Power of the Force* green
  holo header card (Collection 1, #69578) [.01]
  with 2nd hook, in stand-up bubble 5.00
  Variation, without holo sticker. 5.00
  Loose, with dark gray bowcaster and heavy
    blaster rifle. 3.00

Chewbacca Bounty Hunter Disguise

The Shadows of the Empire storyline takes place between *The Empire Strikes Back* and before *Return of the Jedi*. Chewbacca and Leia go to Coruscant to try to find out who has been attempting to assassinate Luke. Chewbacca disguises himself as Snoova, a Wookiee bounty hunter. Leia is captured by Prince Xizor and Chewbacca contacts Luke and Lando. The three of them and Dash Rendar proceed to rescue the princess.

Classic:
None

New:
Chewbacca in Bounty Hunter Disguise, with "Vibro
  Axe and Heavy Blaster Rifle" on a purple
  Shadows of the Empire card (#69562,
  June 1996) [531618.00]. $7.00
  Loose, with black axe and heavy blaster rifle 3.00

CHIEF CHIRPA

Chief Chirpa is an Ewok, one of eight issued in the *Return of the Jedi* series.

Classic:
Chief Chirpa (#70690, 1983)
  Original *Return of the Jedi* header card $30.00
  Reissue on Tri-Logo header card 17.00
  Loose, with long club 10.00

New:
None

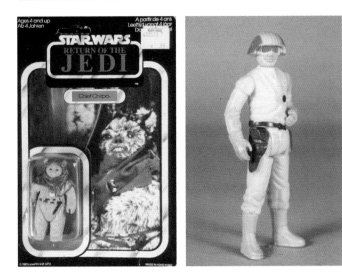

*Chief Chirpa and Cloud Car Pilot, loose
(Kenner 1983 and 1980)*

C-3PO (Kenner 1978 and 1996)

CLOUD CAR PILOT

This figure has not been heavily collected, and like several similar figures from the classic series, it will only be issued with a vehicle in the new series.

Classic:
Cloud Car Pilot (Twin Pod) (#69630, 1982)
    Original *The Empire Strikes Back* header card. . . $60.00
    Reissue on *Return of the Jedi* header card 40.00
    Reissue on Tri-Logo header card 30.00
    Loose, with pistol and light 15.00

New:
    None, but look for Cloud Car vehicle

C-3PO (SEE-THREEPIO)

C-3PO is a Cybot Galactica 3PO Human Cyborg Relations Droid and needs no introduction, but he could use a few more buyers. He generally ranks about last in his class in price.

Classic:
See-Threepio (C-3PO) (#38220, 1978)
    Original *Star Wars* "12 back" header card. $150.00
    Reissue on *Star Wars* "20/21 back" header
        card. 100.00
    Reissue on *The Empire Strikes Back* header card . . 60.00
    Reissue on Tri-Logo header card 45.00
    Loose, no accessories 10.00

New:
C-3PO with "Realistic Metalized Body" on *New Power of the Force* red header card
    (#69573, July 1995) [521785.00] 10.00
C-3PO with "Realistic Metalized Body" on *New Power of the Force* green holo header card
    (Collection 1, #69573) [.01] with 2nd hook, in original or stand-up bubble. 5.00
    Loose, without accessories 3.00

C-3PO (Removable Limbs)

The removable limbs version of C-3PO is based on his dismemberment and subsequent rescue in the second movie. C-3PO has not been a popular character with collectors.

Classic:
C-3PO (Removable Limbs) (#69600, 1982)
    Original *The Empire Strikes Back* header card. . . $60.00
    Reissue on *Return of the Jedi* header card as
        See-Threepio (C-3PO) (#69430) "now
        with removable arms, legs and back pack". . . . 35.00
    Reissue on *Power of the Force* header card
        as **See-Threepio (C-3PO)** with removable
        limbs (#69430) 75.00
    Reissue on Tri-Logo header card 25.00
    Loose, with back pack and limbs 10.00

New:
C-3PO with "Realistic Metalized Body and Cargo Net" and sticker saying "New Pull-Apart Feature" on *New Power of the Force* green Freeze Frame header card (Collection 1, #69832) [.00] 7.00
    Loose, with Cargo Net 3.00

C-3PO with Removable Limbs (Kenner 1983 and 1985)

Darth Vader (Kenner 1978 and 1998)

DARTH VADER

The front photo was changed during the *Return of the Jedi* series. The original photo shows Darth holding his lightsaber. The new photo is more of a close-up and no lightsaber is visible.

The telescoping lightsaber is a really scarce variation which came with just a few of the earliest versions of Obi-Wan Kenobi, Luke Skywalker and Darth Vader. It adds about $2,000 to its value, but beware of fakes.

In the new series, his lightsaber was shortened, along with Luke's and Obi-Wan's, resulting in two different versions of his figure and the packaging variation of a short lightsaber in a long lightsaber clear plastic tray.

Classic:
Darth Vader (#38230, 1978) 4¼" figure
  Original *Star Wars* "12 back" header card..... $200.00
  Variation, with telescoping lightsaber, scarce . . 2,250.00
  Loose, with telescoping lightsaber 400.00
  Reissue on *Star Wars* "20/21 back" header card . 100.00
  Reissue on *The Empire Strikes Back* header card . . 75.00
  Reissue on *Return of the Jedi* header card 45.00
  Reissue on *Return of the Jedi* header card,
    new package. 45.00
  Reissue on *Power of the Force* header card. 90.00
  Reissue on Tri-Logo header card 40.00
  Loose, with lightsaber 10.00

New:
Darth Vader with "Lightsaber and Removable
  Cape" 4¼" on *New Power of the Force* red
  header card (#69572, July 1995) with long
  lightsaber [521783.00] 25.00
  Loose, with long red lightsaber. 10.00
  Short lightsaber in long package slot 20.00
  Short lightsaber version 10.00
Darth Vader with "Lightsaber and Removable
  Cape" on *New Power of the Force* green holo
  header card (**Collection 1**, #69572) [.01] with
  2nd hook, in original bubble 10.00
Darth Vader with "Lightsaber and Removable
  Cape" on *New Power of the Force* green
  holo header card (Collection 3, #69802) [.02]
  with 2nd hook, in original or stand-up bubble 5.00

  Retooled, *Shadows of the Empire* two-pack
    style figure [.02]. 8.00
  Reissue, on Freeze Frame header card [.03] 6.50
  Loose, with red lightsaber with black handle. 3.00

Darth Vader (Removable Helmet)

With his helmet off, Darth reveals what's left of his original face. There is no equivalent figure from the classic series. The Anakin Skywalker figure, listed previously, is the ghostly version seen only at the end of the third movie.

Classic:
  None

New:
Darth Vader with "Removable Helmet and Light-
  saber" and with "Detachable Hand" on *New
  Power of the Force* Freeze Frame header
  card (Collection 3, #69836, 1998) [550630.00] . . . $7.00
  Loose 3.00

*Darth Vader with Removable Helmet and Dash Rendar
(Kenner 1998 and 1996)*

DASH RENDAR

The Shadows of the Empire storyline takes place between *The Empire Strikes Back* and before *Return of the Jedi*. Dash Rendar, an exceptional pilot, is a former Imperial Officer cadet and former smuggler, who fought for the Rebel Alliance in the Battle of Hoth. Leia hired him to help protect Luke from bounty hunters employed by Prince Xizor. When Leia is captured by Prince Xizor, he teams up with Luke, Lando and Chewbacca to rescue the princess. He shoots down many of Xizor's Black Sun starships with his *Outrider* starfighter.

Classic:
  None

New:
Dash Rendar, with "Heavy Weapons Pack" on a
  purple *Shadows of the Empire* card (#69561,
  June 1996) [531616.00] $7.00
  Loose, with grey double-barreled pistol and
    rifle and shoulder mount backpack 3.00

Star Destroyer Commander and Death Star Droid
(Kenner 1983 and 1978)

Death Star Gunner (Kenner 1996 and 1997)

DEATH SQUAD COMMANDER

The Death Squad Commander's name was changed to Star Destroyer Commander when he was reissued on *The Empire Strikes Back* header cards.

Classic:
Death Squad Commander (#38290, 1978)
    Original *Star Wars* "12 back" header card $200.00
    Reissue on *Star Wars* "20/21 back" header
        card 100.00
    Reissue on *The Empire Strikes Back* header
        card as **Star Destroyer Commander** 100.00
    Reissue on *Return of the Jedi* header card 65.00
    Reissue on Tri-Logo header card 65.00
    Loose, with pistol 15.00

New:
    None

DEATH STAR DROID

While not exactly a famous character from the movie, the classic Death Star Droid has attracted collector interest and it will be issued late in 1998 in the new series.

Classic:
Death Star Droid (#39080, 1978–79)
    Original *Star Wars* header card $150.00
    Reissue on *The Empire Strikes Back* header card . 130.00
    Reissue on *Return of the Jedi* header card 70.00
    Reissue on Tri-Logo header card 60.00
    Loose, no accessories 10.00

New:
    Scheduled for 4th quarter, 1998

DEATH STAR GUNNER

The Death Star Gunner is a heavy weapons gunner who operates the Death Star superlaser. Operating big guns must make one grow taller because between Collection 1 and Collection 3 their average height, as listed on the header card, increased from 1.8 meters to 1.83 meters.

Classic:
    None

New:
Death Star Gunner with "Radiation Suit and Blaster
    Pistol" (#69608, Oct. 1996) on *New Power of
    the Force* red header card (Collection 1)
    [535194.00] $25.00
    Reissue, now with "Imperial Blaster and
        Assault Rifle" on green header card [.01] 8.00
    Reissue with holographic picture on green
        header card [.01] with 1st hook, in original
        bubble 6.00
Death Star Gunner with "Imperial Blaster and
    Assault Rifle" on *New Power of the Force*
    green holo header card (Collection 3, #69809)
    [.02] with 2nd hook, in original bubble 5.00
    Loose with black assault rifle and blaster pistol . . . 3.00

DENGAR

Dengar is a freelance human bounty hunter. He stands 1.8 meters tall and first appeared in *The Empire Strikes Back*. Darth Vader employs him to find Han Solo.

Dengar (Kenner 1985 and 1997)

Classic:
Dengar (#39329, 1981)
    Original *The Empire Strikes Back* header card . . . $50.00
    Reissue on *Return of the Jedi* header card 35.00
    Reissue on Tri-Logo header card 25.00
    Loose, with rifle 10.00

New:
Dengar with "Blaster Rifle" on *New Power of the
    Force* green holo header card (Collection 2,
    #69687, July 1997) [542903.00] with 2nd
    hook, in stand-up bubble 5.00
    Variation, without holo sticker 5.00
    Loose, with black pistol and blaster rifle 3.00

DROIDS FIGURES

Figures from the *Droids* series are listed only in the Action Figures — Chronological Section.

8D8 carded and loose (Kenner 1984)

8D8

This droid was also available in the Jabba the Hutt Dungeon playset from Sears.

Classic:
8D8 (#71210, 1984)
    Original *Return of the Jedi* header card $30.00
    Reissue on Tri-Logo header card 15.00
    Loose, no accessories 10.00

New:None

EMPEROR PALPATINE

Emperor Palpatine is the human dictator of the Galactic Empire. He stands 1.73 meters tall, but mostly he is stooped over. The figure comes with a walking stick in both the original and new versions. He was initially available loose as a mail-in.

In the new series, the figure initially came on a Collection 1 header card. This was quickly corrected to

Emperor Palpatine (Kenner 1985 and 1998)

Collection 3, making the original ".00" version somewhat scarce. It commands only a slight premium over the more common corrected version.

Classic:
The Emperor (#71240, 1984)
    Original *Return of the Jedi* header card $35.00
    Reissue on *Power of the Force* header card. 75.00
    Reissue on Tri-Logo header card 15.00
    Loose, with cane 10.00

New:
Emperor Palpatine with "Walking Stick" on *New
    Power of the Force* green holo header card
    (**Collection 1**, #69633, April 1997) [538959.00]
    with 1st hook, in original bubble 10.00
Emperor Palpatine with "Walking Stick" on *New
    Power of the Force* green holo header card
    (Collection 3, #69811, 1997) [.01] with 2nd
    hook, in original or stand-up bubble 5.00
    Reissue, on Freeze Frame header card [.02] 6.50
    Loose, with a black walking stick 3.00

EMPEROR'S ROYAL GUARD

The Emperor's guards are human "Sovereign Protectors of the Emperor." They average 1.83 meters tall, about 0.1 meters taller than their Emperor. The figure comes with a force pike

Classic:
Emperor's Royal Guard (#70680, 1983)
    Original *Return of the Jedi* header card $40.00
    Reissue on Tri-Logo header card 20.00
    Loose, with pike. 10.00

New:
Emperor's Royal Guard with "Force Pike" on *New
    Power of the Force* green holo header card
    (Collection 3, #69717, Sept. 1997) [542911.00]
    with 2nd hook, in stand-up bubble 5.00
    Reissue, on Freeze Frame header card [.01] 6.50
    Loose, with light gray pike 3.00

Endor Rebel Soldier: *See Rebel Soldier (Endor Gear)*

Emperor's Royal Guard (Kenner 1983 and 1997)   *Ewoks: Wicket & Logray and 4-Lom (Kenner 1998 and 1997)*

EV-9D9

The EV-9D9 is a Merendata EV Supervisor Droid owned by Jabba the Hutt. It is 1.6 meters tall. The figure comes with a data entry terminal on a stand. The figure is 4¾" tall, taller than the average human figure which is not to scale with the 1.6 meter given height.

The classic series figure was also available in the Jabba the Hutt Dungeon playset from Sears.

Classic:
EV-9D9 (#93800, 1985)
  Original *Power of the Force* header card $150.00
  Reissue on Tri-Logo header card 100.00
  Loose, no accessories 75.00

New:
EV-9D9 with Datapad 4¾" on *New Power of the Force* green holo header card (Collection 2, #69722, Oct. 1997) [542919.00] with 2nd hook, in stand-up bubble 5.00
  Variation, without holo sticker................ 5.00
  Reissue, on Freeze Frame header card [.01] 6.50
  Loose, with black data terminal on stand 3.00

EV-9D9 (Kenner 1985 and 1997)

EWOKS FIGURES

Figures from the *Ewoks* series are listed only in the Action Figures — Chronological Section.

EWOKS: WICKET & LOGRAY

These two characters were previously issued separately in the *Return of the Jedi* figure line and are listed later.

Classic: Separate Figures

New:
Ewoks: Wicket & Logray with "Staff, Medicine Pouch and Spear" on *New Power of the Force* green Freeze Frame header card (Collection 2, #69711) [550383.00] $7.00
  Loose Wicket, with hood and spear 2.00
  Loose Logray, with mask, medicine pouch and staff 2.00

4-LOM (Classic)

Kenner reversed the names of 4-LOM and Zuckuss in the original figure line-up and corrected it in the new figures. The original figure was available as a mail-in.

Classic:
4-LOM (#70010, 1982)
  Original *The Empire Strikes Back* header card .. $150.00
  Reissue on *Return of the Jedi* header card 30.00
  Reissue on Tri-Logo header card 25.00
  Loose, with weapon....................... 10.00

New:
  See Zuckuss

4-LOM (formerly Zuckuss)

The real 4-LOM is a an industrial protocol droid working as a freelance bounty hunter. He makes his first appearance in *The Empire Strikes Back* and somewhat resembles another protocol droid — C-3PO. His programming was altered and he became a thief and eventually a bounty hunter, working with Zuckuss for Jabba the Hutt.

Zuckuss and FX-7 Medical Droid (Kenner 1980)

Classic:
See Zuckuss

New:
4-LOM with "Blaster Pistol and Blaster Rifle" on *New Power of the Force* green holo header card (Collection 2, #69688, July 1997) [542905.00] with 2nd hook, in stand-up bubble. . . $5.00
Variation, without holo sticker. 5.00
Loose, with black pistol and blaster rifle 3.00

FX-7

The FX-7 is a medical droid, but not a popular figure with collectors.

Classic:
FX-7 (Medical Droid) (#39730, 1980)
    Original *The Empire Strikes Back* header card. . . $50.00
    Reissue on *Return of the Jedi* header card 40.00
    Reissue on Tri-Logo header card 50.00
    Loose, no accessories 10.00

New:
None

GAMORREAN GUARD

The Gamorrean guards work as palace guards for Jabba the Hutt. They are 1.8 meters tall and only slightly less in girth. If they have keen minds and pleasant dispositions, they keep them well hidden beneath their horns, snout and tusks.

Classic:
Gamorrean Guard (#70670, 1983)
    Original *Return of the Jedi* header card $25.00
    Reissue on *Power of the Force* header card,
        foreign release only 150.00
    Reissue on Tri-Logo header card 18.00
    Loose, with axe 10.00

New:
Gamorrean Guard with Vibro Ax on *New Power of the Force* green holo header card (Collection 2, #69693, Oct. 1997) [542909.00] with 2nd hook, in original bubble 6.00
Reissue, on Freeze Frame header card [.01] 6.50
Loose, with black vibro ax with bone handle. 3.00

GARINDAN

Garindan is a Kubaz spy who sells his services to the highest bidder, like all good spys. He is seen in the Mos Eisley spaceport in the original movie, but he had to wait until the new figures to appear in plastic.

Classic:
None

New:
Garindan (Long Snout) with "Hold-Out Pistol" on *New Power of the Force* green holo header card (Collection 3, #69706, July 1997) [542907.00] with 2nd hook, in stand-up bubble. . . $5.00
Reissue, on Freeze Frame header card (#69706) [.01] 6.50
Loose, with black hold-out pistol 3.00

GENERAL MADINE

General Madine is from the planet Corellia. He was an

Gamorrean Guard (Kenner 1985 and 1997)   *Garindan and General Madine (Kenner 1997 and 1983)*

Grand Moff Tarkin, holo picture and plain picture (Kenner 1997)

Greedo (Kenner 1978 and 1997)

Imperial officer, but now fights for the Rebel Alliance. He helped to devise the plan to attack the second Death Star.

Classic:
General Madine (#70780, 1983)
    Original *Return of the Jedi* header card $30.00
    Reissue on Tri-Logo header card 15.00
    Loose, with staff. 10.00

New:
None

GRAND MOFF TARKIN

Grand Moff Tarkin is the human commander of the Death Star. He is 1.8 meters tall.

The figure is supposed to come with a blaster rifle and pistol, but actually it just has a large and a small pistol. His figure appeared briefly on a Collection 2 header card before being changed to Collection 3. The original version is quite scarce, accounting for its value.

Classic:
None

New:
Grand Moff Tarkin with "Imperial Issue Blaster Rifle
    and Pistol" and sticker on plastic bubble
    which says "Never Before Offered in any
    Kenner Collection" on *New Power of the
    Force* green holo header card (**Collection 2**,
    #69702, 1997) [540897.00] with 2nd hook,
    in stand-up bubble $20.00
Grand Moff Tarkin with "Imperial Issue Blaster Rifle
    and Pistol" and sticker on plastic bubble
    which says "Never Before Offered in any
    Kenner Collection" on *New Power of the
    Force* green holo header card (Collection 3,
    #69702, July 1997) [.01] with 2nd hook, in
    stand-up bubble. 5.00
    Variation, without holo sticker. 5.00
    Reissue, on Freeze Frame header card [.02] 6.50
    Loose, with large and small black blaster
       pistols 3.00

GREEDO

Greedo is a freelance Rodian bounty hunter. He stands 1.65 meters tall in his green skin, not counting his antenna. He died early in the Cantina scene in the first movie. He should have checked under the table for Han Solo's gun.

Despite this brief movie appearance, he has been a popular figure and appeared fairly early in both the new and the original figure lines.

Classic:
Greedo (#39020, 1978–79)
    Original *Star Wars* header card $150.00
    Reissue on *The Empire Strikes Back* header card . 125.00
    Reissue on *Return of the Jedi* header card 55.00
    Reissue on Tri-Logo header card 60.00
    Loose, with blaster pistol 10.00

New:
Greedo, with "Rodian Blaster Pistol" (#69606, Oct.
    1996) on *New Power of the Force* red header
    card (Collection 1) [535190.00] 25.00
    Reissue, now with "Blaster Pistol" on green
       header card [.01]. 8.00
    Reissue with holographic picture on green
       header card [.01]. 6.00
    Loose, with black Rodian blaster rifle and pistol . . . 3.00

Hammerhead: *See Momaw Nadon*

HAN SOLO

In the original series, Luke Skywalker had two hair colors, but Han Solo changed his whole head. He may have gotten the large head in the movies when Leia kissed him. The small head is more common on the earlier cards, but was phased out. The large head is more common on later cards and loose figures. The front picture of Han was changed during the *Return of the Jedi* series. His original picture shows him with his pistol held in his right hand, pointing up. The new picture shows him his gun pointing directly at you, held in both hands.

Han Solo (Kenner 1978 and 1997)

Classic:

Han Solo with **large head** (#38260, 1978) dark brown hair
   Original *Star Wars* "12 back" header card. $575.00
   Reissue on *Star Wars* "20/21 back" header
      card. 400.00
   Reissue on *The Empire Strikes Back* header card . 250.00
   Reissue on *Return of the Jedi* header card,
      new photo 175.00
   Reissue on Tri-Logo header card 125.00
   Loose, with pistol. 25.00
Han Solo with **small head** (#38260) brown hair
   Original *Star Wars* "12 back" header card. 500.00
   Reissue on *Star Wars* "20/21 back" header
      card. 400.00
   Reissue on *The Empire Strikes Back* header card . 300.00
   Reissue on *Return of the Jedi* header card. 150.00
   Reissue on *Return of the Jedi* header card,
      new photo 200.00
   Reissue on Tri-Logo header card 150.00
   Loose, with pistol. 35.00

New:

Han Solo with "Heavy Assault Rifle and Blaster" on
   New Power of the Force red header card
   (#69577, July 1995) [521793.00] 12.50

Han Solo with "Heavy Assault Rifle and Blaster" on
   New Power of the Force green holo header
   card (Collection 1, #69577) [.01] with 2nd
   hook, in original or stand-up bubble 5.00
   Variation, without holo sticker. 5.00
   Loose, with black blaster pistol and rifle 3.00

Han Solo (Bespin Outfit)

On the back of header card version ".01" for the new Freeze Frame issue of this figure "Saelt-Marae" is misspelled as "Sealt-Marie" — two errors in just 10 letters. Version ".02" corrects this error.

Classic:
Han Solo (Bespin Outfit) (#39339, 1981)
   Original *The Empire Strikes Back* header card . . $125.00
   Reissue on *Return of the Jedi* header card 75.00
   Reissue on Tri-Logo header card 40.00
   Loose, with pistol. 12.50

New:
Bespin Han Solo with "Heavy Assault Rifle and
   Blaster" on *New Power of the Force* green
   holo header card (Collection 1, #69719,
   Sept. 1997) [542913.00] with 2nd hook, in
   stand-up bubble. 5.00
   Reissue, on Freeze Frame header card [.01] 7.00
   Reissue [.02] corrected spelling 6.00
   Loose, with black blaster pistol and rifle 3.00

Han Solo (Carbonite)

Han Solo was flash frozen in a carbonite chamber and turned over to Boba Fett who delivered him to Jabba the Hutt where he became Jabba's favorite wall decoration. All this was just a test run. Darth Vader's plan was to freeze Luke and turn him over to the Emperor. Kenner keeps changing its mind, from Carbonite Chamber, to Carbonite Freezing Chamber to Carbonite Block, but you get the block and the figure for the price of the figure.

On the back of header card version ".04" for the new Freeze Frame issue of this figure "Saelt-Marae" is misspelled

Han Solo Bespin Outfit (Kenner 1997 and 1998)   *Han Solo Carbonite (Kenner 1985 and 1998)*

as "Sealt-Marie" — two errors in just 10 letters. Version ".05" corrects this error.

Classic:
Han Solo (in Carbonite Chamber) (#93770, 1985)
    Original *Power of the Force* header card $225.00
    Reissue on Tri-Logo header card, figure on top . 175.00
    Loose, with carbonite sheet 100.00

New:
Han Solo in Carbonite with "Carbonite Freezing
    Chamber" on *New Power of the Force* red
    header card (#69613, June 1996) [532826.00]. . . 20.00
    Reissue with "Carbonite Block" [.01]. 7.50
Han Solo in Carbonite with "Carbonite Block" on
    New Power of the Force green holo header
    card (Collection 2, #69613, 1997) [.02] with
    2nd hook, in original or stand-up bubble. 7.00
    Reissue, Collection 1 (#69613, 1997 [.03]
      with 2nd hook, in stand-up bubble 5.00
    Reissue, on Freeze Frame header card
      (#69817, 1998) [.04] 7.00
    Reissue, [.05] corrected spelling 6.00
    Loose, with carbonite block and black blaster
      pistol 3.00

Han Solo (Endor Gear/Trench Coat)

Han Solo Trench Coat carded and loose (Kenner 1984)

In early 1998, Han changed from Navy blue pants to tan or brown pants. These figures have only appeared on plain picture header cards, although these two changes should be independent of each other and brown pants on a holo card is possible. Since there are no text or graphics changes on the printed card, the new version is still numbered version ".00." All of the figures are now being issued on "Freeze Frame" cards, so this particular version should remain quite scarce.

The initial Freeze Frame version misspelled "Saelt-Marae" and this makes it worth somewhat more than the corrected version. Both versions come with brown pants, so the loose brown pants figure is not scarce.

Classic:
Han Solo (in Trench Coat) (#71300, 1984)
    Original *Return of the Jedi* header card $50.00
    Reissue on *Power of the Force* header card. . . . 500.00

Han Solo Endor Gear, blue pants and brown pants
(Kenner 1997)

    Reissue on Tri-Logo header card 25.00
    Loose, with camo coat and pistol 15.00

New:
Han Solo in Endor Gear with "Blaster Pistol" on
    New Power of the Force green holo header
    card (Collection 1, #69621, April 1997)
    [538957.00] with 1st hook, in original bubble or
    with 2nd hook, in stand-up bubble, navy blue pants . 5.00
    Loose, blue pants, with black blaster pistol. 3.00
    Reissue, brown pants, plain picture 20.00
    Reissue, on Freeze Frame header card
      (#69621, 1998) [.01] brown pants 7.00
    Reissue, [.02] corrected spelling 6.00
    Loose, brown pants, with black blaster pistol 3.00

Han Solo (Hoth Outfit)

The new Han Solo in Hoth Gear originally came with an open hand, which was too open to hold his blaster pistol. The hand was changed for later versions of the figure. It's called a "closed hand," or a "gripping hand" but there is still an opening between the thumb and fingers.

Han Solo Hoth Gear (Kenner 1980 and 1996)

Classic:
Han Solo (Hoth Outfit) (#39790, 1980)
    Original *The Empire Strikes Back* header card . . . $75.00
    Reissue on *Return of the Jedi* header card 75.00
    Reissue on Tri-Logo header card 40.00
    Loose, with pistol 15.00

New:
Han Solo in Hoth Gear with "Blaster Pistol and
    Assault Rifle" on *New Power of the Force* red
    header card (#69587, March 1996) [.00] with
    open hand 25.00
    Loose, with open hand 8.00
    Variation, with closed hand 15.00
    Loose, with closed hand, black blaster pistol
        and assault rifle 3.00

Hoth Rebel Soldier: *See Rebel Soldier (Hoth Gear)*

IG-88, carded and loose (Kenner 1980)

IG-88

IG-88 is a freelance assassin droid created by Holowan scientists at Darth Vader's request to work as a bounty hunter. Because of its programming, it values Imperial credits much more than organic life, making it a "devastatingly efficient hunting machine." *See also: Two-packs*

Classic:
IG-88 (Bounty Hunter) (#39770, 1980) 4½" figure
    Original *The Empire Strikes Back* header card . . . $95.00
    Reissue on *Return of the Jedi* header card 75.00
    Reissue on Tri-Logo header card 75.00
    Loose, with rifle and pistol 15.00

New:
    None, but see Shadows of the Empire two-packs.

IMPERIAL COMMANDER

The Imperial Commander figure has not been issued in the new series. His place has been taken by Captain Piett

Classic:
Imperial Commander (#39389, 1980)
    Original *The Empire Strikes Back* header card . . . $45.00

Imperial Commander and Imperial Dignitary
(Kenner 1983 and 1985)

    Reissue on *Return of the Jedi* header card 35.00
    Reissue on Tri-Logo header card 25.00
    Loose, with pistol 10.00

New:
    None

IMPERIAL DIGNITARY

The tall, skinny and effeminate Imperial Dignitary first appeared in the Power of the Force series and has not been issued in the new series.

Classic:
Imperial Dignitary (#93850, 1985)
    Original *Power of the Force* header card $75.00
    Reissue on Tri-Logo header card 45.00
    Loose, no accessories 30.00

New:
    None

IMPERIAL GUNNER

The Imperial Gunner was originally available in the Power of the Force series and has not been issued in the new series. The closest equivalent is the Death Star Gunner.

Classic:
Imperial Gunner (#93760, 1985)
    Original *Power of the Force* header card $150.00
    Reissue on Tri-Logo header card 125.00
    Loose, with pistol 75.00

New:
    None

Imperial Stormtrooper: *See Stormtrooper*

Imperial Stormtrooper (Hoth Gear): *See Snowtrooper*

Imperial TIE Fighter Pilot: *See TIE Fighter Pilot*

Imperial Gunner and Ishi Tib (Kenner 1985 and 1998)

ISHI TIB

Ishi Tib comes from Planet Tibrin, where everyone lives in cities build on coral reefs. He, and others from his planet, joined the Rebel Alliance because they are ardent freedom lovers.

Classic:
None

New:
Ishi Tib with "Blaster Rifle" on *New Power of the Force* green Freeze Frame header card (Collection 3, #69754, March 1998) [550621.00] .... $ 7.00
Loose, with all equipment 3.00

JAWAS

The Jawas are hardware traders on Tatooine. They average just 1 meter in height, but drive a big sandcrawler. The original Jawa came with a vinyl cape, but this was quickly changed to cloth. The few vinyl-caped Jawas are the most valuable of all the *Star Wars* figures. Care in buying is essential, because a fake vinyl cape is not hard to make and a loose

Jawas (Kenner 1978 and 1997)

Jawa in cloth cape is cheap. Even carded figures can be altered with skillful re-gluing of the bubble.

Classic:
Jawa (#38270, 1978) **vinyl cape**, 2¼" figure
    Original *Star Wars* "12 back" header card . . . $2,500.00
    Loose, with weapon and vinyl cape 300.00
Jawa (#38270) **cloth cape**
    Original *Star Wars* "12 back" header card..... 200.00
    Reissue on *Star Wars* "20/21 back" header
        card........................... 90.00
    Reissue on *The Empire Strikes Back* header card .. 75.00
    Reissue on *Return of the Jedi* header card 45.00
    Reissue on *Power of the Force* header card..... 75.00
    Reissue on Tri-Logo header card 65.00
    Loose, with weapon and cloth cape 13.00

New:
Jawas with "Glowing Eyes and Ionization Blasters"
    2½" and 2¼" (Collection 2, #69607, Nov.
    1996) on *New Power of the Force* red header
    card [535183.00] 20.00
    Reissue, now with "Glowing Eyes and Blaster
        Pistols" on green header card [.01] 6.00
    Reissue with holographic picture on green
        header card [.02] with 2nd hook, in
        stand-up box........................... 6.00
    Loose, two figures with small pistol and large
        ionization blaster 3.00

Jedi Knight Luke Skywalker: *See Luke Skywalker
(Jedi Knight Outfit)*

KLAATU

Klaatu can be found with either tan limbs or gray limbs and sometimes with some of each. The price is the same in all cases, but a difference might start to show up if the figures becomes more valuable.

If you don't know where this character's name comes from then you don't know your classic science fiction movies very well. "Klaatu Barada Nikto" was the phrase which Patricia Neal said to the robot in *The Day the Earth Stood Still* to stop it from destroying the world after Michael Rennie (Klaatu) was shot. You can find it on a lot of T-shirts at science fiction conventions.

Classic:
Klaatu (#70730, 1983) with **tan arms** or **gray arms**
    Original *Return of the Jedi* header card $30.00
    Reissue on Tri-Logo header card 15.00
    Loose, with apron and spear 10.00

New:
None

Klaatu in Skiff Guard Outfit

Klaatu is one of Jabba the Hutt's skiff guards. Along with Barada and Nikto, he makes up the famous phrase that Patricia Neal is taught by Michael Rennie to say to stop Gort, the evil eyed robot, from destroying the Earth in the 1950s classic movie *The Day the Earth Stood Still*. The original figure was also available in the Jabba the Hutt Dungeon playset from Sears.

Klaatu and Klaatu Skiff Guard (Kenner 1983 and 1985)

*Lak Sivrak and Lando Calrissian, General Pilot
(Kenner 1998 and 1985)*

Classic:
Klaatu (in Skiff Guard Outfit) (#71290, 1984)
    Original *Return of the Jedi* header card $30.00
    Reissue on Tri-Logo header card 15.00
    Loose, with weapon 10.00

New:
    None

LAK SIVRAK

Lak Sivrak is a "Shistavanen Wolfman, expert hunter, tracker and Imperial world scout." He fought for the Rebels at the Battle of Hoth and dies in the Battle of Endor.

Classic:
    None

New:
Lak Sivrak with "Blaster Pistol and Vibro-Blade" on
    New Power of the Force green Freeze Frame
    header card (Collection 2, #69753) [550380.00] . $7.50
    Loose, with black blaster pistol and rifle 3.00

LANDO CALRISSIAN

Lando is the former captain of the *Millennium Falcon*. He lost the ship in a high-stakes game of sabacc to you know who, but eventually became Baron Administrator of the Cloud City mining and gambling establishment.

There are two versions of the character. In one, there is some white showing in his mouth and the figure is variously described as having teeth or smiling. The other version has the mouth closed and no white teeth or smile is visible.

Classic:
Lando Calrissian
Lando Calrissian (#39800, 1980) **no teeth** version
    Original *The Empire Strikes Back* header card . . . $60.00
    Loose, with pistol 12.50

Lando Calrissian (#39800, 1980) **white teeth** version
    Original *The Empire Strikes Back* header card 65.00

Reissue on *Return of the Jedi* header card 45.00
Reissue on Tri-Logo header card 45.00
Loose, with pistol 12.50

New:
Lando Calrissian with "Heavy Rifle and Blaster
    Pistol" on *New Power of the Force* red header
    card (#69583, Feb. 1996) [526523.00] with
    1st hook, in original bubble 7.50
    Reissue on *New Power of the Force* green
      header card, Collection 1 (#69583) [.01] (in
      Wholesale Club three figure packages only)
      with 2nd hook and stand-up bubble 25.00
    Loose, with heavy pistol and light hold-out
      pistol, plus blue and black cape 3.00

Lando Calrissian (General)

On the back of header card version ".00" for the new issue of this figure "Saelt-Marae" is misspelled as "Sealt-Marie" — two errors in just 10 letters. Version ".01" corrects this error. The error version is scarce.

Classic:
Lando Calrissian (General Pilot) (#93820, 1985)
    Original *Power of the Force* header card $110.00
    Reissue on Tri-Logo header card 70.00
    Loose, with cape and pistol 50.00

New:
Lando Calrissian in General's Gear with "Blaster
    Pistol" on *New Power of the Force* green
    Freeze Frame header card (Collection 1,
    #69756) [547101.00] 7.00
    Reissue, Saelt Marae spelling corrected [.01] 6.00
    Loose, with black blaster pistol and tan cape 3.00

Lando Calrissian (Skiff Guard)

Lando wears his skiff guard outfit when he works with Leia, Chewbacca, Luke and R2-D2 to rescue Han from Jabba the Hutt.

Lando Calrissian Skiff Guard (Kenner 1983 and 1998)

Lobot and Logray (Kenner 1981 and 1983)

On the back of header card version ".01" for the new Freeze Frame issue of this figure "Saelt-Marae" is misspelled as "Sealt-Marie" — two errors in just 10 letters. Version ".02" corrects this error.

Classic:
Lando Calrissian (Skiff Guard Disguise) (#70830, 1983)
    Original *Return of the Jedi* header card $45.00
    Reissue on Tri-Logo header card 20.00
    Loose, with spear. 15.00

New:
Lando Calrissian as Skiff Guard with "Skiff Guard
    Force Pike" on *New Power of the Force* green
    holo header card (Collection 1, #69622, April
    1997) [538961.00] 2nd hook, gold circles 5.00
    Variation, without holo sticker. 5.00
    Reissue, on Freeze Frame header card [.01] 7.00
    Reissue, [.02] corrected version 6.00
    Loose, with gray force pike and helmet 3.00

LOBOT

Lobot is the chief aid to Lando Calrissian in the administration of Cloud City. He is a human/cyborg originally from Bespin.

Classic:
Lobot (#39349, 1981)
    Original *The Empire Strikes Back* header card . . . $45.00
    Reissue on *Return of the Jedi* header card 35.00
    Reissue on Tri-Logo header card 25.00
    Loose, with pistol. 8.00

New: Scheduled for 1998

LOGRAY

Logray is an Ewok Medicine Man. He was issued with Wicket, as part of the Ewok pack in the New Power of the Force line-up.

Classic:
Logray (Ewok Medicine Man) (#70710, 1983)
    Original *Return of the Jedi* header card $30.00
    Reissue on Tri-Logo header card 15.00

    Loose, with mask, staff and pouch 10.00

New:
    None, but see Ewoks two-pack

See also: EWOKS series

LUKE SKYWALKER

Luke Skywalker was included in the Early Bird Package and many of these figures, plus a few of the original carded figures have a telescoping lightsaber. A genuine telescoping lightsaber adds about $1,000 to the figure's value, but many fakes are believed to exist. Both blond-haired and brown-haired Lukes were made throughout the original series. Blondes may or may not have more fun, but blond Lukes came in both tan pants and lighter colored pants. Brown Lukes only had tan pants. The header card picture was changed during the *Return of the Jedi* series from the original contemplative Tatooine picture to an action gunner picture. Both cards are common and there is little or no difference in price, although the new photo should be slightly preferable to collectors who have earlier versions of the original photo.

Luke Skywalker and Luke Skywalker with Long Lightsaber
(Kenner 1978 and 1995)

In the new series, his lightsaber was shortened, along with Darth's and Obi-Wan's, resulting in two different versions of his figure and the packaging variation of a short lightsaber in a long lightsaber clear plastic tray.

Classic:
Luke Skywalker (#38180, 1978) **blond hair**
Original *Star Wars* "12 back" header card..... $325.00
Reissue on *Star Wars* "20/21 back" header
card.................................. 250.00
Reissue on *The Empire Strikes Back* header card . 200.00
Reissue on *Return of the Jedi* header card..... 175.00
Reissue, gunner picture, on *Return of the Jedi*
header card.......................... 165.00
Reissue on Tri-Logo header card 125.00
Loose, with lightsaber 35.00
Luke Skywalker (#38180) **brown hair**
Reissue on *The Empire Strikes Back* header card . 225.00
Reissue on *Return of the Jedi* header card..... 160.00
Reissue, gunner picture, on *Return of the Jedi*
header card.......................... 150.00
Reissue on Tri-Logo header card 135.00
Loose, with lightsaber 25.00
Variation, carded, with telescoping lightsaber,
blond or brown hair, scarce 1,250.00
Loose, with telescoping lightsaber 200.00

New:
Luke Skywalker with "Grappling-Hook Blaster and
Lightsaber" on *New Power of the Force* red
header card (#69571, July 1995) [521781.00]
with long lightsaber 30.00
Loose, with long lightsaber and blaster........ 12.50
Short lightsaber in long slot version, scarce 75.00
Short lightsaber version 15.00
Loose, with short lightsaber and blaster 4.00

Luke (Battle Poncho)

Luke Skywalker in Battle Poncho was issued in the original Power of the Force series, but he has not been issued in the new series. The closest equivalent is the Luke Sky-walker in Endor Gear which came with the Speeder Bike vehicle.

Classic:
Luke Skywalker (in Battle Poncho) (#93710, 1985)
Original *Power of the Force* header card $100.00
Reissue on Tri-Logo header card 60.00
Loose, with poncho and pistol 50.00

New:
None

Luke (Bespin)

The front photo was changed during *The Empire Strikes Back* series. The original photo shows Luke standing in front of a white background, preparing to draw his gun. The new photo shows him facing forward with gun drawn in front of a blue background.

On the back of header card version ".00" for the Freeze Frame issue of this figure "Saelt-Marae" is misspelled as "Sealt-Marie." Version ".01" corrects this error. The error version is scarce, and expensive.

Classic:
Luke Skywalker (Bespin Fatigues) (#39780, 1980)
Original *The Empire Strikes Back* header card .. $100.00
Reissue on *The Empire Strikes Back* header
card, new package 145.00
Reissue on *Return of the Jedi* header card,
yellow hair........................... 140.00
Reissue on Tri-Logo header card 125.00
Loose, with pistol and lightsaber 15.00
Reissue on *Return of the Jedi* header card,
brown hair............................ 90.00
Reissue on Tri-Logo header card 125.00
Loose, with pistol and lightsaber 20.00

New:
Luke Skywalker in Bespin Gear with "Detachable
Hand" on *New Power of the Force* green
Freeze Frame header card (Collection 1,
#69713) [.00] 7.00
Reissue, [.01] "Saelt-Marae" spelling corrected ... 6.00
Loose, with all equipment 3.00

Luke Skywalker Battle Poncho and Luke Skywalker Bespin Fatigues (Kenner 1985)   *Luke Skywalker Ceremonial and Luke Skywalker Dagobah (Kenner 1997 and 1996)*

Luke (Ceremonial Outfit)

The ceremonial outfit is the one worn by Luke when he receives a medal (along with Han and Chewbacca) after destroying the first death star. He must be proud, because (if you believe the figures) he grows from his original 1.72 meters to 1.75 meters. He stays that height while on Hoth, but shrinks back to 1.72 meters after he becomes a Jedi and feels the weight of the universe on his shoulders.

The figure originally appeared on a Collection 2 card, but this error was soon corrected and the Collection 1 version is the more common. There is only a slight premium for the error card.

Classic:
None

New:

Luke Skywalker in Ceremonial Outfit with "Medal of Valor and Blaster Pistol" and "All New Likeness of Luke" on sticker on *New Power of the Force* green holo header card (**Collection 2**, #69691, Nov. 1997) [540895.00] with 1st hook, in stand-up bubble $10.00
Luke Skywalker in Ceremonial Outfit with "Medal of Valor and Blaster Pistol" and "All New Likeness of Luke" on sticker on *New Power of the Force* green holo header card (Collection 1, #69691) [.01] with 2nd hook, in stand-up bubble . . 5.00
Variation, without holo sticker 5.00
Loose, with black blaster pistol and gold medal on brown strap 3.00

Luke (Dagobah)

This figure is based on the period in *The Empire Strikes Back* when Luke is in Jedi training on Dagobah. He is pictured on the header card with Yoda on his back and Yoda figure from the same series comes with a backpack which would allow you to recreate this.

Classic:
None

New:

Luke Skywalker in Dagobah Fatigues with "Lightsaber and Blaster Pistol" on *New Power of the Force* red header card (#69588, March 1996) with long lightsaber [527601.00] $25.00
Loose, with long lightsaber. 6.00
Short lightsaber in long package slot [.01] 15.00
Short lightsaber [.01] 15.00
Loose, with short lightsaber and black blaster pistol 3.00

Luke (Hoth Gear)

In the new series, the figure initially came on a Collection 2 header card. This was quickly corrected to Collection 1, making the original ".00" version somewhat scarce.

Classic:

Luke Skywalker (Hoth Battle Gear) (#69610, 1982)
Original *The Empire Strikes Back* header card . . . $75.00
Reissue on *Return of the Jedi* header card 40.00
Reissue on Tri-Logo header card 35.00
Loose, with rifle 15.00

New:

Luke Skywalker in Hoth Gear with "Blaster Pistol and Lightsaber" on *New Power of the Force* green holo header card (**Collection 2**, #69619, Feb. 1997) [537997.00] 1st hook, in original bubble 10.00
Variation, without holo sticker 10.00
Luke Skywalker in Hoth Gear with "Blaster Pistol and Lightsaber" on *New Power of the Force* green holo header card (Collection 1, #69822) [.01] with 2nd hook, in original or stand-up bubble . 5.00
Variation, without holo sticker 6.00
Loose, with black blaster pistol and blue lightsaber with silver handle 3.00

Luke (Imperial Guard Disguise)

The Shadows of the Empire storyline takes place between *The Empire Strikes Back* and before *Return of the Jedi*. Luke and Lando go to the Imperial Center of Coruscant

Luke Skywalker Hoth Gear and Luke Skywalker Imperial Guard (Kenner 1997 and 1996)   *Luke Skywalker Jedi Knight (Kenner 1983 and 1996)*

where Leia is held prisoner by Prince Xizor. They steal Imperial Guard uniforms and team up with Dash Rendar and Chewbacca to rescue the princess.

Classic:
None

New:
Luke Skywalker in Imperial Guard Disguise, with "Taser Staff Weapon" on a purple *Shadows of the Empire* card (#69566, June 1996) [531622.00] $7.00
Loose, with dark red helmet and gray staff....... 3.00

Luke (Jedi Knight)

Both the original and the new figures had variations. In the original series, the figure came most frequently with a green lightsaber, but some figures had a blue lightsaber instead. In the new series, the first figures to appear had a brown tunic or vest, but most of the figures have a black tunic that is the same color as the rest of the figure. In both series, the variation is an important factor in value. A Jedi Knight Luke Skywalker, in common black vest, was also used as a give-away at the *Star Wars Special Edition* premiere in early 1997. This figure came on a special header card and is listed in the previous section of this book under Mail-In and Exclusive figures.

Classic:
Luke Skywalker (Jedi Knight Outfit) with **green lightsaber** (#70650, 1983)
Original *Return of the Jedi* header card $100.00
Reissue on *Power of the Force* header card.... 175.00
Reissue on Tri-Logo header card 60.00
Loose, with cloak, pistol and green lightsaber.... 40.00
With **blue lightsaber**, scarce
Original *Return of the Jedi* header card 175.00
Reissue on Tri-Logo header card 90.00
Loose, with cloak, pistol and blue lightsaber..... 60.00

New:
Jedi Knight Luke Skywalker with "Lightsaber and Removable Cloak" on *New Power of the Force* red header card (#69596, June 1996) [532822.00] with **brown tunic** 75.00

Loose, brown tunic, with cloak and green lightsaber............................. 12.00
With **black tunic** [.00] 8.00
Loose, black tunic, with cloak and green lightsaber............................. 3.00
Jedi Knight Luke Skywalker with "Lightsaber and Removable Cloak" on *New Power of the Force* green holo header card (**Collection 2**, #69816, 1997) [.01] with 2nd hook, in original bubble 10.00
Variation, without holo sticker............... 10.00
Jedi Knight Luke Skywalker with "Lightsaber and Removable Cloak" on *New Power of the Force* green holo header card (Collection 1, #69816, 1997) [.02] with 2nd hook, in stand-up bubble............................. 5.00
Loose, with silver-handled green lightsaber and black cloak 3.00

Luke (Stormtrooper)

On the back of header card version ".03" for the new Freeze Frame issue of this figure "Saelt-Marae" is misspelled as "Sealt-Marie" — two errors in just 10 letters. Version ".04" corrects this error.

Classic:
Luke Skywalker, Imperial Stormtrooper Outfit (#93780, 1985)
Original *Power of the Force* header card $400.00
Reissue on Tri-Logo header card 225.00
Loose, with removable helmet and pistol 150.00

New:
Luke Skywalker in "Stormtrooper Disguise with Imperial Issue Blaster" (#69604, Nov. 1996) on *New Power of the Force* red header card (Collection 2) [535181.00] 25.00
Reissue on green header card [.01] with 1st hook, in original bubble 12.00
Reissue, with holographic picture on green header card [.01]....................... 10.00
Luke Skywalker in "Stormtrooper Disguise with Imperial Issue Blaster" on *New Power of the Force* green holo header card (Collection 1, #69819) [.02] with 2nd hook, in original bubble.... 5.00

Luke Skywalker Stormtrooper (Kenner 1985 and 1997)   *Luke Skywalker (X-Wing Fighter Pilot) (Kenner 1985 and 1996)*

Variation, without holo sticker. 6.00
Reissue, on Freeze Frame header card [.03] 7.00
Reissue, [.04] spelling corrected 6.00
Loose, with white helmet and black blaster
  pistol 3.00

Luke (X-Wing Pilot)

Between header cards ".00" and ".01" in the new series the word "Fighter" was changed to "fighter" in three places.

Classic:
Luke Skywalker: X-Wing Pilot (#39060, 1978–79)
  Original *Star Wars* header card $150.00
  Reissue on *The Empire Strikes Back* header
    card as **Luke Skywalker (X-Wing Pilot)** 115.00
  Reissue on *Return of the Jedi* header card as
    Luke Skywalker (X-Wing Fighter Pilot) 50.00
  Reissue on *Power of the Force* header card. . . . 100.00
  Reissue on Tri-Logo header card 80.00
  Loose, with pistol. 15.00

New:
Luke Skywalker in X-wing Fighter Pilot Gear with
  "Lightsaber and Blaster Pistol" on *New Power
  of the Force* red header card (#69581, Feb.
  1996) with long lightsaber [526517.00]
  "Fighter" and [.01] "fighter". 25.00
  Loose, with long blue lightsaber. 8.00
  Short lightsaber in long package slot 20.00
  Short lightsaber 10.00
Luke Skywalker in X-wing Fighter Pilot Gear with
  "Lightsaber and Blaster Pistol" on *New Power
  of the Force* green holo header card (Col-
  lection 1, #69581) [.02] with 2nd hook, in
  original bubble. 5.00
Luke Skywalker in X-wing Fighter Pilot Gear with
  "Lightsaber and Blaster Pistol" on *New Power
  of the Force* green holo header card (Collection 1, #69581) [.02] with 2nd hook, in
  stand-up bubble. 5.00
  Loose, with black pistol and blue lightsaber
    (short) with silver handle 3.00

LUMAT

Lumat is an Ewok, one of eight issued in the *Return of the Jedi* series.

Classic:
Lumat (#93670, 1984)
  Original *Return of the Jedi* header card $40.00
  Reissue on *Power of the Force* header card. 50.00
  Reissue on Tri-Logo header card 25.00
  Loose, with bow. 15.00

New:
  None

MALAKILI (RANCOR KEEPER)

Malakili is Jabba the Hutt's Rancor wrangler. He is a portly human and shows an unnaturally close emotional attachment to his Rancor after Luke kills it.

Classic:
Rancor Keeper (#71350, 1984)
  Original *Return of the Jedi* header card $30.00
  Reissue on Tri-Logo header card 15.00
  Loose, with prod 10.00

New:
Malakili (Rancor Keeper) with "Long-Handled Vibro-Blade" on
  New Power of the Force green holo
  header card (Collection 2, #69723, Oct. 1997)
  [542921.00] with 2nd hook, in stand-up bubble. . . . 5.00
  Reissue, on Freeze Frame header card [.01] 6.50
  Loose, with a brown-handled silver vibro-blade . . . 3.00

MOMAW NADON (HAMMERHEAD)

The Momaw Nadon, the hammerhead, is an Ithorian scout affiliated with the Rebel Alliance. He is 1.95 meters tall and is first seen in the Mos Eisley Cantina.

His original figure carried a pistol. Now he carries a blaster rifle (called a "Laser Canon" on the first 1996 card).

Classic:
Hammerhead (#39030, 1978–79) 4" figure
  Original *Star Wars* header card $130.00

Rancor Keeper/Malakili (Kenner 1985 and 1998)   *Hammerhead/Momaw Nadon (Kenner 1978 and 1997)*

Reissue on *The Empire Strikes Back* header card . 115.00
Reissue on *Return of the Jedi* header card 75.00
Reissue on Tri-Logo header card 60.00
Loose with Imperial blaster pistol 12.50

New:
Momaw Nadon "Hammerhead" with "Double-Barreled Laser Canon" (Collection 2, #69629, Nov.
1996) on *New Power of the Force* red header
card [535187.00] warning on sticker........... 20.00
Reissue, now with "Double-Barreled Blaster
Rifle" on green header card [.01] printed
warning 6.00
Reissue, with holographic picture on green
header card [.01] with 1st hook, in original
bubble, with printed warning 6.00
Loose, with double-barreled blaster rifle........ 3.00

Nien Nunb and Nikto (Kenner 1998 and 1984)

NIEN NUNB

Nien Nunb is a Sullustan, who acts as a rebel pilot and
navigator. He is listed as 1.6 meters tall. In the *Return of the
Jedi* movie, he is Lando's co-pilot during the Battle of Endor.
The figure was initially available loose as a mail-in.

Classic:
Nien Nunb (#70840, 1983)
    Original *Return of the Jedi* header card $35.00
    Reissue on Tri-Logo header card 20.00
    Loose, with pistol....................... 10.00

New:
Nien Nunb with "Blaster Pistol and Blaster Rifle" on
New Power of the Force green holo header
card (Collection 2, #69694, Oct. 1997)
[542917.00] with 2nd hook, in stand-up bubble.... 5.00
    Reissue, on Freeze Frame header card [.01] 6.50
    Loose, with black blaster pistol and blaster rifle ... 3.00

NIKTO

The figure was also available in the Jabba the Hutt Dungeon playset from Sears.

Classic:
Nikto (#71190, 1984)
    Original *Return of the Jedi* header card $30.00

Reissue on *Power of the Force* header card,
    foreign release only 300.00
Reissue on Tri-Logo header card 15.00
Loose, with staff........................ 10.00

New:
    None

PAPLOO

Paploo is an Ewok, one of eight issued in the *Return of
the Jedi* series.

Classic:
Paploo (#93680, 1984)
    Original *Return of the Jedi* header card $40.00
    Reissue on *Power of the Force* header card..... 45.00
    Reissue on Tri-Logo header card 25.00
    Loose, with staff....................... 15.00

New:
    None

PONDA BABA (WALRUS MAN)

Ponda Baba is an Aqualish smuggler and pirate. He is
the partner of Dr. Evazan. He strongly resembles the Walrus
Man from the original figures, but is dressed differently.
Perhaps this is to hide his replacement arm. Ben Kenobi
sliced off the original in the Mos Eisley Cantina.

In the new series, Ponda Baba initially came on a
Collection 2 header card. This was quickly corrected to
Collection 3, making the original ".00" version scarce.

Classic:
Walrus Man (#39050, 1978–79)
    Original *Star Wars* header card $135.00
    Reissue on *The Empire Strikes Back* header card . 125.00
    Reissue on *Return of the Jedi* header card 60.00
    Reissue on Tri-Logo header card 60.00
    Loose, with stormtrooper blaster 12.50

New:
Ponda Baba with "Blaster Pistol and Rifle" on *New
Power of the Force* green holo header card
(**Collection 2**, #69708, July 1997)
[540903.00] with 1st hook, in stand-up bubble ... 20.00

Walrus Man/Ponda Baba (Kenner 1984 and 1997)

Ponda Baba with "Blaster Pistol and Rifle" on *New Power of the Force* green holo header card (Collection 3, #69708 July 1997) [.01] with
2nd hook, in stand-up bubble 5.00
Loose, with black blaster pistol and rifle 3.00

POWER DROID

The Power Droid figure is box shaped and gets around on two mechanical feet. It closely resembles the robots Hewie, Dewie and Louie from the movie *Silent Running* starring Bruce Dern.

Classic:
Power Droid (#39090, 1978–79) 2¼" figure
Original *Star Wars* header card $135.00
Reissue on *The Empire Strikes Back* header card . 125.00
Reissue on *Return of the Jedi* header card 55.00
Reissue on Tri-Logo header card 60.00
Loose, no accessories 10.00
New:
None

Power Droid and Prince Xizor (Kenner 1978 and 1996)

PRINCE XIZOR

The Shadows of the Empire storyline takes place between *The Empire Strikes Back* and before *Return of the Jedi*. Prince Xizor runs the Black Sun criminal organization and wants to ruin Darth Vader and take over his position as the second most powerful figure in the empire. He tries to eliminate Luke Skywalker before Lord Vader can fulfill his promise to deliver Luke alive to the Emperor. He captures Leia, but Luke, Lando, Chewbacca and Dash Rendar rescue her and get away.

Classic:
None

New:
Prince Xizor, with "Energy Blade Shields" on a purple *Shadows of the Empire* card (#69594, June 1996) [531620.00] $7.00
Loose with blue energy blade shields with black base 3.00

Princess Leia Organa (Kenner 1978 and 1996)

PRINCESS LEIA ORGANA

Luke changes his hair color and pants and Han Solo gets a big head, but Princess Leia's basic figure says the same through out the original series. Of course she does get other outfits, but they are different figures.

Classic:
Princess Leia Organa (#38190, 1978) 3½" figure
Original *Star Wars* "12 back" header card. $300.00
Reissue on *Star Wars* "20/21 back" header
card 250.00
Reissue on *The Empire Strikes Back* header card . 295.00
Reissue on *Return of the Jedi* header card. 400.00
Reissue on Tri-Logo header card 150.00
Loose, with pistol 40.00

New:
Princess Leia Organa with "'Laser' Pistol and Assault Rifle" on *New Power of the Force* red header card (#69579, July 1995) [523211.00]
3 band belt 20.00
Variation, 2 band belt (Nov. 1996) 10.00
Variation, with holo sticker 10.00
Princess Leia Organa with "Laser Pistol and Assault Rifle" on *New Power of the Force* green holo header card (Collection 1, #69579) [.01] with 2nd hook, in original bubble 5.00
Variation, without holo sticker 5.00
Loose with black laser pistol and short rifle 4.00
Princess Leia Organa with "Blaster Rifle and Long-Barreled Pistol" and with sticker saying "All New Likeness" on *New Power of the Force* green Freeze Frame header card (Collection 1) [.00] 7.00
Loose, with all equipment 3.00

Princess Leia (Bespin Gown)

There are two versions of this figure. In one the neck is flesh colored (crew neck) and in the other the neck is the same color as the rest of the costume or outfit (turtle neck). Both versions come with the same distinctive cloak. The front photo on the header card was changed during *The Empire*

*Princess Leia Bespin Gown and Boushh Disguise
(Kenner 1980 and 1983)*

Princess Leia Combat Poncho (Kenner 1984 and 1985)

Strikes Back figure series. The original photo shows Leia turned to the left, looking back at the camera. The new photo shows her directly facing the camera.

Classic:
Leia Organa (Bespin Gown) (#39720, 1980)
    Original *The Empire Strikes Back* header
      card, **turtle neck** version $175.00
    Original *The Empire Strikes Back* header
      card, turtle neck, new package 150.00
    Reissue on *Return of the Jedi* header card 150.00
    Reissue on Tri-Logo header card 125.00
    Loose, in cloak with pistol 20.00
Leia Organa (Bespin Gown) (#39720, 1980)
    Original *The Empire Strikes Back* header
      card, **crew neck** version 125.00
    Original *The Empire Strikes Back* header
      card, crew neck, new package 90.00
    Reissue on *Return of the Jedi* header card 60.00
    Loose, in cloak with pistol 20.00

New:
    None

Princess Leia (Boushh Disguise)

The Shadows of the Empire storyline takes place between *The Empire Strikes Back* and before *Return of the Jedi*. Leia Chewbacca go to Coruscant to try to find out who has been attempting to assassinate Luke. Leia disguised herself as the Ubesian bounty hunter, Boushh. Leia is captured by Prince Xizor and rescued by Chewbacca, Luke, Lando and Dash Rendar. Leia keeps the disguise and uses it again attempting to rescue Han Solo from Jabba the Hutt.

Classic:
Princess Leia Organa (Boushh Disguise) (#70660, 1983)
    Original *Return of the Jedi* header card $50.00
    Reissue on Tri-Logo header card 25.00
    Loose, with helmet and weapon 20.00

New:
Leia in Boushh Disguise, with "Blaster Rifle and
    Bounty Hunter Helmet" on a purple *Shadows*

of the Empire card (#69602, June 1996)
    [532824.00] 8.00
Leia in Boushh Disguise, with "Blaster Rifle and
    Bounty Hunter Helmet" on a *Shadows of the
    Empire* purple holo header card (**Col-
    lection 1**, #69818, 1997) [.01] with 2nd hook 50.00
Leia in Boushh Disguise, with "Blaster Rifle and
    Bounty Hunter Helmet" on *New Power of the
    Force* green holo header card (Collection 1,
    #69818, 1997) [.02] with 2nd hook, in original
    or stand-up bubble 7.00
    Variation, without holo sticker 7.00
    Loose, with grey and brown helmet and long
      black blaster rifle 3.00

Princess Leia (Combat Poncho)

Princess Leia Combat Poncho was issued in the *Return of the Jedi* series, but she has not been issued in the new series. The closest equivalent is the Princess Leia in Endor Gear which came with the Speeder Bike vehicle.

Classic:
Princess Leia Organa (in Combat Poncho) (#71220, 1984)
    Original *Return of the Jedi* header card $60.00
    Reissue on *Power of the Force* header card 100.00
    Reissue on Tri-Logo header card 25.00
    Loose in poncho with pistol 20.00

New:
    None

Princess Leia (Ewok Celebration Outfit)

This is a new outfit for the Princess, and a new waist-length hair style, too. The Princess Leia collection figures, with four other outfits and hair styles, came out at about the same time. On the back of header card version ".00" for the new issue of this figure "Saelt-Marae" is misspelled as "Sealt-Marie" — two errors in just 10 letters. Version ".01" corrects this error. The error version is scarce.

Classic:
    None

*Princess Leia Ewok Celebration and Jabba's Prisoner
(Kenner 1998 and 1997)*

New:
Princess Leia Organa in Ewok Celebration Outfit,
  on *New Power of the Force* green Freeze
  Frame header card (Collection 1, #69714,
  Feb. 1998) [547095.00] $15.00
  Variation [.01] corrected 6.50
  Loose, with black pistol 3.00

Princess Leia (Hoth Outfit)

Princess Leia has appeared in a lot of new outfits in the new series, but this classic figure has not appeared. It's probably just as well. There were so many figures in Hoth outfits in the classic series that it was hard to tell them apart.

Classic:
Leia Organa (Hoth Outfit) (#39359, 1981)
  Original *The Empire Strikes Back* header card . . $125.00
  Reissue on *Return of the Jedi* header card 100.00
  Reissue on *Return of the Jedi* header card,
    new package 75.00
  Reissue on Tri-Logo header card 60.00
  Loose, with pistol 20.00

New:
  None

Princess Leia (Jabba's Prisoner)

Princess Leia appeared in a very skimpy and unprincess-like outfit after she was captured by Jabba the Hutt at the beginning of *Return of the Jedi*. She uses her slave chain to strangle the ugly slug before she escapes.

There is nothing quite like a little bondage to warm up red-blooded collectors and so Princess Leia as Jabba's Prisoner, or Princess Leia Slave Girl as she is sometimes called, was heavily collected when she first appeared. This pushed her price up to $15.00, but the price fell as more and more supply appeared and now she hardly more valuable than other figures. Near the end of 1997 she was available without holo sticker, and this version is both scarce and more attractive than the holo sticker version.

On the back of header card version ".01" for the new Freeze Frame issue of this figure "Saelt-Marae" is misspelled as "Sealt-Marie" — two errors in just 10 letters. Version ".02" corrects this error.

Classic:
  None

New:
Princess Leia Organa as Jabba's Prisoner, on
  New Power of the Force green holo header
  card (Collection 1, #69683, Sept. 1997)
  [542899.00] with 2nd hook, in stand-up bubble . . . $6.00
  Variation, without holo sticker 10.00
  Reissue on Freeze Frame header card [.01] 7.00
  Reissue [.02] spelling corrected 6.00
  Loose, with gray chain and collar 3.00

PRINCESS LEIA COLLECTION

Figures from the Princess Leia Collection are listed under Two-Packs.

PRUNE FACE

Prune Face is scheduled to reappear in 1998. As with Momaw Nadon (Hammerhead) and Saelt Marae (Yak Face) he is scheduled to appear under his real name, "Orrimaarko."

Classic:
Prune Face (#71320, 1984)
  Original *Return of the Jedi* header card $30.00
  Reissue on Tri-Logo header card 15.00
  Loose, with cloak and rifle 10.00

New:
  Scheduled for 1998 as Orrimaarko.

Rancor Keeper: *See Malakili*

Prune Face and Rebel Commando (Kenner 1984 and 1983)

REBEL COMMANDER

The figure was also available loose with the MLC-3 vehicle.

Classic:
Rebel Commander (#39369, 1981)
    Original *The Empire Strikes Back* header card . . . $40.00
    Reissue on *Return of the Jedi* header card 30.00
    Reissue on Tri-Logo header card 25.00
    Loose, with rifle 10.00

New:
    None

REBEL COMMANDO

The Rebel Commando is based on the Rebel troops who fought in the Battle of Endor. There is no equivalent figure in the New Power of the Force line-up, but the Endor Rebel Soldier is similar.

Classic:
Rebel Commando (#70740, 1983)
    Original *Return of the Jedi* header card $30.00
    Reissue on Tri-Logo header card, new package . .   15.00
    Loose, with rifle 10.00

New:
    None

REBEL FLEET TROOPER

Initially the Rebel Fleet Trooper came on a Collection 2 header card. This was quickly corrected to Collection 1, making the original ".00" version scarce.

Classic:
    None

New:
Rebel Fleet Trooper with "Blaster Pistol and Rifle" on *New Power of the Force* green holo header card (**Collection 2**, #69696, May 1997) [540905.00] with 1st hook, in stand-up bubble $20.00

Rebel Fleet Trooper and Hoth Rebel Soldier
(Kenner 1997 and 1998)

Rebel Fleet Trooper with "Blaster Pistol and Rifle" on *New Power of the Force* green holo header card (Collection 1, #69696, July 1997) [.01] with 2nd hook, in stand-up bubble 5.00
    Reissue, on Freeze Frame header card [.02 sticker] 6.50
    Loose, with 3.00

REBEL SOLDIER (ENDOR)

The Endor Rebel Soldier was not included in the classic figure line-up, but the Rebel Commando is similar, and fought in the same battle.

On the back of header card version ".00" for the Freeze Frame issue of this figure "Saelt-Marae" is misspelled as "Sealt-Marie." Version ".01" corrects this error. The original error version is scarce and this is the initial appearance of the figure, which accounts for the price.

Classic:
    None

New:
Endor Rebel Soldier with "Survival Backpack and Blaster Rifle" on *New Power of the Force* green Freeze Frame header card (Collection 1, #69716, 1998) [547098.00] $15.00
    Reissue, [.01] "Saelt-Marae" spelling corrected . . .   6.50
    Loose, with all gear 3.00

REBEL SOLDIER (HOTH GEAR)

These are rebel soldiers in their ice planet Hoth uniforms. The figure was also available loose with the Snowspeeder vehicle.

In the new series, the Hoth Rebel Soldier initially came on a Collection 2 header card. This was soon corrected to Collection 1, but there is little difference in price between the two versions.

On the back of header card version ".02" for the new Freeze Frame issue of this figure "Saelt-Marae" is misspelled as "Sealt-Marie" — two errors in just 10 letters. Version ".03" corrects this error.

Classic:
Rebel Soldier (Hoth Battle Gear) (#39750, 1980)
    Original *The Empire Strikes Back* header card . . . $50.00
    Reissue on *Return of the Jedi* header card 35.00
    Reissue on Tri-Logo header card 25.00
    Loose, with pistol 10.00

New:
Hoth Rebel Soldier with "Survival Backpack and Blaster Rifle" on *New Power of the Force* green holo header card (**Collection 2**, #69631, Feb. 1997) [538004.00] with 1st hook and original bubble 10.00
    Variation, without holo sticker 10.00
Hoth Rebel Soldier with "Survival Backpack and Blaster Rifle" on *New Power of the Force* green holo header card (Collection 1, #69821, 1997) [.01] with 2nd hook and stand-up bubble 5.00

Ree-Yees and Romba (Kenner 1983 and 1985)

R2-D2 and R2-D2 Sensorscope (Kenner 1978 and 1985)

Reissue, on Freeze Frame header card [.02] 7.00
Reissue, [.03] "Saelt-Marae" spelling corrected . . . 6.00
Loose, with white backpack and black blaster rifle . 3.00

REE-YEES

Ree-Yees is a Gran for Kinyen and is last seen on Jabba's sail barge when it is blown to bits. He is scheduled to reappear in 1998 so you can pretend to blow him up again.

Classic:
Ree-Yees (#70800, 1983)
    Original *Return of the Jedi* header card $30.00
    Reissue on Tri-Logo header card 15.00
    Loose, with weapon 10.00

New:
    Scheduled for 1998

ROMBA

Romba is an Ewok, one of eight issued in the *Return of the Jedi* series.

Classic:
Romba (#93730, 1985)
    Original *Power of the Force* header card $50.00
    Reissue on Tri-Logo header card 30.00
    Loose, with spear 20.00

New:
    None

Sandpeople: *See Tusken Raider*

R2-D2

R2 units are tripodal computer repair and information retrieval robots, or astromech droids. They act as navigators and in-flight repair droids on Rebel X-wing fighters. R2-D2 is 0.96 meters tall, a little taller then Yoda.

Classic:
Artoo-Detoo (R2-D2) (#38200, 1978) 2¼" figure
    Original *Star Wars* "12 back" header card $150.00

Reissue on *Star Wars* "20/21 back" header
    card 100.00
Reissue on *The Empire Strikes Back* header card . . 50.00
Reissue on Tri-Logo header card 35.00
Loose, no accessories 12.50

New:
R2-D2 with "Light Pipe Eye Port and Retractable
    Leg" 2½" on *New Power of the Force* red
    header card (#69574, July 1995) [521787.00] . . . 10.00
R2-D2 with "Light-Pipe Eye Port and Retractable
    Leg" on *New Power of the Force* green holo
    header card (Collection 1, #69574) [.01] with
    2nd hook, in original or stand-up bubble 5.00
Loose, without accessories 3.00

R2-D2 (Sensorscope)

Like C-3PO, R2-D2 is a popular character, but not always a popular action figure collectible. This figure has never drawn much interest from collectors.

Classic:
Artoo-Detoo (R2-D2) (with Sensorscope) (#69590, 1982)
    Original *The Empire Strikes Back* header card . . . $50.00
    Reissue on *Return of the Jedi* header card
        (#69420) 35.00
    Reissue on Tri-Logo header card 28.00
    Loose, with scope 12.50

New:
R2-D2 with "Spring-Loaded, Pop-Up Scanner,
    Remote Action Retractable Scomp Link,
    Grasper Arm and Circular Saw" on *New
    Power of the Force* green Freeze Frame
    header card (Collection 1) [.00] 7.00
Loose, ... 3.00

R2-D2 (Pop-up Lightsaber)

Classic:
Artoo-Detoo (R2-D2) with Pop-up Lightsaber (#93720, 1985)
    Original *Power of the Force* header card $150.00
    Reissue on Tri-Logo header card 100.00
    Loose, with lightsaber 75.00

Artoo-Detoo R2-D2 (#71780) Droids 1985 with pop-
up lightsaber 45.00
Loose 15.00

New:
None

R5-D4 (Kenner 1978 and 1996)

R5-D4

The R5-D4 is a Modified Astromech Droid used in
combat by the Rebel Alliance. It is 1 meter tall. The 1996 figure comes with a yellow projectile and has a concealed
launcher which is revealed when the droid is opened at the
top. The word "Photon" was dropped from the description of
the missile launcher, undoubtedly because it sounded more
like *Star Trek* than *Star Wars*.

Classic:
R5-D4 (#39070, 1978–79) 2½" figure
Original *Star Wars* header card $135.00
Reissue on *The Empire Strikes Back* header card . 125.00
Reissue on *Return of the Jedi* header card as
   Arfive Defour (R5-D4) 60.00
Reissue on Tri-Logo header card 60.00
Loose, no accessories 10.00

New:
R5-D4 with "Concealed Photon Missile Launcher"
   3" (Collection 2, #69598, Nov. 1996) on *New
   Power of the Force* red header card
   [535185.00] no small parts warning 20.00
Reissue on red header card, with small parts
   warning, straight latch [.01] 15.00
Reissue, now with "Concealed Missile
   Launcher" on green header card
   [535185.01], with warning on sticker and
   hooked latch, 1st hook, in original bubble 6.00
Reissue with holographic picture on green
   header card, with warning, hooked latch or
   straight latch 6.00
Loose, with yellow launching missile 3.00

Yak Face/Saelt-Marae (Kenner 1985 and 1997)

SAELT-MARAE (YAK FACE)

Saelt-Marae, better known to classic series collectors as
Yak Face is and informant working for Jabba the Hutt. He
stands 2.2 meters tall, which helps him keep tabs on people.
The original figure was primarily available overseas, which
has kept its price quite high.

Classic:
Yak Face (#93840, 1985) foreign release
Original *Power of the Force* header card $1,500.00
Reissue on Tri-Logo header card 325.00
Loose, with staff 150.00

New:
Saelt-Marae (Yak Face) with "Battle Staff" 4½" on
   New Power of the Force green holo header
   card (Collection 2, #69721, Oct. 1997)
   [542923.00] with 2nd hook, in stand-up bubble 5.00
Reissue, on Freeze Frame header card [.01] 6.50
Loose, with dark gray battle staff 3.00

SANDTROOPERS

These are human stormtroopers in desert gear. The original name of the figure, Tatooine Stormtrooper, was changed
almost immediately to Sandtrooper. The weapon was also
changed, but in name only.

Classic:
None

New:
Tatooine Stormtrooper with "Concussion Grenade
   Cannon" (Collection 1, #69601, Oct. 1996) on
   New Power of the Force red header card
   [535192.00] $25.00
Reissue as **Sandtrooper**, with "Heavy Blaster
   Rifle" (#69601) on green header card [.01] 8.00
Reissue with holographic picture on green
   header card 6.00
Sandtrooper with "Heavy Blaster Rifle" on *New
   Power of the Force* green holo header card
   (Collection 3, #69808) [.02] with 2nd hook,
   in stand-up bubble 5.00

Sandtroopers (Tatooine Stormtrooper) and Snowtrooper (Kenner 1996 and 1997)

Snaggletooth, loose and Squidhead (Kenner 1978 and 1985)

Loose, with black heavy blaster rifle and black
    backpack with grey highlights. 3.00

See-Threepio: *See C-3PO*

SNAGGLETOOTH

The blue Snaggletooth was only available in the Cantina Adventure Set, which was a Sears exclusive. He is full sized and he wears boots and a blue suit. The figure came polybagged with a Han Solo-style blaster in this set. The only Snaggletooth on a header card is in a red suit and he is the correct smaller size and bare-footed. There is no difficulty in distinguishing between them.

Snaggletooth (blue)
Classic:
Snaggletooth (**blue**) (Sears Exclusive) 3¾" figure
    loose only, from Cantina Adventure Set $150.00

Snaggletooth (red)
Classic:
Snaggletooth (**red**) (#39040, 1978–79) 2¾" figure
    Original *Star Wars* header card 125.00
    Reissue on *The Empire Strikes Back* header card . 100.00
    Reissue on *Return of the Jedi* header card 55.00
    Reissue on Tri-Logo header card 60.00
    Loose, with pistol. 10.00

New:
    None

SNOWTROOPER

Snowtroopers are human cold assault stormtroopers. This new name replaces the original "Imperial Stormtrooper (Hoth Battle Gear)." They average 1.83 meters in height and carry an Imperial issue blaster rifle.

The classic figure came with a rifle, but the new figure carries a backpack and pistol, not a rifle, despite its header card description.

Classic:
Imperial Stormtrooper (Hoth Battle Gear) (#39740,
    1980)
    Original *The Empire Strikes Back* header card. . . $60.00
    Reissue on *Return of the Jedi* header card 50.00
    Reissue on Tri-Logo header card 50.00
    Loose, with rifle 10.00

New:
Snowtrooper with "Imperial Issue Blaster Rifle" on
    New Power of the Force green holo header
    card (Collection 3, #69632, Sept. 1997)
    [542915.00] with 2nd hook, in original or
    stand-up bubble. 5.00
    Reissue, on Freeze Frame header card
      (#69632) [.01] 6.50
    Loose, with black pistol and white backpack. 3.00

SQUID HEAD

Squidhead from the classic series has not received much collector interest to date and he has not been issued in the new series.

Classic:
Squid Head (#70770, 1983)
    Original *Return of the Jedi* header card $30.00
    Reissue on Tri-Logo header card 15.00
    Loose, with pistol and cloak 10.00

New:
    None

Star Destroyer Commander: *See Death Squad Commander*

STORMTROOPER

Stormtroopers are humans used as elite Imperial shock troops by the Galactic Empire. They carry a variety of weapons, including an Imperial issue blaster, blaster rifle and heavy infantry cannon.

Stormtroopers (Kenner 1996 and 1997)

Classic:
Stormtrooper (#38240, 1978)
   Original *Star Wars* "12 back" header card. $225.00
   Reissue on *Star Wars* "20/21 back" header
     card. 150.00
   Reissue on *The Empire Strikes Back* header card . . 80.00
   Reissue on *Return of the Jedi* header card 50.00
   Reissue on *Power of the Force* header card
     as **Imperial Stormtrooper**. 150.00
   Reissue on Tri-Logo header card, new package. . . 60.00
   Loose with weapon 15.00

New:
Stormtrooper with "Blaster Rifle and Heavy Infantry
   Cannon" on *New Power of the Force* red
   header card (#69575, July 1995) [521789.00] . . . 10.00
   Reissue, with holo sticker [.00]. 9.00
Stormtrooper with "Blaster Rifle and Heavy Infantry
   Cannon" on *New Power of the Force* green
   holo header card (Collection 3, #69803, 1997)
   [.01] with 2nd hook, in stand-up bubble 5.00
   Reissue, on Freeze Frame header card [.02] 6.50
   Loose, with black pistol and blaster rifle 3.00

TEEBO

Teebo is an Ewok, one of eight issued in the *Return of the Jedi* series.

Classic:
Teebo (#71310, 1984)
   Original *Return of the Jedi* header card $40.00
   Reissue on *Power of the Force* header card. . . . 200.00
   Reissue on Tri-Logo header card 20.00
   Loose, with club, mask and pouch 12.50

New:
   None

TIE FIGHTER PILOT

These elite imperial pilots are human and fly the Twin Ion Engine (TIE) Fighter for the Galactic Empire. They also carry a blaster pistol, but there doesn't seem to be much they could do with it while flying. They average 1.7 meters in height, about 0.1 meters shorter than Stormtroopers.

In the new series, the first TIE Fighter Pilot figures came with a small-parts warning on a sticker. This was quickly changed to a printed warning on the ".01" header card. The original version is scarce and valuable. The first green card issue was in Collection 2, but this was corrected to Collection 3. There is only a small premium for the Collection 2 version.

Classic:
Imperial Tie Fighter Pilot (#70030, 1982)
   Original *The Empire Strikes Back* header card . . $100.00
   Reissue on *Return of the Jedi* header card 55.00
   Reissue on Tri-Logo header card 55.00
   Loose, with pistol 15.00

New:
TIE Fighter Pilot with "Imperial Blaster Pistol and
   Rifle" on *New Power of the Force* red header
   card (#69584, March 1996) with small-parts
   warning printed on sticker [527597.00] 25.00
   Warning printed on header card [.01] 6.00
   Reissue on red header card (#69673) [.02] 6.00

Teebo (Kenner 1984 and 1985)   *Tie Fighter Pilot and 2-1B (Kenner 1996 and 1980)*

TIE Fighter Pilot with "Imperial Blaster and Rifle" on *New Power of the Force* green holo header card (**Collection 2**, #69673) [.03] with 2nd hook, in original bubble 10.00
TIE Fighter Pilot with "Imperial Blaster Pistol and Rifle" on *New Power of the Force* green holo header card (Collection 3, #69806, 1979) [.04] with 2nd hook, in stand-up bubble 5.00
Reissue, on Freeze Frame header card (#69806) [.05] 6.50
Loose, with black pistol and rifle. 3.00

2-1B

2-1B is an industrial automaton surgical droid. His new version is supposed to have a medical diagnostic computer, but it looks a lot like a weapon. Classic series figures also came with some of the PDT-8 vehicles.

Classic:
2-1B (#39399, 1981)
Original *The Empire Strikes Back* header card . . $50.00
Reissue on *Return of the Jedi* header card as
Too-Onebee (2-1B) (#71600) 40.00
Reissue on Tri-Logo header card 40.00
Loose, with grey staff. 10.00

New:
2-1B Medic Droid with "Medical Diagnostic Computer" on *New Power of the Force* green holo header card (Collection 2, #69618, Feb. 1997) [537994.00] with 1st hook, in original bubble . 5.00
Variation, without holo sticker. 5.00
Reissue [.01] with 2nd hook, in original or stand-up bubble 5.00
Loose, with blue-gray gun-shaped medical computer 3.00

TUSKEN RAIDER (SAND PEOPLE)

The Tusken Raiders are humanoid nomadic warriors. They average 1.9 meters tall and just about kicked Luke Skywalker's butt in the early stages of the first movie.

The figure comes with a "gaderffi" stick weapon, which seems to have almost as many spellings as *Momar Quadaffi*.

It's spelled "gaderffii" some places. The first version of the new figure came with a closed hand. This was replaced with a more open hand. A scarce few of the reissue figures still had the closed hand, making this a valuable variation.

Classic:
Sand People (#38280, 1978)
Original *Star Wars* "12 back" header card. $225.00
Reissue on *Star Wars* "20/21 back" header card. 150.00
Reissue on *The Empire Strikes Back* header card as **Sandpeople** (#38280). 125.00
Reissue on *Return of the Jedi* header card as **Tusken Raider** (Sand People)" (#38280). 75.00
Reissue on Tri-Logo header card 65.00
Loose, with cloak and weapon 15.00

New:
Tusken Raider with "Gaderffi Stick Battle Club" on *New Power of the Force* red header card (Collection 2, #69603, Nov. 1996) [535179.00] closed hand 25.00
Variation, open hand 25.00
Reissue, now with "Gaderffii Stick" on green header card with plain picture [.01] 6.00
Variation, closed hand 30.00
Reissue on green header card with holographic picture [.01] open hand 6.00
Loose, with brown-handled silver gaderffi stick:
Closed hand. 6.00
Open hand. 3.00

UGNAUGHTS

Ugnaughts work in Cloud City mining Tibanna gas and doing other manual labor. Two versions are available, Lavender Smock and Blue Smock, but they generally sell for the same price.

Classic:
Ugnaught (#39319, 1981)
Original *The Empire Strikes Back* header card . . $45.00
Reissue on *Return of the Jedi* header card 35.00
Reissue on Tri-Logo header card 25.00
Loose, in blue smock with white tool case 10.00
Loose, in lavender smock with white tool case . . . 12.50

Tusken Raider/Sand People (Kenner 1978 and 1996)   *Ugnaught, loose and Warok (Kenner 1981 and 1985)*

New:
Ugnaughts, with "Tool Kit" on *New Power of the Force* green Freeze Frame header card (Collection 2) [.00] scheduled for June 1998...... 7.50
Loose, with Tool Kit...................... 3.00

Walrus Man: *See Ponda Baba*

WAROK

Warok is an Ewok, one of eight issued in the *Return of the Jedi* series.

Classic:
Warok (#93810, 1985)
Original *Power of the Force* header card...... $50.00
Reissue on Tri-Logo header card............. 30.00
Loose, with bow and pouch................. 20.00

New:
None

WEEQUAY

Weequays are from the planet Sriluur and several work for Jabba the Hutt as guards.

The new version of Weequay identifies him as a skiff guard and adds a "blaster rifle" to his weaponry. It's more like the size of a large pistol and very similar weapons are frequently just called "Blasters" by Kenner. Initially Weequay came on a Collection 2 header card. This was quickly corrected to Collection 3, making the original ".00" version scarce.

Classic:
Weequay
Original *Return of the Jedi* header card....... $30.00
Reissue on Tri-Logo header card............. 15.00
Loose, with spear........................ 12.50

New:
Weequay Skiff Guard with "Force Pike and Blaster Rifle" on *New Power of the Force* green holo

Weequay/Weequay Skiff Guard (Kenner 1985 and 1997)

header card (**Collection 2**, #69707, May 1997) [540901.00] with 1st hook, in stand-up bubble.................................. 20.00
Weequay Skiff Guard with "Force Pike and Blaster Rifle" on *New Power of the Force* green holo header card (Collection 3, #69707, July 1997) [.01] with 2nd hook, in stand-up bubble......... 5.00
Loose, with brown force pike and blaster........ 3.00

Wicket W. Warrick and Yoda (Kenner 1985 and 1981)

WICKET W. WARRICK

Wicket is the first Ewok that Princess Leia meets on Endor, right after she crashes her speeder bike. He was also issued as part of the Ewok pack in the New Power of the Force line-up and, at virtually the same time in early 1998, with Princess Leia in the Princess Leia collection.

Classic:
Wicket W. Warrick (#71230, 1984)
Original *Return of the Jedi* header card....... $50.00
Reissue on *Power of the Force* header card.... 200.00
Reissue on Tri-Logo header card............. 25.00
Loose, with spear........................ 12.50

New:
None, but see Ewoks: Wicket & Logray

See also: EWOKS *series*

YODA

Yoda, the diminutive Jedi master, is of an unknown race and lives on the swamp planet, Dagobah. He is over 900 years old, so he needs a gimer stick to help him walk.

In the original series, Yoda comes with a snake which fits around his neck as well as a gimer stick. The front photo on the header card was changed during the *Return of the Jedi* figure series. The original photo shows Yoda holding his stick and facing somewhat to the left. The new photo shows him facing significantly to the right. Yoda originally had a brown

Yoda (Kenner 1985 and 1996)   *Yoda and Zuckuss (Kenner 1997 and 1998)*

snake, but some of *The Empire Strikes Back* figures came with an orange snake. The gimer stick is roughly the same color as the snake in each version.

Classic:
Yoda (with **orange snake**) (#38310, 1981)
   Original *The Empire Strikes Back* header card . . $75.00
   Loose, with orange snake 20.00
Yoda (with **brown snake**) (#38310, 1981)
   Original *The Empire Strikes Back* header card . . . 90.00
   Reissue on *Return of the Jedi* header card 65.00
   Reissue on *Return of the Jedi* header card as
      Yoda, The Jedi Master 60.00
   Reissue on *Power of the Force* header card. . . . 350.00
   Reissue on Tri-Logo header card 50.00
   Loose, with brown snake 20.00

New:
Yoda with "Jedi Trainer Backpack and Gimer Stick"
   2" on *New Power of the Force* red header
   card (#69586, March 1996) [527603.00]. 7.50
   Reissue, red header card (#69672) [.00] or
      [.01] with holo sticker. 6.00
Yoda with "Jedi Trainer Backpack and Gimer Stick"
   on *New Power of the Force* green holo header card (**Collection 2**, #69672) [.02] with 2nd
   hook, in original bubble 10.00
   Variation, without holo sticker. 10.00
Yoda with "Jedi Trainer Backpack and Gimer Stick"
   on *New Power of the Force* green holo header card (Collection 1, #69586) [.03] with 2nd
   hook, in original bubble 5.00
   Loose, with brown gimer stick and blue-gray
      backpack 3.00

ZUCKUSS (Classic)

Kenner reversed the names of 4-LOM and Zuckuss in the original figure line-up and corrected it in the new figures.

Classic:
Zuckuss (#70020, 1982)
   Original *The Empire Strikes Back* header card . . $75.00
   Reissue on *Return of the Jedi* header card 35.00
   Reissue on Tri-Logo header card 25.00
   Loose, with rifle 10.00

New:
   See 4-LOM

ZUCKUSS (formerly 4-LOM)

The real Zuckuss is from the planet Gand and was one of the bounty hunters who answered Darth Vader's call-up to help in locating the Millennium Falcon and its crew. He worked with 4-LOM, the droid turned bounty hunter.

Classic:
   See 4-LOM

New:
Zuckuss with "Heavy Blaster Rifle" on *New Power
   of the Force* Freeze Frame header card
   (#69747, 1998) [550627.00] $7.00

collected by science fiction fans. Many of them usually look down on media tie-in books, but they make an exception for *Star Wars*. For one thing, they all saw the movie several times, and, for another, George Lucas sent a delegation to the 1980 World Science Fiction Convention in Boston to present a free showing of the movie. The movie had played in many theaters from 1977 all the way into late 1978, but it had been off the screens for about two years at the time of the convention.

While the first paperback edition and the hardcover edition enjoy crossover collector interest from persons who are not primarily *Star Wars* fans, book club editions have no collector following whatever apart from die-hard *Star Wars* fans. Consequently the book club edition of the original *Star Wars* novel, and for that matter, any *Star Wars* novel, is not valuable. The one exception might be the very first printing of the book club edition of *Star Wars*. This can be identified by the printing code "S27" in the gutter on page 183. It appeared before the trade hardcover, making it the first hardcover edi-

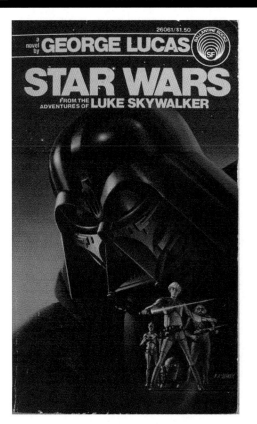

Star Wars, *1st paperback (Del Rey 1976)*

BOOKS

Star Wars mass market Collectible #1, the very first mass market *Star Wars* item produced, was the movie novelization paperback book which appeared in late November 1976, seven months before the movie opened. No one knew how big the movie would be and the book had a very normal first print run. Of course, it's been reprinted many times, so the first edition is the one to get. It can be identified by the line "First Edition: December 1976" at the bottom, on the copyright page. As the movie became a hit, the paperback was reprinted many times, with huge print runs — 3.5 million copies in the first year. None of these reprintings is scarce, and none is valuable.

The novel appeared in hardcover in the fall of 1977. The trade hardcover is scarce and valuable. It has a gold dust jacket, and says "Hardbound Ballantine Books Edition: October 1977/First Edition: December 1976" in two lines on the copyright page. First edition hard cover science fiction books are

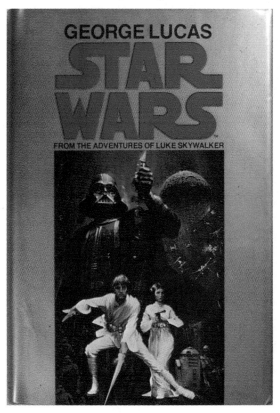

Star Wars, *1st Hardcover (Del Rey 1977)*

tion of the book. The book is supposed to be by George Lucas, but just about everyone in the science fiction community believes that it was ghost written by Alan Dean Foster, from the screenplay, a fact now confirmed by Lucas.

Each of the other movies was novelized in turn. Other original novels followed for a few years from Ballantine Del Rey. They were written by Alan Dean Foster, Brian Daley and L. Neil Smith. Then there was a slack period until Bantam got the *Star Wars* novels license. Comics tapered off at this time as well. In mid 1991, *Star Wars* novels returned with Timothy Zahn's *Heir to the Empire*. This book made it to the top of the *New York Times* bestseller lists. Bantam continued a successful publishing program with a number of new novels and juvenile adaptations. Lucas Films licensing has insisted on overall continuity in the storylines for both the books and the comics, so that they constitute a consistent "expanded universe." This makes these novels important in the *Star Wars* universe, because there are only about six hours of actual films. The earlier Del Rey novels were mostly written before the movie series was completed, and thus lack this continuity. The lives of subsidiary characters such as Boba Fett and new characters such as Grand Admiral Thrawn are only covered in the novels and the comics.

In 1997, Del Rey got the *Star Wars* license back. They intend to continue publishing *Star Wars* novels aggressively; they will have to in order to cover all the money they paid.

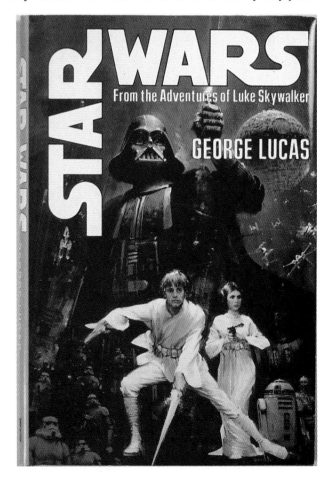

*Star Wars, 1st Book Club Edition
(Science Fiction Book Club 1977)*

FICTION

Movie Novelizations:

Star Wars, by Alan Dean Foster, uncredited ghost writer, from screenplay by George Lucas
1st PB: $1.50, 220pp, Ballantine #26061-9, Dec. 1976, Ralph McQuarrie cover $25.00
2nd PB: $1.95, 220pp, Ballantine-Del Rey #26079-1, Aug. 1977, Movie tie-in, John Berkey cover 10.00
1st SFBC: $2.49, 183pp, Del Rey #2403-4, Aug. 1977, with 16 pages of color photos from the movie, printing code S27, John Berkey cover 15.00
Later SFBC: later printing codes 5.00
1st HC: $6.95, 183pp, Del Rey #27476-8, Oct. 1977, with 16 pages of color photos from the movie, John Berkey cover 60.00
Later PB: 220pp, Ballantine-Del Rey #29368-1 Oct. 1980 . . . . 3.00
Later PB: $2.75, 220pp, Ballantine-Del Rey #30735-6, June 1984 . . . . 3.00
Recent PB: retitled *Star Wars: A New Hope*, $4.99, Ballantine-Del Rey #34146-5 . . . . 5.00
Recent HC: as *Star Wars: A New Hope*, $16.00, 224p, Ballantine-Del Rey #40077-1, Oct. 1994, new intro by George Lucas, Tom Jung cover 16.00

The Empire Strikes Back, by Donald F. Glut from story by George Lucas and screenplay by Lawrence Kasdan and Leigh Brackett
1st PB: $2.25, 214pp, Ballantine-Del Rey #28392-9, May 1980, Roger Kastel cover 15.00
Later PB: 214pp, Ballantine-Del Rey #29209-X, Aug. 1980, Roger Kastel cover. 5.00

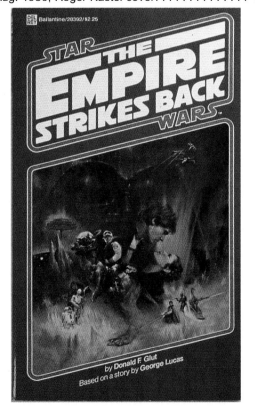

The Empire Strikes Back, *by Donald F. Glut,
1st Paperback (Del Rey 1980)*

1st SFBC: $2.49, Del Rey #3863-8, Aug.
  1980, printing code K29, Roger Kastel cover . . 10.00
Later SFBC: later printing codes 5.00
Later PB: $3.50, 214pp, Ballantine-Del Rey
  #32022-0, 1980s 3.00
Recent PB: Del Rey #32022-0, trilogy logo
  cover, in silver 5.00
still in print
Recent HC: $16.00, 224pp, Ballantine-Del
  Rey #40078-X, Oct. 1994, new introduc-
  tion by George Lucas, Roger Kastel cover 16.00

Return of the Jedi, by James Kahn, from screen
  play by Lawrence Kasdan and George Lucas
1st PB: $2.95, 181pp, Ballantine-Del Rey
  #30767-4, June 1983, Movie Tie-in 10.00
Current PB: #30767-4, trilogy logo cover, in gold
SFBC: $3.98, Del Rey #2144-4, Aug. 1983,
  printing code N31 . . . . 12.00
HC: $16.00, 240p, Ballantine-Del Rey #40079
  -8, Oct. 1994, Kazuhiko Sano cover 16.00

Star Wars Trilogy by George Lucas, Donald F.
  Glut and James Kahn
TPB: $8.95, 471p, Del Rey #34806-0, May
  1987, Sylvain Michaels cover 10.00
TPB: retitled: *Classic Star Wars: The Star
  Wars Trilogy*, $10.00, 480p, Del Rey
  #34806-0, April 1995, Tom Jung cover 10.00
1st PB: $5.99, 480p, Del Rey #38438-5,
  March 1993, John Berkey cover 6.00
still in print

Movie Novelizations: Illustrated Editions
The Empire Strikes Back: The Illustrated Edition,
  by Donald F. Glut, $4.95, 213pp, Del Rey
  #28831-9, Aug. 1980, Ralph McQuarrie
  illustrations and cover 10.00
Return of the Jedi Illustrated Edition, by James
  Kahn, Del Rey #30960-X, June 1983 . . . . 10.00

Novels (1978–89)
Splinter of the Mind's Eye, by Alan Dean Foster
1st HC: $7.95, 216pp, Del Rey #27566-7,
  Feb. 1978, Ralph McQuarrie cover 20.00
1st PB: $1.95, 199pp, Ballantine-Del Rey
  #26062-7, April 1978, Ralph McQuarrie cover. . . 5.00
SFBC: $1.98, Del Rey #2597-3, May 1978,
  Ralph McQuarrie cover 5.00
Later PB: $2.50, 199pp, Ballantine-Del Rey
  #32023-9, 1984, Ralph McQuarrie cover 4.00
Later PB: $5.99, 224p, Del Rey #32023-9,
  May 1994, Ralph McQuarrie cover,
  different design 5.00

Han Solo Series, by Brian Daley
Han Solo at Stars' End
HC: $8.95, 198pp, Del Rey #28251-5, April
  1979, Wayne Barlowe cover 20.00
SFBC: $2.49, Del Rey #3356-3, printing code
  J28, Aug. 1979, Wayne Barlowe cover. 5.00
1st PB: $2.25 Ballantine-Del Rey #29664-8,
  Oct. 1979, Wayne Barlowe cover 5.00
Recent PB: $5.99, 192p, Del Rey #29664-8,
  July 1997, Dave Dorman cover 5.00

Classic Star Wars, The Star Wars Trilogy,
Trade Paperback (Del Rey 1995)

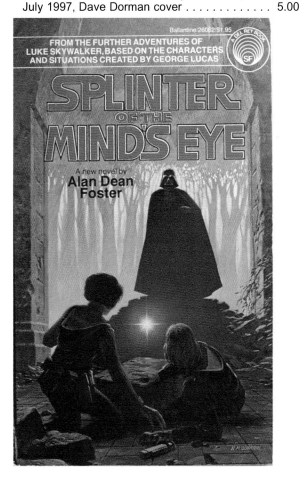

Splinter of the Mind's Eye, *by Alan Dean Foster,*
1st Hardcover (Del Rey 1980)

Han Solo at Star's End *and* Han Solo's Revenge, *1st Edition Hardcovers, and* Han Solo and the Lost Legacy, *SFBC Edition, by Brian Daley (Del Rey 1979–80)*

Han Solo's *Revenge*
    1st HC: $8.95, 198pp, Del Rey #28475-5,
      Nov. 1979, Dean Ellis cover 20.00
    SFBC: $2.98, Del Rey #3670-7, Feb. 1980,
      Dean Ellis cover 5.00
    1st PB: $2.25, 199pp, Ballantine-Del Rey
      #28840-8, June 1980, Dean Ellis cover 5.00
    Recent PB: Del Rey #28840-8, Dave Dorman
      cover. 5.00

Han Solo and the Lost Legacy
    1st PB: $2.25, 187pp, Ballantine-Del Rey
      #28710-X, Sept. 1980, William Schmidt cover . 10.00
    SFBC: $3.98, Del Rey #3398-5, printing code
      K42, Dec. 1980, William Schmidt cover 7.50
    Recent PB: Del Rey #34514-2, Dave Dorman
      cover. 5.00

Combined edition: *The Han Solo Adventures*
    1st PB: $5.99, 576p, Del Rey #37980-2, June
      1992, William Schmidt cover 6.00
    Recent PB: *Classic Star Wars: The Han Solo
      Adventures*, $10.00, 576p, Del Rey
      #39442-9, April 1995, William Schmidt cover . . 10.00

Lando Calrissian Series, by L. Neil Smith
Lando Calrissian and the Mindharp of Sharu
    1st PB: $2.50, 182pp, Ballantine-Del Rey
      #31158-2, July 1983, William Schmidt cover . . . 15.00
    1st SFBC: $4.98, Del Rey #3639-2, Jan. 1984 . . . . 5.00
Lando Calrissian and the Flamewind of Oseon
    1st PB: $2.50, 181pp, Ballantine-Del Rey
      #31163-9, Oct. 1983, William Schmidt cover . . . 15.00
    1st SFBC: $4.98, Del Rey #3588-1, Apr. 1984 . . . . 5.00

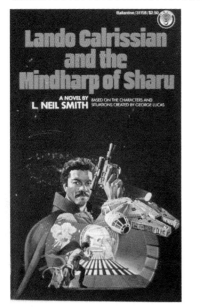

Lando Calrissian and the Mindharp of Sharu, Lando Calrissian and the Flamewind of Oseon, *and* Lando Calrissian and the Starcave of ThonBoka, *by L. Neil Smith, Paperback 1st Editions (Del Rey 1983)*

Lando Calrissian and the Starcave of ThonBoka
    1st PB: $2.50, 181pp, Ballantine-Del Rey
        #31164-7, Dec. 1983, William Schmidt cover . . 15.00
    SFBC: none
all out of print, but combined as:
Classic Star Wars: The Lando Calrissian Adventures
    1st combined PB: $5.99, Del Rey #39110-1,
        July 1994, William Schmidt cover 6.00
    Current TPB: $10.00, 416p, Del Rey
        #39443-7, April 1995, William Schmidt cover . . 10.00

Novels (1990–98)

Timothy Zahn's *Heir to the Empire* launched the current phase of *Star Wars* publishing. It appeared about six months before the first Dark Horse Comic — *Dark Empire* and it reached #1 on the *New York Times* bestseller's list. The story takes place five years after the death of Darth Vader and recounts the efforts of your favorite heroes to bring as many planets as possible into the New Republic and the emergence of Grand Admiral Thrawn as leader of the remnants of the Empire in a counter-revolution.

As the first collectible of the 1990s, after the 1985 to 1990 dark ages, this book is highly collectible. However, it would be an overstatement to say it caused the rebirth of *Star Wars*. Rather, it is just the first item in a well-orchestrated plan to bring *Star Wars* back; a plan in which we have all been entirely willing participants. New novels and comics are a critical part of the plan, because there is such as shortage of actual movie material — only about six hours. Brief appearances by crucial characters leaves many, many stories to tell!

The novels and story collections are listed below in their approximate order of appearance, based on the first book in the series. Titles first published in hardcover are listed first, followed by paperback series. Generally, better or more important authors and stories are published in hardcover, while paperback originals are considered to be of lesser importance by the publisher. Of course, this decision is generally reached before the novel is completed. After publica-

tion, fans judge for themselves.

It has been common for the Science Fiction Book Club to reprint three-book paperback original series in one omnibus book club edition. For a collector, however, a first edition paperback is more valuable than a hardcover reprint, because it is the true first edition of the work.

In order to be worth collecting, any hardcover book must be in near mint condition, with dust jacket in similar shape. The only defect in a dust jacket that does not significantly reduce value is "price-clipping," where a small portion of the inside front flap of the dust jacket is cut to remove the original price. This was commonly done to books given as gifts and by some used book dealers who wanted to charge more than original price. It is a pointless practice today, because the price is also printed on the bar code box in back.

Now that publication of new *Star Wars* novels is in full swing, print runs are large and price appreciation is unlikely. The best way to collect is to wait until the hardcover book you want is available for half price or less on the remainder tables at your favorite book store; and then look through all of them to find a first edition. You can accumulate a handsome hardcover collection this way, at reasonable prices.

Novels and Story Collections (1990–98)

Hardcover originals:
Grand Admiral Thrawn series by Timothy Zahn
Heir to the Empire
    1st HC: $15.00, 361p, Bantam Spectra
        #07327-3, June 1991, Tom Jung cover $30.00
    Limited Ed. HC $125.00, Bantam June 1991,
        signed, in slipcase 150.00
    1st SFBC: $5.98, Bantam #18382-2, Summer
        1991, Tom Jung cover 5.00
    1st PB: $4.99, 404p, Bantam Spectra
        #29612-4, June 1992, Tom Jung cover 6.00
Dark Force Rising
    1st HC: $18.50, 376p, Bantam Spectra
        #08574-3, June 1992, Tom Jung cover 25.00

Heir to the Empire, Dark Force Rising *and* The Last Command, *by Timothy Zahn, 1st Hardcovers (Bantam Spectra 1991–93)*

Limited Ed. HC, $125.00, Bantam #08907-2,
   June 1992, signed, in slipcase 140.00
1st SFBC: $7.98, Bantam #19949-7, Summer
   1992 . . . . 7.50
1st PB: $5.99, 439p, Bantam Spectra
   #56071-9, March 1993, Tom Jung cover 5.00
The Last Command
1st HC: $21.95, 407p, Bantam Spectra
   #09186-7, May 1993, Tom Jung Cover 25.00
Limited Ed. HC, not seen 140.00
SFBC: $8.98, 349p, Bantam #00913, July
   1993, Tom Jung cover 7.50
1st PB: $5.99, 467p, Bantam Spectra
   #56492-7, Feb. 1994, Tom Jung cover 5.00

The Truce At Bakura, by Kathleen Tyers
1st HC: $21.95, 311p, Bantam Spectra
   #09541-2, Jan. 1994, Drew Struzan cover 25.00
SFBC: $7.98, 246p, Bantam #02501, Drew
   Struzan cover 7.50
1st PB: $5.99, 341p, Bantam Spectra
   #56872-8, Dec. 1994, Drew Struzan cover 5.00

The Courtship Of Princess Leia, by Dave Wolverton
1st HC: $21.95, 327p, Bantam Spectra
   #08928-5, May 1994, Drew Struzan cover 25.00
SFBC: $7.98, 327p, Bantam #03409, Drew
   Struzan cover 7.50
1st PB: $5.99, Bantam Spectra #56937-6,
   May 1995, Drew Struzan cover 5.00

The Crystal Star, by Vonda N. McIntyre
1st HC: $21.95, 309p, Bantam Spectra
   #08929-3, Dec. 1994, Drew Struzan cover 25.00
SFBC: $7.98, 260p, Bantam #06637, Feb.
   1995, Drew Struzan cover 7.50
1st PB: $5.99, 413p, Bantam Spectra
   #57174-5, Dec. 1995, Drew Struzan cover 5.00

Children of the Jedi, Barbara Hambly
1st HC: $21.95, 345p, Bantam Spectra
   #08930-7, May 1995, Drew Struzan cover 25.00

SFBC: $8.98, 330p, Bantam #07692, Aug.
   1995, Drew Struzan cover 8.00
1st PB: $5.99, 409p, Bantam Spectra
   #57293-8, July 1996, Drew Struzan cover 5.00
Star Wars Darksaber, by Kevin J. Anderson
1st HC: $22.95, Bantam Spectra #09974-4,
   Nov. 1995, Drew Struzan cover 25.00
SFBC: $8.98, Bantam, Drew Struzan cover 8.00
1st PB: $5.99, Bantam Spectra #56611-9,
   Nov. 1996, Drew Struzan cover 5.00

Shadows Of The Empire, by Steve Perry
1st HC: $22.95, Bantam Spectra #10089-0,
   May 1996, Drew Struzan cover 25.00
SFBC: $8.98, Bantam, Drew Struzan cover 8.00
1st PB: $5.99, Bantam Spectra #57413-2,
   April 1997, Drew Struzan cover 5.00

The New Rebellion, by Kristine Kathryn Rusch
1st HC: $22.95 Bantam Spectra #10093-9,
   Dec. 1996, Drew Struzan cover 25.00
SFBC: $8.98, 386p, Bantam #14441, Jan.
   1997, Drew Struzan cover 8.00
1st PB: $5.99, Bantam Spectra #57414-0,
   Oct. 1997, Drew Struzan cover 5.00

Planet of Twilight, by Barbara Hambly
1st HC: $22.95, 312p, Bantam Spectra
   #09540-4, May 1997, Drew Struzan cover 25.00
SFBC: Bantam 8.00
1st PB: $5.99, Bantam Spectra #57517-1,
   Apr. 1998, Drew Struzan cover 6.00

Specter of the Past, by Timothy Zahn
1st HC: $23.95, 344p, Bantam Spectra
   #09542-0, Nov. 1997, Drew Struzan cover 24.00
SFBC: Bantam. 8.00
1st PB: 1998 . . . . 6.00

I, Jedi, by Michael Stackpole
1st HC: $23.95, Bantam Spectra #10820-4,
   Feb. 1998 . . . . 24.00

 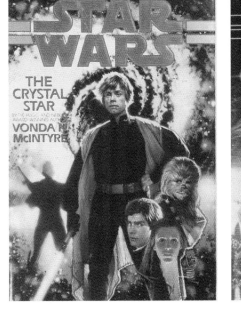 

The Truce at Bakura, *by Kathleen Tyers,* The Crystal Star, *by Vonda N. McIntyre and* Children of the Jedi, *by Barbara Hambly,*
1st Hardcovers (Bantam Spectra 1994–95)

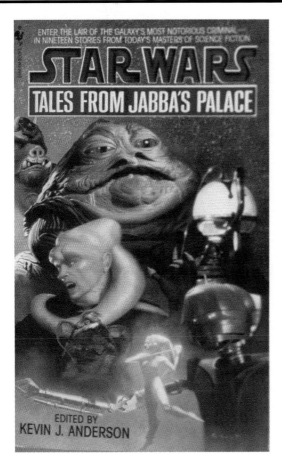

Tales From Jabba's Palace, *edited by Kevin J. Anderson*
1st Paperback (Bantam Spectra 1996)

Paperback originals:
The Jedi Academy Trilogy by Kevin J. Anderson
#1 *Jedi Search*
1st PB: $5.99, 354p, Bantam Spectra #29798-8,
    March 1994, John Alvin cover 6.00
#2: *Dark Apprentice*
1st PB: $5.99, 354p, Bantam Spectra #29799-6,
    July 1994, John Alvin cover 5.00
#3: *Champions of the Force*
1st PB: $5.99, 324p, Bantam Spectra #29802-X,
    Oct. 1994, John Alvin cover 5.00
Boxed Set: 18.00
The Jedi Academy Trilogy, combined edition
SFBC: $14.98, Bantam #0562 . . . . 10.00

The Corellian Trilogy by Roger McBride Allen
#1: *Ambush At Corellia*
1st PB: $5.99, 308p, Bantam Spectra #29803-8,
    March 1995, Drew Struzan cover 5.00
#2: *Assault At Selonia*
1st PB: $5.99, 289p, Bantam Spectra #29805-4,
    July 1995, Drew Struzan cover 5.00
#3: *Showdown At Centerpoint*
1st PB: $5.99, 301p, Bantam Spectra #29806-2,
    Oct. 1995, Drew Struzan cover 5.00
Boxed Set: 18.00
The Corellian Trilogy, combined edition
SFBC: Bantam 10.00

Star Wars Tales edited by Kevin J. Anderson
Star Wars: Tales from the Mos Eisley Cantina
    1st PB: $5.99, Bantam Spectra #56468-4

Aug. 1995, Anthology of 16 stories, Steve
    Youll cover 5.00
Star Wars Tales From Jabba's Palace
    1st PB: $5.99, Bantam Spectra #56815-9, Jan
    1996, Anthology, Steve Youll cover 5.00
Star Wars: Tales of the Bounty Hunters
    1st PB: $5.99, 339p, Bantam Spectra
    #56816-7, Dec. 1996, Anthology of 5
    stories, Steve Youll cover 5.00

Black Fleet Crisis by Michael Kube-McDowell
#1: *Before The Storm*
    1st PB: $5.99, 309p, Bantam Spectra
    #57273-3, April 1996, Drew Struzan cover 6.00
#2: *Shield of Lies*
    1st PB: $5.99, 340p, Bantam Spectra
    #57277-6, Sept. 1996, Drew Struzan cover 6.00
#3: *Tyrant's Test*
    1st PB: $5.99, 366p, Bantam Spectra
    #57275-X, Jan. 1997, Drew Struzan cover 6.00
Black Fleet Crisis, combined edition
    SFBC: $14.98, 785p, Bantam #15119, Drew
        Struzan cover 10.00

X-Wing series, by Michael A. Stackpole
#1: *Rogue Squadron*
    1st PB: $5.99, 388p, Bantam Spectra
    #56801-9, Feb. 1996, Paul Youll cover 6.00
#2: *Wedge's Gamble*
    1st PB: $5.99, 357p, Bantam Spectra
    #56802-7, June 1996, Paul Youll cover 6.00
#3: *The Krytos Trap*
    1st PB: $5.99, 355p, Bantam Spectra
    #56803-5, Oct. 1996, Paul Youll cover 6.00
#4: *The Bacta War*
    1st PB: $5.99, 349p, Bantam Spectra
    #56804-3, Feb. 1997, Paul Youll cover 6.00

Han Solo Trilogy by A.C. Crispin
#1: *Star Wars The Paradise Snare*
    1st PB: $5.99 Bantam Spectra #57415-7,
    June 1997, Drew Struzan cover 6.00
#2: *Star Wars The Hutt Gambit*
    1st PB: $5.99 Bantam Spectra #57416-7,
    Sept. 1997, Drew Struzan cover 6.00
#3: *Rebel Dawn*
    1st PB: $5.99 Bantam Spectra #57417-5,
    Feb. 1998 . . . . 6.00

Schweighofer, Peter ed.: *Star Wars: Tales from the
    Empire*, $5.99 Bantam Spectra #57876-6,
    Nov. 1997 . . . . 5.00

YOUNG ADULT AND JUVENILE NOVELS

Juvenile and Young Adult books do not draw much collector interest, while kiddie books with pictures are fairly collectible. This has little or nothing to do with the quality of the fiction.

YOUNG ADULT

Young Jedi Knights series by Kevin J. Anderson and
    Rebecca Moesta, featuring the adventures of Jason
    and Jaina at the Luke Skywalker Jedi Academy.
1: *Shadow Academy*
    1st PB: $5.99, Boulevard #16025-1 . . . . $6.00
2: *The Lost Ones*
    1st PB: $5.99, Boulevard #16052-9 . . . . 5.00

3: *Heirs of the Force*
   1st PB: $5.99, Boulevard #16066-9 . . . . 5.00
Boxed Set: #1–#3 . . . . 15.00
4: *Lightsabers*
   1st PB: $5.99, Boulevard #16091-X 5.00
5: *Darkest Knight*
   1st PB: $5.99, Boulevard #16129-0 . . . . 5.00
6: *Jedi Under Seige*
   1st PB: $5.99, Boulevard #16163-0 . . . . 5.00
Combined HC: #1–#6 . . . . 20.00
7: *Shards of Alderaan*
   1st PB: $5.99, Boulevard #16207-6 . . . . 5.00
8: *Diversity Alliance*
   1st PB: $5.99, Boulevard #16234-3, April 1997 . . . 5.00
9: *Delusions of Grandeur*
   1st PB: $5.99, Boulevard #16272-6, June 1997 . . . 5.00
10: *Jedi Bounty*
   1st PB: $5.99, Boulevard #16297-1, Oct. 1997 . . . . 5.00
#11: *The Emperor's Plague*
   1st PB: $5.99, Boulevard #16331-5, Jan. 1998 . . . . 5.00
#12: *Return to Ord Mantell*
   1st PB: $5.99, Boulevard #16362-8, Mar. 1998 . . . 5.00

JUVENILE

Star Wars series by Paul Davids and Hollace Davids
#1: *The Glove of Darth Vader*
   1st PB: $3.99, Bantam Skylark #15887-2, July
   1992 . . . . $3.00
#2: *The Lost City of The Jedi*
   1st PB: $3.99, Bantam Skylark #15888-0, July
   1992 . . . . 3.00
by Paul Davids
#3: *Zorba The Hutt's Revenge*
   1st PB: $3.99, Bantam Skylark #15889-9,
   Aug. 1992 . . . . 3.00
Boxed Set: #1–#3 . . . . 10.00
Combined HC #1–#3 . . . . 10.00
#4: *Mission From Mount Yoda*
   1st PB: $3.99, Bantam Skylark #15890-2,
   Feb. 1993 . . . . 3.00
#5: *Queen Of The Empire*
   1st PB: $3.99, Bantam Skylark #15891-0,
   March 1993 . . . . 3.00
#6: *Prophets Of The Dark Side*
   1st PB: $3.99, Bantam Skylark #15892-9,
   May 1993 . . . . 3.00
Combined HC: #4–#6 . . . . 10.00

Galaxy of Fear series by John Whitman
#1: *Eaten Alive*
   1st TPB: $4.99, Bantam Skylark #48450-8,
   Feb. 1997, 3-D cover 5.00
#2: *City of the Dead*
   1st TPB: $4.99, Bantam Skylark #48451-6,
   Feb. 1997, 3-D cover 5.00
#3: *Planet Plague*
   1st TPB: $4.99, Bantam Skylark #48452-4,
   April 1997, 3-D cover 5.00
#4: *Nightmare Machine*
   1st TPB: $4.99, Bantam Skylark #48453-2,
   June 1997 . . . . 5.00
#5: *Ghost of the Jedi*
   1st TPB: $4.99, Bantam Skylark #48454-0,
   Aug. 1997 . . . . 5.00
#6: *Army of Terror*
   1st TPB: $4.99, Bantam Skylark #, Oct. 1997 . . . . . 5.00
#7: *The Brain Spiders*
   1st TPB: $4.99, Bantam Skylark #, Dec. 1997 . . . . 5.00

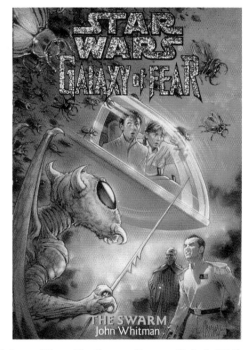

Galaxy of Fear: The Swarm *(Bantam Skylark 1998)*

#8: *The Swarm*
   1st TPB: $4.99, Bantam Skylark #48638-1,
   Feb. 1998 . . . . 5.00
#9: *Spore*
   1st TPB: $4.99, Bantam Skylark #48639-X,
   Feb. 1998 . . . . 5.00
#10: *The Doomsday Ship*
   1st TPB: $4.50, Bantam Skylark #48640-3,
   Apr. 1998 . . . . 4.50

Junior Jedi Knights series by Nancy Richardson
#1: *Golden Globe*
   1st TPB: $4.50, Boulevard #035-9 . . . . 4.00
#2: *Lyric's World*
   1st TPB: $4.50, Boulevard #068-5 . . . . 4.00
#3: *Promises*
   1st TPB: $4.50, Boulevard #097-9 . . . . 4.00

by Rebecca Moesta
#4: *Anakin's Quest*
   1st TPB: $4.50, Boulevard #136-3, Eric Lee
   cover 4.00
#5: *Vader's Fortress*
   1st TPB: $4.50, Boulevard #173-8 . . . . 4.00
#6: *Kenobi's Blade*
   1st TPB: $4.50, Boulevard #208-4 . . . . 4.00

Cruise Along Books
Han Solo's Rescue Mission
   TPB: $6.98, 7"x9", Fun Works #823-7, March
   1998, with Galoob X-Ray vehicle 7.00
Luke Skywalker's Race Against Time
   TPB: $6.98, 7"x9", Fun Works #824-5, March
   1998, with Galoob X-Ray vehicle 7.00

Other Juvenile Books
Golden, Christpoher: *Shadows of the Empire: A
   Star Wars Junior Novelization*
   TPB: $4.50, Dell Yearling 41303-6, Oct. 1996 . . . . 4.00
The Empire Strikes Back Shimmer Book
   HC: $8.98, 24pg, 9"x9", Fun Works #860-1,
   March 1998 . . . . 9.00

The Art of Star Wars Episode V The Empire Strikes Back
(Ballantine 1994)

NON-FICTION

    Star Wars books come in every conceivable category of non-fiction. There are art books, sketch books, making-of-the-movie books, reference books, humor books and even "fictional" non-fiction books. Many books include elements of several categories, making organization of the following lists problematic. You may have to search a little for the title you are interested in.

Art of... Books
The Art of Star Wars, edited by Carol Titelman, plus
    script by George Lucas, includes sketches,
    costume designs, blueprints, production paintings
    and photos.
    1st HC: $17.95, 175p, Ballantine #28273-6,
      Nov. 1979. . . . . $25.00
    1st TPB: $10.95, 175p, Ballantine #27666-3,
      Nov. 1979 . . . . 15.00
    SFBC: $11.98, Ballantine #3823-2, Summer
      1980 . . . . 15.00
    Later TPB: $12.95, Ballantine #29565-X, Nov.
      1980 . . . . 15.00
    Reissue TPB: *The Art of Star Wars, Revised*
      Edition, Ballantine #30627-9, 1982 . . . . 15.00
Retitled: *The Art of Star Wars, Episode IV, A New Hope*
    TPB: $18.00, 176p Del Rey #39202-7, Oct.
      1994, 9"x12", Ralph McQuarrie cover 20.00

    TPB: Ballantine #40980-9, 1996, 2nd edition 19.00

Revised as: *Second Edition of The Art of Star Wars:*
    A New Hope, by Carol Titelman and George Lucas:
    1st TPB: $18.95, 192p Del Rey #39202-7,
      Feb. 1997, Ralph McQuarrie cover, revised
      with material from the special edition 19.00
The Art of the Empire Strikes Back, edited by Deborah
    Call, with text by Valerie Hoffman and Vick Bullock
    1st HC: Del Rey #29335-5, Oct. 1980 . . . . 25.00
    SFBC: $17.50, Del Rey 5579-8, Feb. 1981 . . . . . 15.00
    1st TPB: $15.95, 176p, Ballantine #28833-5,
      Oct. 1980, 9"x12" 15.00
Retitled: *The Art of Star Wars, Episode V, The Empire*
    Strikes Back
    TPB: $18.00, 160p, Ballantine/Del Rey
      #39203-5, Oct. 1994, repackaged 20.00
    TPB: Ballantine #41088-2, 1996, 2nd edition 19.00
Revised as: *Second Edition of The Art of Star Wars*
    The Empire Strikes Back, edited by Deborah Call
    1st TPB: $18.95, 192p, Del Rey #39203-5,
      Feb. 1997, revised, with material from the
      special edition 19.00
The Art of Return of the Jedi, edited by Anonymous,
    including the film script by Lawrence Kasdan and
    George Lucas
    1st HC: $19.95, Del Rey #30957-X, Nov.
      1983, 9"x12" 25.00
    SFBC: $19.98, Del Rey 5393-4, Fall 1984 . . . . . . 15.00
Retitled: *The Art of Star Wars, Episode VI, Return*
    of the Jedi
    TPB: $19.00, 160p, Del Rey #39204-3, Oct.
      1994, repackaged 20.00
    TPB: Ballantine #41089-0, 1996, 2nd ed. 19.00

Revised as: *Second Edition of The Art of Star Wars:*
    Return of the Jedi, edited by Anonymous
    1st TPB: $18.95, 192p, Del Rey #39204-3,
      Feb. 1997, revised, with material from the
      special edition 19.00

The Art of Dave Dorman *(Friedlander 1996)*

The Art of Star Wars Galaxy edited by Gary Cerani
   TPB: 9"x12", 132p, Topps #01-5, 1993, Ken
      Steacy cover 20.00
   HC: $150.00, Underwood Miller March 1994,
      limited to 1,000 copies, boxed, signed,
      with special card 150.00
   2nd TPB: $25.00, 1996 . . . . 20.00
   QVC exclusive 25.00
The Art of Star Wars Galaxy, Volume Two by C.
   Cerani and Gary Cerani
   TPB: $19.95, 132p, Topps #03-1, Nov. 1994,
      Boris Valejo cover 20.00
Star Wars: The Art of the Brothers Hildebrandt, by
   Bob Woods
   TPB: Ballantine #42301-1, Oct. 1997 . . . . 25.00
Star Wars: The Art of Dave Dorman, edited by
   Stephen D. Smith and Lurene Haines, Dave
   Dorman illustrations and text
   HC: 128p, Friedlander #38-3, Dec. 1996,
      signed, limited to 2,500 copies 75.00
   TPB: $24.95, Friedlander #37-5, Dec. 1996 . . . . . 25.00
Star Wars: The Art of Ralph McQuarrie Artbox
   includes 48-page book, 15 postcards, and 6
   postage stamps in a box
   HC: $18.95, Chronicle #1320-7, 1996 . . . . 20.00
The Illustrated Star Wars Universe, edited by
   Martha Banta
   HC: Bantam #03925-4, 1995 . . . . 20.00
The Illustrated Star Wars Universe, by Kevin J.
   Anderson, illustrated by Ralph McQuarrie
   1st HC, $35.00, 192p, Bantam Spectra
      #09302-9, Dec. 1995, 8½"x11" 35.00
   1st TPB, $17.95 Bantam 37484-2, Oct. 1997 . . . . 18.00
Industrial Light & Magic: The Art of Special Effects,
   by Thomas G. Smith
   1st HC:, Del Rey #32263-0, Nov. 1986 . . . . 25.00

Illustrated Screenplays
Star Wars: A New Hope Illustrated Screenplay
   TPB: Ballantine #42069-7, 1998, 5"x8" 12.00
Star Wars: The Empire Strikes Back Illustrated Screenplay
   TPB: Ballantine #42070-5, 1998, 5"x8" 12.00
Star Wars: Return of the Jedi Illustrated Screenplay
   TPB: Ballantine #42079-9, 1998, 5"x8" 12.00

Guide to
A Guide to the Star Wars Universe, by Raymond L.
   Velasco
   1st PB, $2.95, Ballantine-Del Rey #31920-6,
      1984 . . . . 7.50
*A Guide to the Star Wars Universe, Second Edition,
   Revised & Expanded*, by Bill Slavicsek
   1st TPB: $10.00, 448p, Del Rey #38625-6,
      1996, 5"x8" Ralph McQuarrie cover 10.00
Star Wars: The Essential Guide To Characters, by
   Andy Mangels
   1st TPB: $18.00, 208p, Del Rey #39535-2,
      Nov. 1995, Reference 18.00
*Star Wars: The Essential Guide To Vehicles and
   Vessels*, by Bill Smith
   1st TPB: $18.00, 224p, Del Rey #39299-X,
      March 1996, Reference 18.00
*Star Wars: The Essential Guide to Weapons and
   Technology*, by Bill Smith
   1st TPB: $18.00, 200p, Del Rey #41413-6,
      Oct. 1997 . . . . 18.00
Star Wars Technical Journal, by Shane Johnson
   1st HC: $35.00, 192p, Del Rey #40182-4,
      Oct. 1995, combination of the three Starlog
      technical journals, includes schematics,
      fold -out blueprints, photos, etc. 35.00
   2nd Edition, Del Rey #9127909, 1997 . . . . 35.00
The Secrets of Star Wars: Shadows of the Empire,
   by Mark Cotta Vaz, interviews, guide to
   characters and places, black and white
   illustrations, with 8 pages in color, 7½"x9¼"
   TPB: $15.00, 320p, Del Rey #40236-7, May
      1996 . . . . 15.00

Making of
The Star Wars Album, edited by Anonymous
   1st TPB: Nov. 1977, $5.95, 76p, Ballantine
      27591-8, 8½"x11", Bros. Hildebrandt covers . . . 20.00

*Once Upon a Galaxy: A Journal of the Making of
   The Empire Strikes Back*, by Alan Arnold
   1st PB: $2.75, Del Rey #29075-5, Sept. 1980,
      photo cover 10.00

The Essential Guide to Characters, *by Andy Mangels;* The Essential Guide to Vehicles and Vessels *and*
The Essential Guide to Weapons and Technology, *by Bill Smith, Trade Paperbacks (Del Rey 1995–97)*

The Making of Return of the Jedi, by John Philip
Peecher
1st PB, Del Rey #31235-X, Sept. 1983 . . . . 10.00

Pop-Up Books
Star Wars: The Rebel Alliance, Ships of the Fleet,
by Bill Smith, with 6 pop-up paintings by
Barbara Gibson, diagrams by Troy Vigil, fold-
outs, 10p, 11¼"x8¾"
HC: $15.95, Little Brown #53509-5, 1995 . . . . 16.00
Star Wars: The Galactic Empire, Ships of the Fleet,
by Bill Smith, with 6 pop-up paintings by
Barbara Gibson, diagrams by Troy Vigil, fold-
outs, 10p, 11¼"x8¾"
HC: $15.95, Little Brown #53510-9, 1995 . . . . 16.00
Star Wars: The Mos Eisley Cantina Pop-up Book by
Kevin J. Anderson and Rebecca Moesta,
illustrated by Ralph McQuarrie, 16p, 8½"x12¾"
HC: $19.95, Little Brown #53511-7, 1995 . . . . 20.00
Star Wars: Jabba's Palace Pop-up Book by Kevin
J. Anderson and Rebecca Moesta, illustrated
by Ralph McQuarrie, 16p, 8½"x12¾"
HC: $19.95, Little Brown #53513-3, 1995 . . . . 20.00

Scripts/Dramatizations
*Star Wars: The National Public Radio Dramatiza-
tion*, by Brian Daley
TPB: $11.00, 352p, Del Rey #39109-8, Oct.
1994, Illustrated. 12.00
*The Empire Strikes Back: The National Public
Radio Dramatization*, by Brian Daley
TPB: $11.00, 352p, Del Rey #39605-7, June
1995, illustrated 11.00
*Return of the Jedi: The National Public Radio
Dramatization*, by Brian Daley
TPB: $11.00, 208p, Del Rey #40782-2, Dec.
1996, Illustrated. 12.00
Star Wars: The Three-In-One Annotated Scripts,
annotated by Laurent Bouzereau
TPB: $, Del Rey #40981-7, May 1997 . . . . 13.00
Star Wars: A New Hope, facsimile script
TPB: One Stop Publishing #306-4, 1994 . . . . 20.00
The Empire Strikes Back, facsimile script
TPB: One Stop Publishing #307-2, 1994 . . . . 20.00

Return of the Jedi, facsimile script
TPB: One Stop Publishing #304-8, 1994 . . . . 20.00
Star Wars Trilogy, facsimile scripts
TPB: 1-56693374-9, 1995 . . . . 50.00

Sketchbook
The Star Wars Sketchbook, by Joe Johnston
1st TPB: $4.95, 65 original sketches, Ballan-
tine #27380, 1977, 8½"x11" 25.00
The Empire Strikes Back Sketchbook, by Joe
Johnston and Rodis Jamero
1st TPB: $5.95, 95p, Ballantine #28836-X,
July 1980, sketches 35.00
Return of the Jedi Sketchbook, by Joe Johnston
1st TPB: Ballantine, 1983. . . . . 25.00

Smithsonian
*Star Wars: The Magic of Myth: Companion to the
Exhibition at the National Air and Space
Museum, Smithsonian Institution*, by Mary
Henderson
1st HC: $49.95, Bantam Broadway #10206-0,
Nov. 1997 . . . . 50.00
1st TPB: $24.95, Bantam Broadway
#37810-4, Nov. 1997 . . . . 25.00

Misc.
*The Quotable Star Wars: I'd Just as Soon Kiss a
Wookiee!*, by Stephen J. Sansweet
TPB: $6.00, 128p, Del Rey #40760-1, Oct.
1996 . . . . 6.00
*The Ultimate Unauthorized Star Wars Trilogy Trivia
Challenge* by James Hatfield & George "Doc" Burt
TPB: Kensington #185-3, 1997 . . . . 15.00
Star Wars Diplomatic Corps Entrance Exam, by
Kathryn Rusch
TBP: $12.00, 176p, Del Rey #41412-8, June
1997 . . . . 12.00
The Jedi Master's Quiz Book, by Rusty Miller
TPB: Del Rey #30697-X, Nov. 1982 . . . . 5.00
Star Wars Classic Characters, 1998 edition
TPB: Cedco #55912520-9, 1997 . . . . 13.00
The Star Wars Diaries
TPB: Cimino 90167422-8, 1997 . . . . 25.00

*Star Wars Album, Trade Paperback (Ballantine 1977); Star Wars: The Mos Eisley Cantina Pop-up Book and
Star Wars: Jabba's Palace Pop-Up Book, by Kevin J. Anderson and Rebecca Moesta (Little Brown 1995)*

Star Wars Storybook, The Empire Strikes Back Storybook, Return of the Jedi Storybook *(Scholastic 1977–84)*

Star Wars: A Storybook, by J. J. Gardner
  (Scholastic #06654-4, 1996) 6.00
Star Wars little chronicles (Chronicle #1480-7, Jan.
  1997). 10.00
The Empire Strikes Back Storybook, by Shep
  Steneman (Random House 84414-9, Aug. 1980) . 10.00
  TPB: (Scholastic Book Service) 5.00
The Empire Strikes Back Storybook by J.J.
  Gardner (Scholastic #06656-0, 1996). 5.00
The Empire Strikes Back little chronicles (Chronicle
  #4182-3, Jan. 1997). 10.00
Return of the Jedi Storybook, by Joan D. Vinge
  (Random House 1983). 12.50
  TPB: (Scholastic Book Service) 4.00
Return of the Jedi Storybook by J.J. Gardner
  (Scholastic #06659-5, 1996) 6.00
Return of the Jedi little chronicles (Chronicle
  #4194-7, Jan. 1997). 10.00

Story Books
The Wookiee Storybook, illustrated by Patricia
  Wynne (Random House 1979). 7.50
The Mystery of the Rebellious Robot, illustrated by
  Mark Corcoran (Random House 1979). 6.00
The Maverick Moon, illustrated by Walter Wright
  (Random House 1979). 6.00
The Droid Dilemma (Random House 1979). 6.00

Droid Story Books
The Pirates of Tarnoonga, by Ellen Weiss (Random
  House 1986). 5.00
The Lost Prince, by Ellen Weiss (Random House
  1985). 5.00
Escape from the Monster Ship, by Bonnie Bogart
  (Random House 1986). 5.00
The White Witch, by Emily James (Random House
  1986). 5.00
Shiny as a Droid (Random House 1985-6) 5.00

Ewoks Story Books
Wicket Goes Fishing, by Melinda Luke (Random
  House 1986) 5.00
Wicket and the Dandelion Warriors, by Larry
  Weinberg (Random House 1985). 5.00

The Ring, the Witch, and the Crystal, by Cathy E.
  Dubowski (Random House 1986) 5.00
The Shadow Stone, by Cathy E. Dubowski
  (Random House 1986) 5.00
The Ewoks and the Lost Children, by Amy Ehrlich
  (Random House 1985). 5.00
Three Cheers for Kneesaa!, by Jane E. Gerver
  (Random House 1984). 5.00
The Ewoks' Hang Gliding Adventure, by Judy
  Herbstman (Random House 1984). 5.00
The Adventures of Teebo, by Joe Johnston
  (RandomHouse 1984) 5.00
The Baby Ewoks' Picnic Surprise, by Melinda Luke
  (Random House 1984). 5.00
Wicket Finds a Way, by Melinda Luke (Random
  House 1984) 5.00
The Red Ghost, by Melinda Luke and Paul Dini
  (Random House 1986). 5.00

The Mystery of the Rebellious Robot (Random House 1979)

How the Ewoks Saved the Trees, by James Howe
(Random House 1984). 5.00
Fuzzy as an Ewok (Random House 1985-6) 5.00
Learn-to-Read Activity Book (Random House 1985) . . . 5.00
ABC Fun (Random House 1985–86). 5.00
School Days (Random House 1985–86) 5.00

Other Children's Books

Star Wars: Pilots and Spacecraft Glow-in-the-Dark
(Golden Book #13480-6, 1997) 6.00
Star Wars: A New Hope, Golden Book and Tattoos
(Golden Book #13067-3, 1997) 6.00
Star Wars: The Empire Strikes Back, Golden Book
and Tattoos (Golden Book #13068-1, 1997) 6.00
Star Wars: Return of the Jedi, Golden Book and
Tattoos (Golden Book #13069-X, 1997) 6.00
Star Wars: Return of the Jedi by Elezabeth Levy
(Random House #87205-1, 1995) 4.00
Star Wars Compendium (Paradise Press). 15.00
The Empire Strikes Back by Larry Weinberg
(Random House #87204-3, 1995) 4.00
Star Wars Princess Leia, Rebel Leader, illustrated
by Ken Steacy (Golden Book #10105, 1997) 4.00
The Mos Eisley Cantina Scratch and Sniff Book
(Golden Book #13552, 1997) 5.00
Return of the Jedi Giant Collector's Compendium
(Paradise Press 1983) 10.00
Star Wars: Battling the Empire by Stephen R.
Covey (Golden Books #75704-8, 1997) 17.00
The Empire Strikes Back Panorama Book, illus.
GerryDaly (Random House). 15.00
The World of Star Wars (Paradise Press 1981) 10.00
The Jedi Master's Quizbook 8.00
My Jedi Journal (Ballantine) 6.00
*How to Draw Star Wars Heroes, Creatures,
Spaceships and other Fantastic Things*, by J.
Lee Ames 15.00
Han Solo's Rescue 10.00
*The Star Wars Question and Answer Book about
Space* (Random House). 7.00

*The Star Wars Question and Answer Book about
Computers* (Random House) 7.00

Posterbooks, Scrapbooks

Star Wars Pull-out Posterbook (Scholastic
#06655-2, 1996) 5.00
The Empire Strikes Back Pull-out Posterbook
(Scholastic #06657-9, 1996) 5.00
Return of the Jedi Pull-out Posterbook (Scholastic
#06663-3, 1996) 5.00
Star Wars Treasy (Scholastic #39635-8) 5.00
The Empire Strikes Back (Scholastic #31791-1) 4.00
The Complete Star Wars Trilogy Scrapbook by
Mark Cotta Vaz (Scholastic #06653-6, 1996) 8.00
*The Star Wars Trilogy Scrapbook: The Rebel
Alliance* by Mark Cotta Vaz, $6.99, Scholastic
(64p #12051-4, Nov. 1997) 7.00

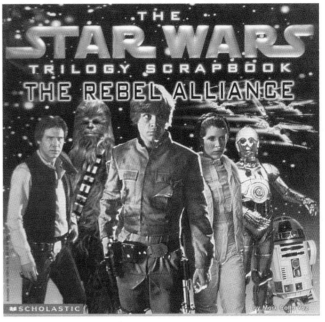

*Star Wars Trilogy Scrapbook: The Rebel Alliance,
by Mark Cotta Vaz (Scholastic 1997)*

*The Star Wars Trilogy Scrapbook: The Galactic
Empire* by Mark Cotta Vaz, $6.99, 64p
(Scholastic #12051-4, Nov. 1997). 7.00

Mouse Works

Star Wars: A Shimmer Book by Ken Steacy (Mouse
Works #82567-X, 1997) hardcover. 9.00
Rescue Han Solo (Mouse Works #82823-7, 1998) 7.00
Return of the Jedi, A Flip Book (Mouse Works
#82579-3,1997) 3.00
The Empire Strikes Back, A Flip Book (Mouse
Works #82578-5, 1997) 3.00

Blank Books (1996–97)

Star Wars Journal, Return of the Jedi space battle
scene (#78840, 1996) 8.00
Star Wars Journal, Hildebrandt poster art (#78859,
1996). 8.00
Star Wars 20th Anniversary Journal (#79898, 1997) . . . 8.00
Star Wars 20th Anniversary Journal with bookmark
(7988X, 1997) 8.00

Star Wars Princess Leia Rebel Leader *(Golden Book 1997)*

CERAMICS

Yoda Ceramic Bank (Sigma 1982)

BANKS

The Roman Ceramics Company was the first to manufacture ceramic banks. These, like all 1977 collectibles, appeared before the action figures, but many collectors passed them up at the time and they were available at retail for several years. Each bank came in a white box and was hand painted. Sigma made three ceramic banks for the later movies. See also plastic and metal banks under DOLLS AND FIGURES and talking banks under ELECTRONICS.

Ceramic Banks (1977–82):
C-3PO Ceramic Bank, 8" tall, waist up, metallic gold
    (Roman Ceramics 1977) boxed $75.00
Darth Vader Ceramic Bank, 7" tall, head (Roman
    Ceramics 1977) boxed. 85.00
R2-D2 Ceramic Bank, 8" tall, full figure (Roman
    Ceramics 1977) boxed. 75.00

Chewbacca Ceramic Bank, 10fi" tall, kneeling with
    gun (Sigma 1982) 45.00
Jabba the Hutt Ceramic Bank, 6" tall, figural (Sigma
    1982). 45.00
Yoda Ceramic Bank, 8" tall, figural (Sigma 1982) 45.00

R2-D2 Cookie Jar (Roman Ceramics 1977)

COOKIE JARS

Ceramic cookie jars were another early collectible from Roman Ceramics. R2-D2 is just the right shape to hold a lot of cookies. Cookie jars will be making a comeback in a big way in 1998, with over a dozen scheduled from Star Jars. They also make similar items for *Star Trek* and other licenses. Only 1,000 of each will be produced and they look very attractive in the pictures that they sent me. They can be reached at (561) 622-7693.

Cookie Jars (1977–82):
C-3PO, 10fl" gold metallic glaze (Roman Ceramics
    Corp. 1977) $140.00
Darth Vader (Roman Ceramics Corp. 1977) 140.00

Chewbacca Cookie Jar (Star Jars 1998)
Photo courtesy of Star Jars

R2-D2 13" tall, in white cardboard box with blue
   printing (Roman Ceramics Corp. 1977) 150.00
C-3PO/Darth Vader/R2-D2 Hexagon Cookie Jar
   (Sigma 1982) 100.00

Cookie Jars by Star Jars, limited editions of 1,000 jars
First Batch, First Quarter 1998
Obi-Wan Kenobi (Star Jars #026, 1998) 250.00
Jabba the Hutt (Star Jars #027, 1998) 250.00
Chewbacca (Star Jars #028, 1998) 250.00

Second Batch, Second Quarter 1998
C-3PO (Star Jars #029, Sept. 1998) 250.00
Princess Leia (Star Jars 1998) 250.00
Boba Fett (Star Jars 1998) 250.00

Projected, later in 1998
Wicket the Ewok (Star Jars 1998) 250.00
R2-D2 (Star Jars 1998) 250.00
Han Solo (Star Jars 1998) 250.00
Luke Skywalker (Star Jars 1998) 250.00
Stormtrooper (Star Jars 1998) 250.00
Lando Calrissian (Star Jars 1998) 250.00
Darth Vader (Star Jars 1998) 250.00
Yoda (Star Jars 1998) 250.00

Possible Editions (but not certain)
Gamorrean Guard (Star Jars 1998–99) 250.00
Death Star (Star Jars 1998–99) 250.00
Imperial AT-AT (Star Jars 1998–99) 250.00

Bookends
Chewbacca/Darth Vader Figural Bookends (Sigma
   1983) 75.00

FIGURES

Sigma produced a dozen 7" ceramic bisque figures in
1983. The faces on the human figures are somewhat juvenile;
the non-humans are better sculpted.

Return of the Jedi, bisque figures
Bib Fortuna (Sigma 1983) $50.00
Boba Fett (Sigma 1983) 65.00
C-3PO and R2-D2 (Sigma 1983) 60.00
Darth Vader (Sigma 1983) 60.00
Galactic Emperor, seated (Sigma 1983) 65.00
Gamorrean Guard (Sigma 1983) 60.00
Han Solo (Sigma 1983) 50.00
Klaatu (Sigma 1983) 50.00
Lando Calrissian (Sigma 1983) 50.00
Luke Skywalker, Jedi Knight (Sigma 1983) 50.00
Princess Leia, Boushh disguise (Sigma 1983) 65.00
Wicket W. Warrick (Sigma 1983) 50.00

HOUSEHOLD AND OFFICE ITEMS

These ceramic items range from bookends to tape dis-
pensers and from toothbrush holders to music boxes.

Ceramic figural items
Chewbacca and Darth Vader bookends (Sigma 1983) $75.00
C-3PO pencil tray (Sigma 1983) 40.00
C-3PO, seated figural tape dispenser (Sigma 1983) . . 40.00
C-3PO, in pieces, "Help" picture frame (Sigma 1983) . 30.00
Darth Vader picture frame (Sigma 1983) 45.00
Darth Vader mirror (Sigma 1983) 45.00
Ewok music box radio (Sigma 1983) 30.00
Gun Turret with C-3PO music box (Sigma 1983) 45.00
Landspeeder soap dish, with C-3PO and Obi-Wan
   (Sigma 1983) 40.00
Luke (Hoth Gear) and Tauntaun teapot set (Sigma
   1983) 150.00
R2-D2 picture frame (Sigma 1983) 45.00
R2-D2 and R5-D4 figural salt and pepper shakers
   (Sigma 1983) 125.00
R2-D2 figural string dispenser, with scissors (Sigma
   1983) 40.00
Rebel Snowspeeder toothbrush holder (Sigma 1983) . 40.00
Sy Snootles & Rebo Band music box (Sigma 1983) . . 90.00
Wicket and Kneesa music box (Sigma 1983) 75.00
Yoda pencil cup (Sigma 1983) 35.00
Yoda figural salt and pepper shakers (Sigma 1983) . . . 35.00
Yoda and tree figural vase (Sigma 1983) 35.00
Yoda in backpack box (Sigma 1983) 20.00

Gamorrean Guard and Lando Calrissian Mugs (Sigma 1983)

MUGS — FIGURAL

Ceramic Drinking Mugs
1st Batch (Sigma 1983) in white corrugated box
C-3PO $30.00
Chewbacca. 30.00
Darth Vader 30.00
Han Solo 30.00
Princess Leia 30.00
Luke Skywalker 30.00
Yoda. 30.00

2nd Batch (Sigma 1983) in *Return of the Jedi* color photo box
Biker Scout. 30.00
Gamorrean Guard. 30.00
Klaatu. 30.00
Lando Calrissian. 30.00
Stormtrooper 30.00
Wicket W. Warrick. 30.00

Ceramic Mugs (Rawcliffe 1995)
Star Wars. 13.00
The Empire Strikes Back 13.00
Return of the Jedi. 13.00
Shadows of the Empire. 13.00
Rebel Logo. 13.00
Darth Vader 13.00
Obi-Wan Kenobi 13.00
Yoda. 13.00
AT-AT 13.00
AT-ST 13.00
Shuttle *Tyderium*. 13.00
TIE Fighter 13.00

Boba Fett Mug and Box (Applause 1995)

14oz. Mugs, (Applause 1995) boxed, with certificate of authenticity
Darth Vader (#46044) 15.00
Boba Fett (#46045). 15.00
Stormtrooper (#46046) 15.00
C-3PO (gold) (#46047) 15.00

Second batch (Applause 1996)
Bib Fortuna (#46225) 15.00
Gamorrean Guard (#46226) 15.00
Han Solo (#46227) 15.00
Tusken Raider (#46228) 15.00
Emperor Palpatine (#46235) 15.00

Third batch (Applause 1997)
Chewbacca (#42679) 15.00
Luke Skywalker (#42680) 15.00
Obi-Wan Kenobi (#42681). 15.00
Princess Leia Organa (#42682) 15.00

15" Decal Mugs (Applause 1998)
Darth Vader (#42983) 9.00
Boba Fett (#42984). 9.00
Galactic Empire (#42985) 9.00
Jedi Knights (#42986). 9.00

PLATES

The first *Star Wars* collector plates were made in the late 1980s by the Hamilton Collection. There were eight plates, plus a larger 10th anniversary plate in 1987. The plates originally came in a styrofoam sandwich box.

8¼" Plates, First Series (1985–87)
Han Solo, pictured seated in Mos Eisley Cantina . . . $50.00
Princess Leia, pictured holding blaster 50.00
Luke Skywalker and Darth Vader, pictured fighting
    with lightsabers 60.00
Five heroes, pictured in the *Millennium Falcon* cockpit 50.00
Luke and Yoda, pictured seated on ground in
    Dagobah swamp 50.00
R2-D2 and Wicket the Ewok. 50.00
AT-ATs, pictured shooting 50.00
X-Wings and TIE Fighters pictured in front of Death
    Star. 50.00

10th Anniversary commemorative plate
1977–87 Commemorative, picturing Han, Luke,
    Leia and Darth's head in foreground with
    robots, Chewbacca & Obi-Wan in background . . . 60.00

Second Series, Star Wars Trilogy, 8¼" art by
    Morgan Weistling (Hamilton Collection 1993)
Star Wars, featuring Luke Skywalker in X-Wing Pilot
    outfit in foreground. 40.00
The Empire Strikes Back, featuring Luke Skywalker
    with Yoda on his back at top, Han Solo and
    Leia kissing underneath. 40.00
Return of the Jedi, featuring Luke Skywalker and
    Leia in Jabba's prisoner outfit swinging on rope . . 40.00

Third Series
These plates were originally offered at $40.00, but by 1997 Previews was still distributing them, now for $35.00. The advertisements say they are limited to 28 firing days, but that is not quite the same thing as limiting to a specific quantity. In any event, just about everyone who wants one of them has bought it already, so price appreciation will be slow.

Third Series: Space Vehicles 8¼", art by Sonia Hillios
    (Hamilton Collection 1995–96) 23K gold border
Millennium Falcon (EW1MF, 1995) $35.00
Imperial Shuttle *Tyderium* and landing pad 35.00
TIE Fighters in front of Cloud City 35.00
Red Five X-Wing Fighter pursued by TIE Fighter in
    Death Star trench. 35.00
Imperial Star Destroyer orbiting planet (EW5MF, 1996) 35.00
Rebel Snowspeeder circling AT-AT feet (EW6MF,
    1996). 35.00
B-wing (EW7MF, 1996). 35.00
Slave-1 (1996) 35.00

The Empire Strikes Back *Plate, Second Series and TIE Fighter/Cloud City Plate, Third Series (Hamilton Collection 1993–95)*

Fourth Series: Space Vehicles, 9", art by Sonia Hillios (Hamilton Collection 1997–98) 24K gold border

Medical Frigate (#13609)	35.00
Jabba's Sail Barge (#13602)	35.00
Y-Wing Fighter (#13604)	35.00

Star Wars Heroes and Villains, 8¼" art by Keith Birdsong (1997–98) bordered in 24k gold

Luke Skywalker (#, 1997)	35.00
Han Solo (#13661)	35.00
Darth Vader (#13662)	35.00
Princess Leia (#13663)	35.00
Obi Wan Kenobi (#13664)	35.00
Emperor Palpatine (#13665)	35.00
Boba Fett (#13667)	35.00
Yoda (#13666)	35.00

STEINS

Lidded Steins 6" (Metallic Impressions 1995) with solid pewter lid

Star Wars: A New Hope	$34.00
Star Wars: The Empire Strikes Back	34.00
Star Wars: Return of the Jedi	34.00

Deep Relief Stoneware (Dram Tree 1995) boxed

Star Wars, heroes picture	25.00
Star Wars: The Empire Strikes Back	25.00
Star Wars: Return of the Jedi	25.00

Lidded Steins 9½" (Dram Tree 1997–98)

Unique Darth Vader Stein, solid pewter lid with figure, limited to 1977 pieces, with Jason Palmer artwork	85.00
Unique Yoda Stein, solid pewter and lid, limited to 3,000 pieces, with Tsuneo Sanda artwork	80.00
Unique Boba Fett Stein, solid pewter and lid, limited to 3,000 pieces, with Dave Dorman artwork	85.00

TANKARDS

Ceramic "Toby" Tankard, sculpted by Jim Rumph (California Originals 1977) in white cardboard shipping box

Chewbacca, 6¾" tall, 36oz. brown	$60.00
Darth Vader 7¼" tall, 52oz. glossy black	60.00
Obi-Wan-Kenobi, 6¾" tall, 36oz, brown	60.00

Star Wars *Stoneware Stein (Dram Tree 1995)*

CLOTHING AND ACCESSORIES

CLOTHING

You can outfit yourself from head to toe with *Star Wars* clothes, and they are listed here in that order. While many collectors own items of *Star Wars* apparel, few would consider themselves collectors of it. Rather, they own some items that they wear when the occasion arises or the mood hits them. While some accessories, such as belt buckles or watches, have developed a collector following, the general rule can be summed up as "Don't expect to make a killing on your *Star Wars* T-shirts."

Most of the items listed here are designed for adults, and are priced accordingly. Most of the prices are the original retail price. All this really tells you is that you shouldn't pay $30.00 for a T-shirt if you can get a hundred different styles of T-shirts of the same type for under $20.00 retail at the local shopping mall.

See also: Masks and Costumes

Rebel Forces Logo cap (Thinking Cap Co. 1981)

Caps and Hats
The Empire Strikes Back logo cap, red/white embroidery and black emblem (Thinking Cap Co. 1980–81) $15.00
Imperial Guard hat, black with silver medallion on front (Thinking Cap Co. 1980–81) 25.00
Rebel Forces Logo cap, tan billed cap with flap in back, red/blue/yellow round patch (Thinking Cap Co. 1980–81) 20.00
Yoda Ear Cap, red, green cloth ears and artificial hair, yellow/black Yoda patch on front (Thinking Cap Co. 1980–81) 20.00

Admiral Ackbar cap (Sales Corp. of America 1983) . . . 15.00
Darth Vader and Emperor's Royal Guards cap (Sales Corp. of America 1983) 15.00
Gamorrean Guard (Sales Corp. of America 1983) 15.00
Jabba the Hutt (Sales Corp. of America 1983) 15.00
Luke and Darth (Sales Corp. of America 1983) 15.00
Return of the Jedi logo (Sales Corp. of America 1983) 15.00
Jedi Ski cap (white with red and black trim, Sales Corp. of America 1983) 20.00
Ewok knit child's hat (Sales Corp. of America 1983) . . 15.00

"Star Tours" logo embroidered on baseball cap (Star Tours) 8.00
Star Tours logo hat (orange burst design artwork on black cap, Star Tours) 8.00
Star Tours logo hat (orange and blue on white cap, Star Tours) 9.00
"Star Tours and Disney-MGM" logos hat (Droids on side, color artwork on white painter's cap, Star Tours) 9.00
Star Wars Fan Club Hat (special promo. hat) 15.00

Star Wars Embroidered Border Logo Hat (Ralph Marlin #690210, 1996) black 16.00
Star Wars Embroidered Border Logo Hat (Ralph Marlin #690220, 1996) white 16.00
Darth Vader Face cap (#825, 1997) 13.00
Star Wars 20 Years Logo cap (#845, 1997) 12.00
Darth Vader marble cap (#855, 1997) 12.00
Boba Fett marble cap (#865, 1997) 13.00
Sun-Visor (Star Tours logo on white plastic visor, Star Tours) 5.00

Star Wars Illusion logo cap (#348115, 1997) 12.00
Darth Vader Movie Cap "Never underestimate the Dark Side" (#348065, 1997) 12.00
Stormtrooper Movie Cap "Freeze you rebel scum" (#348085, 1997) 12.00
Yoda Movie Cap "May the force be with you" (#348075, 1997) 12.00
X-Wing Glitter Cap (#348095, 1997) 12.00
Star Wars tie-top ski hat (1997) 13.00
Star Wars Illusion logo cap (1997) 10.00
Star Wars 20 years logo cap (1997) 12.00
Darth Vader black mesh cap (1997) 16.00

Outerwear
Poncho, children's plastic with Jedi logo (Adam Joseph 1983) 30.00
Raincoat, plastic children's with Jedi logo (Adam Joseph 1983) 30.00
C-3PO and R2-D2 blue rain jacket 30.00
C-3PO and R2-D2 blue poncho 30.00
Darth Vader and Guards poncho 30.00

Jackets

Luke Skywalker Bespin Jacket, tan, resembling one worn by Luke in *The Empire Strikes Back* (Fan Club promotion)	90.00
Star Tours Jacket, pocket logo on black/blue nylon jacket (Star Tours)	50.00
Star Tours Jacket, pocket front logo & full back logo, silver satin jacket with blue piping (Star Tours)	90.00
Star Wars X-Wing Rogue Squadron Bomber Jacket, black leather with three patches (1997)	300.00
Luke Skywalker Bespin Jacket (1997)	80.00

Sweatshirts

Sweatshirt (Star Tours logo in glitter on black shirt, Star Tours)	35.00
Darth Vader Sweatshirt, black (AME 1995)	28.00
Star Wars Sweatshirt, black with Tom Cantrell poster art (AME 1995)	28.00
Boba Fett Sweatshirt, white (AME 1995)	28.00
Yoda Sweatshirt, white (AME 1995)	28.00
Star Wars Galaxy Jawa Wrench Sweatshirt	28.00

Vest

Han Solo Vest (black vest resembling. one worn by Han Solo in movies, Fan Club promotion)	100.00
Han Solo Vest (1997)	60.00

T-Shirts

Almost all T-shirts are bought to be worn, not collected. The earliest T-shirts were produced using Iron-on transfers made by Factors, Inc. Enough of these were still around in 1994 for T-shirts to be offered to comic shops with the original 1977 transfers.

In 1994, American Marketing Enterprises produced a line of T-shirts using the images from the Topps Galaxy trading cards which had appeared in 1993. Recent T-shirts have used the images from the *Star Wars Special Edition* video tape boxes and images of the Kenner action figures. I have also seen images of cards from Decipher's various collectible

card games. Maybe someone is interested in using the cover of this book for a T-shirt; who knows?

These days there is a brisk business in this icon of the American popular culture, with several new *Star Wars* T-shirt designs available just about every month. The following list includes primarily ones offered to comic shops through Diamond Previews, and so the items and prices are for teenage and adult sizes. The product numbering contains gaps indicating that many more styles were probably also available. Generally, the product number appears in the catalog, but not on the T-shirt. Most of the recent T-shirts were made by Changes, but other brand names and store brands appear on many of the shirts. No attempt has been made to list children's and department store items. As with most *Star Wars* items, very few were available in the dark times, from 1985 to 1994, but now the flood has begun and there will be no letup as the new movies appear.

Light grey T-Shirt with original 1977 Iron-On transfer

Star Wars Han and Chewie (1994)	$20.00
Luke and C-3PO (1994)	20.00
C-3PO and R2-D2 (1994)	20.00
Darth Vader (1994)	20.00
Han Solo (1994)	20.00
Hildebrandt Movie Poster (1994)	20.00
Chewbacca (1994)	20.00
Stormtroopers in Battle (1994)	20.00
Space Battle with Darth Vader (1994)	20.00

Star Wars Galaxy card image on T-Shirt, American Marketing Enterprises (AME)

George Lucas (AME 1994) card #2	19.00
Han Solo (AME 1994) card #7	19.00
Chewbacca (AME 1994) card #8	19.00
Boba Fett (AME 1994) card #13	19.00
Emperor Palpatine (AME 1994) card #14	19.00
Battle Scene (AME, 1994) card #16	19.00
Rancor Beast (AME 1994) card #44	19.00

Jawa with Wrench Star Wars Galaxy *Card T-Shirt (AME 1994); Boba Fett T-shirt (Liquid Blue 1998)*

Artoo T-shirt (Star Wars Fan Club 1997); TIE Fighters T-shirt (Liquid Blue 1998)

Swinging Luke and Leia (AME 1995) card #53 . . . . . . 19.00
Tom Cantrell (AME 1994) card #54 . . . . 19.00
Darth Vader (AME, 1994) card #59 . . . . 19.00
Villains of the Evil Empire (AME 1995) card #62 . . . . . 19.00
Boris Vallejo (AME 1994) card #71 . . . . 19.00
Return of the Jedi (AME 1994) card #74 . . . . 19.00
Bounty Hunters (AME 1995) card #. 19.00
Jim Sterenko (AME 1994) card #80 . . . . 19.00
Jawa with Wrench (AME 1994) card #130 . . . . 19.00

T-Shirts (Changes 1993–1998)
Tusken Raider picture 16.00
Star Wars Villains 16.00
Darth Vader Embroidered T-shirt (1996) 19.00
Stormtrooper Embroidered T-shirt (1996) 19.00
Yoda Embroidered T-shirt (1996) 19.00
Star Wars Hildebrandt 1977 art Iron-on T-shirt
    (Changes #29346-9, 1995) 15.00
Luke and Leia Ringer T-shirt (#29346-41, 1996) 16.00
Jawa Ringer T-shirt (#29346-42, 1996) 16.00
Darth Vader Ringer T-shirt (#29346-43, 1996) 16.00
Stormtrooper Ringer T-shirt (#29346-44, 1996) 16.00
Princess Leia Ringer T-shirt (#29346-45, 1996) 16.00
Han and Chewie Ringer T-shirt, white shirt with blue
    trim, transfer image (1996) 16.00
Luke and C-3PO Ringer T-shirt, white shirt with blue
    trim, transfer image (1996) 16.00
R2-D2 and C-3PO Ringer T-shirt, white shirt with
    blue trim, transfer image (1996) 16.00
Chewbacca (#29301-1) black and white 15.00
Darth Vader (#29301-2) black and white 15.00
Boba Fett (#29301-3) black and white 15.00
Princess Leia (#29301-4) black and white 15.00
Yoda (#29301-5, 1996) black and white 15.00
Stormtrooper (#29301-13, 1996) black and white 15.00
X-Wing Fighter (#29301-19, 1996) 15.00
Darth Vader with lightsaber (#29301-22, 1996) 15.00
Darth Vader "I Want You for the Imperial Forces"
    (#29301-23, 1996) 15.00
Boba Fett with Gun (#29301-23, 1996) 15.00
C-3PO (#29301-24, 1996) black and white 15.00

Darth Vader/*Star Wars* video tape (#29301-26, 1996) . 15.00
Stormtrooper/Empire video tape (#29301-27, 1996) . . 15.00
Stormtrooper/Empire two-sided (#29301-28, 1996) . . . 16.00
Darth Vader/*Star Wars* two-sided (#29301-29, 1996) . . 16.00
Yoda/Jedi two-sided (#29301-30, 1996) 16.00
Yoda/Jedi video tape (#29301-31, 1996) 15.00
Star Wars: *The Empire Strikes Back* International
    Video T-shirt (#331-38) 16.00
Star Wars: A New Hope International Video T-shirt
    (#331-39) 16.00
Star Wars: *Return of the Jedi* International Video
    T-shirt (#331-40) 16.00
Emperor Lightning portrait (#29301-55, 1996) 15.00
Princess Leia and Jabba the Hutt (#29301-56,
    1996) two-sided image 17.00
Han Solo in Carbonite (#29301-57, 1996) 15.00
R2-D2 and C-3PO (#29301-59, 1996) 15.00
Tusken Raider (#29301-60, 1996) 15.00
Shadows of the Empire (#29301-61, 1996) two-
    sided image 16.00
Han Solo and Stormtroopers (#29301-62, 1996) 15.00
Boba Fett BF BobaWear Logo (Parody of Calvin
    Klein logo) (#29301-63, 1996) two-sided image . . 17.00
Star Wars SW RebelWear Logo (Parody of Calvin
    Klein logo) (#29301-64, 1996) two-sided image . . 17.00
Darth Vader DV ImperialWear Logo (Parody of Calvin
    Klein logo) (#29301-65, 1996) two-sided image . . 17.00
Darth Vader & Fighters (29331-96, 1997) 16.00
Mos Eisley Cantina Bar and Grill (29331-100, 1997) . . 16.00
Darth Vader Silhouette (#29331-102, 1997) 16.00
Death Star Battle (#29331-103, 1997) 16.00
Jedi Gathering (#29331-104, 1997) 16.00
Stormtrooper Silhouette (#29331-105, 1997) 16.00
C-3PO and R2-D2 Silhouette (#29331-106, 1997) 16.00
Luke and Darth Vader Action Figures T-shirt
    (#29331-114, 1997) 16.00
Star Wars Creatures (#29331-115, 1997) 16.00
Han & Leia (#29331-117, 1997) 16.00
Han & Leia Action Figures T-shirt (#29331-125, 1997) . 16.00
Star Wars: A New Hope Special Edition Movie
    Poster (#29331-128, 1997) 16.00

Star Wars: *Return of the Jedi* Special Edition Movie
    Poster (#29331-129, 1997) 16.00
Star Wars: *The Empire Strikes Back* Special Edition
    Movie Poster (#29331-130, 1997) 16.00
Boba Fett Taking Off (#29301-132, 1997) 15.00
Star Wars Dark and Darker (#29331-134, 1997) 16.00
Boba Fett Designerwear (#29331-140, 1997) 16.00
Han Solo Designerwear (#29331-141, 1997). 16.00
Mos Eisley Designerwear (#29331-142, 1997) 16.00
Princess Leia Designerwear (#29331-143, 1997) 16.00
Luke Skywalker Designerwear (#29331-144, 1997). . . 16.00
Star Wars Bounty Hunters Action Figures T-shirt
    (1997) 16.00
Star Wars Group Action Figures T-shirt (1997) 16.00

Here Comes Vader T-shirt (#340S100, 1997) 16.00
Yoda Solo Force (#340SW42, 1997) 17.00
C-3PO Solo Force (#340SW43, 1997) 17.00
Stormtrooper Solo Force (#340SW44, 1997) 17.00
Boba Fett Solo Force (#340SW45, 1997) 17.00
Darth Vader Solo Force (#340SW46, 1997) 17.00

Cantina Band (1997). 15.00
Speeder Bike, two-sided (1997) 16.00
Hoth Battle, two sided (1997) 16.00
Darth Vader (1997) 15.00
Yoda (1997) 15.00
Tusken Raider (1997). 15.00
Boba Fett (1997). 15.00
The Emperor (1997) 15.00
Luke Skywalker Caricature (#LUF2565, 1997) 17.00
Stormtrooper Caricature (#LUF2566, 1997). 17.00
Princess Leia Caricature (#LUF2567, 1997) 17.00
Star Wars Trooper (#LUF2568, 1997) 17.00
Chewbacca Rocks (#LUF2569, 1997). 17.00
Lord Vader (#LUF2570, 1997). 17.00
Chewie Glitter (#LUF2597, 1997) 20.00
Artoo Glitter (#LUF2598, 1997). 20.00
Leia Glitter (#LUF2599, 1997). 20.00
Max Rebo Band (#LUF2618, 1997). 18.00

Mos Eisley Cantina Live (#LUF2619, 1997). 18.00
All I Need To Know About Life I Learned From Star
    Wars T-shirt (#920, 1997). 17.00
Artoo Ringer t-shirt (1997). 18.00
Princess Leia Ringer t-shirt (1997) 18.00
Chewie Ringer T-shirt (1997) 18.00
Darth Vader T-shirt, one sided with raised inks
    (Winterland 1997) 17.00
Princess Leia, two-sided image, purple shirt
    (Winterland 1997) 18.00
Stromtrooper two-sided image, lime green shirt
    (Winterland 1997) 18.00
Luke Skywalker two-sided image, orange shirt
    (Winterland 1997) 18.00

Tie-Dye T-shirts
Chewbacca Tie Dye T-shirt (#11901, 1997). 25.00
Boba Fett Tie Dye T-shirt (#11902, 1997). 25.00
Star Wars Droids Tie Dye T-shirt (#11903, 1997). . . . 30.00
Planet Hoth Tie Dye T-shirt (#11904, 1997). 27.00
Death Star Battle Tie Dye T-shirt (#11905, 1997). . . . 25.00
Star Wars TIE-Fighters Tie Dye T-shirt (#11906, 1997) 27.00
Star Wars Poster Tie Dye T-shirt (#11907, 1997). . . . 25.00
Sand People Tie Dye T-shirt (#11908, 1997). 27.00
Yoda Tie-Dye T-Shirt (#11909, 1997). 26.00
Desert Droids Tie Dye T-shirt (#11910, 1997) 27.00
Star Wars: Darth Vader Tie Dye T-Shirt, image
    from *Star Wars* Special Edition Boxed Set
    (#31966, 1998) 28.00

Silkscreened T-shirts
Death Star, two-sided (Liquid Blue 1997) 27.00
Planet Hoth, two-sided (Liquid Blue 1997). 27.00
Sand People, two-sided (Liquid Blue1997) 27.00
Boba Fett (Liquid Blue 1997) 25.00
Chewbacca (Liquid Blue 1997) 25.00
TIE Fighter (Liquid Blue 1997) 27.00
Yoda (Liquid Blue 1997) 25.00

Polo Shirts
Star Tours Polo Shirt, color pocket logo (Star Tours) . . 25.00

Stormtrooper T-shirt (Oneita 1996); B-Wing and Death Star (Hanes 1991)

Underwear

Boba Fett Underoos (Union Underwear 1983). 20.00
C-3PO Underoos (Union Underwear 1983) 20.00
Darth Vader Underoos (Union Underwear 1983) 20.00
Han Solo Underoos (Union Underwear 1983) 20.00
Luke Skywalker Underoos (Union Underwear 1983) . . 20.00
Leia Underoos (Union Underwear 1983) 20.00
R2-D2 Underoos (Union Underwear 1983) 20.00
Wicket Underoos (Union Underwear 1983) 20.00
Yoda Underoos (Union Underwear 1983) 20.00

Star Wars: Darth Vader Repeat Silk Boxers (Ralph
    Marlin #53464, 1998) 17.00
Star Wars ships, cotton boxers 15.00

Sleepwear

Pajamas, *Star Wars*, C-3PO and X-Wing, gold 20.00
Pajamas, *Star Wars*, Darth Vader, C-3PO and
    R2D2, blue 20.00
Pajamas, "May the Force Be With You, Darth and
    R2-D2, blue" 20.00
Rebel Alliance Pajamas, 2 piece, kids sizes (1997) . . . 16.50
Galactic Empire Pajamas, 2 piece, kids sizes (1997) . . 16.50
Darth Vader Short Sleeve pajamas with cape, 3-
    piece, kids sizes (1997) 13.50

Leg Warmers

Leg Warmers, 22" long, black with red/white
    stitching, Jedi knit into them (Sales Corp. of
    America 1983) 20.00

Socks

C-3PO Slipper Socks (Stride Rite 1983) 15.00
Darth Vader Slipper Socks (Stride Rite 1983) 15.00
R2-D2 and Wicket Socks (Charleston Hosiery 1983) . . 10.00
R2-D2 and Darth Vader Socks (Charleston Hosiery
    1983) 10.00

OTHER CLOTHING ITEMS

The Ralph Marlin *Star Wars* collection started with one tie in 1992 and has now grown to a whole wardrobe of silk and polyester ties, caps, silk boxer shorts and embroidered T-shirts. Despite the quality, most of these items are still clothing, and thus not very collectible. After all, no one will buy your used boxer shorts, even if they are silk. Ties, belts, belt buckles and the other items listed here at least have some collector potential.

Ties — Silk

Star Wars collectors silk tie in tin litho box (Ralph
    Marlin #600020, 1995) $40.00
Darth Vader collectors silk tie (Ralph Marlin
    #306210, 1996) 25.00
Darth Vader Pattern, silk tie (Ralph Marlin 1997) 25.00
Star Wars Fighters collectors silk tie (Ralph Marlin
    #306220, 1996) 25.00
Star Wars: Cantina Silk tie (Ralph Marlin #32505) 25.00
Star Wars: Vehicles II Black Silk tie (Ralph Marlin
    #32505) 25.00

Ties — Polyester

Imperial AT-AT tie, polyester (Ralph Marlin
    #151070, 1997) 15.00
Death Star Assault tie, polyester (Ralph Marlin
    #151110, 1997) 15.00
Darth Vader Line Art polyester tie (Ralph Marlin
    #151089, 1997) 15.00
Star Wars International Video tie (Ralph Marlin
    #151036, 1997) 15.00
The Empire Strikes Back International Video tie
    (Ralph Marlin #151037, 1997) 15.00
Return of the Jedi International Video tie (Ralph
    Marlin #151038, 1997) 15.00
Star Wars Yoda Line Art polyester tie (Ralph Marlin
    #151086, 1997) 15.00
Star Wars Droids Line Art polyester tie (Ralph
    Marlin #151087, 1997) 15.00
Star Wars Death Star Rising polyester tie (Ralph
    Marlin #151091, 1997) 15.00
Chewbacca & Han, polyester tie (Ralph Marlin 1997) . 13.00
Luke and Yoda, polyester tie (Ralph Marlin 1997) 13.00
R2-D2 and C-3PO Line Art, polyester tie (Ralph
    Marlin 1997) 13.00
Characters, polyester tie (Ralph Marlin 1997) 14.00
Trench Scene, polyester tie (Ralph Marlin 1997) 14.00
Star Wars Original Illustration, polyester tie (Ralph
    Marlin 1997) 14.00
Star Wars Poster, polyester tie (Ralph Marlin 1997) . . 14.00
Characters II, polyester tie (Ralph Marlin 1997) 13.00
Star Wars Video tie (Poly Ties #136230, 1996) 16.00
The Empire Strikes Back Video tie (Poly Ties
    #136240, 1996) 16.00
Return of the Jedi Video tie (Poly Ties #136250,
    1996) 16.00

Leather Belt, Yoda round buckle (Lee Co. 1983); C-3PO and R2-D2 Belt Buckle (unknown manufacturer, possibly unlicensed)

Suspenders

Darth Vader Suspenders, circular plastic badge with raised Empire logo and color pic. of Darth Vader (Lee Co. 1980). 20.00
Yoda Suspenders, circular plastic badge with raised Empire logo and color pic. of Yoda (Lee Co. 1980). 20.00

Belts

May the Force Be With You Elastic Belt (Lee Co. 1983). 25.00
Star Wars Elastic Belt, tan or blue with magnetic enamel *Star Wars* logo buckle (Lee Co. 1983) . . . 25.00
Star Wars/The Empire Strikes Back Elastic Belt, alternating logos on belt, tan or blue (Lee Co. 1983). 25.00
Star Wars/Return of the Jedi Elastic Belt, alternating logos on belt, tan or blue with round character-buckle (Lee Co. 1983) 25.00
Leather Belt, Darth Vader oval buckle (Lee Co. 1983) . 30.00
Leather Belt, Jabba the Hutt rectangular buckle (Lee Co. 1983). 30.00
Leather Belt, Yoda round buckle (Lee Co. 1983) 30.00
Leather Belt, brown child-size with red enamel Empire logo buckle (Lee Co. 1983) 30.00
Star Wars belt, illustrated 12.00
Star Wars stretch belt 8.00
Return of the Jedi belt, illustrated 5.00

Belt Buckles

C-3PO and R2-D2 Belt Buckle (Basic Tool & Supply 1977). 20.00

Return of the Jedi *shoelaces (Stride Rite 1983)*

Darth Vader Belt Buckle (Basic Tool & Supply 1977) . . 20.00
Star Wars logo Belt Buckle (Basic Tool & Supply 1977). 20.00
X-Wing with *Star Wars* logo Belt Buckle (Basic Tool & Supply 1977) 20.00
C-3PO and R2-D2 Belt Buckle (3" rectangular. blue enamel background, Lee Co. 1979) 15.00
Star Wars belt buckles (Leather Shop 1977)
    Star Wars logo. 20.00
    R2-D2 . . . . 20.00
    R2-D2 & C-3PO. 20.00
    Darth Vader 20.00

Shoes and Footwear

Darth Vader Sandals, Vader head and *Star Wars* logo (1977) 20.00
Yoda Sandals, "May the Force Be With You" on sides . 20.00
Sneakers, cutouts of characters on sides, assort. colors (Stride Rite) 25.00
Chewbacca booties 25.00
Darth Vader booties 25.00

Shoelaces

Star Wars logo/Darth Vader Shoelaces, blister packed on card with spaceships and Jedi logo (Stride Rite 1983) 5.00
Star Wars logo/R2-D2 and C-3PO Shoelaces blister packed on card with spaceships and Jedi logo (Stride Rite 1983) 5.00
Return of the Jedi logo Shoelaces, blister packed on card with spaceships and Jedi logo (Stride Rite 1983) several lengths and styles, each 5.00
Ewoks Shoelaces, blister packed on card with spaceships and Jedi logo (Stride Rite 1983) 5.00

Umbrellas

Darth Vader Umbrella (Adam Joseph 1983) 25.00
R2-D2 Umbrella (Adam Joseph 1983). 25.00

ACCESSORIES

PINS — JEWELRY — WATCHES — WALLETS

Clothes make the man, but accessories make the clothes! Also, it makes a lot more sense to collect accessories than clothes. You can wear them occasionally without damage or reduction in value.

PINS

The market for attractive pins, ones that you might actually wear somewhere other than to a *Star Wars* fan club meeting, has been owned by Hollywood Pins. They also make a very attractive line of *Star Trek* pins. These pins are sold through comic shops and specialty dealers and are available over the internet. The company has not continued their license for the original movies and, as of this writing, may or may not make pins for the new trilogy. Existing stocks will be available for a while, but when they are gone, prices may start to rise.

Hollywood Pins (1994–97)

Rebel Alliance New Republic Pin (large) (#SW001) . . . $7.00
Rebel Alliance New Republic Pin (small) (#SW005) . . . 5.00
Rebel Alliance Logo cut-out pin (large) (#SW030) 9.00

Assortment of Star Wars *pins (Hollywood Pins 1995–97)*

Rebel Alliance Logo cut-out pin (small) (#SW035) 5.00
Rebel Alliance mini-logo (#SW036) 3.50
Star Wars 20th Anniversary (#SW041) 6.00
Star Wars Special Edition (#SW042S) 6.00
Star Wars: A New Hope Theme pin (#SW051) 13.00
The Empire Strikes Back Theme pin (#SW052) 13.00
Return of the Jedi Theme pin (#SW053) 13.00
May The Force Be With You pin (#SW052) 6.00
Star Wars Far Star pin (#SW070) 6.00
Imperial Emblem Pin (#SW160) 7.00
Darth Vader black pin (#SW205) 11.00
Darth Vader 3-D Face cut-out pin (#SW206) 6.00
Luke on Tauntaun cut-out pin (#SW255) 13.00
Yoda cut-out pin (#SW263) 9.00
Chewbacca cut-out pin (#SW275) 11.00
Princess Leia (Jabba's Prisoner) cut-out pin (#SW280) . 9.00
Ben (Obi-Wan) Kenobi cut-out pin (#SW286) 9.00
Lando Calrissian cut-out pin (#SW290) 9.00
Emperor Palpatine cut-out pin (#SW293) 9.00
Rebo Band cut-out pin (#SW320) 11.00
Jabba the Hutt cut-out pin (#SW325) 8.00
Jabba the Hutt tattoo pin (#SW326) 6.00
Boba Fett cut-out pin (#SW330) 11.00
Boba Fett Insignia pin (#SW331) 7.00
Boba Fett Skull pin (#SW332) 7.00
Emperor's Royal Guard cut-out pin (#SW333) 7.00
Stormtrooper cut-out pin (#SW335) 9.00
Gamorrean Guard cut-out pin (#SW340) 6.00
C-3PO cut-out pin (#SW455) 7.00
R2-D2 cut-out pin (#SW456) 7.00
Admiral Ackbar (#SW460) 7.00
Ewok cut-out pin (#SW480) 8.00
AT-AT cut-out pin (#SW520) 9.00
X-Wing Fighter cut-out pin (#SW540) 7.00
X-Wing Fighter antique silver cut-out pin (#SW541) . . . 7.00
Millennium Falcon cut-out pin (#SW552) 9.00
TIE Fighter cut-out pin (#SW561) 9.00

Stormtrooper icon pin (#SW604) 6.00
Boba Fett icon pin (#SW605) 6.00
Millennium Falcon round pin (#SW652) 6.00
Crossed Lightsabers logo cut-out pin (#SW752) 9.00
R2-D2 cut-out pin (#SW840) 7.00
Black Sun logo (#SW901) 6.00

Keychains Hollywood Pins 1994
Star Wars New Republic key chain (#SW801) 7.00
Yoda portrait key chain (#SW805) 7.00
Darth Vader portrait key chain (##SW810) 7.00
Millennium Falcon cut-out key chain (#SW815) 7.00

JEWELRY

Star Wars head pendants (Weingeroff Ent. 1977) boxed
    R2-D2 . . . . $25.00
    C-3PO 25.00
    Chewbacca 25.00
    Stormtrooper 25.00
    Darth Vader 25.00
Star Wars earrings
    R2-D2 . . . . 10.00
    C-3PO 10.00
    Darth Vader 10.00
Star Wars stickpins
    R2-D2 . . . . 8.00
    C-3PO 8.00
    Darth Vader 8.00
Charm bracelet 15.00
The Empire Strikes Back (W.Berrie 1980)
    X-Wing medal 8.00
    Chewbacca medal 8.00
    Darth Vader 8.00
Return of the Jedi pendants (Adam Joseph 1983)
    Darth Vader 8.00
    Yoda 8.00
    R2-D2 . . . . 8.00
    Salacious Crumb 8.00

Imperial Guard. 8.00
Wicket stickpin. 6.00
Princess Kneesa stickpin. 6.00
R2-D2 Pendant pin and chain, sterling silver, 1¾"
    tall, with chain 100.00
Wicket the Ewok jewelry (Adam Joseph 1983) 7.50

Wicket the Ewok Jewelry (Adam Joseph 1983)

WALLETS
Return of the Jedi Wallets and Coin Holders
Vinyl Wicket the Ewok Wallet, cartoon Ewok artwork
    (Adam Joseph 1983) $15.00
Darth Vader and Imperial Guards Wallet, black
    (Adam Joseph 1983) 15.00
R2-D2 and C-3PO Wallet, blue (Adam Joseph 1983) . 15.00
Yoda Wallet, red (Adam Joseph 1983) 15.00
Star Tours Wallet, black nylon with velcro closure
    ("Star Tours" printed in corner) 8.00
Darth Vader and Imperial Guards Pocket Pal, black
    (Adam Joseph 1983) 10.00
R2-D2 and C-3PO Pocket Pal, blue (Adam Joseph
    1983). 10.00
Yoda Pocket Pal, red (Adam Joseph 1983) 10.00
Darth Vader and Imperial Guards Coin Holder, black
    (Adam Joseph 1983) 10.00
R2-D2 and C-3PO Coin Holder, blue (Adam Joseph
    1983). 10.00
Yoda "May The Force Be With You" Coin Holder, red
    (Adam Joseph 1983) 10.00

WATCHES

As with most collectibles, the best way to collect a watch is in its original packaging. Bradley Time made most of the *Star Wars* watches in the 1970s and 1980s. There are quite a number of styles. Digital watches generally sell for a little less than analog watches and 1980s watches based on the second and third movies sell for a little less than those based on the first movie from the 1970s.

C-3PO and R2-D2 child's watch, vinyl band (Bradley Time 1977)

Recently, plastic figural head watches have been made by Hope Industries and sold in toy stores. They have not developed a following among regular watch collectors, but they are reasonably attractive as *Star Wars* toy items.

Official Star Wars Watches (Bradley Time 1977-83)
Star Wars
Analog Watches
C-3PO and R2-D2 drawing, adult size analog
    watch, gold metal case, dark blue vinyl black
    strap, in plastic box $100.00
C-3PO and R2-D2 drawing, child size analog watch,
    silver metal case, light blue vinyl strap in blue
    plastic box with clear plastic lid 90.00
R2-D2 & C-3PO, black face, black vinyl band 100.00
R2-D2 & C-3PO, black face, silver bezel ring 120.00
Darth Vader, white face, red logo, black vinyl band . . 100.00
Darth Vader, gray face, white logo, black vinyl band . 100.00
Darth Vader, stars & planet on face. 120.00
Digital Watches
C-3PO & R2-D2 round digital, red logo, black vinyl
    strap 90.00
C-3PO & R2-D2 oval digital, red logo, black vinyl
    strap 100.00
C-3PO & R2-D2 rectangular digital, X-Wing and TIE
    fighters, musical. 125.00
C-3PO & R2-D2 oval digital, X-Wing fighters. 75.00
Star Wars logo/Darth Vader round digital, blue face,
    black vinyl band. 100.00

The Empire Strikes Back and Return of the Jedi
Analog Watches
Yoda, gray face, black vinyl band 80.00
Yoda, white face, blue logo, black band. 90.00
Jabba the Hutt, vinyl band 75.00
Ewoks, vinyl band. 65.00
Wicket the Ewok, stars & planet on face 65.00
Digital Watches
Yoda round digital. 75.00
Jabba the Hutt, digital. 65.00
Droids, digital 50.00
Ewoks, digital 50.00

Plastic Watches (Hope Industries 1990s)
Imperial Forces Collector Timepiece Gift Set, includ-
    ing 2 watches and Death Star Collector Case
    in window box (Hope Industries #46101)
    Darth Vader and Boba Fett watches. 15.00
    Darth Vader and Stormtrooper watches 15.00
Rebel Alliance Collector Timepiece Gift Set,
    including 2 watches and *Millennium Falcon*
    Collector Case in window box (Hope
    Industries #46102)
    C-3PO and R2-D2 watches 15.00
    C-3PO and Yoda watches 15.00

*C-3PO figural plastic watch with Millennium Falcon case
(Hope Industries 1996)*

Imperial Forces Collector Timepiece 4-piece Gift
Set, including 3 watches and Death Star
Collector Case in window box (Hope
Industries #46103) 20.00
Rebel Alliance Collector Timepiece 4-piece Gift Set,
including 3 watches and *Millennium Falcon*
Collector Case in window box (Hope
Industries #46104) 20.00
Star Wars Collector Timepiece C-3PO watch in
Millennium Falcon watch case in window box
(Hope Industries #46212, 1996) 10.00
Star Wars Collector Timepiece Darth Vader watch in
Millennium Falcon watch case in window box
(Hope Industries #46211, 1996) 10.00
Star Wars Collector Timepiece R2-D2 watch in
Millennium Falcon watch case in window box
(Hope Industries 1996) 10.00
Star Wars Collector Timepiece Boba Fett watch in
Millennium Falcon watch case in window box
(Hope Industries 1997) 10.00
Star Wars Collector Timepiece Stormtrooper watch
in *Millennium Falcon* watch case in window
box (Hope Industries 1997) 10.00
Star Wars Collector Timepiece Yoda watch in
Millennium Falcon watch case in window box
(Hope Industries 1997) 10.00

Watches, with face/head cover (Hope Industries 1996)
Darth Vader 7.00
C-3PO 7.00
R2-D2 . . . . 7.00
Boba Fett 7.00
Stormtrooper (#97004) 7.00
Yoda 7.00

Hologram Watches (1990s)
Darth Vader Hologram Watch (A.H. Prismatic
#8000/SW 1995) 25.00

Darth Vader *Star Wars* Plastic Holographic Watch
(Third Dimension 1994) 35.00
Yoda *Star Wars* Plastic Holographic Watch (Third
Dimension 1994) 45.00
X-Wing *Star Wars* Plastic Holographic Watch (Third
Dimension 1995) 45.00
Boba Fett *Star Wars* Plastic Holographic Watch
(Third Dimension 1995) 40.00

Collector Watches (1990s)
Millennium Falcon Watch (Fantasma #90WA-MLF-
LE, 1993) deluxe analog, brass case with
flip-up lid, limited to numbered 10,000 pieces 65.00
Darth Vader Watch (Fantasma #90WA-DV-LE,
1993) deluxe analog, black coin dial, limited
to 7,500 numbered pieces 65.00
Battle of the Force Collectors Limited Edition Watch
(Fantasma #90WA-DV-LE, 1993) limited
to 7,500 numbered pieces 65.00
Star Wars: A New Hope quartz analog watch, gold-
tone buckle (#46240, 1997) 25.00
Star Wars: The Empire Strikes Back quartz analog
watch, chrome tone buckle (#46240, 1997) 25.00
Star Wars Death Star analog wristwatch, limited to
10,000 copies (1997) 90.00
Darth Vader Collector's Watch, analog, black
leather band, silver bezel in Darth Vader
helmet container, silver edition, limited to
15,000 copies (Fossil LI-1604) 85.00
Darth Vader Collector's Watch, analog, black
leather band, silver bezel in Darth Vader
helmet container, gold edition, limited to 1,000
copies (Fossil LI-1604) 120.00
Official limited edition Boba Fett watch, limited to
10,000 pieces, in tin case with litho image and
with certificate of authenticity (Fossil #LI-1619) . . . 75.00
Official limited edition Boba Fett gold edition watch,
23k gold plated limited to 1,000 pieces, in tin
case with litho image and with certificate of
authenticity (Fossil #LI-1620) 120.00

TOTE BAGS
Tote Bags
R2-D2 and C-3PO Duffel Bag, blue (Adam Joseph
1983) $30.00
Yoda Duffel Bag, red (Adam Joseph 1983) 30.00

Star Tours Fanny Pack, black with blue/silver "Star
Tours" logo (Star Tours) 15.00
Star Tours Gym Bag, horizontal design with
blue/silver "Star Tours" logo (Star Tours) 30.00
Star Tours Toilette Case, black with blue/silver "Star
Tours" logo (Star Tours) 15.00
Darth Vader and Imperial Guards Tote Bag, red
canvas (Adam Joseph 1983) 25.00
R2-D2 and C-3PO Tote Bag, blue canvas (Adam
Joseph 1983) 25.00
Star Tours Tote Bag, black design with blue/silver
"Star Tours" logo (Star Tours) 20.00

OTHER ACCESSORIES

BUTTONS, PATCHES, PINS & KEYCHAINS

Buttons are popular, but they are easy to make and most
are unlicensed. As such, they can be accumulated, but no
accurate list can be compiled. Just about any such button can

be bought for about $1.00 for regular size and about $2.00 for large size. Selling later at a profit is another matter. The most fun way to collect them is to look for free ones, which are often available at movie openings or shows. A few licensed items which have developed a collector following are listed below.

Buttons, Badges & Tabs
Fan Club membership buttons. . . . . $5.00 to 10.00
Fan Club character set, 25 buttons 50.00
Various movie & slogan buttons . . . . 1.00 to 2.00
Revenge of the Jedi logo buttons (1982). 10.00
Star Wars Trilogy Special Edition give-away 1.00

Patches, movies, characters . . . . 3.00 to 10.00
Patches (**Revenge of the Jedi**) 25.00
Star Wars Trilogy Patch Set, reproduction of
    cast/crew movie patches, 5" long, limited to
    1,000 sets (1997). 12.00

Holographic Pins (A.H. Prismatic 1994)
B-Wing Fighter 2.50
Millennium Falcon and TIE Fighter 2.50
TIE Fighter and X-Wing 2.50
Millennium Falcon and *Star Wars* logo 2.50
Darth Vader 2.50
Imperial Star Destroyer. 2.50
X-Wing Fighter. 2.50
TIE Fighter 2.50
AT-AT & Snowspeeder 2.50

Star Wars 3-D Square Pins, moving image, 2"x2"
    (A.H. Prismatic #1016SWX 1997)
        Darth Vader 3.00
        Millennium Falcon 3.00
        R2-D2 and C-3PO 3.00
        X-Wing Fighter. 3.00

KEYCHAINS

Keychains, die-cast metal (1996)
See-Threepio (Playco 03110) $3.00
Artoo-Deetoo (Playco 03110) 3.00
Darth Vader (Playco 03110) 3.00
Han Solo (Playco 03110) 3.00
Luke Skywalker (Playco 03110) 3.00
Star Wars Keychain four-pack, Artoo-Deetoo, See
    Threepio, Darth Vader and Luke Skywalker
    (Playco Toys #03120) 10.00

Second Series die-cast gold painted, display box,
    2"x3" (Playco #3115, 1997)
Luke Skywalker 3.00
C-3PO 3.00
R2-D2 . . . . 3.00
Darth Vader 3.00

Third Series (Asst. #3118, Playco 1998)
Chewbacca, with crossbow. 3.00
Imperial Stormtrooper with blaster. 3.00
Imperial TIE-Fighter pilot. 3.00
Greedo with blaster 3.00

Fourth Series (Asst. #3200, Playco 1998)
Emperor Palpatine 3.00
Admiral Ackbar 3.00
Princess Leia 3.00
Luke Skywalker in pilot gear 3.00

Return of the Jedi metal keychains (Adam
    Joseph 1983) 4 different, each. 8.00

Vinyl Keychains (Applause 1996)
Darth Vader (#46221) 3.00
Greedo (#46222) 3.00
Stormtrooper (#46223) 3.00
Boba Fett (#46224). 3.00

Millennium Falcon Keyring (1983, reoffered in 1994). . 20.00

Millennium Falcon pewter keychain (Rawcliffe 1998)

Pewter Keychains
Rebel Alliance, Blue Card (Rawcliffe Feb. 1998)
Millennium Falcon (#00942, 1998) 7.00
R2-D2 (Rawcliffe #00977, 1998) 7.00
Princess Leia (#00940, 1997) 7.00
Obi-Wan Lightsaber (#00941, 1997) 7.00

Galactic Empire, Red Card (Rawcliffe, Feb. 1998)
Stormtrooper (#00801, 1997) 7.00
Darth Vader Helmet (#00937, 1998). 7.00
Boba Fett Helmet (#00938, 1997) 7.00
Boba Fett with Gun (#00939, 1997) 7.00
Darth Vader Fist (#00943, 1997). 7.00
Boba Fett (#00944, 1997). 7.00
Vader Lightsaber (#00945, 1997) 7.00
TIE Squadron (#00946, 1997). 7.00
Death Star Pewter (#00999, 1998) 7.00

Star Wars Pewter Keychains (Rawcliffe)
20 year anniversary logo (#00947, 1997) 7.00
Trilogy Special Edition (#00948, 1997) 7.00

Star Wars 3-D square keychains, 2"x2" (A.H.
    Prismatic, 1997)
        Darth Vader. 5.00
        Millennium Falcon 5.00
        R2-D2 & C-3PO. 5.00
        X-Wing Fighter. 5.00

COINS

A-Wing Pilot, Amanaman, Anakin Skywalker, AT-AT
AT-ST Driver and B-Wing Pilot coins (Kenner 1985)

Barada, Bib Fortuna, Biker Scout Boba Fett
Chewbacca and Chief Chirpa coins (Kenner 1985)

COINS

There were two ways to get one of the Kenner Power of the Force coins — with a figure, or by mailing in a proof of purchase. The figures came with a coin which related to the figure, but when you mailed in a proof of purchase, you got a random coin. Consequently, the coins that came with a figure are a lot more common than the ones that did not. The action figure section in this book lists both the new and reissued figures which came on Power of the Force header cards, with coins. More of the new figures were issued, so their coins are the most common. The exceptions are the Anakin Skywalker and Yak Face coins, since their figures were only available overseas. There are a total of 37 Power of the Force figures, but only 35 coins. The AT-AT Driver and Nikto had Warok coins.

Kenner planned to issue Power of the Force figures for Chief Chirpa, Emperor's Royal Guard, Luke, Lograyay and TIE Fighter Pilot, but did not. The coins for these figures were probably struck in anticipation of this, because they were commonly used to fulfill the mail-in requests. Interest in the *Star Wars* line was waning in 1985, and thus relatively few people mailed-in, so these coins are still scarce.

The more expensive coins were rarely used to fulfill the mail-in offer. They mostly got on the market from sources within Kenner. There was one other way, however, to get them all. Collectors who pestered Kenner about the missing coins were eventually given the right to buy a whole set, for $29.00! The offer was never made to the public. It turned out to be one of the better purchases of all time, as a complete set is worth more than 100 times that amount today.

Creatures, C-3PO, Darth Vader, Droids
Emperor and Emperor's Royal Guard coins (Kenner 1985)

EV-9D9, FX-7, Gamorrean Guard, Greedo,
Imperial Commander and Imperial Dignitary coins (Kenner 1985)

Han Solo: Rebel Fighter, Rebel Hero, Carbon Freeze, Hero Imperial Gunner and Jawas coins (Kenner 1985)

Lando Calrissian (Cloud City and Millennium Falcon), Logray Luke Skywalker: Jedi and Jedi Knight coins (Kenner 1985)

All these coins are from the collection of Rob Johnson. Thanks again, Rob!

Star Wars Coins, Silver Color (Kenner 1985) Set . $3,000.00
Amanaman. 20.00
Anakin Skywalker, Jedi. 125.00
AT-AT, *Star Wars*, mail-in, scarce 100.00
AT-ST Driver, Empire 10.00
A-Wing Pilot, Rebel. 10.00
Barada, Skiff Sentry 10.00
Bib Fortuna, Major Domo, mail-in, very scarce 125.00
Biker Scout, Empire 25.00
Boba Fett, Bounty Hunter 200.00
B-Wing Pilot, Rebel. 10.00
Chewbacca, Wookiee. 20.00
Chief Chirpa, Ewok Leader, mail-in 40.00
Creatures, *Star Wars*, "at local cantinas". 90.00
   Variation "at local cafes". 150.00
C-3PO, Protocol Droid 20.00
Darth Vader, Lord of the Sith. 20.00
Droids, *Star Wars*, mail-in, scarce 75.00
Emperor, Galactic Ruler 20.00
Emperor's Royal Guard, Empire, mail-in 75.00
EV-9D9, Torture Droid. 10.00
FX-7, Medical Droid, mail-in, very scarce 125.00
Gamorrean Guard, Palace Sentry. 20.00
Greedo, Bounty Hunter, mail-in, very scarce 125.00
Han Solo, Carbon Freeze. 20.00
Han Solo, Rebel. 15.00
   Variation, "Hans Solo" 75.00
Han Solo, Rebel Fighter 15.00
Han Solo, Rebel Hero (Hoth gear) mail-in, scarce. . . . 75.00

Hoth Stormtrooper, Empire, mail-in, very scarce 150.00
Imperial Commander, Empire, mail-in, scarce 75.00
Imperial Dignitary, Empire. 10.00
Imperial Gunner, Empire. 15.00
Jawas, Desert Scavengers 15.00
Lando Calrissian, Rebel General (with *Millennium Falcon*) 10.00
Lando Calrissian, Rebel General (with Cloud City) mail-in, scarce 60.00
Logray, Ewok, mail-in 40.00
Luke Skywalker, Rebel Leader, mail-in 25.00
Luke Skywalker, Rebel Leader (on Tauntaun) mail-in, scarce 125.00
Luke Skywalker, Rebel Leader (with landspeeder) . . . 10.00
Luke Skywalker, Rebel Leader (on scout bike) 12.00
Luke Skywalker, Jedi (with X-Wing). 25.00
Luke Skywalker, Jedi Knight (head) 15.00
Luke Skywalker, Jedi Knight (bust, on Dagobah) mail-in, very scarce 150.00
Lumat, Ewok Warrior 10.00
Millennium Falcon, *Star Wars*, mail-in, scarce 120.00
Obi-Wan Kenobi, Jedi Master 25.00
Paploo, Ewok 10.00
Princess Leia, Boushh, mail-in, very scarce 125.00
Princess Leia, Rebel Leader (in Endor outfit) 20.00
Princess Leia, Rebel Leader (head, with R2-D2). 125.00
Romba, Ewok. 10.00
R2-D2, Rebel Droid 10.00
Sail Skiff, *Star Wars*, mail-in, very scarce 150.00
   Variation, Does not say "*Star Wars*" 300.00
Star Destroyer Commander, Empire, mail-in, scarce . 100.00
Stormtrooper, Empire 25.00

Luke Skywalker Rebel Leader (five variations) and Luke Skywalker Jedi Knight (bust) coins (Kenner 1985)

Lumat, Millennium Falcon, Obi-Wan Kenobi, Princess Leia: with R2-D2, Boushh, and Endor outfit coins (Kenner 1985)

Paploo, R2-D2, Romba, Sail Skiff
Stormtrooper and Hoth Stormtrooper coins (Kenner 1985)

Star Destroyer Commander, Teebo, TIE Fighter Pilot
Too-Onebee, Tusken Raider and Warok coins (Kenner 1985)

Teebo, Ewok. 25.00
TIE Fighter Pilot, Empire, mail-in. 75.00
Too-One Bee, Medical Droid, mail-in, very scarce . . . 150.00
Tusken Raider, Sand People, mail-in, very scarce . . . 150.00
Warok, Ewok 10.00
Wicket The Ewok 15.00
Yak Face, Bounty Hunter 125.00
Yoda, The Jedi Master 20.00
Zuckuss, Bounty Hunter, mail-in, very scarce 150.00

Droids Coins, Gold Color (Kenner 1985)
Kea Moll, Freedom Fighter 5.00
Thall Joben, Speeder Racer 5.00
Jann Tosh, Adventurer 5.00
A-Wing Pilot, Rebel. 25.00
C-3PO, Protocol Droid 10.00
     Variation, C-3PO, Droids 10.00
Boba Fett, Bounty Hunter 50.00
Tig Fromm, Techno Villain. 5.00
Jord Dusat, Thrill Seeker 5.00
Kez-Iban, Lost Prince 5.00
Sise Fromm, Gang Leader 5.00
R2-D2, Droids. 10.00
Uncle Gundy, Prospector 5.00

Ewoks Coins, Bronze Color (Kenner 1985)
Dulok, Scout. 5.00
King Gorneesh, Dulok. 5.00
Dulok Shaman 5.00
Logray, Ewok Shaman 5.00
Wicket, Ewok Scout 8.00
Urgah (Lady Gorneesh) Dulok 5.00

Bend-Em coins (JustToys 1994) from 4-packs
Millennium Falcon. 5.00
TIE Fighter 5.00
X-Wing Fighter 5.00
Star Wars 15th Anniversary Silver Coin (Catch a
     Star 1992) limited to 5,000 . . . . 45.00

MILLENNIUM MINTED
COIN COLLECTION

Kenner began to reissue Power of the Force coins in 1998. These coins are gold-colored, so they will not be mistaken for the originals, which were silver. The coins come with figures and are mounted in a stand-up display holder. So far three have appeared and four more are listed on the package. If they sell, you can expect to see more of them. Coin and figure come in a window box, which has a back window as well so you can see the reverse of the coin. The package sells for $10.00, so I have valued the coin at $5.00. Will avid exonumia collectors bid the price up? Who knows. Action figure collectors consider it a shameless gimmick to sell them another copy of a figure that they already own.

Gold-colored Coins (Kenner 1998)
Han Solo Rebel Fighter, with Bespin Han Solo (#84022) $5.00
Hoth Stormtrooper, Empire, with Snowtrooper (#84028) 5.00
Chewbacca Wookiee, with Chewbacca (#84023) 5.00
Emperor Palpatine 5.00
Luke Skywalker in Endor Gear 5.00
Princess Leia in Endor Gear 5.00
C-3PO 5.00

Wicket, Yak Face, Yoda and Zuckuss coins (Kenner 1985)

Han Solo, Rebel Fighter coin, close-up (Kenner 1985)

COMICS

COMICS

Star Wars collectible Number 2 is the comic book adaptation of the movie. It also appeared prior to the movie premiere, just prior. The first six issues of the comic follow the plot of the movie and the adventures continue on their own until issue #39 when the second movie adaptation begins. One interesting feature of the comic version of the movie is the appearance of Biggs Darklighter, Luke's friend. He was originally seen with Luke in the movie, but was edited out to keep the pace of the action as fast as possible. He does appear in the movie, as the last pilot killed by Darth Vader in the final battle against the Death Star, but he is not fully identified. The comic was adapted from a "rough cut" of the movie before the character was eliminated. He is somewhat restored in the 1997 updated version of the movie and now even has an action figure.

Star Wars #1 (Marvel Comics 1977)

There were two versions of the first issue of the comic book. The more common version has the price of 30¢ in a white box while the rare version has a price of 35¢ in a white diamond.

There were no comics from 1987, when the Marvel series ended, until December 1991 when Dark Horse comics started the current explosion with the publication of *Star Wars Dark Empire*.

It is hard to believe, but there are only six hours of actual *Star Wars* film footage to date, less than half as many hours as *Star Trek's* movies alone, not counting the over 300 hours of *Star Trek* TV shows (and, yes, completely ignoring the made-for-children *Ewoks* and *Droids* TV shows). Avid fans have made up for this by seeing each of the movies numerous times. Still, comics, and books, supply much needed additional material to the *Star Wars* saga and therefore play a correspondingly greater role than in other series.

The *Shadows of the Empire* book and comic storyline has generated its own supply of action figures. Characters from the books and comics are included as major characters in the *Star Wars* universe in such books as *Star Wars, The Essential Guide to Characters* by Andy Mangels.

CLASSIC STAR WARS
Dark Horse Comics (Aug. 1992 – June 1994)

The events in this series take place between those in the first film *Star Wars: A New Hope* and the second film *The Empire Strikes Back*. The stories were written by Archie Goodwin and the art is primarily by Al Williamson, with occasional help from Allen Nunis. The covers are all new and are mostly by Williamson, with a couple by Nunis, George Evans, Mark Schultz, Tom Yeates or Bret Blevins. The material was originally published from 1981 to 1984 in newspaper strips, and has been reformatted and newly colored for this series.

Comics
1 Archie Goodwin, Al Williamson art and cover...... $8.00
2 Archie Goodwin, Al Williamson art and cover....... 4.00
3 Archie Goodwin, Al Williamson art and cover 4.00
4 Archie Goodwin, Al Williamson art and cover 4.00
5 Archie Goodwin, Al Williamson art and cover 4.00
6 Archie Goodwin, Allen Nunis, Al Williamson art
   and cover 4.00
7 Archie Goodwin, Allen Nunis, Al Williamson art
   and cover 4.00

8 Archie Goodwin, Al Williamson & Allen Nunis art,
  Mark Schultz cover 4.00
8 bagged with *Star Wars* Galaxy promo card 15.00
9 Archie Goodwin, Allen Nunis, Al Williamson art
  and cover 3.50
10 Archie Goodwin, Allen Nunis, Al Williamson art
   and cover 3.50
11 Archie Goodwin, Al Williamson & Allen Nunis cover . 3.00
12 Archie Goodwin, Al Williamson & Allen Nunis,
   Bret Blevins cover 3.00
13 Archie Goodwin, Al Williamson & AN, Tom Yeats
   cover 3.00

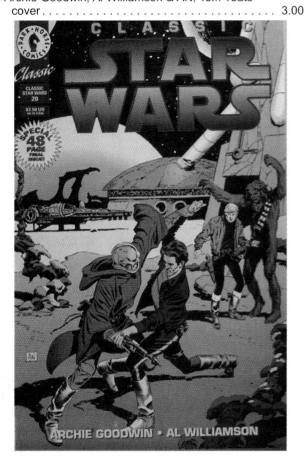

Classic Star Wars #20 (Dark Horse Comics 1994)

14 Archie Goodwin, Allen Nunis, Al Williamson art
   and cover 3.00
15 Archie Goodwin, Al Williamson art and cover 3.00
16 Archie Goodwin, Al Williamson & Allen Nunis cover . 3.00
17 Archie Goodwin, Al Williamson, Mark Schultz cover . 3.00
18 Archie Goodwin, Al Williamson, Allen Nunis cover . . 3.00
19 Archie Goodwin, Al Williamson, George Evans
   cover 3.00
20 Archie Goodwin, Allen Nunis, Al Williamson art
   and cover, final issue 4.00
20 bagged with *Star Wars* Galaxy promo card 10.00

Trade Paperbacks
Vol. 1 In Deadly Pursuit, Al Williamson cover, reprint
  #1–#7 . . . . 15.99
Vol. 1, rep. 2nd edition (#45043) 16.95
Vol. 2 The Rebel Storm, Al Williamson cover, reprint
  #8–#14 (#44-422) 16.95
Vol. 3 Escape to Hoth, Al Williamson cover, reprint
  #15–#20 . . . . 16.95

CLASSIC STAR WARS:
A NEW HOPE
Dark Horse Comics (June and July, 1994)

The classic Marvel Comics adaptation of the first movie from 1977 was newly colored by Pamela Rambo and issued in a two-part prestige-format. The story is written by Roy Thomas and drawn by Howard Chaykin and inked primarily by Steve Leialoha.

Comics
1 Art Adams cover, reprint $4.25
2 Adam Hughes cover, reprint 3.95

Trade Paperback
Series reprint 9.95

CLASSIC STAR WARS:
DEVILWORLDS
Dark Horse Comics (Aug. and Sept. 1996)

The following two issues are reprints from Marvel U.K. comics from the early 1980s. They feature work by writer Alan Moore and others. Covers are by Christopher Moeller.

Comics
1 Four Stories: "The Flight of the Falcon," "Blind
  Fury," Dark Lord's Conscience," "Dark Knight's
  Devilry" $2.50
2 Three Stories: "Rust Never Sleeps," "The Pan-
  dora Effect," "Tilotny Throws a Shape" 2.50

*Classic Star Wars The Early Adventures #3
(Dark Horse Comics 1995)*

CLASSIC STAR WARS:
THE EARLY ADVENTURES
Dark Horse Comics (Aug. 1994–April 1995)

This is a reprint of the classic 1979–80 newspaper strips written and drawn by Russ Manning and featuring, in the last issue, the first appearance of Boba Fett. The strips were reformatted, colored and expertly retouched by Rick Hoberg, who worked with Manning on the originals.

Comics
```
1 Mike Allred cover, Gambler's World . . . . . . . . . . . $3.00
2 Rick Hoberg & Mike Grell cover, Blackhole. . . . . . .  2.50
3 Eric Shanower cover, Rebels of Vorzyd-5. . . . . . . .  2.50
3 bagged with trading card DH2 . . . . . . . . . . . . . . .  5.00
4 Rick Hoberg cover, Tatooine . . . . . . . . . . . . . . . . .  2.50
5 Rick Hoberg cover, A: Lady Tarkin . . . . . . . . . . . . .  2.50
6 Weather Dominator . . . . . . . . . . . . . . . . . . . . . . .  2.50
7 Rick Hoberg cover, Vs. Darth Vader. . . . . . . . . . . .  2.50
8 Kilian Plunkett cover, X-Wing Secrets . . . . . . . . . .  2.50
9 Killian Plunkett cover, Boba Fett appears . . . . . . . .  2.50
```

Trade Paperback
```
Series reprint, Al Williamson cover . . . . . . . . . . . . . . 19.95
```

CLASSIC STAR WARS:
THE EMPIRE STRIKES BACK
Dark Horse Comics (Aug. and Sept. 1994)

These two issues reprint the 1980 Marvel Comics adaptation (issues #39 to #44) of the second movie and are written

Classic Star Wars: Han Solo at Star's End #2
(Dark Horse Comics 1997)

by Archie Goodwin with art and covers by Al Williamson. They are newly colored for this series.

Comics
```
1 . . . . . . . . . . . . . . . . . . . . . . . . . . . . . . . . . . . . $4.00
2 . . . . . . . . . . . . . . . . . . . . . . . . . . . . . . . . . . . .  4.00
```

Trade Paperback
```
Series reprint Al Williamson & Carlos Garzon cover . . .  9.95
Special reprint, Bros. Hildebrandt cover . . . . . . . . . . .  9.95
```

CLASSIC STAR WARS:
HAN SOLO AT STAR'S END
Dark Horse Comics (March–May 1997)

This series was written by Archie Goodwin and features art by Alfredo Alcala from the original newspaper strips. It's an adaptation of Brian Daley's classic novel and takes place before the adventures in the first movie.

Comics
```
1 Igor Kordey cover . . . . . . . . . . . . . . . . . . . . . . . . $2.95
2 Stan and Vince cover. . . . . . . . . . . . . . . . . . . . . . .  2.95
3 Stan and Vince cover. . . . . . . . . . . . . . . . . . . . . . .  2.95
```

Trade Paperback
```
Series reprint, Al Williamson cover . . . . . . . . . . . . . .  6.95
```

CLASSIC STAR WARS:
RETURN OF THE JEDI
Dark Horse Comics (Oct. and Nov. 1994)

The third classic movie adaptation by Archie Goodwin and Al Williamson.

Comics
```
1 Movie Adaptation. . . . . . . . . . . . . . . . . . . . . . . . . $4.00
1 bagged with trading card DH3 . . . . . . . . . . . . . . . .  5.00
2 Movie Adaptation. . . . . . . . . . . . . . . . . . . . . . . . .  3.50
```

Trade Paperback
```
Series reprint (1995). . . . . . . . . . . . . . . . . . . . . . . . .  9.95
Special reprint, Bros. Hildebrandt cover . . . . . . . . . . .  9.95
```

CLASSIC STAR WARS:
VANDELHELM MISSION
Dark Horse Comics (March 1995)

This takes place after the events in the third movie and was written by Archie Goodwin with art by Al Williamson.

Comics
```
1 Han Solo, Lando and Nien Nunb . . . . . . . . . . . . . . $3.95
```

DARK HORSE CLASSICS:
STAR WARS — DARK EMPIRE
Dark Horse Comics (March–Aug. 1997)

This series reprints the original Dark Horse 1991–92 series written by Tom Veitch with art by Cam Kennedy and covers by Dave Dorman.

Comics
```
1 Reprint. . . . . . . . . . . . . . . . . . . . . . . . . . . . . . . . $2.95
2 Reprint . . . . . . . . . . . . . . . . . . . . . . . . . . . . . . . .  2.95
3 Reprint . . . . . . . . . . . . . . . . . . . . . . . . . . . . . . . .  2.95
4 Reprint . . . . . . . . . . . . . . . . . . . . . . . . . . . . . . . .  2.95
```

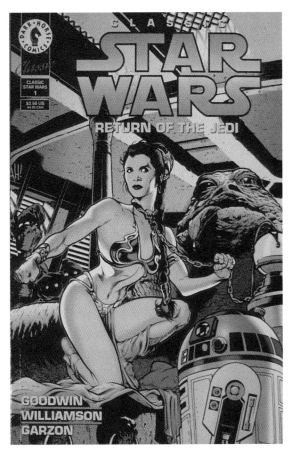

Classic Star Wars Return of the Jedi #1
(Dark Horse Comics 1994)

5 Reprint	2.95
6 Reprint	2.95

DARK HORSE COMICS
Dark Horse Comics (1993–94)

Dark Horse Comics had two series of *Star Wars* stories. In issues #7 through #9, Tom Veitch scripted a three-part *Tales of the Jedi* story, to introduce readers to the regular comic book series of the same name which debuted in October 1993.

In issues #17 through #19, Dan Thorsland did the same thing as an introduction to the Droids comics which first appeared in Jan. 1994.

Comics

7 Featuring: Mad Dogs, Robocop, Predator and *Star Wars*	$12.00
8 Featuring: X, Robocop, James Bond and *Star Wars*	14.00
9 Featuring: X, Robocop, James Bond and *Star Wars*	8.00
17 Featuring: *Star Wars*, Aliens and Predator	2.75
18 Featuring: *Star Wars*, Aliens and Predator	2.75
19 Featuring: Alien, X, and *Star Wars*	2.75

A DECADE OF DARK HORSE
Dark Horse Comics (Aug. 1996)

This series was to celebrate 10 whole years of Dark Horse comics with some of the best of their best stories. Issue #2 featured the *Star Wars* story "This Crumb for Hire," which

chronicles the first meeting of Jabba the Hutt and his annoying pet, Salacious Crumb.

Comics

2 Allen Nunis cover	$2.95

DROIDS
Star/Marvel Comics (April 1986 – June 1987)

The comics were written by Dave Manak and feature art work by John Romita, Al Williamson, Ernie Colon and Jon D'Agostino.

Comics

1 John Romita	$3.00
2 Al Williamson	3.00
3 John Romita/Al Williamson	3.00
4 Al Williamson	3.00
5 Al Williamson	3.00
6 Ernie Colon/Al Williamson, A: Luke Skywalker	3.00
7 Ernie Colon/Al Williamson, A: Luke Skywalker	3.00
8 Ernie Colon/Al Williamson, A: Luke Skywalker	3.00

EWOKS
Star/Marvel Comics (June, 1985 – Sept., 1987)

The comics were written by Dave Manak and feature art work by Warren Kremer, Jacqueline Roettcher and Jon D'Agostino.

Comics

1 Based on TV Series	$3.00
2	2.50
3	2.50
4 A: Foonars	2.50
5 Wicket vs. Ice Demon	2.50
6 Mount Sorrow, A: Teebo	2.50
7 A: Logray, V: Morag	2.50
8	2.50
9 Lost in Time	2.50
10 Lost in Time	1.50
11 Kneesaa Shrunk, A: Fleebogs	1.50
12	1.50
13	1.50
14 Teebo — King for a Day	1.50
15	1.50

MARVEL MOVIE SHOWCASE
FEATURING STAR WARS
Marvel Comics (November, 1982)

Comics

1 Reprint, Stars Wars #1-6	$4.00
2 December, 1982	4.00

RETURN OF THE JEDI
Marvel Comics (Oct. 1983–Jan. 1984)

A four part adaptation of the movie, written by Archie Goodwin, with art by Al Williamson.

Comics

1 Archie Goodwin, Al Williamson	$3.00
2 Archie Goodwin, Al Williamson	3.00
3 Archie Goodwin, Al Williamson	3.00
4 Archie Goodwin, Al Williamson	3.00

Star Wars Return of the Jedi #2 (Marvel Comics 1980)

Star Wars #2 (Marvel Comics 1977)

STAR WARS
Marvel Comics (July, 1977)

Although dated July 1977, the first comics actually appeared before the movie opened. The first six issues adapted the movie based on a "rough cut." This has led to considerable wonder about the "missing scenes" where, at the beginning of the movie, Luke goes to see his Tatooine pal, Biggs Darklighter, who tells him that he is going to join the Rebel forces. This scene was cut from the final version of the movie. A later reunion scene between Luke and Biggs, just before they fly off in their X-wing fighters to attack the Death Star, was also cut. It was restored in the 1997 *Special Edition*. Biggs is killed by Darth Vader, but Luke's other wing-mate, Wedge Antilles, survives. In 1998, Biggs was finally immortalized in plastic as an action figure.

The most valuable comic in the Marvel series is the 35 cent version of issue Number 1. Only a very few were printed, as a price increase test. The test must have been successful, because the price has increased over 1,000 fold since then. The second and third movies were adapted in turn and the series finished out its nine-year run with issue number 107. There was no at coordination between the few *Star Wars* novels being published and the comic book series and the comics issued between the movies did not have the benefit of knowledge of the movie plots. That innovation did not come until the 1990s, with the many Dark Horse comics series. Marvel used its better artists on these comics, at least for the first six years or so, and both comic collectors and *Star Wars*

collectors have considered these stories to be worthy additions to their collections.

Comics

1 Howard Chaykin, 30 Cent, begin: movie adaptation.	$65.00
1a Howard Chaykin, 35 Cent (square Box).	400.00
1b "Reprint"	7.50
2 Howard Chaykin, movie adaptation, pt. 2	25.00
2b "Reprint"	4.00
3 Howard Chaykin, movie adaptation, pt. 3	25.00
3b "Reprint"	4.00
4 Howard Chaykin, Steve Leialoha, movie adaptation, pt. 4 (low distribution.)	20.00
4b "Reprint"	4.00
5 Howard Chaykin, Steve Leialoha, movie adaptation, pt. 5.	20.00
5b "Reprint"	3.00
6 Howard Chaykin, Dave Stevens, end: movie adaptation	20.00
6b "Reprint"	3.00
7 Howard Chaykin, Frank Springer, Featuring Luke & Chewbacca	18.00
7b "Reprint"	2.50
8 Howard Chaykin, Tony DeZuniga, Eight against a World	18.00
8b "Reprint"	2.50
9 Howard Chaykin, Tom Palmer, V: Cloud Riders . . .	18.00
9b "Reprint"	2.50
10 Howard Chaykin, Tom Palmer, Behemoth from Below	18.00
11 Carmine Infantino, Tom Palmer, Fate of Luke Skywalker	15.00

12 Terry Austin, Carmine Infantino, Doomworld 15.00
13 Terry Austin, John Byrne, Carmine Infantino,
　　Deadly Reunion 15.00
14 Terry Austin, Carmine Infantino 15.00
15 Carmine Infantino, V: Crimson Jack 15.00
16 Walt Simonson, V: The Hunter 15.00
17 Crucible, Low Distribution 16.00
18 Carmine Infantino, Empire Strikes (Low Distribution) . .   16.00
19 Carmine Infantino, Ultimate Gamble (Low Distribution)   16.00
20 Carmine Infantino, Death Game (Scarce) 16.00
21 Terry Austin, Carmine Infantino, Shadow of a
　　Dark Lord (Scarce) 16.00
22 Carmine Infantino, Han Solo vs. Chewbacca 12.00
23 Carmine Infantino, Flight Into Fury 12.00
24 Carmine Infantino, Ben Kenobi Story 12.00
25 Carmine Infantino, Siege at Yavin 12.00
26 Carmine Infantino, Doom Mission 10.00
27 Carmine Infantino, V: The Hunter 10.00
28 Carmine Infantino, Cavern of the Crawling Death . .   10.00
29 Carmine Infantino, Dark Encounter 10.00
30 Carmine Infantino, A Princess Alone 10.00
31 Carmine Infantino, Return to Tatooine 10.00
32 Carmine Infantino, The Jawa Express 10.00
33 Carmine Infantino, Gene Day, V: Baron Tagge 10.00
34 Carmine Infantino, Thunder in the Stars 10.00
35 Carmine Infantino, V: Darth Vader 10.00
36 Carmine Infantino, V: Darth Vader 10.00
37 Carmine Infantino, V: Darth Vader 10.00
38 Terry Austin, Mike Gustovich, Riders in the Void . . .   10.00
39 Al Williamson, Begin: *The Empire Strikes Back* . . .   15.00
40 Al Williamson, Battleground Hoth 14.00
41 Al Williamson, Imperial Pursuit 14.00
42 Al Williamson, Bounty Hunters 14.00

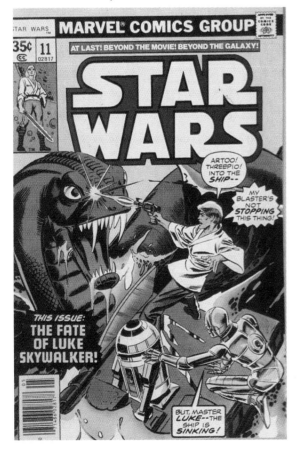

Star Wars #11 (Marvel Comics 1978)

Star Wars #30 (Marvel Comics 1980)

43 Al Williamson, Betrayal at Bespin 14.00
44 Al Williamson, End: *The Empire Strikes Back* 14.00
45 Carmine Infantino, Gene Day, Death Probe 10.00
46 Tom Palmer, V: Dreamnaut Devourer 10.00
47 Carmine Infantino, Gene Day, Droid World 10.00
48 Carmine Infantino, Leia vs. Darth Vader 10.00
49 Scott Williams, Tom Palmer, The Last Jedi 10.00
50 Walt Simonson, Al Williamson, Tom Palmer,
　　Giant size issue 12.00
51 Walt Simonson, Tom Palmer, "Resurrection of Evil" .   9.00
52 Walt Simonson, Tom Palmer 9.00
53 Carmine Infantino, Walt Simonson 9.00
54 Carmine Infantino, Walt Simonson 9.00
55 Walt Simonson, Tom Palmer 9.00
56 Walt Simonson, Tom Palmer 9.00
57 Walt Simonson, Tom Palmer, "Battle on Bespin" 9.00
58 Walt Simonson, Tom Palmer 9.00
59 Walt Simonson, Tom Palmer 9.00
60 Walt Simonson, Tom Palmer 9.00
61 Walt Simonson, Tom Palmer 9.00
62 Walt Simonson, Tom Palmer, "Luke Skywalker:
　　Pariah" 9.00
63 Walt Simonson, Tom Palmer 9.00
64 Walt Simonson, Tom Palmer, "Serphidian Eyes" 9.00
65 Walt Simonson, Tom Palmer, "Golrath Never
　　Forgets" 9.00
66 Walt Simonson, Tom Palmer 9.00
67 Tom Palmer 9.00
68 Gene Day, Tom Palmer, Boba Fett cover 9.00
69 Gene Day, Tom Palmer 9.00
70 A: Han Solo 9.00
71 A: Han Solo 7.00
72 . . . .   7.00

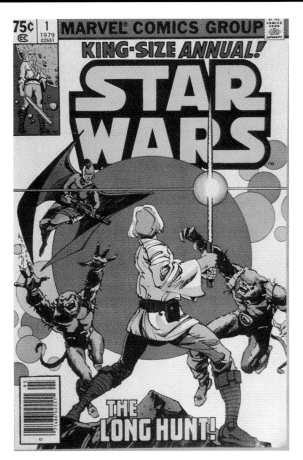

Star Wars King Size Annual #1 (Marvel Comics 1979)

73 Secret of Planet Lansbane	7.00
74.	7.00
75.	7.00
76.	7.00
77.	7.00
78.	7.00
79.	7.00
80.	7.00
81.	7.00
82.	7.00
83.	7.00
84.	7.00
85.	7.00
86.	7.00
87.	7.00
88.	7.00
89.	7.00
90 "The Choice"	7.00
91.	7.00
92 Bill Sienkiewicz cover.	7.00
93.	7.00
94.	7.00
95.	7.00
96.	7.00
97.	7.00
98 Al Williamson.	7.00
99	7.00
100 Painted cover, double-size	15.00
101 Bill Sienkiewicz	12.00
102 Kiro's Back	12.00
103.	12.00
104.	12.00
105.	12.00

106.	12.00
107 Whilce Portacio inks, last issue	30.00
Ann.#1 Walt Simonson cover, V: Winged Warlords, "The Long Hunt"	10.00
Ann.#2 Rudy Nebres	8.00
Ann.#3 Rudy Nebres, Darth Vader cover.	8.00

Star Wars 3-D #1 & #2 (Blackthorne Comics 1987–88)

STAR WARS IN 3-D
Blackthorne Publishing (Dec. 1987 – Fall 1988)

3-D comics have never been all that popular with comics collectors or *Star Wars* collectors.

Comics

1	$3.50
2 through 7, each	2.50

STAR WARS: BATTLE OF THE BOUNTY HUNTERS
Dark Horse Comics (July 1996)

This is a pop-up comic book featuring Boba Fett battling other bounty hunters for his prize: Han Solo encased in carbonite! It was written by Ryder Windhan, with artwork and cover by Christopher Moeller.

Comics

Pop-up comic	$17.95

STAR WARS: A NEW HOPE THE SPECIAL EDITION
Dark Horse Comics (Jan.–April 1997)

An all new adaptation of the special edition of the movie. The series was written by Bruce Jones, pencilled by Deuardo Barreto and inked by Al Williamson and others. The four Dave Dorman covers can be placed together to form one large image with the Death Star at the center.

The trade paperback of the first movie was released at the same time as the first comic and sports a cover by the famous Brothers Hildebrandt. In August, they released a spe-

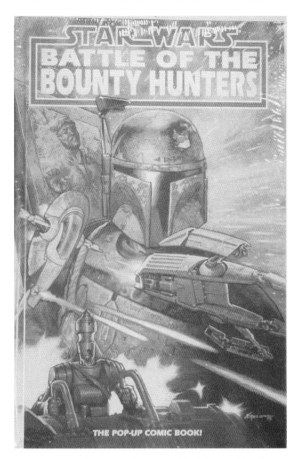

Star Wars Battle of the Bounty Hunters (Dark Horse Comics 1996)

cial edition boxed set of this trade paperback plus reprints of classic adaptations from the other two movies.

Comics

1	$3.50
2	3.25
3	3.25
4	3.25

Trade Paperback

A New Hope, Tim and Gret Hildebrandt cover	10.00
Special Edition boxed set	30.00

STAR WARS: BOBA FETT —
BOUNTY ON BAR-KOODA
Dark Horse Comics (Dec. 1995)

First of a series of one-shot comics featuring your favorite bounty hunter, Boba Fett. This one follows the events in Dark Empire II. It was written by John Wagner and contains art and a cover by Cam Kennedy.

Comics

1-shot 48pg	$3.95

STAR WARS: BOBA FETT —
WHEN THE FAT LADY SWINGS
Dark Horse Comics (Sept. 1996)

Second in the series of one-shot comics featuring Boba

Fett. This one was also written by John Wagner and contains art by Cam Kennedy and a cover by Mathieu Lauffray.

Comics

1-shot	$3.95

STAR WARS: BOBA FETT —
MURDER MOST FOUL
Dark Horse Comics (Aug. 1997)

Third in the series of one-shot comics featuring Boba Fett. This one was also written by John Wagner and contains art by Cam Kennedy and a cover by Mathieu Lauffray.

Comics

1-shot	$3.95

STAR WARS: BOBA FETT —
DEATH, LIES & TREACHERY
Dark Horse Comics (Jan. 1998)

Trade Paperback

TPB, reprints Bounty on Bar-Kooda, When the Fat Lady Swings and Murder Most Foul	$12.95

STAR WARS: BOBA FETT —
TWIN ENGINES OF DESTRUCTION
Dark Horse Comics (Jan. 1997)

A one-shot comic featuring Boba Fett. This one was written by Andy Mangles with art by John Nadeau and Jordi Ensign and a cover by John Nadeau. It was previously serial-

Star Wars Crimson Empire #3 (Dark Horse Comics 1998)

ized in Topps' *Star Wars Galaxy* magazine.

Comics

1-shot 32pg.	$2.95

STAR WARS: CRIMSON EMPIRE
Dark Horse Comics (Dec. 1997–May 1998)

This story line begins immediately after the events in Empire's End and tells the tale of Kir Kanos, the last remaining member of Emperor Palpatine's Royal Guard. It was written by Mike Richardson and Randy Stradley, with art by Paul Gulacy and P. Craig Russell. Painted covers by Dave Dorman.

Comics

1	$2.95
2	2.95
3	2.95
4	2.95
5	2.95
6 Final battle against Carnor Jax.	2.95

STAR WARS: DARK EMPIRE
Dark Horse Comics (Dec. 1991–Oct. 1992)

This was the first *Star Wars* series done by Dark Horse Comics. The story takes place six years after the Battle of Endor and the death of Darth Vader. The fighting continues and Luke and Lando are shot down over the former Imperial capitol. Naturally Han, Leia and Chewie try to rescue them. While massive dark side World Devistators ravage entire planets, Leia has to protect her unborn child and Luke is seduced by the dark side. The Emperor wields a mysterious and intelligent artifact called the Jedi Holocron, which delivers a thousand-year-old prophecy. The Battle of Calimari rages to a climax and everything depends on the data carried by one little robot!

The comics were written by Tom Veitch, with art by Cam Kennedy and covers by Dave Dorman.

Comics

1 Destiny of a Jedi	$35.00
1a 2nd Printing	5.00
1b Gold edition	35.00
2 World Destroyer, very low print run.	30.00
2a 2nd Printing	5.00
2b Gold edition	35.00
3 Battle for planet Calamari.	20.00
3a 2nd printing	4.00
3b Gold edition	20.00
4 Pursued by a bounty hunter	15.00
4a Gold edition	20.00
5 Captured by the Emperor.	15.00
5a Gold edition	20.00
6 The Jedi Holocron	10.00
6a Gold edition	18.00
Gold editions, embossed foil logo, set	125.00
Platinum editions, embossed foil logo, set	200.00

Trade Paperbacks

Preview 32pg.	.99
Dark Empire series reprint, #1–#6 Dave Dorman cover.	20.00
Dark Empire 2nd ed. (#44-848).	17.95

Star Wars Dark Empire II, Hero Special
(Dark Horse Comics 1994)

Limited Edition Hardcover

Leather bound, foil-stamped, with slipcase	125.00

STAR WARS: DARK EMPIRE II
Dark Horse Comics (Dec. 1994 – May 1995)

In the second Dark Empire series, Luke tries to rebuild the Jedi Knights while the remains of the Empire still hopes to destroy the New Republic with a new super-weapon. In the meantime, Han keeps one step ahead of Boba Fett while he tracks down an old Jedi woman. Luke looks for the Jedi Holocron on the planet Ossus. Lando hides in a shipment of War Droids for an attack on the Empire. Han rejoins Leia as they protect their young twins from the Emperor on New Alderaan.

Written again by Tom Veitch, with art by Cam Kennedy and covers by Dave Dorman.

Comics

1 2nd chapter	$7.50
2 F: Boba Fett	4.00
3 V: Darksiders	4.00
4 Luke Vs. Darksiders.	3.50
5 Creatures	3.50
6 Cam Kennedy & Dave Dorman cover, save the twins	3.50
Platinum editions, embossed foil logo, set	50.00

Ashcan

Hero Special ashcan.	5.00

Trade Paperback
Dark Empire II series reprint, plus cover paintings . . . 17.95

Limited Edition Hardcover
Leather bound, foil-stamped, with slipcase 100.00

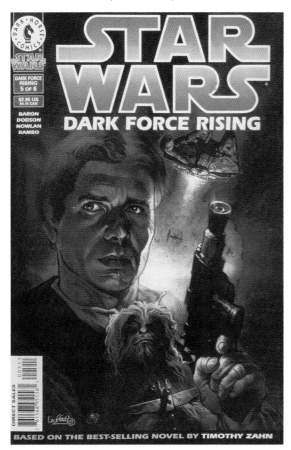

Star Wars Dark Force Rising #5 (Dark Horse Comics 1997)

STAR WARS: DARK FORCE RISING
Dark Horse Comics (May–Oct. 1997)

The ruthless Grand Admiral Thrawn of the dying Empire looks for 200 Dreadnaught heavy cruisers, which were lost to hyperspace in the time of the Old Republic. Luke finds a new Jedi mentor named C'Baoth, and learns new ways to use the force. But are they good ways, or dark ways? Only Talon Karrde knows where the ships are. When both sides find them, Grand Admiral Thrawn uses a trick not seen since the end Clone Wars.

Written by Mike Baron, pencils by Terry Dodson, inked by Kevin Nowlan and covers by Mathieu Lauffray.

Comics
1 . . . . $2.95
2 . . . . 2.95
3 . . . . 2.95
4 . . . . 2.95
5 . . . . 2.95
6 . . . . 2.95
Trade Paperback
Series Reprint 17.95

STAR WARS: DARK FORCES — SOLDIER FOR THE EMPIRE
Dark Horse Comics (Feb. 1997)

First in a planned trilogy of graphic novels based on *Star Wars: Dark Forces* interactive games. The story features Kyle Katarn, a graduate of the Imperial Military Academy, who becomes a spy for the Rebel Alliance.

Hardcover
HC, black and white, by William C. Dietz and Dean
    Williams $25.00

STAR WARS: DARK FORCES — REBEL AGENT
Dark Horse Comics (March 1998)

Second part of the adventures of Kyle Katarn, based on the *Star Wars*: Dark Forces interactive game.

Hardcover
HC by William C. Dietz and Dean Williams $24.95

Star Wars: Droids #3 (Dark Horse Comics 1994)

STAR WARS: DROIDS
Dark Horse Comics (April – Sept. 1994)

These whimsical misadventures of Artoo-Detoo and See-Threepio take place years before the events in the *Star Wars: A New Hope* movie. They journey to the Kalarba system where they are acquired by the Pitareeze family. They encounter IG-88 and the notorious Olag Greck plus a variety of pirates, bounty-hunters and rock monsters.

The adventures actually begin in Dark Horse Comics #17 through #19, and this story is included in the series trade paperback. Most of the stories were written by Dan Thorsland, with one by Ryder Windham. Art was supplied by Bill Hughes, Andy Mushynsky and Ian Gibson. Covers are by Kilian Plunkett.

The regular series continues these stories, with tales written by Ryder Windham and Jan Strnad. Art is by Ian Gibson, Bill Hughes, Keith Williams and Rich Perrotta. Covers are again by Kilian Plunkett.

Comics
```
1 Featuring C-3PO and R2-D2 . . . . . . . . . . . . . . . . . $3.50
2 Interplanetary thieves steal our droids . . . . . . . . . .  2.75
3 A droid battle arena the Hosk moon . . . . . . . . . . .   2.75
4 Leased to Jace Forno . . . . . . . . . . . . . . . . . . . .   2.75
5 A meeting with model E droids . . . . . . . . . . . . . .   2.50
6 A power core rupture . . . . . . . . . . . . . . . . . . . . .  2.50
Spec.#1 Introducing Olag Greck, reprint DHC #17–#19. .  2.50
```

Trade Paperback
```
The Kalarba Adventures, reprint of #1–#6, the
    Special and an 8-page story from Topps Star
    Wars Galaxy magazine (#44-489) . . . . . . . . . . .  17.95
```

Limited Edition Hardcover
```
Leather bound, foil-stamped, with slipcase . . . . . . .  100.00
Regular Series Comics (April 1995 – Dec. 1995)
    1 Deputized Droids . . . . . . . . . . . . . . . . . . . . . .  3.00
    2 Marooned on Nar Shaddaa . . . . . . . . . . . . . . . .  2.50
    3 C-3PO to the Rescue . . . . . . . . . . . . . . . . . . . .  2.50
    4 . . . . . . . . . . . . . . . . . . . . . . . . . . . . . . . . . . . . 2.50
    5 Caretaker virus . . . . . . . . . . . . . . . . . . . . . . . .  2.50
    6 Revolution . . . . . . . . . . . . . . . . . . . . . . . . . . . .  2.50
    7 . . . . . . . . . . . . . . . . . . . . . . . . . . . . . . . . . . . . 2.50
    8 . . . . . . . . . . . . . . . . . . . . . . . . . . . . . . . . . . . . 2.50
```

Trade Paperback
```
TPB Droids — Rebellion, Reprints #1 through #4 . . . .  14.95
```

STAR WARS: EMPIRE'S END
Dark Horse Comics (Oct.–Nov. 1995)

Following the events in *Dark Empire II*, The Emperor needs a new Jedi clone body to replace his rapidly failing and inferior clone body. Han and Leia's child, Anakin, would do very nicely.

Written by Tom Veitch, art by Jim Baikie and covers by Dave Dorman.

Comics
```
1 Return of Emperor Palpatine . . . . . . . . . . . . . . . . $2.95
2 conclusion . . . . . . . . . . . . . . . . . . . . . . . . . . . . . 2.95
```

Trade Paperback
```
Series Reprint . . . . . . . . . . . . . . . . . . . . . . . . . . . . 5.95
```

STAR WARS:
HEIR TO THE EMPIRE
Dark Horse Comics (Oct. 1995 – April 199)

Five years after the death of Darth Vader, Grand Admiral Thrawn has control of the Imperial Fleet in this adaptation of Timothy Zahn's novel.

Written by Mike Baron, with art by Olivier Vatine and Fred Blanchard and covers by Mathieu Lauffray.

Comics
```
1 I: Grand Admiral Thrawn . . . . . . . . . . . . . . . . . . . $2.95
2 . . . . . . . . . . . . . . . . . . . . . . . . . . . . . . . . . . . . . 2.95
3 . . . . . . . . . . . . . . . . . . . . . . . . . . . . . . . . . . . . . 2.95
4 Luke looses his Jedi powers . . . . . . . . . . . . . . . .  2.95
5 Mara Jade captures Luke . . . . . . . . . . . . . . . . . .  2.95
6 Luke goes to rescue Han . . . . . . . . . . . . . . . . . . .  2.95
```

Trade Paperback
```
Heir to the Empire, from novel by Timothy Zahn . . . . . 19.95
```

Limited Edition Hardcover
```
Foil-stamped, 160 pgs, tipped-in art plate with
    signatures, in slipcase . . . . . . . . . . . . . . . . . . .  100.00
```

STAR WARS: JABBA THE HUTT —
THE GARR SUPPOON HIT
Dark Horse Comics (April 1995)

Jabba lives for the art of the deal. Here he barters with Garr Suppoon, an absolute devil at the negotiating table. Which one will live long enough to write his memoirs as the Art of the Comeback? Written by Jim Woodring, with art by Art Wetherell and Monty Sheldon and a cover by Steve Bissette and Cam Kennedy.

Star Wars: Heir to the Empire #4 (Dark Horse Comics 1996)

Comics
1 Featuring Garr Suppoon $2.50

STAR WARS: JABBA THE HUTT — THE HUNGER OF PRINCESS NAMPI
Dark Horse Comics (June 1995)

The second Jabba the Hutt one-shot, written by Jim Woodring, with art by Art Wetherell and Monty Sheldon and a cover by Mark Harrison.

Comics
1 Wheel and Deal. $2.50

STAR WARS: JABBA THE HUTT — THE DYNASTY TRAP
Dark Horse Comics (Aug. 1995)

Jabba tries to employ Cabrool Nuum to sell a hot freighter, but he falls into a trap set by Cabrool's offspring. Written by Jim Woodring, with art by Art Wetherell and Monty Sheldon and a cover by Mark Harrison.

Comics
1 Featuring: Cabrool Nuum. $2.50

STAR WARS: JABBA THE HUTT — BETRAYAL
Dark Horse Comics (Feb. 1996)

Bib Fortuna plots a revolt against Jabba. Written by Jim

Star Wars: The Last Command #2 (Dark Horse Comics 1997)

Woodring, with art by Art Wetherell and Monty Sheldon and a cover by Mark Harrison.

Comics
1 Featuring Bib Fortuna $2.50

STAR WARS: THE LAST COMMAND
Dark Horse Comics (Nov. 1997 – May 1998)

Six-part comic adaptation of Timothy Zahn's *The Last Command*. Grand Admiral Thrawn creates an army of clones, while Leia gives birth to twins, Jacen and Jaina Solo. Imperials try to steal the kids, but are confronted by Han and Mara Jade. The last of these comics was just appearing as this book was completed.

Written by Mike Baron, with art by Edvin Biukovic, Eric Shanower and Pamela Rambo. Covers by Mathieu Lauffray.

Comics
1 . . . . $2.95
2 . . . . 2.95
3 . . . . 2.95
4 . . . . 2.95
5 . . . . 2.95
6 . . . . 2.95

STAR WARS: THE PROTOCOL OFFENSIVE
Dark Horse Comics (Sept. 1997)

This comic was plotted by Brian Daley, author of *Han Solo at Stars' End* and written by Anthony Daniels (C-3PO in the movies) and Ryder Windham. Art and cover by Igor Kordey. If you guessed that it stars C-3PO, you would be right.

Comics
1-shot $4.95

STAR WARS: RIVER OF CHAOS
Dark Horse Comics (May – Nov. 1995)

Leia is on a spy mission with a small band of rebels, but one of they turns out to be Ranulf, an Imperial counter-spy. Eventually Ranulf must choose between his Imperial allies and the Rebel he has come to love. Written by Louise Simonson with art and covers by June Brigman and Roy Richardson.

Comics
1 LSi, JBr, Emperor sends spies $2.50
2 Imperial in Allies Clothing. 2.50
3 . . . . 2.50
4 F: Ranulf 2.50

STAR WARS: SHADOWS OF THE EMPIRE
Dark Horse Comics (May – Oct. 1996)

This comic, based on the novel by Steve Perry, takes place between the events in *The Empire Strikes Back* and *Return of the Jedi*. It pits the underworld against the Rebel Alliance against the Empire. Prince Xizor controls the largest

Star Wars: Shadows of the Empire #6 (Dark Horse Comics 1996)

*Star Wars: Shadows of the Empire: Evolution #1
(Dark Horse Comics 1998)*

merchant fleet in the Empire, and also its largest criminal organization. Darth Vader resents the Prince's power, the Prince wants Darth's power, while Dash Rendar just resents the Prince. Our heroes want to rescue Han, but every bounty hunter in the galaxy want him for Jabba's reward, alive or dead. The Emperor wants Luke, alive, while the Prince wants Luke (and Darth, for that matter) dead. Xizor captures Leia on general principals, leaving almost as many heroes needing rescue as there are in disguise, doing the rescuing.

This story is the only one, so far, which has generated its own group of action figures: Prince Xizor, Dash Rendar, Chewbacca disguised as a bounty hunter, Luke disguised as an Imperial Guard and Leia in Boushh disguise.

The comics were written by John Wagner, with art by Kilian Plunkett and P. Craig Russell and covers by Hugh Fleming.

Comics
1 The Emperor enlists the criminal underworld	$2.95
2 Prince Xizor.	2.95
3 Surprise attack on Luke	2.95
4 Bounty hunters try to steal Han	2.95
5 Bounty hunters seek Luke	2.95
6 Leia a captive	2.95

Trade Paperback
Shadows of the Empire, Christopher Moeller cover . . .	17.95

Limited Edition Hardcover
Deluxe, signed, with original plate.	80.00

STAR WARS: SHADOWS OF THE EMPIRE — EVOLUTION
Dark Horse Comics (Feb. – June 1998)

Guri, a human replicant droid was Xizor's personal assassin. Now that her boss has been destroyed, she goes looking for her human side. This series was written by Steve Perry, author of *Shadows of the Empire*. It's adapted by Ron Randall, Tom Simmons, Dave Netelle, with covers by Duncan Fegredo. It's a five issue mini-series and should be concluded by the time this book goes to press.

Comics
1	$2.95
2 thru 5.	2.95

STAR WARS: SHADOW STALKER
Dark Horse Comics (Nov. 1997)

This one-shot collects a story which was serialized in Topps' *Star Wars Galaxy* magazine. It features Jix, a covert agent whom Darth Vader sends to take care of a defecting Imperial governor. It's written by Ryder Windham, with art and cover by Nick Choles.

Comics
1-shot.	$2.95

STAR WARS: SPLINTER OF THE MIND'S EYE
Dark Horse Comics (Dec. 1995 – June 1996)

This series is adapted from the Alan Dean Foster novel, which was originally published in 1978. The Kaiburr crystal, "capable of magnifying and clarifying one's perception of the Force," is hidden somewhere on the planet Mimban. Luke and Leia battle massive creatures called yuzzem, wormlike wandrella and a subterranean race of aboriginals to find the crystal before Darth Vader does.

Written and inked by Terry Austin, pencilled by Chris Sprouse, with covers by Hugh Fleming (first two) and Mark Harrison (last two).

Comics
1	$2.95
2	2.95
3	2.95
4	2.95

Trade Paperback
Splinter of the Mind's Eye series reprint, Duncan
Fegredo cover 14.95

STAR WARS: TALES FROM MOS EISLEY
Dark Horse Comics (March 1996)

Bruce Jones and Brett Blevins bring you these tales of the Mos Eisley Spaceport, infamous as a "wretched hive of scum and villainy."

Comics
1-shot, from *Star Wars* Galaxy Mag. #2–#4	$2.95

STAR WARS: TALES OF THE JEDI
Dark Horse Comics (Oct. 1993 – Feb. 1994)

These tales take place 4, 000 years in the past, when the Jedi Knights were supreme. The first two comics feature Ulic Qel-Droma, a young Jedi Knight in training, as he battles against the Dark Side to stop a war. The last three focus on Nomi Sunrider, who reluctantly takes up a lightsaber to avenge her husband's death at the hands of Bogga the Hutt.

The comics were written by Tom Veitch, and have covers by Dave Dorman.

Comics
1 Pencils by Chris Grossett, Inks by Mike Barreiro	$7.00
Gold foil edition	15.00
2 Pencils by Chris Grossett, Inks by Mike Barreiro	6.00
Gold foil edition	15.00
3 Art by Janine Johnston	4.00
Gold foil edition	15.00
4 Art by David Roach	3.50
Gold foil edition	15.00
5 Art by David Roach	3.50
Gold foil edition	15.00
Gold foil set	65.00

Trade Paperback
Knights of the Old Republic, series reprint, Hugh

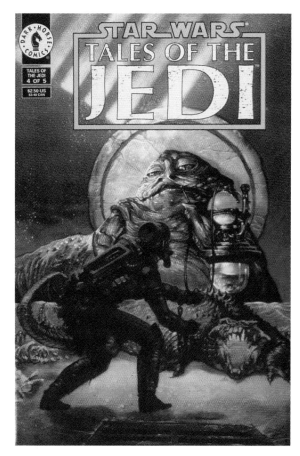

Star Wars: Tales of the Jedi #4 (Dark Horse Comics 1993)

Fleming cover	16.00
2nd printing (#44-164)	14.95

STAR WARS: TALES OF THE JEDI: THE FREEDON NADD UPRISING
Dark Horse Comics (Aug. and Sept. 1994)

This two-part miniseries brings Ulic and Nomi together to battle Freedon Nadd and save the planet Onderon. Its a prequel to the Dark Lords of the Sith.

Written by Tom Veitch, with art by Tony Atkins and Denis Rodier and covers by Dave Dorman.

Comics
1	$2.75
2	2.50

Trade Paperback
Series reprint, ... 5.95

STAR WARS: TALES OF THE JEDI: DARK LORDS OF THE SITH
Dark Horse Comics (Oct. 1994 – March 1995)

The adventures of Ulic and Nomi continue, as Exar Kun threatens to use ancient Sith magic to take over the universe, if it doesn't take him over first.

The series was written by Tom Veitch and Kevin J. Anderson, with art by Chris Grossett, Art Wetherell, Mike   /

Star Wars: Tales of the Jedi: Dark Lords of the Sith,
Trade Paperback (Dark Horse Comics 1995)

Barreiro and Jordi Ensign. Dave Dorman produced the first
cover and Hugh Fleming did the rest.

Comics

1	$3.00
1 Bagged with a trading card DH1	5.00
2	2.50
3 Krath Attack...........................	2.50
4	2.50
5	2.50
6 Final battle.............................	2.50

Trade Paperback
Series reprint, Hugh Fleming cover............... 17.95

STAR WARS:
TALES OF THE JEDI:
THE SITH WAR
Dark Horse Comics (Aug. 1995 – Jan. 1996)

Continuing the Sith saga, Ulic and Exar join up to use
their Dark Side power, but they have somewhat different purposes in mind. Its Jedi against Jedi and brother against brother, while Nomi stands firm against Ulic's plan.

The stories were written by Kevin J. Anderson, with art
by Jordi Ensign, Dario Carrasco, Jr., Mark Heike, Bill Black
and David Jacob Beckett. Covers are by Hugh Fleming.

Comics
1 Exar Kun and Ulic Qel-Droma's plans $2.50

2 The power of the Dark Side	2.50
3 Exar Kun turns novices into assassins	2.50
4 Jedi assassination pogrom.....................	2.50
5 Ulic vs. his brother Cay	2.50
6 Final battle over Yavin Four	2.50

Trade Paperback
The Sith War, Mathieu Lauffray cover 17.95

STAR WARS:
TALES OF THE JEDI —
THE GOLDEN AGE OF THE SITH
Dark Horse Comics (Oct. 1996 – Feb. 1997)

A thousand years before the Sith Empire fell, it had a
golden age. This story is told in issue #0. In issue #1, two war-
ring factions hope to fill the void left by the death of Marka
Ragnos, Dark Lord of the Sith. Gav and Jori Daragon, two
innocent hyperspace explorers, get caught between them,
with crucial maps that both sides want.

Written by Kevin J. Anderson, with art by Chris
Gossett, Stan Woch, Mark G. Heike, Bill Black and Jacob
Beckett. Cover #0 is by Christopher Moeller, while the others
are by Russell Walks.

Comics

0 The golden age	$1.00
1 Gav and Jori Daragon	2.95
2	2.95
3	2.95

Star Wars: Tales of the Jedi: The Golden Age of the Sith #1
(Dark Horse Comics 1996)

*Star Wars: Tales of the Jedi: The Fall of the Sith Empire #5
(Dark Horse Comics 1997)*

4 Captured by Naga Sadow 2.95
5 Battle for control of the Sith 2.95

Trade Paperback
Series reprint, Duncan Fegredo cover 16.95

STAR WARS:
TALES OF THE JEDI —
THE FALL OF THE SITH EMPIRE
Dark Horse Comics (June – Oct. 1997)

Naga Sadow, leads the Sith Empire in an all-out assault on the Old Republic. Jori Daragon, an explorer, stumbles on his plans, but as she tries to warn Empress Teta, she ends up on trial instead. This is the story of how the Old Republic wins the battle, but ends up doomed anyway.

Written by Kevin J. Anderson, with art by Dario Carrasco, Jr. Mark G. Heike, Bill Black and David Jacob Beckett. Covers are by Duncan Fegredo.

Comics
1 Naga Sadow prepares his fleet $2.95
1 variant cover, signed by Kevin J. Anderson 20.00
2 Jori on trial. 2.95
3 First Encounter 2.95
4 The Sith invasion rages on. 2.95
5 The Fall of the Sith 2.95

Trade paperback
Series reprint, Duncan Fegredo cover 15.95

STAR WARS:
X-WING ROGUE SQUADRON
Dark Horse Comics (July 1995 – 1998)

This continuing series stars Wedge Antilles, X-wing pilot who survived both Death Star missions and now leads the Rogue Squadron. The series is divided into mostly 4-part story arcs, with separate titles, as noted. They are solicited in Diamond Previews as if they were separate 4-issue series, so I have included brief plot descriptions and credits for each arc.

Michael A. Stackpole is the principal writer, with different co-authors and artists on each story arc. He also wrote several of the paperback novelizations.

THE REBEL OPPOSITION

Wedge goes to rescue goes on a rescue mission to the planet Mrlsst, where he joins in an uneasy alliance with the Cilpari natives against the Empire. Tycho Celchu infiltrates the Imperial Forces, but ends up going into battle against his friends. Mike Baron co-authored the series, with art by Allen Nunis and Andy Mushynski and covers by Dave Dorman.

Comics
fi Wizard limited exclusive $15.00
1 The Rebel Opposition, Pt.1 . . . . 4.00
2 The Rebel Opposition, Pt.2 . . . . 3.00
3 The Rebel Opposition, Pt.3 . . . . 3.00
4 The Rebel Opposition, Pt.4 . . . . 3.00

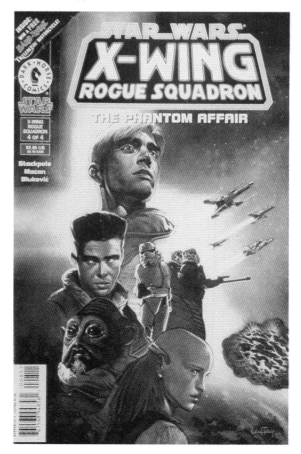

*Star Wars: X-Wing Rogue Squadron #8
(Dark Horse Comics 1996)*

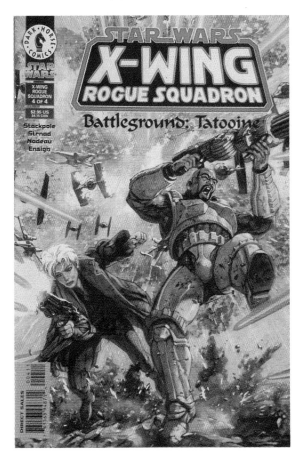

Star Wars: X-Wing Rogue Squadron #12
(Dark Horse Comics 1996)

THE PHANTOM AFFAIR

Wedge negotiates for a Mrlssti cloaking device with Loka Hask, the pirate chieftain who killed Wedge's parents. Darko Macan co-authored the series, with art by Edvin Biukovic, John Nadeau, Jordi Ensign and Gary Erskin, and covers by Mathieu Lauffray.

Comics

5 The Phantom Affair, Pt.1	3.00
6 The Phantom Affair, Pt.2	3.00
7 The Phantom Affair, Pt.3	3.00
8 The Phantom Affair, Pt.4	3.00

BATTLEGROUND TATOOINE

Wedge must find Jabba the Hutt's hidden weapons cache on Tatooine. Jan Strnad co-authored the series, with art by John Nadeau and Jordi Ensign, and covers by Mark Harrison.

Comics

9 Battleground Tatooine, Pt.1	3.00
10 Battleground Tatooine, Pt.2	3.00
11 Battleground Tatooine, Pt.3	3.00
12 Battleground Tatooine, Pt.4	3.00

THE WARRIOR PRINCESS

How did Plourr Ilo, a royal princess of Eiattu, end up in the Rogue Squadron and what will she do with her power now that she's been recalled to the throne? Scott Tolson co-authored, with art by John Nadeau and Jordi Ensign and covers by Mark Harrison.

Comics

13 The Warrior Princess, Pt.1	3.00
14 The Warrior Princess, Pt.2	3.00
15 The Warrior Princess, Pt.3	3.00
16 The Warrior Princess, Pt.4	3.00

REQUIEM FOR A ROGUE

Rogue Squadron must rescue a group of Bothan castaways on Malrev 4. It would be a lot easier if they hadn't turned out to be spies instead. Jan Strnad co-authored, with art by Gary Erskin and covers by Kevin Ryan.

Comics

17 Requiem for a Rogue, Pt.1	3.00
18 Requiem for a Rogue, Pt.2	3.00
19 Requiem for a Rogue, Pt.3	3.00
20 Requiem for a Rogue, Pt.4	3.00

IN THE EMPIRE'S SERVICE

Its Wedge versus Baron Fel, the Empire's greatest fighter ace. Art by John Nadeau and Jordi Ensign and covers by John Nadeau and Timothy Bradstreet.

Comics

21 In the Empire's Service, Pt.1	3.00
22 In the Empire's Service, Pt.2	3.00

Star Wars: X-Wing Rogue Squadron #25
(Dark Horse Comics 1997)

23 In the Empire's Service, Pt.3 . . . . 3.00
24 In the Empire's Service, Pt.4 . . . . 3.00

MAKING OF BARON FEL

Baron Fel is captured by the Rebel Alliance. One-shot, with art by Steve Crespo and Chip Wallace and cover by Timothy Bradstreet.

Comics
25 The Making of Baron Fel 3.00

FAMILY TIES

Art by Jim Hall, Gary Martin and Drew Johnson, with covers by John Nadeau.

Comics
26 Family Ties, Pt.1 . . . . 3.00
27 Family Ties, Pt.2 . . . . 3.00

MASQUERADE

Art by Drew Johnson and Gary Martin, with covers by John Nadeau.

Comics
28 Masquerade, Pt.1 . . . . 3.00
29 Masquerade, Pt.2 . . . . 3.00
30 Masquerade, Pt.3 . . . . 3.00
31 Masquerade, Pt.4 . . . . 3.00

Trade Paperbacks
The Phantom Affair, reprint #5–#8, Edvin Biukovic
    cover 12.95
Battleground Tatooine, reprint #9–#12, ... 12.95

GRAPHIC NOVELS
Dark Horse Comics

Film Adaptations
Star Wars, 104 pages $10.00
The Empire Strikes Back, 104 pages 10.00
Return of the Jedi, 104 pages 10.00

Classic Star Wars
Vol. 1 In Deadly Pursuit, 192 pages 17.00
Vol. 2 The Rebel Storm, 208 pages 17.00
Vol. 3 Escape to Hoth, 192 pages 17.00

Star Wars Droids
The Kalarba Adventures, 200 pages 18.00
    Hardcover edition, signed & numbered 100.00
Rebellion, 112 pages 15.00

Star Wars: Tales of the Jedi
Tales of the Jedi, 136 pages 15.00
Dark Lords of the Sith, 160 pages 18.00
The Sith War, 152 pages 18.00

Star Wars: Dark Empire
Dark Empire (2nd. Edition), 184 pages 18.00
Dark Empire II, 184 pages 18.00

Novel Adaptations
Star Wars: Heir to the Empire, 160 pages 20.00
    Hardcover edition, signed & numbered 80.00
Star Wars: Splinter of the Mind's Eye, 112 pages 15.00

Star Wars: Battle of the Bounty Hunters, pop-up
    comic, 12 pages, hardcover 18.00

Special comic
Star Wars
fi limited edition (Wizard). 10.00

COMIC STRIP REPRINTS

Star Wars, written by Archie Goodwin and drawn by Al Williamson, black and white comic strip reprints, hardcovers, three volumes, (Russ Cochran 1991) boxed set $150.00

Star Wars comic strip reprints, 3 volumes (Russ Cochran)

CRAFT AND ACTIVITY

CRAFT AND ACTIVITY TOYS

In toy industry terminology, Craft and Activity Toys are those that involve painting, coloring, baking, stamping, stickering, etc. MODEL KITS, which might fall into this category, have their own section and coloring books are listed under BOOKS.

There is some collector interest in the early Kenner items, but whether anybody really collects any other activity toys is questionable. Still, there are some interesting, but generally cartoonish, graphics to be found.

Coloring
Color N' Clean Machine, 50" roll of scenes to color,
    4 crayons & wipe cloth (Craft Master 1980) $45.00
Pen and Poster Set, two 17" x 22" posters & 6 pens,
    (Craft Master 1980) 20.00
Pen and Poster Set, two 11½" x 18" posters & 8
    crayons (Craft Master 1982)................. 20.00
Star Wars Mega-Fuzz Coloring Set, small (Craft
    House #51473, 1996) 3.00
Star Wars Mega-Fuzz Coloring Set, AT-AT picture
    (Craft House #51462, 1996)................. 4.00
Star Wars Mega-Fuzz Coloring Set, Darth Vader
    picture (Craft House #51463, 1996) 4.00
Star Wars, A New Hope 3-D Crayon by Number
    (Rose Art #01629) 4.00
Star Wars Poster Art coloring set (Craft Master 1978) . 20.00

Display Making
Star Wars Wonder World display tank, gel, ships,
    tweezers (Kenner 09955, 1995) 15.00

Star Wars Wonder World (Kenner 1995)

Drawing
Star Wars Trilogy Light-Up Drawing Desk (Rose Art
    #01671)................................... 10.00
Star Wars Trilogy Deluxe Light-Up Drawing Desk
    (Rose Art #1630) 15.00

Slave 1 Figure Maker (Kenner 1996)

Figure Making
Millennium Falcon Figure Maker, including 2 cans of
    air hardening compound & 6 markers (Kenner
    #22161, 1996)............................. 15.00
Droids Kit Figure Maker (Kenner #22185/22183, 1996) 15.00
Slave 1 Figure Maker (Kenner #22175, 1996)....... 15.00

Painting
Playnts Poster Set, 15½"x23½" posters and paints,
    5 different posters, 6 paints, 2 brushes, (Kenner
    1977)..................................... 35.00
Paint-By-Number, 8" x 10" scene & supplies (Craft
    Master 1980)
        Darth Vader............................ 20.00
        Han & Leia 20.00
        Luke 20.00
        Yoda 20.00
Paint-by Number, scenes from Empire 10" x 14"
    scene plus 12 paints, brush (Craft Master 1980)
        The Battle on Hoth...................... 25.00
        The Chase Through the Asteroids 25.00
Paint-By-Number, scenes from Jedi 4 different.
    (Craft Master 1983)
        C-3PO/R2-D2 .... 20.00
        Jabba the Hutt......................... 20.00
        Lando and Boushh...................... 20.00
        Sy Snootles............................ 20.00

Star Wars Acrylic Paint By Number Set (Craft
    House #51451, 1996) 4.00
Darth Vader Dimensional Mask poster set. 20.00
Battle on Hoth paint set 15.00
The Empire Strikes Back Glow-in-the-Dark paint sets
    Luke 10.00
    Leia & Han Solo. 10.00
    Darth Vader 10.00
    Yoda 10.00
Star Wars Paint-by-number, 16"x20" b&w image
    plus paints (#1411, 1997). 12.00

Painting: Figurines
Figurine Painting Set, 5½" plastic figurine, 4 differ-
    ent paints & brush (Craft Master 1980)
    Leia. 40.00
    Luke on Tauntaun 40.00
    Yoda 40.00
    Han Solo. 40.00
Figurine Painting Set, plastic figures, paints, and
    brush (Craft Master 1983)
    C-3PO/R2-D2 . . . . 35.00
    Admiral Ackbar 35.00

Painting: Water Colors
Dip Dots *Star Wars* Painting Set, 8½"x11" scenes,
    water color (Kenner 1977) 40.00
Water Color Paint Set, 8"x10" Ewok scene, 8 paints,
    brush (Fundimensions 1983)
    Ewok. 20.00
    Ewok village 20.00
    Ewok flyer 20.00
Star Wars Watercolor by Number (Craft House
    #51472, 1996). 3.00

Play Doh Sets
Star Wars Action Play Set (Kenner 1977) 30.00
Star Wars: *The Empire Strikes Back* Play-Doh Yoda
    Playset, with molds for four figures and plastic
    X-Wing fighter and 16"x10" playmat, 3 cans of
    Play-Doh and trimmer (Kenner 1980). 25.00
Star Wars: *The Empire Strikes Back* Play-Doh Ice
    Planet Playset, with molds for five figures and
    plastic Snowspeeder and playmat, 3 cans of
    Play-Doh, rolling pin and trimmer 15.00
Star Wars: *Return of the Jedi* Play-Doh Playset, with
    molds for nine figures and plastic vehicle and

Figurine Stampers Gift Set (Rose Art 1996)

playmat depicting Jabba the Hutt, 3 cans of
    Play Doh and roller (Kenner 1983) 15.00
Ewoks Playset (Kenner 1985) 15.00

Presto Magix (American Publishing)
Presto Magix, poster from *The Empire Strikes Back*
    and six different transfer sheets (1980)
    Asteroid Storm. 5.00
    Beneath Cloud City 5.00
    Dagobah Bog Planet 5.00
    Deck of the Star Destroyer. 5.00
    Ice Planet Hoth 5.00
    Rebel Base 5.00
Presto Magix, poster of *Return of the Jedi* scenes
    and transfer sheets (1983)
    Death Star. 4.00
    Ewok village 4.00
    Jabba's throne room 4.00
    Sarlaccs Pit. 4.00
Presto Magix, 16" x 24" scene & transfer sheets (1983)
    Jabba's throne room 25.00
    Endor 25.00
    Ewok village 25.00
Return of the Jedi Color Transfers (1983) 24"x5"
    back-ground scene plus 30 full color transfers . . . 15.00

Rug Making
Latch Hook Rug Kit, 6 different. (Lee Wards 1980)
    C-3PO/R2-D2 . . . . 40.00
    Chewbacca 40.00
    Darth Vader 40.00
    R2-D2 . . . . 40.00
    Stormtrooper 40.00
    Yoda 40.00

Stamp Collecting
Stamp Collecting Kit, stamp album, 24 Star War
    seals, 35 stamps (H.E. Harris 1977) 25.00

Stamping (1980s)
1983 rubbers stamps, several different. 7.50
Wicket 3-1 stamp set 5.00
Star Tours stamp set. 6.00

Stamping (1990s)
C-3PO Figurine Stamper (Rose Art #01676, 1996)
    carded. 4.00
Darth Vader Figurine Stamper (Rose Art #01676,
    1996) carded. 4.00
R2-D2 Figurine Stamper (Rose Art #01676, 1996)
    carded. 4.00

Star Wars *Postage Stamp Collecting Kit (H.E. Harris 1977)*

R2-D2 Suncatcher, baked (Fundimensions 1983)

Stormtrooper Figurine Stamper (Rose Art #01676, 1996) carded 4.00
Yoda Figurine Stamper (Rose Art #01676, 1996) carded 4.00
Star Wars Figurine Stampers Gift Set, including Darth Vader, Stormtrooper, Yoda, C-3PO and R2-D2 stamps (Rose Art #01674, 1996) boxed . . 15.00

Sticking
Wicket the Ewok Transfer Set (Kenner 1985) 12.00
Star Wars Sticker Studio, over 300 stickers (Rose-Art#1648, 1997) 6.00
Star Wars Sticker Value Pack, 150 stickers (Rose-Art #1664, 1997) 4.00
Star Wars Push Pin assortment, 12 pins per set (RoseArt #1666, 1997) 4.00

Sticking: Magnetic
Star Wars Mix 'N' Match Adventure Playset, magnetic pieces and background (ATA-Boy Inc.) 20.00

Suncatchers (Lee Wards 1980) *Empire Strikes Back* cards
C-3PO 12.00
Darth Vader head 12.00
Darth Vader figure 12.00
IG-88 . . . . 12.00
Luke Skywalker 12.00
Luke Skywalker and TaunTaun 12.00
Millennium Falcon 12.00
Princess Leia 12.00
Snowspeeders 12.00
Stormtrooper 12.00
X-Wing Fighter 12.00
Yoda and R2-D2 . . . . 12.00

Suncatchers Makit & Bakit "Stained Glass" (Fun-dimensions 1983) *Return of the Jedi* header cards
R2-D2 . . . . 10.00
Darth Vader 10.00
Gamorrean Guard 10.00
Jabba and Salacious Crumb 10.00

OTHER ACTIVITIES

While skating, kite flying and yo-yoing are not really like the artistic activities listed previously, these toys have to be listed somewhere.

Biking
Riding Speeder Bike (Kenner 1983) $1,000.00

Boping
Inflatable Bop Bags (Kenner 1977) boxed
Chewbacca, 50" tall (#63050) 60.00
Darth Vader, 50" tall 60.00
Jawa, 36" tall 70.00
Artoo-Detoo, 36" tall 45.00

Kite Flying
Darth Vader Parasail Kite (SpectraStar 1997) 15.00

Skating
Ice Skates (BrookfieldAthletic Show 1983) Darth Vader and Imperial Guard 75.00
Wicket 75.00
Darth and Imperial Guard Roller Skates (Brookfield Athletic Shoe 1983) 75.00
Wicket Roller Skates (Brookfield Athletic Shoe 1983) . 75.00

Yo-Yoing
Star Wars 3D Sculpted Yo Yo (SpectraStar 1995)
Darth Vader (#1624) 5.00
Stormtrooper (#1623) 5.00

Darth Vader Parasail Kite (SpectraStar 1997)

DIE-CAST

DIE-CAST FIGURES AND SHIPS

Like ceramics, die-cast figures and ships are their own collecting category. Unlike ceramics, die-cast spaceships are figural. However, they are generally not scaled to fit the characters in the same line nor each other. Typically a die-cast Death Star, Star Destroyer and X-wing are all about the same size. Die-cast figures and ships which were designed for gaming are listed under "Games." See also "Micro" for Kenner's small die-cast figures designed for plastic playsets.

DIE-CAST SHIPS
Kenner (1978–80)

Kenner issued die-cast ships on header cards and in open boxes. The latter are much more valuable. Several of the boxed ships also came with backgrounds. These say "Special Offer" prominently in red in a yellow oval on the left and right sides of the package.

Ships (Carded)

Darth Vader TIE Fighter (#39160) (removable figure of Darth Vader).	$50.00
Loose	25.00
Variation, small wings, scarce	500.00
Imperial TIE Fighter (#38590)	40.00

Y-Wing Fighter die-cast ship, with background (Kenner 1979)

TIE Bomber die-cast ship (Kenner 1980)

Loose	15.00
Land Speeder (#38570) (Luke and C-3PO in cockpit)	100.00
Loose	35.00
Rebel Armored Snowspeeder (#39680).	125.00
Loose	45.00
Slave I (#39670).	90.00
Loose	35.00
Twin-Pod Cloud Car (#39660).	95.00
Loose	35.00
X-Wing Fighter (#38680) wings and cockpit open	75.00
Loose	25.00

Ships (Boxed)

Millennium Falcon (#39210) with swiveling cannon and antennae dish	150.00
Loose	50.00
Reissue, with background	500.00
Imperial Cruiser (#39230)	200.00
Loose	65.00
Reissue, with background	500.00
Y-Wing Fighter (#39220)	150.00
Loose	50.00
Reissue, with background	500.00
TIE Bomber (#39260) test market figure, scarce	800.00
Loose	275.00

Metal Figurines (Heritage 1977)

Bantha Set, Bantha with 2 Sand people	45.00
C-3PO	15.00
Chewbacca	20.00
Darth Vader	20.00

Han Solo 15.00
Jawa 15.00
Luke Skywalker 20.00
Obi-Wan Kenobi 20.00
Leia 20.00
R2-D2 .... 20.00
Sand Person, different from Bantha set 15.00
Snitch 15.00
Storm Trooper 20.00

Action Master 4 Pack (Kenner 1994)

ACTION MASTERS
Kenner (1994–96)

Kenner's Action Masters figures were issued on a header card with an exclusive trading card. A Predator, two Terminators, four Aliens and several DC Superheroes were also available in the Action Masters series. There was a gold C-3PO available as a free mail-in for six proof of purchase points. I mailed-in but I never received the figure, which is one reason you won't find a picture of it here.

Die-Cast Figures
Darth Vader Action Masters figure, with card
  (#62671, 1994) $10.00
Luke Skywalker Action Masters figure, with card
  (#62672, 1994) 10.00
C-3PO Action Masters figure, gold, with card
  (#62673, 1994) 10.00
R2-D2 Action Masters figure, with card (#62674, 1994). 10.00
Stormtrooper Action Masters figure, with card
  (#62675, 1994) 10.00
Chewbacca Action Masters figure, with card (1994) .. 10.00
Snowtrooper Action Masters figure, with card (1994).. 10.00
Special Edition Action Masters "Gold" C-3PO
  mail-in figure 25.00
Star Wars Action Masters Collectors Set (4 Pack):
  C-3PO, Princess Leia Organa, R2-D2 and
  Obi-Wan Kenobi, with four trading cards
  (#62634, 1994) 30.00
Star Wars Action Masters Collectors Set (6 Pack):
  Han Solo, Chewbacca, Stormtrooper, Boba
  Fett, Darth Vader and Luke Skywalker, with
  six trading cards (#62640, 1994) 45.00

R2-D2 Action Master figure (Kenner 1994)

Star Wars The Power of the Force 6 Pack set: Han
  Solo, Chewbacca, Stormtrooper, Boba Fett,
  Darth Vader and Luke Skywalker, with six
  trading cards (#69782, 1995) 45.00

MICRO MACHINE DIE-CAST
Galoob (1996–98)

The original packaging for these figures was an oval-shaped header card. The packaging was changed in 1997 to a rectangular card with stripes, similar in design to the action fleet packages (see MicroMachines). The Jawa Sandcrawler was discontinued, however, sufficient stock remained available and in early 1998 I was able to purchase a Sandcrawler at a local Toys "R" Us store for $1.98. Die-cast figures have interested collectors over the years, and these figures, particularly on the original header cards, might turn out to be a good buy at current prices.

First Batch (Asst. #66260, 1996)
X-Wing Starfighter (#66261) $6.00
  Reissue on striped card 5.00
Millennium Falcon (#66262) 6.00
  Reissue on striped card 5.00
Imperial Star Destroyer (#66263) 6.00
  Reissue on striped card 5.00
TIE Fighter (#66264). 6.00
  Reissue on striped card 5.00
Y-Wing Starfighter (#66265) 6.00
  Reissue on striped card 5.00
Jawa Sandcrawler (#66266) original card only 9.00

Jawa Sandcrawler Micro Machine die-cast (Galoob 1996)

Y-Wing Starfighter Micro Machine die-cast (Galoob 1997)

Second Batch (Asst. #66260, 1997)

Death Star	6.00
Reissue on striped card	5.00
Executor with Star Destroyer	6.00
Reissue on striped card	5.00
Landspeeder	6.00
Reissue on striped card	5.00
Millennium Falcon	6.00
Reissue on striped card	5.00
Slave I	6.00
Reissue on striped card	5.00
Snowspeeder	6.00
Reissue on striped card	5.00
TIE Bomber	6.00
Reissue on striped card	5.00
Y-Wing Starfighter	6.00
Reissue on striped card	5.00

PEWTER FIGURES
Rawcliffe (1993–95)

Star Wars Characters

Admiral Ackbar (#RF969)	$15.60
C-3PO	15.60
Chewbacca (#RF963)	22.00
Lando Calrissian	15.60
Princess Leia (#RF958)	14.00
Luke Skywalker (#RF959)	14.00
Obi-Wan Kenobi (#RF961)	22.00
R2-D2 (#RF957)	14.00
Han Solo (#RF960)	14.00
Ewok-Wicket	10.00
Yoda (#RF955)	10.00

Characters, Darkside

Bib Fortuna (#RF970)	15.60
Boba Fett (#RF966)	15.60
Emperor Palpatine (#RF968)	15.60
Gamorrean Guard (#RF971)	15.60
Stormtrooper (#RF965)	15.60
Darth Vader (#RF962)	24.00

PEWTER VEHICLES
Rawcliffe (1993–95)

Star Wars Vehicles

A-Wing (#RF953)	$32.00
B-Wing (#RF954)	32.00
Millennium Falcon	30.00
Outrider	36.00
Snow Speeder (#RF972)	30.00
X-Wing, 3" tall (#RF975)	36.00
Y-Wing (#RF973)	36.00

Vehicles Darkside

Sail Barge	34.00
Star Destroyer (#RF964)	60.00
Slave I	28.00
TIE Fighter (#RF974)	32.00
Shuttle *Tydirium* (#RF967)	36.00
TIE Bomber	36.00

Vehicles Special Limited Edition, with base

Death Star	160.00
Millennium Falcon (#RF951, 1993)	140.00
TIE Interceptor	76.00
Vader's Custom TIE Fighter (#RF950, 1993)	108.00
X-Wing (#RF952, 1993)	76.00

DOLLS AND FIGURES

DOLLS

Between 1979 and 1980, Kenner produced a dozen Large Size Action Figures, (i.e. dolls) in window boxes with a flap. All the figures were made to the same 12" scale, but R2-D2 and the Jawa were small characters and so their dolls are about 8" tall, while Chewbacca, Darth Vader and IG-88 were about 15" tall. These are highly prized collectibles, both in and out of box (loose). The Radio Control R2-D2, listed under ELECTRONICS, was made to the same scale as the listed figures.

DOLLS
Kenner (1979–80)

Jawa doll, boxed and loose (Kenner 1979)

Large Figures, *Star Wars* logo (1979)

Princess Leia Organa (#38070) 11½" tall.	$225.00
Loose, in Alderaanian cape, royal belt, long socks and shoes with comb, brush and booklet.	125.00
Luke Skywalker (#38080) 11¾" tall	350.00
Loose, in Tattooine desert costume with light saber, grappling hook, boots and utility belt . .	185.00
Chewbacca (#38600) 15" tall	150.00
Loose, with ammunition belt with removable cartridges and crossbow laser rifle	85.00
Darth Vader (#38610) 15" tall	225.00
Loose, with lightsaber and removable cloth cape	100.00

See-Threepio (C-3PO) (#38620) 12" tall	150.00
Loose, issued without equipment	50.00
Artoo-Detoo (R2-D2) (#38630) 7½" tall	130.00
Loose, with removable Death Star Plans	50.00
Han Solo (#39170) 11¾" tall	500.00
Loose, with shirts, pants, vest, boots, laser pistol, holster and belt, and Rebel Alliance Medal of Honor	230.00
Stormtrooper (#39180) 12" tall	300.00
Loose, with laser rifle	130.00
Ben (Obi-Wan) Kenobi (#39340) 12" tall	325.00

Luke Skywalker, Princess Leia, Han Solo and Chewbacca dolls, loose (Kenner 1979)

Ben (Obi-Wan) Kenobi doll, boxed and Boba Fett doll, loose (Kenner 1979)

Loose, in hooded cloak and boots, with lightsaber	150.00
Jawa (#39350) 8" tall	175.00
Loose, with laser rifle, ammunition belt and hooded cloak	75.00
Boba Fett (#39140) 13" tall	375.00
In *The Empire Strikes Back* box	325.00
Loose, with cape, Wookiee scalps, utility belts, laser pistol and rocket backpack	150.00

Large Figure, *The Empire Strikes Back* logo (1980)

IG-88 (Bounty Hunter) (#39960) 15" tall	600.00
Loose, with rifle, pistol and cartridge belt with four cartridges	250.00

STAR WARS: COLLECTOR SERIES — 12" DOLLS
Kenner (1996–98)

Kenner began issuing Collector Series dolls in 1996. The first series of dolls had a dark blue background card inside the package. In December, light blue cards appeared. Obi-Wan Kenobi was scarce and almost impossible to find in stores from the very first. He was just as difficult to locate later with the light blue backing card. Chewbacca is pictured on the back of the boxes, but he was not included in the series. He was scheduled for the second series, but again didn't appear and he did not actually arrive until the fourth series. Instead of Chewbacca, the second series had two Tusken Raiders, with different weapons — one with a blaster and one with a more authentic Gaderffii Stick. Lando Calrissian from this batch did not sell out as quickly as the other dolls and could still be found in many stores well into 1998.

12" Dolls (Aug. 1996) in window box with flap cover

Luke Skywalker (#27724)

On original dark blue package card, binoculars on belt, black lightsaber handle	$55.00
Reissue, binoculars on card	35.00
Reissue, on light blue package card	25.00
Reissue, black and silver lightsaber handle	20.00
Loose, in shirt, pants, boots and utility belt, with lightsaber, blaster and electro binoculars on belt	12.50
Loose figure with loose binoculars	9.00

Han Solo (#27725)

On original dark blue package card	35.00
Reissue, on light blue package card, painted or unpainted belt pouch	20.00
Loose, in shirt, vest, pants, holster and boots with blaster pistol and blaster rifle	12.50

Darth Vader, Luke Skywalker and Han Solo Collector Series dolls (Kenner 1996)

Luke Skywalker doll, reissue binoculars on card (Kenner 1996)

Obi Wan Kenobi doll, on original dark blue package card
(Kenner 1996)

Darth Vader (#27726)
　　On original dark blue package card, black
　　　lightsaber handle. 25.00
　　Reissue, on light blue package card, black
　　　lightsaber handle. 25.00
　　Reissue, black and silver lightsaber handle 20.00
　　Loose, black helmet, outfit, cape, boots, and
　　　gloves, with red lightsaber, either handle 10.00

Obi-Wan Kenobi (#27719)
　　On original dark blue package card, black
　　　lightsaber handle and silver belt buckle 60.00
　　Reissue, on light blue package card, black or
　　　black and silver lightsaber handle and silver
　　　buckle. 45.00
　　Reissue, gold buckle 55.00
　　Loose, in hooded robe, shirt, pants, inner robe
　　　and boots, with lightsaber, all variations. 25.00

Second Batch (Asst. #27754, Jan. 1997)
Lando Calrissian (#27755) 18.00
　　Loose, with blaster, cape, shirt, pants, boots
　　　and comlink communicator. 7.50
Luke Skywalker in Bespin Fatigues (#27757) 25.00
　　Loose, in Bespin uniform and boots with utility
　　　belt, blaster and lightsaber. 9.00
Tusken Raider (with Rifle) (#27758, March 1997) 30.00
　　Loose, in robe, wrappings, bandolier, gloves
　　　and boots with blaster and macrobinoculars. . . . 8.00

Tusken Raider (with Gaderffii Stick) (#27758,
　　March 1997) 35.00
　　Loose, in robe, wrappings, bandolier, gloves
　　　and boots with Gaderffii Stick and macro-
　　　binoculars 9.00

Third Batch (Asst. #27690, 1996 i.e. July 1997)
Stormtrooper (#27689) 25.00
　　Loose, with Imperial blaster and ammo belt 9.00
Princess Leia (#27691). 30.00
　　Loose, in royal white hooded tunic, boots and
　　　belt, with blaster. 9.00
Luke Skywalker in X-wing Gear (#27692) 25.00
　　Loose, in orange flight suit and boots, with
　　　helmet and visor, harness, lightsaber and
　　　galaxy map 9.00
Boba Fett (#27693). 25.00
　　Loose, in helmet, cape, scalped Wookiee
　　　braids, battle-scarred Madalorian armor and
　　　boots, with BlasTech EE-3 blaster rifle, wrist
　　　lasers and miniature flame projector, and jet
　　　pack. 10.00

　　Chewbacca, was pictured on the first series packages
and scheduled for early 1997. Collectors kept looking, but he
did not appear until the fall 1997, in the fourth batch. The
package back depicts the three figures in the earlier assortment (plus Chewbacca) and is unlike the other figures in this
assortment, which picture six figures. When Chewbacca did
arrive, he was very short-packed in the assortment and only
12" tall, which is not to scale. I got mine, but half the collectors I know are still looking, which is quite frustrating — for
them anyway.

Fourth Batch (Asst. #27862, Sept. 1997)
TIE Fighter Pilot (#27864). 25.00
　　Loose, with blaster, chest respirator and wrist
　　　comlink 9.00

Tusken Raider, with Gaderffii Stick and Chewbacca dolls
(Kenner 1997)

Yoda, loose, R2-D2, Greedo and AT-AT Driver, boxed Collector Series dolls (Kenner 1998)

C-3PO (#27865) 25.00
    Loose, without accessories, as issued 9.00
Admiral Ackbar (#27866) 25.00
    Loose, in jumpsuit, belt and rank badge, no
      weapon 9.00
Chewbacca (#27756) 65.00
    Loose, with bowcaster, pouch and shoulder
      strap packed with ammo 25.00

Three of the 1998 batches of 12" scale dolls have appeared as of this writing. The packaging has changed somewhat, and no longer includes a front box flap. Gone, too, is the character bio information. However, the quality of the figures has impressed collectors. This is as it should be. Just about the only reason to pay $25.00 or more for a Collector Series doll, is to get a well made, well sculpted, and highly detailed figure.

The three smaller figures seem to have hung around on store shelves for a little longer than the taller ones. R2-D2 is the easiest to find of the three. Nevertheless, the only one of the entire series that has lingered long enough to see a red tag is Lando Calrissian.

Fifth Batch, Star Wars Trilogy (Asst. #27741, Feb. 1998) green background window box, no flap
R2-D2, 6" (#27742) with retractable leg 15.00
    Loose, without accessories 7.50
Yoda, 6" (#27743) 15.00
    Loose, with Gimmer stick 7.50
Jawa, 6" (#27744) with light-up eyes 15.00
    Loose, with gun, cartridge and harness 7.50

Sixth Batch, A New Hope (Asst. #27903, April 1998) in green background window box, no flap
Greedo (#27904) 25.00
    Loose, in jumpsuit, vest and boots with blaster 9.00
Grand Moff Tarkin with "Interrogation Droid included" (#27905) 30.00
    Loose, with Interrogation Droid, Jacket, Belt,
      Pants and Boots 9.00
Sandtrooper with Imperial Droid (#27906) 25.00
    Loose, in Sandtrooper armor with white
      shoulder pauldron, backpack and blaster rifle . . . 9.00
Luke Skywalker in Ceremonial Gear, with Ceremonial Medal (#27907) 25.00
    Loose, in shirt, pants, jacket and boots, with
      lightsaber, blaster and holster 9.00

Seventh Batch, The Empire Strikes Back (Asst. #27915, April 1998) in green background window box, no flap
Han Solo in Hoth Gear with "Firing Rebel Blaster included" (#27916) 30.00
    Loose, with Blaster and Ammo, Pistol, Holster,
      Helmet and Goggles, Hoth Jacket, Pants
      and Boots 12.00
Luke Skywalker in Hoth Gear with "Firing Rebel Blaster included" (#27917) 30.00
    Loose, with Blaster and Ammo, Pistol, Holster,
      Helmet and Goggles, Hoth Jacket, Pants
      and Boots 12.00

AT-AT Driver with "Firing Imperial Blaster included" (#27918) 25.00
    Loose, with Blaster and Ammo, Helmet,
      Breathing Apparatus, Armored Outfit and
      Boots 9.00

Snowtrooper with "Firing Imperial Blaster included"
   (#27919) 25.00
      Loose, with Blaster and Ammo, Helmet, Belt,
        Armored Outfit and Boots. 9.00

Eighth Batch, Return of the Jedi (Catalog price)
Emperor Palpatine 24.00
Luke in Jedi Gear 24.00
Chained Chewbacca. 24.00
Cantina Band Alien 24.00

14" Electronic (Catalog price)
Darth Vader 40.00

COLLECTOR SERIES — EXCLUSIVES

While all the collectors were looking for Chewbacca, some of them were lucky enough to find one or more of the 1997 store exclusives. Many of these had store shelf-lives of less than one day. The first to appear was the Han and Luke Stormtrooper two-pack at Kay-Bee stores. Target stores got an exclusive Luke Skywalker and Wampa, while Toys "R" Us had Han Solo mounted on a Tauntaun. During the one day that these figures were available at retail, they sold for about $50.00 each. It was more like $150.00 within a week. The demand for each figure is different, depending on which stores are nearby. In any give area, exclusive figures from out-of-town stores are usually more in demand, because few, if any, local collectors have one.

Recently, Kenner has sent additional shipments of some of the exclusive dolls and re-issued others as part of its regular Collector Series. The dolls in the additional shipments are identical to the originals and the re-issues differ only slightly from the originals. Many collectors are annoyed that Kenner even considered reissuing the figures that they were lucky enough to acquire, but feel that it's not such a bad idea for

Kenner to produce a few more of the ones they haven't found yet — just enough for them to get one and no more!

12" Special Dolls/Exclusives
Han Solo & Luke Skywalker in Stormtrooper Gear
   (KB Limited Edition of 20,000) (#27867, July
   1997) in window box with flap cover $175.00
     Loose, with helmets, each 15.00
Grand Moff Tarkin & Imperial Gunner with Interrog-
   ator Droid (#27923, Aug. 1997) FAO Schwarz . . 150.00
     Loose, each 25.00
Luke Skywalker vs. Wampa (27947, Aug. 1997)
   Target stores 125.00
   Loose, pair. 35.00
Han Solo & Tauntaun (#27834, Aug. 1997) Toys "R"
   Us stores 125.00
   Loose, pair. 60.00
Cantina Band (Aug. 1997) WalMart stores
   Doikk Na'ts with Fizzz 45.00
   Figrin D'an with Kloo Horn 50.00
   Ickabel with Fanfar. 45.00
   Nalan with Bandfill 45.00
   Tech with Ommni Box 45.00
   Tedn with Fanfar 45.00
Greedo (#27976, Aug. 1997) J.C. Penney stores 70.00
   Loose 35.00
Sandtrooper (#27928, Aug. 1997) direct market 60.00
   Loose, with concussion-grenade launcher,
     environmental survival pack and orange
     shoulder pauldron 25.00
AT-AT Driver (#27977, Oct. 1997) Service
   Merchandise stores. 80.00
   Loose, with helmet, chest respirator, boots,
     comlink and Imperial blaster. 15.00
Jedi Knight Luke Skywalker & Bib Fortuna (#27924,
   Nov. 1997). 125.00
   Loose, each. 15.00

Han Solo and Luke Stormtrooper in Stormtrooper Gear and Han Solo & Tauntaun, exclusive figures (Kenner 1997)

Classic Collectors Series PVC Figures (Applause 1995)

Boxed Set
Star Wars Classic Collectors Series (6 figures):
   Luke Skywalker, Darth Vader, Han Solo,
   C-3PO, R2-D2 and Chewbacca with Bespin
   Display Platform (Applause #46038, 1995). $20.00

3½" figures, First Batch (1995)
Darth Vader (#46104) 5.00
Luke Skywalker (#46105) 3.00
Han Solo (#46106) 3.00
Chewbacca (#46107) 4.00
C-3PO (#46108) 3.00
R2-D2 (#46109) 3.00

Second Batch (1996)
Emperor Palpatine (#46214) 3.00
Princess Leia (#46216) 3.00
Stormtrooper (#46218) 3.00
Boba Fett (#46239) 3.00

Third Batch (1997)
Obi-Wan Kenobi as ghostly Jedi (#42676) 4.00
Lando Calrissian (#42675) 3.00
Greedo (#42677) 3.00
Yoda (#42678) 3.00
Wedge Antilles (#42707) 4.00
TIE-Fighter pilot (#42708) 3.00
Store Assortment Box, 10¾"x15¼"x10" listing all
   16 figures from 1995–97 (#42674) empty 5.00

Fourth Batch (1998)
Admiral Ackbar (#42946) 3.00
Bossk (#42947) 3.00
Snowtrooper (#42948) 3.00
Tusken Raider (#42949) 3.00
Obi-Wan Kenobi (#42965) 3.00

Gift Boxes
Han Solo, Chewbacca, Boba Fett, Darth Vader and
   Luke Skywalker (#42989) 20.00

Jumbo Dioramas (Jan. 1997)
Han Solo and Jabba the Hutt, 4½"x6¼"x4" (#42691) . . 10.00
R2-D2 and C-3PO, 4¾"x3½"x2½" (#42690) 10.00

Read-Along Play Packs
Star Wars, A New Hope Cassette and 3 PVCs
   (Stormtrooper, R2-D2, C-3PO) (Walt Disney
   Records #02844, 1997) 10.00
Star Wars, The Empire Strikes Back Cassette and
   3 PVCs (Han Solo, Chewbacca, Boba Fett)
   (Walt Disney Records #02854, 1997) 10.00
Star Wars, Return of the Jedi Cassette and 3 PVCs
   (Luke Skywalker, Emperor, Princess Leia)
   (Walt Disney Records #02834, 1997) 10.00

PVC SHIPS
Applause (1995)

Star Wars Danglers, on a wire hanger, with suction-cup, in
   clear acetate box, 1¾"x1¾"x3¾"
X-Wing Fighter (#46098) $4.00
Millennium Falcon (#46099) 4.00
Rebel Y-Wing Fighter (#46100) 4.00
Death Star (#46101) 4.00
Imperial Star Destroyer (#46102) 4.00
TIE Fighter (#46103) 4.00
Set of six 20.00
Store Display Box (#46037) empty 3.00

VINYL FIGURES
Suncoast Vinyl Dolls (1993)

Darth Vader $20.00
Luke Jedi Knight 20.00
Luke X-Wing Pilot 20.00
Han Solo 20.00
Chewbacca 20.00
R2-D2 . . . . 20.00
C3-PO 20.00
Leia in white gown 20.00

VINYL FIGURES
Applause (1995–98)

   Most of the vinyl figures produced by Applause are sold
loose, with only a folded wrist tag or card to identify the figure and contain the UPC code for scanning. The figures are
generally available in comic shops and specialty stores like
Spencer Gifts, but not in toy stores. They are not articulated,
although sometimes the arms or waist allows some motion,
but this does not detract from their collectibility. In early
1998, Spencer Gifts was selling much of their stock for about
$10.00, making them an attractive purchase. Applause also
issued boxed figures of Darth Vader and Luke Skywalker in
X-wing gear, plus a series of boxed resin figurines and dioramas. These are reasonably priced when compared to expensive statues and fine replicas sold by other manufacturers.

9"–11" Figures, First Batch (August 1995)
Darth Vader, limited to 20,000 pieces (#46039) $20.00
Luke Skywalker with Yoda, 9¼" (#46040) 15.00
Princess Leia with R2-D2, 8½" (#46041) 15.00
Han Solo as Stormtrooper, 10" (#46042) 15.00
Chewbacca, with C-3PO, 11" (#46043) 15.00

Second Batch (1996)
Darth Vader, 2nd edition, removable helmet, 11"
   (#46234) 17.00
Boba Fett (#46238) 15.00

Princess Leia, Boba Fett and Wedge Antilles vinyl figures (Applause 1995–97)

Princess Leia in poncho with removable helmet 15.00
Emperor Palpatine (*Star Wars* Classic) 10½"
    (#46240) with glow-in-the-dark hands. 16.00
Tusken Raider, 11" (#46241). 15.00
Dash Rendar (Shadows of the Empire) 10½" (#46243). 17.00
Prince Xizor (Shadows of the Empire) 11" (#46244) . . 17.00

Third Batch (1997)
TIE Fighter Pilot, 10" (#42688) 15.00
Wedge Antilles, 11" (#42689) 17.00
Greedo, 10" (#42670) 15.00
Lando Calrissian, skiff guard, 10" (#42671) 15.00
Obi-Wan Kenobi, 10" (#42672) 15.00
R2-D2 with sensor scope, 5½" (#42673) 15.00

Fourth Batch (1998)
Luke in Jedi Training, glow-in-the-dark lightsaber
    and removable helmet, 9" (#42945) 15.00
C-3PO, 9½" (#42955) 15.00

Figures in Large Box
Darth Vader, 12" (#61096) 25.00
Luke Skywalker, in X-wing Pilot Gear, 9" (#61091) . . . 20.00

DIORAMAS AND FIGURINES
Applause (1995–97)

Resin Figurines
Darth Vader Limited Edition Resin Figurine, limited
    to 5,000 pieces (Applause #46048, Aug. 1995)
    light-up base $50.00
Luke Skywalker Limited Edition Resin Figurine,
    limited to 5,000 pieces (Applause #46049,
    Aug. 1995) light-up base 50.00
Bounty Hunters Resin Diorama, includes Boba
    Bossk and Zuckuss, limited to 5,000 pieces
    Fett, (#46196, Sept. 1996) 60.00

Jabba and Leia, with Salacious Crumb, limited to
    5,000 pieces (#46197, Sept. 1996). 60.00
Shadows of the Empire, includes Emperor
    Palpatine, Darth Vader and Prince Xizor,
    limited to 5,000 pieces (#46199, Oct. 1996) 60.00
Leia's Rescue Statuette, includes Luke, Leia, Han
    and Chewbacca (#42669, 1997) 70.00
Han Solo Release From Carbonite Statue, with
    built-in light source, limited to 2,500 copies
    (#61064, 1997) Diamond Previews exclusive . . . 110.00

Sandtrooper and Dewback (Applause 1997)

Star Wars Rancor Statuette (#42735, 1997) 60.00
Star Wars Sandtrooper on Dewback cold-cast resin
    statuette (#42687, 1997) 60.00

FIGURAL BANKS

Plastic (Adam Joseph 1983)
Darth Vader, 9" tall $25.00
Emperor's Royal Guard, 9" tall 25.00
Gamorrean Guard, 9" tall, rare, ... 50.00
R2-D2, 6" tall 30.00
Princess Kneesa, 6" tall, playing tambourine 15.00
Wicket, 6" tall, playing drum 15.00

Metal
Darth Vader Bust Metal Bank, 6" high (Leonard
    Silver Mfg. 1981) 65.00
Darth Vader Metal Bank, tin litho box with combin-
    ation dials (Metal Box Co. 1980) 50.00
Yoda Metal Bank, tin litho box with combination
    dials (Metal Box Co. 1980) 50.00
The Empire Strikes Back Metal Bank, tin octagonal
    bank with photos of characters (Metal Box Co.
    1980) 40.00

PLUSH FIGURES

Plush
Chewbacca (Regal) $60.00
Chewbacca, 20" tall (Kenner 1977) 35.00
R2-D2, 10" tall (Kenner 1977) 50.00
Ewoks (Kenner 1983)
       18" Zephee 40.00
       14" Wicket 30.00
       14" Princess Kneesa 30.00
       14" Paploo 40.00
       14" Latara 40.00
       8" Woklings, six different, each. 15.00
Ewok, 12", light brown with green cowl (Disney) 15.00
Ewok, 8", dark brown with pink cowl (Disney) 12.00

PUPPETS

Yoda Hand Puppet, plastic, 8½" tall (Kenner 1981) . . $40.00
Chewbacca Hand Puppet (Regal) 50.00

STAR WARS BUDDIES
Kenner (1997–98)

Everyone who thinks that Kenner would have made *Star Wars* Buddies even if Beanie Babies were not enjoying their 15 minutes of collecting fame please raise your hand. Thank you. If both of you would write to me care of the publisher and include your unbiased opinions on these toys, I will attempt to include them in the next edition of this book. For everyone else, these Beanie Baby knock-offs are either cute and imaginative or a curse, depending on your view of the real thing. Most collectors that I have met do not utter the words "Beanie Babies" without adding an "expletive deleted."

Buddies (Bean Bag)
C-3PO $8.00
Chewbacca, original black bandolier strap 15.00
Chewbacca, new brown bandolier strap 8.00
Darth Vader 8.00
Figrin D'An 8.00
Gamorrean Guard 8.00
Jabba the Hutt 8.00
Jawa 10.00
Luke Skywalker 8.00
Max Rebo 8.00
Princess Leia 8.00
R2-D2 . . . . 8.00
Salacious Crumb 10.00
Stormtrooper 8.00
Wampa 8.00
Wicket the Ewok 9.00
Yoda 8.00

Star Wars Buddies: Wicket and Max Rebo (Kenner 1998)

ELECTRONIC
AND COMPUTER

ELECTRONIC AND COMPUTER

This section covers electronic and computer games and toys, plus related items. Other types of games are covered in the GAMES section. The electronic toys generally produce recorded sound effects, music or short sound bites from the movies. Actual sound tracks, audio performances and *Star Wars* music are listed in the RECORDINGS section.

The earliest electronic games and toys were made by Kenner. They still make radio and remote controlled toys.

Currently, the predominant manufacturer of *Star Wars* electronic hand-held games and other items is Tiger Electronics, Inc. By 1997, they had produced a large number of such games. There were no new ones for 1998, and Toys "R" Us has discounted some of their existing stock, so this may be the time to buy. In 1999, they will produce many new games based on the new movie and this may create interest in the earlier games. Their Stormtrooper Laser Target Game contains a 13½" Stormtrooper figure which has drawn some interest from doll and figure collectors. The original remote controlled R2-D2 is also sometimes considered a figure for

collecting purposes.

Walkie Talkies: see Role Play

Radio-Controlled/Remote Controlled
Radio Controlled R2-D2, 8", *Star Wars* logo
(Kenner #38430, 1979) $150.00
    Loose 65.00
Radio Controlled Imperial Speeder Bike with figure
(Kenner #27846, 1997) 25.00
Electronic Remote Control R2-D2 (Kenner #27736,
Sept. 1997) 20.00

Classic Electronic Games
Electronic Battle Command Game, 9½" x 7" box,
Star Wars logo (Kenner #40370, 1977) battery
powered 75.00
Electronic Laser Battle Game, 20" x 6½" box, *Star
Wars* logo (Kenner #40090, 1977) 100.00
X-Wing Aces Target Electronic Game, plug-in, *Star
Wars* logo (Kenner 1978) very rare, offered in
mini-catalog 1,000.00

Remote Control R2-D2 (Kenner 1979)

Star Wars *Intimidator (Micro Games of America 1995)*

Stormtrooper Room Alarm (Tiger Electronics 1997)

Destroy Death Star Electronic Game, 17" x 25" box
(Palitoy 1978) 150.00

Electronic Games (Micro Games of America 1995)
Star Wars Shakin' Pinball (MGA 207) (#22623, 1995) . 17.00
Star Wars Electronic Game (MGA 220) (#02033, 1995) 10.00
The Empire Strikes Back Electronic Game
(MGA 222) (#02034, 1995) 10.00
Return of the Jedi Electronic Game (MGA 224)
(#02035, 1995) 10.00
Star Wars Intimidator (INT-200) (1995) 10.00

Electronic Games and Toys (Tiger Electronics)
Star Wars Millennium Falcon Challenge R-Zone
Headgear (#71-196, 1997)................. 15.00
Star Wars Jedi Adventure R-Zone Xtreme Pocket
Game (#71-331, 1997).................... 30.00
R-Zone Cartridges :
Millennium Falcon Challenge (#71-316) 10.00
Jedi Adventure (#71-317)................... 10.00
Rebel Forces (#71-319).................... 10.00
Imperial Assault (#71-321)................. 10.00
Star Wars Imperial Assault 3-D Figure Hand Held
Game "Joystick Games" (#88-001, 1997)....... 20.00
Millennium Falcon Challenge Electronic LCD Game
(#88-005, 1997)......................... 20.00
Millennium Falcon Sounds of the Force Electronic
Memory Game (#88-089, 1997).............. 30.00

Boba Fett Room Alarm with Laser Target Game,
13½" figure in window box, with Han Solo
Laser Blaster (#88-080, 1997) 25.00
Stormtrooper Room Alarm with Laser Target Game,
13½" figure in window box, with Han Solo
Laser Blaster (#88-081, 1997) 25.00
Star Wars Rebel Forces Laser Game (#79-212, 1997) 20.00
Star Wars Electronic Galactic Battle game, includes
10 different vehicles & sound effects (#88-088,
1997)................................. 25.00
Star Wars Death Star Escape Game (#88-090)...... 25.00
Star Wars Quiz Whiz (*Star Wars Trilogy* Episode
IV) Electronic Question & Answer Game
(#88-091)............................... 25.00

Video Board Game
Star Wars Interactive Video Board Game (Parker
Bros. #40392, 1996) 32.00

Computer Games/Software
The Software Toolworks *Star Wars* Chess game
(Software Toolworks 1992)................. 15.00
The Lucas Archives, Vol. I, CD-ROM (also includes
non-*Star Wars* disks) (Lucas Arts #80218, 1995) . 30.00
The Lucas Archives, Vol. II, CD-ROM *Star Wars*
Collection (Lucas Arts #80318, 1996).......... 60.00
TIE Fighter Wars, CD-ROM (Lucas Arts #20618, 1995) . 55.00
X-wing vs. TIE Fighter, CD-ROM (Lucas Arts
#20818, 1997) 60.00
Shadows of the Empire, CD-ROM (Lucas Arts
#31218, 1997) 50.00
Rebel Assault, CD-ROM (Lucas Arts #30418, 1993) .. 30.00
Yoda Stories, CD-ROM (Lucas Arts #31118, 1997) ... 20.00
Rebel Assault II, CD-ROM (Lucas Arts #30918, 1995).. 60.00
Dark Forces, CD-ROM (Lucas Arts #30618, 1994) ... 30.00

Electronic Game Cartridges
Star Wars SNES Cartridge (JVC NES 1993)........ 50.00

Star Wars Chess (Software Toolworks 1992)

Star Wars *Gameboy Cartridge (Nintendo 1993)*

Super *Star Wars* SNES Cartridge (JVC NES 1993). . . 60.00
The Empire Strikes Back Nintendo Cartridge (JVC
    NES #91014, 1992) 40.00
Star Wars Gameboy Cartridge (Capcom #12013,
    1993) 30.00
The Empire Strikes Back Gameboy Cartridge
    (Capcom #12014, 1993) 30.00

Radios and Cassette Players
Luke Skywalker AM Headset Radio, battery
    powered (Kenner #38420, 1979) 40.00
Millennium Falcon Cassette Player (Micro Games
    of America #SW-24M, 1995) 30.00
R2-D2 Data Droid Cassette Player (Tiger
    Electronics #88-083) 10" high 27.00
R2-D2 Personal Cassette Player (Tiger Electronics
    #88-087, 1997) 17.00

Darth Vader AM/FM Clock Radio (Micro Games of
    America #SW-3124, 1995) 32.00
Darth Vader FM Bike Radio (Micro Games of
    America #SW-3180, 1995) 37.00
C-3PO AM/FM Radio (Micro Games of America
    #SW-3190, 1995). 27.00
Darth Vader AM/FM Clock Radio, with molded head
    on top, LCD display (#SW-3124) 25.00

"Talking" Toys
Star Wars Electronic Talking Bank with 8" C-3PO
    and 5" R2-D2, plus "dialogue, music & effects
    from the movie soundtrack" (Thinkway #13902,
    1995). 22.00
Star Wars Electronic Talking Bank with Darth Vader
    plus "dialogue, music & effects from the movie
    soundtrack" (Thinkway #13903, 1996) 22.00
R2-D2 Repeating Robot (Micro Games of America
    #SW-3194, 1995). 32.00
Darth Vader Power Talker Voice Changing Mask
    #SW-3815 (Micro Games of America #22586,
    1995). 35.00

R2-D2 Ditto Droid game (Tiger Electronics
    #88-031, 1997) 10.00
Darth Vader Voice Changer (Tiger Electronics #88-
    041, 1997). 15.00

Electronic Keychains (Tiger Electronics Asst. #88-010)
Boba Fett Keychain (#88-012, 1997). 7.00
Jabba the Hutt Keychain (#88-014, 1997) 7.00
Chewbacca Keychain (#88-015, 1997) 7.00
Luke Skywalker Keychain (X-wing) (#88-016, 1997) . . . 7.00

Second Batch (Tiger Electronics Asst. #88-020)
R2-D2 Keychain Clock (#88-021, 1997) 7.00
Star Destroyer Keychain (#88-022 1997) 7.00
Lightsaber Keychain (#88-023, 1997) 7.00
C-3PO Flashlight Keychain (#88-025, 1997) 7.00

Third Batch (Tiger Electronics Asst. #88-019)
Millennium Falcon Keychain, with sound effects
    (#88-026, 1997). 7.00
Darth Vader (head) Keychain, with sound effects
    (#88-027, 1997). 7.00
Death Star Keychain with voice record and
    playback (#88-028, 1997) 7.00
Stormtrooper (head) Keychain, with sound effects
    (#88-029, 1997) 7.00

Electronic Pens (Tiger Electronics 1997
Luke Skywalker Way Cool Sounds FX Pen (#88-051) . . 8.00

C-3PO Flashlight Keychain (Tiger Electronics 1997)

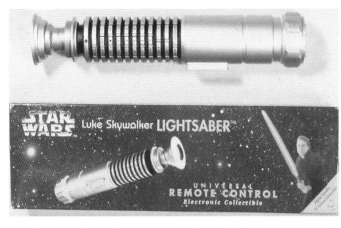

Luke Skywalker Lightsaber Remote Control (Kash 'N' Gold 1997)

Darth Vader Way Cool Sounds FX Pen (#88-052) 8.00
C-3PO Way Cool Sounds FX Pen (#88-054) 8.00
Star Wars Lightsaber FX Recording Pen (#88-055) . . . 25.00

Squawk Boxes (Tiger Electronics 1997)
C-3PO Squawk Box (#88-071) includes 3 movie
  sound effects 15.00
Darth Vader Squawk Box (#88-072) includes 3
  movie sound effects 15.00
Millennium Falcon Squawk Box (#88-073) includes
  3 movie sound effects 15.00

Other Electronic Toys (Tiger Electronics 1997)
A-Wing Calculator (#88-085) 13.00
Star Wars Lightsaber Image Projector (#88-086) 15.00
Star Wars Lazer Tag, Rebel Infantry Deluxe Pack
  (#88-094) 45.00

Electronic Toys
Electronic X-wing Flight Simulator, 30"x10"x17",
  battery powered lights, voices and sounds
  (Kenner #27847, Aug. 1997) green box 23.00
Millennium Falcon Flight Simulator (Kenner 1998) 23.00
Darth Vader 14" Electronic Figure, with removable
  helmet that reveals Anakin Skywalker face,
  says four phrases (Kenner #27729, 1998) 35.00
Electronic Power F/X Obi-Wan Kenobi vs. Darth
  Vader with eight authentic recordings for each
  figure, battery powered, J.C. Penney stores,
  Collector Series (#27661, Aug. 1997) 100.00
*Note: The Electronic Power F/X Obi-Wan Kenobi vs. Darth
  Vader was available in quantity after the 1997 Christmas
  season for $70.00.*

Audioclips
Star Wars Audioclips for IBM-PC 20.00
The Empire Strikes Back Audioclips for IBM-PC 20.00
Return of the Jedi Audioclips for IBM-PC 20.00

Clocks
R2-D2 and C-3PO Talking Alarm Clock, 9" tall
  (Bradley Time 1980) 90.00
R2-D2 and C-3PO Clock Radio (Bradley Time 1984). 100.00
R2-D2 and C-3PO 3-D Sceni-Clock, 8" tall (Bradley
  Time) 75.00
Ewok Teaching Clock, shaped like Ewok village
  with Wicket on face of clock (Kenner Preschool) . 75.00
Star Wars Wall Clock, pictures R2-D2 & C-3PO
  (Welby Elgin 1981) 65.00
The Empire Strikes Back Wall Clock, square, Darth,
  Stormtroopers & logo (Welby Elgin 1981) 65.00

Droid wall clock (Bradley) 25.00
The Empire Strikes Back wall clock (Bradley) 25.00
Portable clock/radio (Bradley 1984) 15.00
Star Wars Special Edition Clock, Drew Struzan art,
  9"x11" battery powered (1997) 40.00
The Empire Strikes Back Special Edition Clock,
  Drew Struzan art, 9"x11" battery powered (1997) . . 40.00
Return of the Jedi Special Edition Clock, Drew
  Struzan art, 9"x11" battery powered (1997) 40.00

Electronic Household Products
Luke Skywalker's Lightsaber Universal (TV) Remote Control (Kash 'N' Gold 2366, 1997) boxed . . 35.00
R2-D2 figural telephone, 12" high, 9¼" wide, 6"
  deep, battery powered with handset in leg,
  droid movements and sound effects (Kash 'N'
  Gold #2363, 1997) boxed 80.00

Mousepads 8½"x11½" (MousTrak 1995)
Darth Vader Mouse Pad (#SW-1) 12.00
Yoda Mouse Pad (#SW-2) 12.00
Millennium Falcon Mouse Pad (#SW-3) 12.00
Luke & Leia, *Return of the Jedi* Mouse Pad (#SW-4) . . 12.00
Rebel Assault Game Art Mouse Pad (#SW-5) 12.00

Giga Pets (Tiger Electronics 1997)
Yoda Giga Pet, Electronic Virtual Pet (#70-135) 7.50
Rancor Giga Pet, Electronic Virtual Pet (#70-136) 10.00
R2-D2 Giga Pet, Electronic Virtual Pet (#70-137) 7.50

Preschool
Ewok Talking Phone, 9" tall (Kenner Preschool 1984) . 70.00
Sit n' Spin (Kenner Preschool 1984) 60.00

R2-D2 Giga Pet (Tiger Electronics 1997)

FOOD COLLECTIBLES

BREAKFAST FOOD, FAST FOOD, JUNK FOOD AND PIZZA

Over the years, *Star Wars* has had promotions with each of the four major food groups — Fast, Junk, Breakfast and Pizza — not to mention a Pet Food promotion in Australia. These promotions generate a variety of collectibles, from food containers, to toys, to mail-in premiums.

BREAKFAST FOOD

Every toy collector should start off with a hearty breakfast. General Mills, who owned Kenner at the time, started promotions off with various *Star Wars* Cheerios boxes beginning in 1978. This was probably the high point of *Star Wars* food products, nutrition-wise, until the 1997 Taco Bell promotion. From then on the offers were on cereals like Boo

Berry, Count Chocula and Lucky Charms. *Star Wars* moved to Kellogg's in 1984 and C-3PO got his own cereal. Finally, in 1996 Froot Loops had its highly successful Han Solo action figure offer. Toocan Sam and R2-D2 — perfect together. The boxes are just as collectible as the premiums.

Listed prices are for complete and clean boxes. A complete box has all four top flaps, all four sides (no missing coupons) and all four bottom flaps. A box that has the top and bottom flaps opened is a "collapsed" box (but still complete). A "Flat" is a mint (usually a file copy) unused cereal box. A flat commands up to 40% more than the listed price.

If you liked a little toast with your cereal, you should have bought Wonder Bread. They offered a series of *Star Wars* trading cards in 1977. Look for them in the TRADING CARDS section.

General Mills Cereal Boxes
Cheerios, with *Star Wars* tumbler offer $35.00
Cheerios, 1978, *Star Wars* Poster in Pack, Space
    Scenes 30.00

Boo Berry, with trading card premium 25.00
Franken Berry, with trading card premium 25.00
Cocoa Puffs, with trading card premium 25.00
Chocolate Crazy Cow, with trading card premium 25.00
Strawberry Crazy Cow, with trading card premium . . . 25.00
Trading Cards, 18 different, see Trading Cards section.

Frankenberry, with sticker premium 25.00
Count Chocula with sticker premium 25.00
Trix, with sticker premium 25.00
Cocoa Puffs, with sticker premium 25.00
Lucky Charms, with sticker premium 25.00
Stickers, 16 different, each 2.00
Lucky Charms, with spaceship hang glider premium . . 25.00

Kellogg's Cereal Boxes
C-3PO Cereal (1984) with sticker trading card offer. . . 20.00
C-3PO Cereal (1984) with Mask on Back, six
    different masks of C-3PO, Chewbacca, Darth
    Vader, Luke Skywalker Stormtrooper or Yoda,
    each 30.00
    Set, 8 different C-3PO Mask boxes 200.00
C-3PO Cereal (1984) with Rebel Rocket in pack
    plus stickers 20.00
    Set, 8 different Boxes + Stickers 200.00

Froot Loops (1996) with Han Solo in Stormtrooper
    outfit mail-in offer 10.00
Apple Jacks (1996) with Dark Horse comic book
    mail-in offer 2.00

Froot Loops with Han Solo action figure offer (Kellogg's 1996)

Corn Pops (1996) with *Star Wars* video offer 2.00
Raisin Bran (1996) with *Star Wars* video offer 2.00

FAST FOOD

The 1970s and 1980s promotions of choice with fast food restaurants were glasses and plastic cups. The most famous of these promotions were the Burger King/Coke four-glass sets sold for each of the three movies. Coke also produced a number of collector plastic cups which were distributed in various fast food chains, both national and regional.

Glassware
Star Wars Promotional Glasses (4 diff. glasses:
   Luke, Han Solo, Darth and R2-D2/C-3PO,
   Burger King/Coca-Cola 1977) each $15.00
   set of 4 . . . . 60.00
The Empire Strikes Back Promotional Glasses (4
   diff. glasses: Luke, Lando, R2-D2/C-3PO and
   Darth, Burger King/Coca-Cola 1980) each 12.00
   set of 4 . . . . 50.00
Return of the Jedi Promotional Glasses (4 diff.:
   Sand barge fight scene, Jabba's palace, Ewok
   village, & Luke/Darth fighting, Burger King/
   Coca-Cola 1983) each 10.00
   set of 4 . . . . 40.00
   Plastic cups, Mass. only, each 12.50
   set of 4 . . . . 50.00

Plastic Coca-Cola Cups 1970s–80s
Star Wars numbered 20-cup set, each 10.00
   Set of 20 . . . . 175.00
Star Wars numbered 8-cup set
   Large, "7–11" or "Coke" each 5.00
   Set of 8 Large cups 30.00
   Small, "Coke" each 5.00
   Set of 8 Small cups 25.00
Star Wars unnumbered 1979 8-cup set, each 5.00
   Set of 8 "Coke" cups 30.00
Return of the Jedi 12-cup set, each 5.00
   Set of 12 "7-11" cups, large or small. 50.00

The Empire Strikes Back movie theater plastic cup
   (Coke 1980) depending on size, each 7.00

Return of the Jedi glasses (Burger King/Coke 1983)

Return of the Jedi movie theater plastic cup (Coke
   1983) depending on size, each 6.00
Star Wars Trilogy Special Edition movie theater
   plastic cup, featuring picture of AT-AT (Pepsi 1997) . 2.00

Taco Bell ran a promotion in late 1996 and early 1997 in conjunction with the release of the *Star Wars Trilogy Special Edition* films. There were a lot of neat toys to collect, along with boxes plus a wrapper and bag. The best part for me is that I get paid to show you pictures of them in this book, enjoy the tacos, and deduct the cost of the meals and toys, all while telling my wife that its not just an excuse to eat at fast food restaurants. This worked for the pizza, Pepsi and junk food just as well. Now if only a beer company would run *Star Wars* promotion...

The toys each came in a plastic bag, with a two page booklet encouraging you to "collect all seven!" They cost about a buck each, but the taco wrapper, bag or box was free.

Star Wars glasses (Burger King/Coke 1977) and The Empire Strikes Back glass (Burger King/Coke 1980)

Balancing Boba Fett toy (Taco Bell 1997)

Fast Food (Taco Bell 1996–97)
Taco Bell taco wrapper picturing C-3PO $1.00
Taco Bell taco bag picturing R2-D2 . . . . 1.00
Taco Bell taco bag picturing C-3PO 1.00

Star Wars Taco Bell food box, with movie scene 2.00
The Empire Strikes Back Taco Bell food box, with
     movie scene 2.00
Return of the Jedi Taco Bell food box, with movie
     scene 2.00

Fast Food Toys (Taco Bell 1996–97)
Millennium Falcon Gyro 3.00
R2-D2 Playset 2.50
Magic Cube, Yoda/Darth Vader 2.50
Floating Cloud City 2.50
Puzzle Cube 2.50
Balancing Boba Fett 2.00
Exploding Death Star Spinner 2.50
Under 3 years old
Yoda figure 5.00

JUNK FOOD

Pepsi had a number of promotional plastic bottles and 12-pack and 24-pack cartons available for the *Star Wars Trilogy Special Edition* movies. The cartons had an offer for three posters for $9.99 plus the order form on the back of the carton.

Lay's Potato Chips had a popular promotion for the *Star Wars Trilogy Special Edition* movies. The UPC symbol from

Spirit of Obi-Wan mail-in figure and Yoda toy (Taco Bell 1997)

two bags of chips plus $1.99 got you the Spirit of Obi-Wan action figure. It's a 3¾" blue-green semi-translucent plastic figure of Obi-Wan and came in a plastic bag in a plain white mailing box with "SKU #69736" on it. The figure does have the magic "Kenner" name on the bottom, but it has no discernable action. The main reason it gets listed with the action figures in many magazines is that the Froot Loops Han Solo in Stormtrooper mail-in, which really is an action figure, gets listed and so they think this mail-in should be too. It belongs in this section, with figures like the Taco Bell under three years old Yoda figure listed above.

The collectible value of the Pepsi cartons, or the Lay's Potato Chip bags listed below are about 90% less if they are not complete. Empty is okay, but cutouts are not, meaning that you can't have a mint bag or box and send away for the mail-in premium too.

Diet Pepsi 12-pack carton (Pepsi 1997)

Soda Containers
Diet Pepsi *Star Wars Trilogy Special Edition*
     12-pack box featuring a Stormtrooper, with
     posters offer (1996) $2.00
Mountain Dew *Star Wars Trilogy Special Edition* 12
     pack box picturing X-wing Fighters, with
     posters offer (1996) 2.00
Diet Pepsi *Star Wars Trilogy Special Edition*
     24-pack box picturing a Stormtrooper, with
     posters offer (1996) 2.00
Pepsi *Star Wars Trilogy Special Edition* 24-pack
     box picturing a C-3PO, with posters offer (1996) . . 2.00
Pepsi *Star Wars Trilogy Special Edition* 24-pack
     box picturing Yoda, with posters offer (1996) 2.00
Pepsi *Star Wars Trilogy Special Edition* 24-pack
     box picturing Darth Vader, with posters offer (1996) . 2.00
Pepsi 20 oz. plastic bottle, picturing Darth Vader 1.00
Pepsi 2-liter plastic bottle, picturing Darth Vader 1.00
Diet Pepsi 20 oz. plastic bottle, picturing C-3PO 1.00
Diet Pepsi 2-liter plastic bottle, picturing C-3PO 1.00

Chips
Lay's Potato Chip bag with "Spirit of Obi-Wan"
     figure offer, various sizes . . . . 1.00 to 2.00
Spirit of Obi-Wan translucent non-action figure, with
     mailer box 10.00
Doritos bag with 3-D Motion card premium 1.00

Star Wars Trilogy Candy Container collection (Topps 1997)

C-3PO, bagged and Chewbacca, carded (Pez 1997)

Candy

Topps Candy Boxes (1980–83)

The Empire Strikes Back figural head candy containers (Topps 1980) box with 18 containers..... 40.00
    Containers, each 2.50
    Set, including Stormtrooper, Boba Fett, Chew-
      bacca, C-3PO and Darth Vader 12.50
    Box, empty 5.00
The Empire Strikes Back figural head candy con-
tainers (Topps 1981) box with 18 containers,
    New Yoda series 40.00
    containers, each 2.50
    Set of six, Tauntaun, Bossk, Yoda, 2-1B........ 12.50
    Box, empty 5.00
Return of the Jedi figural head candy containers
(Topps 1983) box with 18 containers 50.00
    containers, six different, each................. 2.50
    Set of six, Admiral Ackbar, Darth Vader, Ewok,
      Jabba The Hutt, Sy Snootles and Wicket..... 15.00
    Box, empty 5.00

Hersheys Products, 6-pack cartons (1980s) photos on back
Boxes with large C-3PO or Chewbacca photos...... 15.00
Boxes with smaller Luke on Tauntaun, Boba Fett or
    Darth Vader photos 10.00

Star Wars Trilogy Candy Container collection and
card set, 4 head figural candy containers and
10-card set, on header card (Topps 1997) 25.00

Pez Dispensers (Asst #8633, 1997) bagged or carded
C-3PO 3.00
Chewbacca 3.00
Darth Vader 3.00
Stormtrooper 4.00
Yoda... 3.00

PIZZA

In late 1996 and early 1997, Pizza Hut sold its take-out pizzas in coloring boxes with *Star Wars* pictures promoting the *Star Wars Special Edition* movies. The boxes are 12½" square. Too bad they didn't change their company logo to read "Pizza Hutt" for the promotion and use a picture of their "founder," Jabba the Hutt, on the boxes.

Australian "Pizza Hutters" did a little better. In 1995 they got a series of four PVC figures bagged with interlocking cardboard backdrops. The series was distributed to comic shops in the United States through Diamond's Previews catalog/magazine, which is why it is listed in this book. The figures are a little smaller than the U.S. PVC figures made by Applause, and have jagged yellow bases. Incidentally, there is nothing on any of the figures, bags or backdrops which says "Australia" and all the text is in English, even if they pronounce it strangely.

Pizza Hut *Star Wars* coloring box, picturing C-3PO
    and *Millennium Falcon* (1996) $1.00
Pizza Hut *Star Wars* coloring box, picturing R2-D2
    and X-Wing fighters (1996)................... 1.00
Pizza Hut *Star Wars* coloring box, picturing
    Stormtrooper and AT-AT (1996) 1.00
Pizza Hut *Star Wars* coloring box, picturing Darth
    Vader and Star Destroyer (1996) 1.00

Australian Pizza Hut PVC figures with backdrops,
    set of four in original *Star Wars Trilogy/*
    Pizza Hut clear plastic bags (1995) 20.00
Chewbacca, bagged with backdrop............... 5.00
C-3PO, bagged with backdrop 5.00
Darth Vader, bagged with backdrop 5.00
R2-D2, bagged with backdrop................... 5.00

GAMES AND PUZZLES

GAMES

Kenner made the first *Star Wars* games, as well as a variety of jigsaw puzzles, bop bags, vans, and of course, action figures. Many of these were advertised in their various mini-catalogs that came in the boxes for the vehicles. Parker Bros. started making the games in about 1983 and continues to do so today. Kenner is now part of Hasbro as is Parker Bros.

Original Kenner Games (1977–82)
Adventures of R2-D2, board game (Kenner 1977)
    Star Wars logo. $25.00
Destroy Death Star game (Kenner 1979) *Star Wars*
    logo. 30.00
Escape From Death Star board game, 17¾"x17¾"
    playing board, four sets of playing pieces and
    R2-D2 spinner (Kenner 1979) *Star Wars* logo . . . 25.00
Hoth Ice Planet Adventure Game, with board and
    spinner (Kenner 1980) *The Empire Strikes
    Back* logo 25.00
Yoda, The Jedi Master board game (Kenner 1981)
    The Empire Strikes Back logo 25.00
Parker Bros. Games (1982–98)
Star Wars (Parker Brothers 1982) box pictures
    Luke in X-Wing gear 30.00
Wicket the Ewok (Parker Brothers 1983) *Return of
    the Jedi* logo 20.00
The Ewoks Save the Trees! (Parker Brothers 1983)
    Return of the Jedi logo. 20.00
Battle at Sarlacc's Pit (Parker Brothers 1983)
    Return of the Jedi logo. 30.00
Return of the Jedi Card Game, 3½"x4½" box,
    (Parker Brothers 1983). 10.00
Star Wars Death Star Assault Game, board, X-wing
    fighter, 20 TIE fighter pieces (Parker Bros.
    #40390, 1995) 13.00

Star Wars *Monopoly (Parker Bros. 1997)*

Star Wars Monopoly Classic Trilogy Edition (Parker
    Bros #40809, 1997) including 9 pewter figurine
    playing pieces, plastic spaceships, imperial
    currency, etc. 35.00
Ewok Card Games (several different, Parker
    Brothers 1984). 15.00

Other Games
Star Wars Card Trick (Nick Trost 1978). 10.00
Top Trumps New Spacecraft (Waddington) 15.00
Yoda, the Jedi Master magic answer fortune telling
    toy (Kenner 1981) 50.00

PUZZLES

The earliest puzzles came in blue or purple-bordered boxes. Later they were switched to black borders. Several are advertised in Kenner's mini-catalogs. They are among the

Escape From Death Star and Hoth Ice Planet Adventure Games (Kenner 1979–80)

C-3PO & R2-D2, blue box and Trash Compactor, black box,
140-piece puzzles (General Mills 1977)

earliest Kenner products, since it is fairly easy to put a *Star Wars* picture on an existing jigsaw pattern and add a box. You have to sculpt an action figure before it can go into production. Kenner jigsaw puzzles are not titled. The box contained the movie logo, the puzzle's picture and the number of pieces.

140-Piece Puzzles 14"x18" (add $5.00 for blue box)
Sand person atop Bantha $10.00
C-3PO and R2-D2 . . . . 10.00
Han Solo and Chewbacca 10.00
Jawas capture R2-D2 . . . . 10.00
Luke and Han in trash compactor 10.00
Sand person. 10.00
Stormtroopers. 10.00
500-Piece Puzzles 15"x18" (add $5.00 for blue box)
Ben Kenobi and Darth Vader dueling 12.00
Cantina Band 12.00
Luke and Leia. 12.00
Luke on Tatooine 12.00
Jawas selling Droids. 12.00
Space battle 12.00
Victory celebration 12.00
X-Wing Fighter in hanger 12.00
1,000-Piece Puzzles 21½"x27½"
Crew aboard the *Millennium Falcon* 15.00
Movie art poster, Hildebrandt Bros. art 15.00

X-Wing fighters 500-piece puzzle (Kenner 1977–79)

1,500-Piece Puzzles 27"x33"
Millennium Falcon in space. 20.00
Stormtrooper in corridor 20.00

Craft-Master (1983) *Return of the Jedi* logo
Jig-Saw Puzzles
Battle of Endor, 170 pieces 12.00
B-Wings, 170 pieces. 12.00
Ewok leaders, 170 pieces 12.00
Jabba's friends, 70 pieces. 10.00
Jabba's throne room, 70 pieces 10.00
Death Star, 70 pieces 10.00
Wicket and Friends, 3 different, each 5.00

Frame Tray Puzzles
Darth Vader Frame Tray 5.00
Gamorrean Guard Frame Tray 5.00
Jedi Characters Frame Tray 5.00

Movie Poster 1000-piece puzzle (Kenner 1977–79)

Wicket The Ewok Frame Tray puzzles
Ewoks on hang gliders Frame Tray. 5.00
Ewok Village Frame Tray 5.00
Leia and Wicket Frame Tray 5.00
R2-D2 and Wicket Frame Tray 5.00
Wicket Frame Tray 5.00
Match Blocks Puzzles
Ewoks Match Block Puzzle 10.00
Luke and Jabba Match Block Puzzle. 10.00

Jigsaw Puzzles (1995–98)
Star Wars Puzz 3D *Millennium Falcon*, 857 pieces
   (Milton Bradley #04678, 1995) 35.00
Star Wars Puzz 3D Imperial Star Destroyer, 823
   pieces (Milton Bradley #04617, 1996) 35.00
Star Wars Darth Vader 3-D Sculpture, 144 layers
   (Milton Bradley #04737, 1997) 35.00
Star Wars, A New Hope, 550 piece, 18"x24" (Milton
   Bradley #4489-1, 1996) 12.50
Star Wars, The Empire Strikes Back, 550 piece,
   18"x24" (Milton Bradley #4489-2, 1996) 12.50

Star Wars, Return of the Jedi, 550 piece, 18"x24"
(Milton Bradley #4489-3) 12.50
The Empire Strikes Back 1,500 piece jigsaw puzzle,
28¾"x36" (Springbok/Hallmark PZL9028,
#45548, 1997) 17.00
Star Wars: A New Hope 500-piece puzzles
(RoseArt #97033, 1997) 12.00
Star Wars: The Empire Strikes Back 500-piece
puzzles (RoseArt #97033, 1997) 12.00
Star Wars: Return of the Jedi 500-piece puzzles
(RoseArt #97033, 1997) 12.00
Star Wars: A New Hope Poster Illustration Puzzle,
1000 piece (RoseArt #08062, 1997) 7.50

Dark Force Rising Sourcebook *(West End Games 1993)*

ROLE PLAY GAMES

West End Games began producing role playing games in the *Star Wars* universe in 1987. This was in the middle of the dark age, when there were no more action figures produced and no new *Star Wars* novels or comics. During this period, they were the only company keeping the *Star Wars* saga alive with anything like new *Star Wars* storylines.

Role playing games have their own section in most book stores. As such, their books and boxed sets are generally available. Politicians no longer consider them satanic rituals or communist plots. They even have to compete with CCGs (Customizable Card Games) for the game fanatics' attention. Lastly, their fanatics accumulate game modules, rule books, and other items in order to (gasp!) play the games, not collect them. New and revised editions of rule books are much more useful than original editions. The consequences of this are that most of these items, even in near mint condition, are worth little more than their original price!

Boxed Games (9"x11½" boxes)
Star Warriors Role-Playing Board Game, starfighter
combat, with ship counters, game markers,
charts, dice, rules booklet, record sheets and
map (West End Games 40201, 1987) $35.00
Reprint: (West End Games 1992). 20.00
Assault on Hoth, two person board game, with terrain map, many stand-up playing pieces,
cards, dice and rule book (West End Games
40203, 1988) 35.00
Reprint: (West End Games 1992). 20.00
Battle for Endor, board game, with terrain map,
many stand-up playing pieces, cards, dice and
rulebook (West End Games 40206, 1989) 30.00
Reprint: (West End Games 1992). 20.00
Escape From the Death Star, board game, Death
Star schematic, stand-up cards, score pads,
dice and rule book (West End Games 40207
1990). 30.00
Reprint: (West End Games 1992). 20.00

Basic Game and Sourcebooks (8½"x11" hardcovers)
Star Wars, The Role-Playing Game, basic rules
book, 144 pages, 16 pages of color (West End
Games 40001, 1987) 25.00
2nd Edition (West End Games 40055, 1993) 25.00
2nd Edition, Revised and Expanded (West End
Games 40120; #268-X, 1996) 30.00
Star Wars Sourcebook, background supplement,
illustrations, descriptions and statistics, 144
pages in two-color (West End Games 40002,
#066-0, 1988) 20.00
2nd Edition (West End Games 40093, 1994) 22.00
Star Wars Movie Trilogy Sourcebook (West End
Games 40076, #198-5, 1993) 25.00
Imperial Sourcebook, background supplement
(West End Games 40002, #097-0, 1989) 20.00
TPB reissue (West End Games 40051,
#175-6, 1991) 18.00
2nd Edition (West End Games 40092; #210-8,
1994) 22.00
Rebel Alliance Sourcebook, background supple-
ment (West End Games 40007, #109-8, 1991) . . . 20.00
TPB reissue (West End Games 40054, #178-0,
1991) 18.00
2nd Edition (West End Games 40091, #209-4,
1994) 22.00
Heir to the Empire Sourcebook, 144p, from Timothy
Zahn's novel (West End Games 40068, #179-9,
1992). 18.00
Dark Force Rising Sourcebook, by Bill Slavicsek,
142p, from Timothy Zahn's novel (West End
Games 40074, #193-4, 1993) 18.00
Dark Empire Sourcebook (West End Games 40071
#194-2, 1993) 25.00
The Movie Trilogy Sourcebook (West End Games
40089, #506-9, 1997). 28.00
Han Solo and the Corporate Sector Sourcebook
(West End Games 40042, #199-3, 1993) 20.00
Shadows of the Empire Sourcebook (West End
Games 40122, 1996) 20.00
The Jedi Academy Sourcebook (West End Games
40114, #274-4, 1996) from Kevin Anderson
trilogy 22.00
Thrawn Trilogy Sourcebook (West End Games
40131, #280-9, 1996) from Timothy Zahn books. . 25.00
Truce at Bakura Sourcebook (West End Games
40085, #256-6, 1996). 22.00

Star Wars Introductory Adventure Game (West End Games 40602, #298-1, 1997) 20.00
Star Wars X-Wing Rogue Squadron Sourcebook, based on Michael A. Stackpole novels, 144pg. (West End Games 40148, 1998) TPB 25.00
Star Wars Hideouts and Strongholds Sourcebook (West End Games 40111, 1998)............. 22.00

Adventure Modules
Tatooine Manhunt (West End Games 40005, #069-5, 1988) 10.00
Strike Force: Shantipole (West End Games 40009, 1988)..................................... 10.00
Starfall (West End Games 40016, #105-5, 1989) hardcover 10.00
Battle for Golden Sun (West End Games 40017, #103-9, 1988) hardcover 10.00
Otherspace, includes full color map (West End Games 40018, #128-4, 1989) 10.00
Graveyard of Alderaan (West End Games 40019, #116-0, 1990) hardcover 10.00
Scavenger Hunt (West End Games 40020, 1989).... 10.00
Riders of the Maelstrom (West End Games 40021, 1989)..................................... 10.00
Crisis on Cloud City (West End Games 40022, 1989) . 10.00
Otherspace II: Invasion (West End Games 40028, #106-3) hardcover 10.00
Black Ice (West End Games 40030, #107-1, 1990) hardcover 10.00
The Game Chambers of Questal (West End Games 40033, #110-1, 1990) hardcover.............. 10.00
Domain of Evil (West End Games 40034, #148-9, 1991)..................................... 10.00
Isis Coordinates (West End Games 40036, #097-0, 1990) hardcover......................... 10.00
Death in the Undercity (West End Games 40037, 1990).................................... 10.00

Classic Adventures reprints, updated to second edition rules
Classic Adventures, Volume One (West End Games 40083, #261-2, 1995) reprints The Abduction of Crying Dawn Singer and The Politics of Contraband 20.00
Classic Adventures, Volume Two (West End Games #269-8, 1995) 18.00
Classic Adventures, Volume Three (West End Games #282-5, 1996) 18.00
Classic Adventures, Volume Four 18.00

Hardcovers
Bounty Hunters (West End Games #207-8, 1994).... 18.00
Live-Action Roleplaying Game (West End Games #283-3, 1996) 20.00

Softcovers 1991-98
The New Republic: Twin Stars of Kira, 96p (West End Games 40060, #191-8, 1993) 15.00
The New Republic: The Politics of Contraband, 64p (West End Games 40067, #184-5, 1992) 10.00
Planet of the Mists (West End Games 40049, #122-5, 1992) 10.00
Mission to Lianna module, 64p (West End Games 40052, #123-3, 1992)..................... 10.00
Abduction of Crying Dawn Singer (West End Games 40053, #177-2, 1992) 10.00
Heir to the Empire Accessory (West End Games #186-1, 1992) 18.00
The Last Command Accessory (West End Games 40059, #197-7, 1994)..................... 20.00

Instant Adventures (West End Games 40137, #293-0, 1996) 15.00
No Disintegrations (West End Games #296-5, 1997).. 15.00
The Black Sands of Socorro Accessory (West End Games 40154; #503-4, 1997) 18.00
Imperial Double-Cross, solo adventure (West End Games #502-6, 1997) 10.00
Secrets of the Sisar Run, 96pg. (West End Games 40155, 1997) Bros. Hildebrandt cover 12.00
Star Wars Fantastic Technology Personal Gear Sourcebook (West End Games #40158, 1997)... 15.00
Star Wars Adventure Journals #1–#14, 6"x9" (West End Games 41001–14, #400-3–#413-5, 1994–97) articles and fiction, each............ 12.00
Best of *Star Wars* Adventure Journal, Vol. 1, Issue #1 to #4, 128p (West End Games 40129, 1996).. 20.00
Aliens Compendium (West End Games 40166, 1998). 25.00

Star Wars: A New Hope, Galaxy Guide #1
(West End Games 1990s)

Galaxy Guide Books (8½"x11" Trade Paperbacks)
Galaxy Guide 1: A New Hope (West End Games #077-6, 1989) 13.00
  2nd Printing (West End Games 40038, #125-X, 1991)................................... 12.00
  2nd Edition (West End Games 40124, #265-5, 1995)................................... 12.00
Galaxy Guide 2: Yavin and Bespin (West End Games 40023, #126-8, 1989) 13.00
  2nd Edition: (West End Games 40119, #262-0, 1995)................................... 12.00
Galaxy Guide 3: *The Empire Strikes Back* (West End Games 40039, #127-6, 1989) 13.00
  2nd Edition: (West End Games 40094, 1995).... 12.00
Galaxy Guide 4: Alien Races (West End Games 40041, #137-3, 1989)..................... 13.00
  2nd Edition: 96p (West End Games 40094, 1994)................................... 12.00

Galaxy Guide 5: *Return of the Jedi* (West End
  Games 40040 #140-3, 1990) 13.00
  2nd Edition (West End Games 40126, #267-1,
  1995) 15.00
Galaxy Guide 6: Tramp Freighters (West End
  Games 40027, #146-2, 1991) 13.00
  2nd Edition (West End Games 40095, 1995) 15.00
Galaxy Guide 7: Mos Eisley (West End Games
  40069, 1992) 13.00
Galaxy Guide 8: Scouts (West End Games 40061,
  1993) 13.00
Galaxy Guide 9: Fragments From The Rim, 96p
  (West End Games 40063, 1993) 13.00
Galaxy Guide 10: Bounty Hunters (West End
  Games 40073, 1994) 13.00
Galaxy Guide 11: Criminal Organizations (West End
  Games 40075, 1995) 13.00
Galaxy Guide 12: Aliens, Enemies and Allies (West
  End Games 40087, 1995) 13.00

One Player Games
Scoundrel's Luck, one player game (West End
  Games 40102, #112-8, 1990) 13.00
Jedi's Honor, one player game (West End Games
  40103, #111-X, 1990) hardcover 13.00

Other Guide Books (8½"x11" Trade Paperbacks)
Cracken's Rebel Field Guide (West End Games
  40046, #118-7, 1991) 13.00
Death Star Technical Companion (West End Games
  40008, #120-9, 1991) 15.00
Planets of the Galaxy, Volume One (West End
  Games 40050, 1991) 13.00
The New Republic: Planets of the Galaxy, Volume
  Two (West End Games 40057, #180-2, 1992) . . . 13.00
Planets of the Galaxy, Volume Three, 80p (West
  End Games 40072, #169-9, 1992) 15.00
Planets Collection (West End Games 40100,
  #222-1, 1994) hardcover, collects three above . . . 25.00

Shadows of the Empire: Planets Collection (West
  End Games 40134, 1996) 15.00
The New Republic: Wanted by Cracken (West End
  Games 40062, #189-6, 1993) hardcover 15.00
Flashpoint! Brak Sector by Sterling Hersey (West
  End Games 40077, #253-1, 1995) 15.00
Rebel Specforce Handbook (West End Games
  40113 #501-8, 1997) 18.00
Galladinium's Fantastic Technology (West End
  Games #215-9, 1995) 15.00
Platt's Starport Guide (West End Games 40107,
  #224-8, 1995) 25.00
Creatures of the Galaxy (West End Games 40080,
  #221-3, 1994) hardcover 15.00
Classic Campaigns (West End Games #251-5, 1994) . 15.00
Operation: Elrood, 96pg. (West End Games 40132,
  1996) 15.00
Pirates & Privateers (West End Games #294-9, 1996) 18.00
Star Wars Pirates & Privateers Far Orbit Campaign
  (West End Games 40029, 1998) 25.00
Wretched Hives of Scum & Villainy (West End
  Games #500-X, 1997) 18.00
Cracken's Rebel Operatives, 96pg. (West End
  Games 40084 #218-3, 1994) 15.00
Star Wars Miniatures Battle (West End Games
  40044, #144-6, 1994) 18.00
Mos Eisley (West End Games #187-8, 1993) 12.00
Droids (West End Games 40116, #299-X, 1997) 15.00
Stock Ships (West End Games #244-2, 1995) 18.00
Supernova (West End Games #195-0, 1993) 15.00
Goroth: Slave of the Empire (West End Games
  40098, #250-7, 1994) 15.00
The Kathol Outback (West End Games #270-1, 1996) . . 15.00
The Kathol Rift (The Dark Stryder Campaign) (West
  End Games 40121; #273-6, 1996) 15.00
Heroes & Rogues (West End Games 40086,
  #258-2, 1995) 18.00
Cracken's Threat Dossier, 144pg. (West End
  Games 40139; #504-2, 1997) 20.00

Flashpoint! Brak Sector *(West End Games 1995)*

Campaign Pack (West End Games 1990s)

Alliance Intelligence Reports (West End Games
  40109, #260-4, 1995)................... 15.00
Shadows Underworld (West End Games #290-6,
  1997)................................ 15.00
Players Guide to Tapani (40155, 1997)........... 12.00
Live-Action Adventures (West End Games #286-8,
  1996)................................ 15.00
Live-Action Adventures Tool Kit (West End Games
  40152, 1998)......................... 15.00
Starfighter Battle Book (West End Games #092-X,
  1990)................................ 15.00
Imperial Entanglements, 96p (West End Games
  40127, #127-X, 1996) 15.00

Supplements
Star Wars Rules Companion, 80 pages (West End
  Games 40043, 1989)................... 15.00
Campaign Pack, includes floorplans and screen
  (West End Games 1988) 15.00
Lightsaber Dueling Pack, includes two flip books
  and score cards (West End Games #088-1, 1988). 12.00
Starfighter Battle Pack, includes two flip books and
  score cards (1989)..................... 15.00
Gamemaster Kit (West End Games 40048, 1991).... 12.00
Gamemaster Handbook, 128p (West End Games
  40065, #185-3, 1993).................. 18.00
Gamemaster Screen, 2nd edition, with 32-page
  booklet (West End Games 40064, #183-7, 1992). 10.00
Star Wars Miniatures Battles Companion (West End
  Games 40070, 1994)................... 15.00
Expanded Gamemaster Screen, revised (West End
  Games 40135; #288-4, 1996) 10.00

Mos Eisley boxed set (West End Games 40212,
  #295-7, 1997) hardcover 35.00

GAMING MINIATURES
West End Games (1988–97)

West End Games produced 25mm lead miniature figures to accompany its games starting in 1988. They have produced a lot of them, but they are not heavily collected by non-
gamers. They were, however, popular with modelers, who
paint and display them. There are 14 boxed sets, usually containing 10 figures, which were produced from 1988 to 1991.
All of the figures came with statistics for use with West End's
role playing games. Bob Charrette and Julie Guthrie were
credited as sculptors on the first ten packs, while Jonathan
Woods sculpted the last four. In 1993, West End Games began
producing three-figure blister packs of figures. They have
made over fifty different packs to date, plus several sets of
ships.

Miniatures: Figures (25mm figures in 4"x8" boxes)
Heroes of the Rebellion, 10 figures (West End
  Games 40301, #074-1, 1988).............. $25.00
Imperial Forces, 10 figures (West End Games
  40302, #075-X, 1988) 20.00
Bounty Hunters, 10 figures (West End Games
  40303, #076-8, 1988).................. 25.00
A New Hope, 10 figures (West End Games 40304,
  #077-6, 1988) 20.00
The Empire Strikes Back, 10 figures (West End
  Games 40305, #130-6, 1989) 20.00
Return of the Jedi, 10 figures (West End Games
  40306, 134-9 1989) 20.00
Stormtroopers, 10 figures (West End Games 40307,
  #131-4, 1989) 18.00

*The Empire Strikes Back and Heroes of the Rebellion
25mm figure sets (West End Games 1988–89)*

Rebel Characters, 10 figures (West End Games
  40308, #132-2, 1989)................... 18.00
Mos Eisley Cantina, 10 figures (West End Games
  40309, #133-0, 1989).................. 20.00
Jabba's Palace, 8 figures (West End Games 40310,
  #138-1, 1989) 20.00
Rancor Pit, beast keeper and Rancor, in 5 pieces
  (West End Games 40311, #139-X, 1990) 20.00
Rebel Troopers, 10 figures (West End Games
  40312, #141-1, 1990).................. 18.00
Imperial Troops, 8 figures and one laser cannon
  (West End Games #40313, #142-X, 1991) 18.00
Zero-G Assault Troopers, 8 figures (West End
  Games 40314, #142-X, 1992) 18.00

25mm pewter, 3-figure blister packs
Heroes 1 (40401, 1993) Luke, R2-D2 & C-3PO....... 9.00
Heroes 2 (40402, 1993) Han, Chewbacca and Leia ... 9.00
Stormtroopers 1 (40403, 1993)................. 5.00
Stormtroopers 2 (40404, 1993)................. 5.00
Rebel Troopers 1 (40405, 1993) 5.00
Rebel Troopers 2 (40406, 1993) 5.00
Users of the Force (40407, 1993) 5.00
Pilots and Gunners (40408, 1993) 5.00
Stormtroopers 3 (40409, 1993)................. 5.00
Imperial Crew with Heavy Blaster (40410, 1993)...... 5.00
Imperial Army Troopers 1 (40411, 1993) 5.00
Imperial Navy Troopers (40412, 1993) 5.00
Rebel Troopers 3 (40413, 1993) 5.00
Rebel Commandos 1 (40414, 1993) 5.00
Imperial Officers (40415, 1993) 5.00
Stormtroopers 4 (40416, 1993)................. 5.00
Rebel Commandos 2 (40417, 1993) 5.00
Imperial Army Troopers 2 (40418, 1993) 5.00
Imperial Navy Troopers 2 (40419, 1993) 5.00
Bounty Hunters 1 (40420, 1993) 5.00
Rebel Troopers 4 (40421, 1993) 5.00
Bounty Hunters 2 (40422, 1993) 5.00
Droids (40423, 1993) 5.00
Denizens of Cloud City (40424, 1993) 5.00
The Emperor (40425, 1993) 5.00

Stormtroopers 1 and Imperial Speeder Bike 25mm pewter blister packs (West End Games 1993)

Bounty Hunters #3 (40426, 1993) 5.00
Denizens of Tatooine (40427, 1993) 6.00
Jedi Knights (40428, 1993) 5.00
Aliens of the Galaxy #1 (40429, 1993) 5.00
Sandtroopers (40430, 1993) 5.00
Snowtroopers (40431, 1993). 5.00
Hoth Rebels (40432, 1993). 5.00
Scout Troopers (40433, 1994) 6.00
Rebel Operatives (40434, 1994) 6.00
Wookiees (40435, 1994). 6.00
Mon Calamari (40436, 1994) 6.00
Heir to the Empire Villains (40437, 1994) 6.00
Ewoks (40438, 1994) 6.00
Noghri (40439, 1994) 6.00
Luke, Leia and Vader (40440, 1995) 6.00
Zero-G Troopers (40441, 1995) 6.00
Encounter on Hoth (40442, 1995). 6.00
Aliens of the Galaxy 2 (40443, 1995) 6.00
Jabba the Hutt (40444, 1996) 1 figure. 6.00
Jabba's Servants: Bib Fortuna, Ooola and Rancor
    Keeper (40445, 1996) 6.00
Dark Stryder 1 (40446, 1996) 6.00
Dark Stryder 2 (40447, 1996) 6.00
Pirates (40448, 1996). 6.00
Mos Eisley (40449, 1996). 6.00
Gamorrean Guards (40450, 1996) 6.00
Mos Eisley Cantina Aliens (40451, 1996) 6.00
Dark Stryder 3 (40452, 1996) 6.00
Aliens of the Galaxy 3 (40453, 1996) 6.00
Mos Eisley Cantina Aliens 2 (40454, 1996) 6.00
Imperial Troop 12-pack (50455, 1997). 20.00
Rebel Troop 12-pack (50456, 1997) 20.00

Ships/Vehicles
Landspeeder (40501, 1994) 6.00
Imperial Speeder Bikes (40502, 1994) 6.00
Rebel Speeder Bikes (40503, 1994) 9.00
Storm Skimmer (40504, 1994) 9.00
AT-PT (40505, 1994) 9.00
Snowspeeder (40506, 1994). 9.00
Bantha with Rider (40507, 1995) 2-pack 9.00
Tauntaun Patrol (40508, 1996) 10.00

Miniatures Battles (Boxed)
Star Wars Miniatures Battle (West End Games
    40044, #264-7, 1995). 35.00

Star Wars Miniatures Rules, 2nd Edition (West End
    Games 40090, 1994) 18.00
Star Wars Miniatures Battle, Starter Set (West End
    Games 40210, 1995) 12 miniatures 35.00
    2nd Edition (West End Games 1996) 35.00
Vehicles Starter Set, with Rebel Snowspeeder, 2
    speeder bikes and book (West End Games
    40211, #285-X, 1996) 35.00
The DarkStryder Campaign, books, cards, poster
    (West End Games 40209, #254-X, 1995) 30.00
Darkstryder Deluxe Campaign Pack, boxed set,
    includes two 96pg sourcebooks, Timothy Zahn
    story, cards, poster and three supplements
    (West End Games 40220, 1998) 39.00
Darkstryder: Endgame (West End Games 40112,
    #287-6, 1996) 18.00
Lords of the Expanse, books, guides, maps (West
    End Games 40215 #297-3, 1997) 30.00

CUSTOMIZABLE CARD GAMES

Customizable Card Games (CCGs) are one of the 1990s hottest items. There are many players around and lots of new product. Many of the playing cards are quite valuable. The primary reasons for this are scarcity and play value in the game. Scarcity is always a factor in value, but the other factor is usually some kind of intrinsic desirability or charisma in the item. The simple truth is that game cards are not exactly great art, and even if they were great art, too much of the card is taken up by the game text for one to appreciate the art.

As long as the game is played, scarce cards will be valuable. When the world moves on to the next game, they may not be quite so valuable. But then, as Dennis Miller says, that's just my opinion, I could be wrong.

Decipher has the license for *Star Wars* (and *Star Trek*) CCGs. They have produced a lot of games in the last few years and plan for more in 1998. The rarity information is based on their own website (www.decipher.com). Only rare cards are listed and priced individually.

Key to Rarity:
(R) = Rare
(R1) = Rare (one card per sheet)
(R2) = Rare (two cards per sheet)

PREMIERE SET

This initial card set is based on characters and events from the first *Star Wars* movie. It was introduced in December 1995 and was long awaited by Customizable Card Game enthusiasts. It was available in 60-card starter decks, and there are 324 cards in all, divided between light and dark sides. The game is a struggle between the light and dark sides. Each player wields a 60-card deck, either light or dark and the object is to reduce your opponents original force of 60, to zero.

STAR WARS LIMITED

Complete Set: 324 cards. $600.00
Starter Box: 10 starter decks. 110.00
Starter Deck: 60 cards 11.00
Booster Box: 36 packs 140.00
Booster Pack: 15 cards. 4.00

Common Card 0.15–0.40
Uncommon Card 1.00–2.50

RARE CARD CHECKLIST

Admiral Motti (R2) Dark $4.00
Affect Mind (R1) Light 5.00
Alderaan (R1) Dark 3.50
Assault Rifle (R2) Dark 3.00
Beggar (R1) Light 5.50
Biggs Darklighter (R2) Light . . . 5.00
Black 2 (R1) Dark 8.00
Boring Conversation Anyway
    (R1) Dark 4.50
C-3PO [See-Threepio] (R1)
    Light 20.00
Cantina Brawl (R1) Light 4.50
Charming To The Last (R2) Dark 3.00
Dark Collaboration (R1) Dark . . 6.00
Dark Jedi Presence (R1) Dark . 5.50
Darth Vader (R1) Dark 50.00
Death Star Plans (R1) Light . . . 5.50
Demotion (R2) Light 2.50
Devastator (R1) Dark 15.00
Dice Ibegon (R2) Light 2.50
Disarmed (R1) Dark 5.00
Disarmed (R1) Light 5.00
Djas Puhr (R2) Dark 2.50
Don't Get Cocky (R1) Light 5.00
Dr. Evazan (R2) Dark 2.50
DS-61-3 (R1) Dark 9.00
Dutch (R1) Light 8.00
Expand The Empire (R1) Dark . 4.50
Fear Will Keep Them In Line
    (R2) Dark 2.50
5D6-RA-7 [Fivedesix] (R1) Dark 5.00
Full Throttle (R2) Light 2.50
Garindan (R2) Dark 2.50
General Tagge (R2) Dark 4.00
Gift Of The Mentor (R1) Light . . 5.00
Gold 1 (R2) Light 3.50
Gold 5 (R2) Light 3.50
Grand Moff Tarkin (R1) Dark . . 20.00
Han Seeker (R2) Dark 2.00

Han Solo (R1) Light 40.00
Han's Heavy Blaster Pistol
    (R2) Light 3.00
Help Me Obi-Wan Kenobi
    (R1) Light 4.50
I Find Your Lack Of Faith Disturb-
    ing (R1) Dark 5.50
I Have You Now (R2) Dark 2.50
Into the Garbage Chute, Flyboy
    (R2) Light 3.00
Jedi Presence (R1) Light 5.50
Juri Juice (R2) Dark 2.50
K'lor'slug (R1) Light 6.00
Kal'Falnl C'ndros (R1) Light . . 6.00
Kessel Run (R2) Light 3.00
Kitik Keed'kak (R1) Dark 7.50
Krayt Dragon Howl (R1) Light . . 5.50
Labria (R2) Dark 2.50
Lateral Damage (R2) Dark 2.50
Leesub Sirln (R2) Light 2.50
Leia Organa (R1) Light 35.00
Light Repeating Blaster Rifle
    (R1) Dark 5.50
Lightsaber Proficiency (R1) Light 6.00
Local Trouble (R1) Dark 5.00
Lone Pilot (R2) Dark 2.50
Lone Warrior (R2) Dark 2.50
Look Sir, Droids (R1) Dark 5.00
Luke Seeker (R2) Dark 2.00
Luke Skywalker (R1) Light . . . 40.00
Mantellian Savrip (R2) Light . . 2.50
Millennium Falcon (R1) Light . . 30.00
Molator (R1) Dark 5.00
Moment of Triumph (R2) Dark . . 2.00
Move Along... (R1) Light 4.50
Myo (R2) Dark 2.50
Nevar Yalnal (R2) Dark 2.50
Noble Sacrifice (R2) Light 2.50
Obi-Wan Kenobi (R1) Light . . . 40.00

Obi-Wan's Cape (R1) Light 7.00
Obi-Wan's Lightsaber (R1)
    Light 10.00
On The Edge (R2) Light 2.50
Organa's Ceremonial Necklace
    (R1) Dark 4.50
Our Most Desperate Hour
    (R1) Light 4.50
Physical Choke (R1) Dark 5.00
Presence Of The Force (R1)
    Dark 5.00
Rebel Planners (R2) Light 2.50
Red 3 (R2) Light 2.50
Red Leader (R1) Light 9.00
Revolution (R1) Light 6.00
Sandcrawler (R2) Dark 2.50
Sandcrawler (R2) Light 2.50
Send A Detachment Down
    (R1) Dark 4.50
Skywalkers (R1) Light 5.00
Solo Han (R2) Light 2.50
Tactical Re-Call (R2) Dark 2.50
Tagge Seeker (R2) Light 2.50
Tarkin Seeker (R2) Light 2.50
Tatooine: Cantina (R2) Dark . . . 2.50
Tatooine: Cantina (R2) Light . . . 2.50

Tatooine: Obi-Wan's Hut (R1)
    Light 6.50
Thank The Maker (R2) Light . . . 2.50
The Circle Is Now Complete
    (R1) Dark 5.50
The Force Is Strong With This
    One (R2) Light 2.50
Tonnika Sisters (R1) Dark 7.00
Turbolaser Battery (R2) Dark . . 2.50
Utinni! (R1) Dark 4.50
Utinni! (R1) Light 4.50
Vader's Custom TIE (R1) Dark 15.00
Vader's Eye (R1) Dark 8.00
Vader's Lightsaber (R1) Dark . 12.00
Warrior's Courage (R2) Light . . 2.50
We're All Gonna Be A Lot
    Thinner! (R1) Dark 5.00
WED-9-M1 'Bantha' Droid
    (R2) Light 2.50
WED15-1662 'Treadwell' Droid
    (R2) Dark 2.50
Yavin 4: Massassi Throne Room
    (R1) Light 5.00
Your Powers Are Weak, Old Man
    (R1) Dark 5.00

STAR WARS UNLIMITED
Decipher Inc. (1996–98)

Complete Set: 324 cards $400.00
Starter Box: 5 starter decks 85.00
Starter Deck: 120 cards 15.00
Starter Deck: 90 cards 9.50
Booster Box 75.00
Booster Pack: 15 cards 3.00
Star Wars Unlimited Edition Starter Display, 12
    decks and display 114.00
Star Wars Unlimited Edition Booster Display, 36
    packs and display 108.00
Rare and Uncommon cards are worth about 75% of
    the same card in the "Limited Series."

Premiere Set: four light cards and four dark cards (Decipher 1995)

A New Hope *Expansion Set, box (Decipher 1996)*

A NEW HOPE

This initial 162-card limited edition expansion set was introduced in July 1996 and brought Chewbacca and R2-D2 into the game, along with new varieties of cards. The new varieties are creatures, epic events and mobile location cards. Like the original series, it's sold in packs of 15 cards. An unlimited edition is scheduled for summer 1998 release.

A NEW HOPE

Complete Set: 162 cards.	$200.00
Booster Box: 36 pack	95.00
Booster Pack: 15 cards.	3.00
Star Wars: A New Hope Booster Display, 36 packs and display	110.00

RARE CARD CHECKLIST

Attack Run (R2) Light	$5.00	Luke's Cape (R1) Light	6.00
Besieged (R2) Dark	3.00	Magnetic Suction Tube (R2)	
Bowcaster (R2) Light	4.00	Dark	3.00
Brainiac (R1) Light.	10.00	Magnetic Suction Tube (R2)	
Cell 2187 (R1) Light.	5.00	Light	3.00
Chewbacca (R2) Light	20.00	Maneuver Check (R2) Dark . . .	3.00
Clak'dor VII (R2) Light	4.00	Motti Seeker (R2) Light	3.00
Commence Primary Ignition		R2-D2 (Artoo-Detoo) (R2)	
(R2) Dark.	6.00	Light	15.00
Commence Recharging (R2)		R3-T6 (Arthree-Teesix) (R1)	
Light	5.00	Dark	6.00
Conquest (R1) Dark.	12.50	Red 2 (R1) Light	7.50
Corellia (R1) Light	5.00	Red 5 (R1) Light	12.00
Dannik Jerriko (R1) Dark	6.00	Retract The Bridge (R1) Dark. .	5.00
Dark Waters (R2) Dark	4.00	Sandcrawler: Droid Junkheap	
Death Star (R2) Dark	15.00	(R1) Dark	5.00
Death Star Tractor Beam (R2)		Sandcrawler: Loading Bay	
Dark	5.00	(R1) Light	5.00
Death Star: Trench (R2) Light .	5.00	Spice Mines Of Kessel (R1)	
Dejarik Hologameboard (R1)		Dark	5.00
Light	5.00	Superlaser (R2) Dark.	5.00
Dianoga (R2) Dark.	4.00	SW-4 Ion Cannon (R2) Light . .	4.00
Double Agent (R2) Light	4.00	Tantive IV (R1) Light	12.00
DS-61-4 (R2) Dark.	4.00	Tatooine: Bluffs (R1) Dark	5.00
Greedo (R1) Dark	10.00	They're On Dantooine (R1)	
Hem Dazon (R1) Dark	5.00	Light	5.00
Hunchback (R1) Light	5.00	Trooper Davin Felth (R2) Dark .	4.00
Hypo (R1) Light	5.00	Tzizvvt (R2) Light.	3.50
I'm On The Leader (R1) Dark..	5.00	U-3PO (Yoo-Threepio) (R1)	
Imperial Holotable (R1) Dark . .	5.00	Dark	6.00
IT-O (Eyetee-Oh) (R1) Dark...	5.00	Wedge Antilles (R1) Light . . .	15.00
Kiffex (R1) Dark.	5.00	Wookiee Roar (R1) Light	5.00
Leia Seeker (R2) Dark	2.50	You're All Clear Kid! (R1) Light.	5.00
Let The Wookiee Win (R1)			
Light	5.00		

THE EMPIRE STRIKES BACK: HOTH EXPANSION SET

This limited edition expansion set is based on the second movie and was launched in November 1996. AT-ATs and Wampas are added to the *Star Wars* CCG Universe. An unlimited edition is projected for summer 1998 release.

THE EMPIRE STRIKES BACK: HOTH

Complete Set: 162 cards.	$200.00
Booster Box: 36 packs	80.00
Booster Pack: 15 cards.	3.00
The Empire Strikes Back: Hoth Limited CCG Booster Display 36 packs and display	108.00

RARE CARD CHECKLIST

Admiral Ozzel (R1) Dark	$8.00	R-3PO (Ar-Threepio) (R2)	
Anakin's Lightsaber (R1) Light	12.00	Light	5.00
Artillery Remote (R2) Light. . . .	3.00	R-3PO (Ar-Threepio) (R2) Light	
Bacta Tank (R2) Light	4.00	**corrected picture**.	6.00
Blizzard 1 (R1) Dark	10.00	Responsibility Of Command	
Blizzard 2 (R2) Dark	6.00	(R1) Dark	5.00
Blizzard Scout 1 (R1) Dark. . .	10.00	Rogue 1 (R1) Light	10.00
Captain Piett (R2) Dark	5.00	Rogue 2 (R2) Light	5.00
Collapsing Corridor (R2) Dark .	4.00	Rogue 3 (R1) Light	8.50
Commander Luke Skywalker		Rug Hug (R1) Light	6.00
(R1) Light	30.00	Scruffy-Looking Nerf Herder	
Concussion Grenade (R1) Light	6.00	(R2) Dark	4.00
Dack Ralter (R2) Light	3.50	Stalker (R1) Dark.	15.00
Dark Dissension (R1) Light . . .	5.00	Surface Defense Cannon (R2)	
Death Mark (R1) Dark	5.00	Light	3.50
Debris Zone (R2) Dark.	3.00	Tactical Support (R2) Dark. . . .	3.00
Disarming Creature (R1) Light .	5.00	Target The Main Generator	
Echo Base Operations (R2)		(R2) Dark	4.00
Light	4.00	The First Transport Is Away!	
Frozen Dinner (R1) Dark	5.00	(R1) Light	6.00
Furry Fury (R2) Dark	4.00	This Is Just Wrong (R1) Dark..	5.00
General Carlist Rieekan (R2)		Trample (R1) Dark.	5.00
Light	4.00	2-1B (Too-Onebee) (R1) Light..	6.00
General Veers (R1) Dark	10.00	Tyrant (R1) Dark	15.00
High Anxiety (R1) Dark	5.00	Wampa (R2) Dark	4.50
Hoth: Wampa Cave (R2) Dark .	4.00	Weapon Malfunction (R1) Dark	5.00
I Thought They Smelled Bad		Wes Janson (R2) Light	4.00
On The Outside (R1) Light	5.00	Who's Scruffy-Looking? (R1)	
Image of the Dark Lord (R2)		Light	5.00
Dark	3.50	Yaggle Gakkle (R2) Dark	3.50
K-3PO (Kay-Threepio) (R1)		You Have Failed Me For The	
Light	6.00	Last Time (R1) Light	6.00
Major Bren Derlin (R2) Light . .	3.50	You Will Go To The Dagobah	
Meteor Impact? (R1) Dark	5.00	System (R1) Light.	6.00
Mournful Roar (R1) Dark	5.00	Zev Senesca (R2) Light	4.00
Planet Defender Ion Cannon			
(R2) Light	4.00		

The Empire Strikes Back: *Hoth Expansion Set, box (Decipher 1996)*

Hoth Expansion Set, two cards (Decipher 1996)

DAGOBAH

Another expansion set, Dagobah, was introduced in April 1997.This third limited edition expansion set was introduced in April 1997. It is the first set to be sold in packs of 9 cards, rather than 15 and boxes of 60 packs, rather than 36. Both ratios yield the same 540 cards per box. An unlimited edition is projected for summer 1998 release.

Complete Set: 180 cards. $200.00
Booster Box: 60 packs 140.00
Booster Pack: 9 cards (inc. 1 rare) 2.50
Star Wars Dagobah Booster Display, 60 packs and
   display. 150.00

RARE CARD CHECKLIST

Asteroids Do Not Concern Me		IG-2000 (R) Dark.	8.00
(R) Light	$4.00	IG-88 (R) Dark.	12.00
At Peace (R) Light	4.00	IG-88's Neural Inhibitor (R) Dark	5.00
Avenger (R) Dark.	12.00	IG-88's Pulse Cannon (R) Dark	5.00
Bad Feeling Have I (R) Dark . .	5.00	It Is The Future You See (R)	
Bombing Run (R) Dark.	5.00	Light	5.00
Bossk (R) Dark	10.00	Jedi Levitation (R) Light	4.50
Bossk's Mortar Gun (R) Dark . .	5.00	Landing Claw (R) Light	5.00
Broken Concentration (R) Dark	4.00	Lando System? (R) Dark	4.00
Captain Needa (R) Dark	6.00	Lieutenant Suba (R) Dark	5.00
Corrosive Damage (R) Dark. . . .	4.00	Light Maneuvers (R) Light	3.00
Dagobah: Bog Clearing (R) Light	4.50	Location, Location, Location	
Dagobah: Cave (R) Dark	5.00	(R) Dark	4.00
Dagobah: Yoda's Hut (R) Light. .	6.00	Lost In Space (R) Dark	4.00
Dengar (R) Dark	8.00	Luke's Backpack (R) Light	5.00
Dengar's Blaster Carbine (R)		Mist Hunter (R) Dark	7.00
Dark	5.00	Much Anger In Him (R) Dark . .	3.50
Descent Into The Dark (R) Light	4.00	No Disintegrations! (R) Light . .	4.00
Dragonsnake (R) Dark.	4.00	Obi-Wan's Apparition (R) Light .	5.00
Effective Repairs (R) Light	4.00	Order To Engage (R) Light. . . .	4.00
Egregious Pilot Error (R) Light .	4.00	Polarized Negative Power	
Executor (R) Dark	28.00	Coupling (R) Light.	3.50
Executor: Holotheatre (R) Dark	4.00	Punishing One (R) Dark.	7.00
Executor: Meditation Chamber		Raithal (R) Light.	4.00
(R) Dark	5.00	Reflection (R) Light	5.00
Failure At The Cave (R) Dark. .	4.00	Report To Lord Vader (R) Light	5.00
Field Promotion (R) Dark	5.00	Res Luk Ra'auf (R) Dark	4.50
Flagship (R) Dark	5.00	Rycar's Run (R) Light	4.00
4-LOM (R) Dark	6.50	Size Matters Not (R) Light	4.50
4-LOM's Concussion Rifle (R)		Smuggler's Blues (R) Light	4.00
Dark	5.00	Son of Skywalker (R) Light. . .	28.00
Frustration (R) Dark.	3.50	Space Slug (R) Light	4.00
Han's Toolkit (R) Light	4.00	Stone Pile (R) Light	4.00
Hiding In The Garbage (R) Light	4.00	The Dark Path (R) Dark	4.00
Hound's Tooth (R) Dark	7.00	The Professor (R) Light.	4.00
I Have A Bad Feeling About		This Is More Like It (R) Light . .	4.00
This (R) Light	4.00	This Is No Cave (R) Light.	4.00
I Want That Ship (R) Dark	4.50	Through The Force Things You	

Will See (R) Light	4.00	WHAAAAAAAAAOOOOW!	
Tight Squeeze (R) Light	3.00	(R) Light	4.00
Unexpected Interruption (R)		What Is Thy Bidding, My Master?	
Dark	4.00	(R) Light	4.00
Visage Of The Emperor (R) Dark	5.00	Yoda (R) Light	35.00
We Can Still Outmaneuver		Yoda's Gimer Stick (R) Light . .	6.00
Them (R) Light	4.00	Yoda, You Seek Yoda (R) Light	5.00
We Don't Need Their Scum		Zuckuss (R) Dark.	8.00
(R) Light	4.00	Zuckuss' Snare Rifle (R) Dark .	5.00

CLOUD CITY

The Cloud City expansion set appeared in November 1997 and included 180 cards. It introduced bounty hunting and carbon freezing to the game.

Complete Set: 180 cards. $175.00
Booster Box: 60 packs 125.00
Booster Pack: 9 cards (inc. 1 rare) 2.50
Star Wars Cloud City Booster Display, 60 packs and
   display. 150.00

RARE CARD CHECKLIST

Advantage (R) Light	$4.00	I Don't Need Their Scum, Either	
Aiiii! Aaa! Agggggggggg! (R)		(R) Light	4.00
Dark.	4.00	I Had No Choice (R) Dark	4.00
All My Urchins (R) Light	4.00	Impressive, Most Impressive	
All Too Easy (R) Dark	4.00	(R) Light	4.00
Ambush (R) Light.	4.00	Interrogation Array (R) Dark . . .	4.00
Artoo, Come Back At Once! (R)		Into The Ventilation Shaft, Lefty	
Light.	4.00	(R) Light	4.00
Atmospheric Assault (R) Dark .	4.50	Lando Calrissian (R) Dark . . .	20.00
Beldon's Eye (R) Light	4.00	Lando Calrissian (R) Light . . .	20.00
Bionic Hand (R) Light.	5.00	Leia Of Alderaan (R) Light	6.00
Boba Fett (R) Dark.	30.00	Lieutenant Sheckil (R) Dark . .	5.00
Boba Fett's Blaster Rifle (R) Dark	8.00	Lobot (R) Light.	10.00
Brief Loss Of Control (R) Dark .	4.00	Luke's Blaster Pistol (R) Light .	6.50
Bright Hope (R) Light.	5.00	Mandalorian Armor (R) Dark . .	5.00
Captain Bewil (R) Dark	5.00	Mostly Armless (R) Dark	4.00
Captain Han Solo (R) Light . .	28.00	NOOOOOOOOOOOO! (R) Light	4.00
Chief Retwin (R) Dark	5.00	Obsidian 7 (R) Dark.	7.00
Cloud City: Dining Room (R)		Obsidian 8 (R) Dark.	7.00
Dark.	5.00	Off The Edge (R) Light.	4.00
Cloud City: Guest Quarters		Old Pirates (R) Light	4.00
(R) Light	5.00	Point Man (R) Dark	4.00
Courage Of A Skywalker (R)		Princess Leia (R) Light.	25.00
Light	4.00	Protector (R) Light	4.00
Dark Approach (R) Light	4.00	Punch It! (R) Light	4.00
Dark Deal (R) Dark	4.00	Redemption (R) Light.	10.00
Despair (R) Dark	4.00	Release Your Anger (R) Dark. .	4.00
Dismantle On Sight (R) Light . .	4.00	Rendezvous Point On Tatooine	
E-3P0 (R) Dark	6.00	(R) Light	4.00
End This Destructive Conflict		*Slave I* (R) Dark.	15.00
(R) Dark	4.00	Slip Sliding Away (R) Dark	4.00
Epic Duel (R) Dark.	7.00	Smoke Screen (R) Light.	4.00
Flight Escort (R) Dark	4.00	Surprise (R) Dark.	4.00
Focused Attack (R) Dark	4.00	Surreptitious Glance (R) Light .	4.00
Force Field (R) Dark	4.00	The Emperor's Prize (R) Dark .	4.00
Forced Landing (R) Dark	4.00	This Is Even Better (R) Light . .	4.00
Frozen Assets (R) Light	4.00	This Is Still Wrong (R) Dark . . .	4.00
Gambler's Luck (R) Light	4.00	Ugloste (R) Dark	5.00
Glancing Blow (R) Light	4.00	Uncontrollable Fury (R) Light . .	4.00
Haven (R) Light	5.00	Vader's Bounty (R) Dark	5.00
He's All Yours, Bounty Hunter		Vader's Cape (R) Dark.	8.00
(R) Dark	5.00	We'll Find Han (R) Light.	4.00
Higher Ground (R) Light.	4.00	We're The Bait (R) Dark.	4.00
Hindsight (R) Light.	4.00	Why Didn't You Tell Me? (R)	
Hopping Mad (R) Light.	4.00	Dark	4.00
I Am Your Father (R) Dark	5.00	Wookiee Strangle (R) Light . . .	4.00

JABBA'S PALACE

Jabba's Palace expansion set was released on April 29, 1998. All of the individual card prices are estimates, since the set has not been on the market for very long. The set features many cards that can be used to enhance the play value of previously issued cards, permitting the development of new strategies to counteract powerful cards.

```
Complete Set: 180 cards. . . . . . . . . . . . . . . . . . . . $160.00
Booster Box: 60 packs . . . . . . . . . . . . . . . . . . . . 125.00
Booster Pack: 9 cards (inc. 1 rare) . . . . . . . . . . . . 2.50
Jabba's Palace Booster Display, 60 packs & display .  150.00
```

RARE CARD CHECKLIST

8D8 (R) Light	$4.00	Leslomy Tacema (R) Light	4.00
Amanaman (R) Dark	4.00	Life Debt (R) Light	4.00
Ardon "Vapor" Crell (R) Light	4.00	Loje Nella (R) Light	4.00
Artoo (R) Light	15.00	Malakili (R) Dark	4.00
Attark (R) Light	4.00	Max Rebo (R) Light	8.00
Aved Luun (R) Light	4.00	Murttoc Yine (R) Dark	4.00
Bane Malar (R) Dark	4.00	Nal Hutta (R) Dark	4.00
Barada (R) Dark	4.00	Nizuc Bek (R) Dark	4.00
Beedo (R) Dark	4.00	Nysad (R) Dark	4.00
BG-J38 (R) Light	4.00	Oola (R) Light	10.00
Bib Fortuna (R) Dark	8.00	Ortugg (R) Dark	4.00
Blaster Deflection (R) Light	4.00	Palejo Reshad (R) Light	4.00
Dengar's Modified Riot Gun (R)		Pote Snitkin (R) Dark	4.00
Dark	4.00	Princess Leia Organa (R) Light	30.00
Double Laser Cannon (R) Dark	4.00	Pucumir Thryss (R) Light	4.00
Droopy McCool (R) Light	4.00	R'kik D'nec, Hero Of The Dune	
Ephant Mon (R) Dark	4.00	Sea (R) Light	4.00
EV-9D9 (R) Dark	4.00	Rancor (R) Dark	15.00
Fozec (R) Dark	4.00	Rayc Ryjerd (R) Light	4.00
Gailid (R) Dark	4.00	Ree-Yees (R) Dark	4.00
Garon Nas Tal (R) Light	4.00	Rennek (R) Light	4.00
Geezum (R) Light	4.00	Saelt-Marae (R) Light	4.00
Ghoel (R) Light	4.00	Salacious Crumb (R) Dark	8.00
Giran (R) Dark	4.00	Scum And Villainy (R) Dark	4.00
Herat (R) Dark	4.00	Sergeant Doallyn (R) Light	4.00
Hermi Odle (R) Dark	4.00	Shasa Tiel (R) Light	4.00
Hutt Bounty (R) Dark	4.00	Strangle (R) Light	4.00
I Must Be Allowed To Speak (R)		Tamtel Skreej (R) Light	4.00
Light	4.00	Tanus Spijek (R) Light	4.00
J'Quille (R) Dark	4.00	Taym Dren-garen (R) Dark	4.00
Jabba The Hutt (R) Dark	20.00	Tessek (R) Light	4.00
Jabba's Sail Barge (R) Dark	4.00	Thermal Detonator (R) Dark	4.00
Jabba's Sail Barge: Passenger		Thul Fain (R) Dark	4.00
Deck (R) Dark	4.00	Tibrin (R) Light	4.00
Jedi Mind Trick (R) Light	4.00	Unfriendly Fire (R) Light	4.00
Jess (R) Light	4.00	Vedain (R) Dark	4.00
Kalit (R) Light	4.00	Velken Tezeri (R) Dark	4.00
Kiffex (R) Light	4.00	Vizam (R) Dark	4.00
Kirdo III (R) Light	4.00	Vul Tazaene (R) Light	4.00
Kithaba (R) Dark	4.00	Wittin (R) Dark	4.00
Klaatu (R) Dark	4.00	Wooof (R) Dark	4.00
Laudica (R) Light	4.00	Yoxgit (R) Light	4.00

STAR WARS 2-PLAYER CUSTOMIZABLE CARD GAME
Parker Brothers (Feb. 1996)

The Premiere two-player game was introduced in February 1996 and is distributed by Parker Brothers. That means that it found its way into toy stores. The box includes a Light Side and a Dark Side deck, each comprised of 60 common cards, plus a 15-card expansion pack. It's designed to provide the two players with everything they need to begin play. There are three Luke Skywalker and three Darth Vader cards which are exclusive to this set, although they are common within the set. The first 50,000 games distributed had a limited edition expansion pack, while later boxes had unlimited packs.

Star Wars 2-Players Customizable Card Game, licensed from Decipher (#40360, 1996) $20.00

Exclusive Card Checklist

Death Star: Docking Control Room		Luke, Light	4.00
327, Dark	$1.00	Run Luke, Run!, Light	3.00
Death Star: Level 6 Core Shaft Corri-		Vader, Dark	5.00
dor, Light	1.00	Vader's Obsession, Dark	2.50

THE EMPIRE STRIKES BACK INTRODUCTORY TWO-PLAYER GAME

The Empire Strikes Back two-player game was introduced in March 1997 and is also distributed by Parker Brothers. It's the second of a series of three, but I wouldn't bet against others based on the new movies. There are seven unique cards in the set.

Box Set: $20.00

Exclusive Card Checklist

Chewie (3) Light	$4.50	Lone Rogue (3) Light	1.50
Hoth: Mountains (6th Marker)		Rebel Snowspeeder (5) Light	1.00
(2) Dark	1.00	Veers (3) Dark	3.00
Imperial Walker (3) Dark	1.50	Walker Garrison (3) Dark	1.50
Leia (1) Light	4.50		

FIRST ANTHOLOGY SET

The set includes two white border 60-card starter decks, two black border 15-card A New Hope expansion packs, two black border 15-card Hoth expansion packs, a rules supplement, an 11-card Jedi Pack and six rare white border cards previewing the *Star Wars Special Edition* expansion set.

First Anthology Set in a 15"x13"x6" box. $32.00

Decipher also offered a variety of additional items for the discriminating player–collector. A few of the cards were corrected, and players could mail in the old card for a replacement. The first of these was the Dagobah Asteroid Sanctuary card, which didn't work properly in game play. You could also get this card in *Scrye* magazine. Decipher intends to continue to produce and distribute the card, so only the error version should become a collectible. Another replaceable card was the R-3PO card from the Hoth expansion set. It had the wrong image on it (same as the K-3PO card) and you can get a replacement by mail. This is a limited card, so Decipher will destroy the error card when you mail it in and keep the total number in existence at a constant 110,000. The cards have the same play value, but over time there will be more correct cards and less error cards. You can always turn an error card into a correct card for the price of a stamped, self-addressed envelope, but not the other way around.

Decipher distributed Rebel Leader Cards as convention giveaways. There is nothing like a show special freebee to get people to come to your booth. You could also mail-in for one, for $1.00 each, for a short time at the end of 1997 and beginning of 1998. Jedi Packs are available the same way, but without time limit.

Jedi Pack

Eriadu, Dark	$ .30	Leia, Light	1.00
For Luck, Light	.30	Luke's T-16 Skyhopper, Light	.30
Gravity Shadow, Dark	.30	Motti, Dark	1.00
Han, Light	1.00	Tarkin, Dark	1.00
Hyperoute Navigation Chart, Dark	.30	Tedn Dahai, Light	.30

Rebel Leader Checklist

Gold Leader in Gold 1	$4.50	Red Leader in Red 1	5.00

First Anthology Preview Cardlist

Boba Fett, Dark	$12.00	Dark	6.00
Commander Wedge Antilles,		Hit And Run, Light	2.00
Light	8.00	Jabba's Influence, Dark	2.00
Death Star Assault Squadron,		X-wing Assault Squadron, Light	3.00

HOUSEHOLD

HOUSEHOLD

This household section covers *Star Wars* items for use in the Bathroom, Bedroom, Kitchen and other rooms in a house, as well as holiday and party items. See also CERAMICS and ELECTRONICS AND COMPUTER.

BATHROOM

Bathroom products include soaps, grooming products and towels. Some of the combs are designed to be carried in your pocket and some of the towels are designed for the beach, but they are still listed here. Many collectors have one or more of these items in their collections, but they do not seem to be looking for more of them so as to have, for example, every *Star Wars* towel. They just treat what they have as part of their "other *Star Wars* stuff."

Bubble Bath
Bubble Bath Character Containers, 4½" x 9½" tall
    (Omni 1981–83)
       Chewbacca (1981) $15.00

Land Speeder Comb and Keeper (Adam Joseph Industries 1983)

Darth Vader (1981) 15.00
Jabba the Hutt (1981) 15.00
Luke Skywalker in X-Wing Pilot outfit (1981) 15.00
Princess Leia (1981) 15.00
R2-D2 (1981) 15.00
Wicket (1983) 15.00
Yoda (1983) 15.00
Bubble Bath Refueling Station, 6½" tall bottle
    decorated with ships and SW logo (Omni 1981) . . . 5.00
Bubble Bath (Addis 1983)
    Luke 15.00
    Leia 15.00
    R2-D2 . . . . 15.00
    Darth Vader 15.00
    Chewbacca 15.00
    C-3PO 15.00
    Ben Kenobi 15.00
    Wicket 15.00
R2-D2 and C-3PO Bubble Bath Gift Set, with 2
    soaps (Addis 1985) 30.00
Ewoks Bubble Bath Gift Set, with soap (Addis 1985) . . 25.00

Personal Grooming
Comb and Keeper (Adam Joseph Industries 1983)
    Cantina Band (*Return of the Jedi* header card) . . . 15.00
    Land Speeder (*Return of the Jedi* header card) . . 15.00
    Kneesaa (Wicket the Ewok header card) 10.00
R2-D2 and C-3PO Pop-Up Comb, comb comes with
    flip-up mirror, *Star Wars* logo (Adam Joseph
    1983) 15.00
Darth Vader Pop-Up Comb, comb comes with
    flip-up mirror, *Return of the Jedi* logo (Adam
    Joseph 1983) 15.00
Leia Pop-Up Comb, comb comes with flip-up mirror,
    Return of the Jedi logo (Adam Joseph 1983) 15.00
Ewok Personal Care Kit, picture of Princess
    Kneesaa on front of bag, including. comb &
    mirror (Adam Joseph 1983) 25.00

Return of the Jedi Toothbrushes, in box, on header card
Princess Leia Toothbrush (Oral-B 1985) 15.00
Darth Vader Toothbrush (Oral-B 1985) 10.00
Luke Skywalker Toothbrush (Oral-B 1985) 10.00
Ewoks Toothbrush (Oral-B 1985) 12.00
Jedi Master Three-pack, shrink wrapped (Oral-B 1985) 30.00
Electric Toothbrush, battery powered (Kenner 1978) . . 40.00
The Empire Strikes Back Electric Toothbrush, bat-
    tery powered (Kenner 1980) 30.00
Wicket Electric Toothbrush (1984) 25.00

Shampoo
Shampoo Character Containers (Omni 1981-83)
    Chewbacca (1981) 15.00

Darth Vader (1981) 15.00
Jabba the Hutt (1981) 15.00
Luke Skywalker in X-Wing Pilot outfit (1981) 15.00
Princess Leia (1981) 15.00
R2-D2 (1981). 15.00
Wicket (1983) 15.00
Yoda (1983). 15.00
Shampoo Refueling Station, 6½" bottle decorated
  with ships & *Star Wars* logo (Omni 1981) 5.00
Princess Leia Beauty Bag, 2 oz. shampoo, con-
  ditioner, & cologne in SW logo bottles with Leia
  drawings, soap and comb (Omni 1981) 40.00
Luke Skywalker Belt Kit, 2 oz. shampoo, con-
  ditioner & cologne in SW logo bottles with Luke
  drawings, soap, comb & toothbrush (Omni 1981) . 40.00

Soaps
C-3PO Soap, 4" (Cliro 1977). 10.00
R2-D2 Soap, 4" (Cliro 1977) 10.00
Character Soaps, packaged in window boxes with
  Star Wars logo and short description of charac-
  ter on back of box (Omni 1981-83):
  C-3PO. 10.00
  Chewbacca 10.00
  Darth Vader 10.00
  Gamorrean Guard 10.00
  Lando Calrissian 10.00
  Leia 10.00
  Luke 10.00
  R2-D2 . . . . 10.00
  Wicket 10.00
  Yoda 10.00
Star Wars Soap Collection, 4 char. soaps together:
  Leia, Luke, Yoda & Chewbacca (Omni 1981) 30.00
Star Wars Soap Collection, 4 char. soaps together:
  R2-D2, C-3PO, Darth, & Lando (Omni 1981) 30.00

Towels
R2-D2 & C-3PO beach towel (1980s) 15.00
Darth Vader beach towel (1980s) 15.00
R2-D2 & C-3PO hand towel (1980s). 5.00
R2-D2 wash cloth (1980s) 5.00
R2-D2 Bath Towel, 35"x60" (1997) 15.00
Boba Fett Bath Towel, 35"x60" (1997). 15.00
Princess Leia Bath Towel, 35"x60" (1997) 15.00
Darth Vader Bath Towel, 35"x60" (1997) 15.00
Stormtrooper Bath Towel, 35"x60" (1997) 15.00
C-3PO Bath Towel, 35"x60" (1997) 15.00
Darth Vader Beach Towel, 30"x60" (1997). 20.00
C-3PO & R2-D2 Beach Towel, 30"x60" (1997) 20.00
Stromtrooper Beach Towel, 30"x60" (1997). 20.00

BEDROOM

Star Wars bedding was popular from 1978 to 1984 and a variety of sheets, pillowcases, blankets, bedspreads and curtains were made. Most collectors are happy if they still have the ones they slept on as kids, but don't seem to be particularly interested in acquiring the same items in original condition. The problem, I suppose, is that there is little that you can do with a sheet if you don't sleep on it, and if you do sleep on it, it would loose its value as a collectible. For this reason, sheets and similar items, in original packaging are worth, at most, about the same as a new *Star Wars* sheet in its packaging. Your old sheets may be worth something to you, but probably not to anyone else.

Star Wars sleep products made a comeback in 1997 and new ones are available. You can order just about anything you would want from the Jawa Trader, (i.e. the Official *Star Wars* Fan Club). Just pick up a copy of *Star Wars Insider* magazine. More sleep products will undoubtedly come out in time for the new movies. Your kids, or grandkids or nephews will

Princess Leia, C-3PO and Wicket toothbrushes (Oral-B 1985)

Darth Vader Beach Towel (1982)

Star Wars *twin sheet (1978)*

probably want to sleep on the new ones, but you still won't have much you can do with the old designs. If collector interest picks up, today's popular characters such as Boba Fett would probably be the ones to look for.

Bedding

Star Wars sheets (1978–79)	$25.00
Star Wars blanket (1978–79)	35.00
Star Wars pillowcase (1978–79)	7.50
The Empire Strikes Back sheets (1980–82)	20.00
The Empire Strikes Back pillowcase (1980–82)	7.00
The Empire Strikes Back curtains (1980–82)	25.00
The Empire Strikes Back blanket (1980–82)	30.00
Yoda sleeping bag (1980–82)	25.00
Darth Vader pillow (1983–84)	15.00
Return of the Jedi curtains (1983–84)	25.00
Vehicle Diagram Sheets, twin (1997)	35.00
Vehicle Diagram Sheets, full (1997)	45.00
Vehicle Diagram Comforter, twin (1997)	50.00
Vehicle Diagram Comforter, full (1997)	60.00
Character Study sheets, twin (1997)	35.00
Character Study sheets, full (1997)	45.00
Character Study Comforter, twin (1997)	50.00
Character Study Comforter, full (1997)	60.00
Star Wars Dark Side sheets, twin (1998)	30.00
Star Wars Dark Side sheets, full (1998)	50.00
Star Wars Dark Side Comforter, twin (1998)	50.00
Star Wars Dark Side Comforter, full (1998)	60.00
Imperial Forces Blanket, twin (1998)	40.00
Imperial Forces Blanket, full (1998)	50.00
Luke Skywalker/Princess Leia pillowcase (1997)	7.00
Han Solo/Chewbacca pillowcase (1997)	7.00
Yoda/Obi-Wan Kenobi pillowcase (1997)	7.00
Jabba the Hutt/Boba Fett pillowcase (1997)	7.00
C-3PO/R2-D2 pillowcase (1997)	7.00
Symbols of *Star Wars* blanket twin (1997)	40.00
Symbols of *Star Wars* blanket full (1997)	50.00

Sleeping Bags

Star Wars sleeping bag (1978)	25.00
The Empire Strikes Back sleeping bag (1980)	20.00
Star Wars Indoor Sleeping Bag, child's size, Toys "R" Us special (Ero #71924, 1997)	23.00

Nightlights

Return of the Jedi Night Lights (Adam Joseph 1983)

R2-D2	5.00
C-3PO	5.00
Yoda	5.00
C-3PO head	5.00
Yoda head	5.00

Wicket the Ewok Night Lights (Adam Joseph 1983)

Wicket head	5.00
Kneesaa head	5.00

KITCHEN

Star Wars kitchen items includes the usual plates, bowls and mugs plus paper cups and tissues. See also CERAMICS.

Child's Dinnerware

Star Wars china set (Sigma)	$25.00
Return of the Jedi dinnerware set (Deka 1983)	20.00
Wicket the Ewok 3 piece set (Deka 1983)	10.00
Bowls (Deka 1980)	10.00
Cups (Deka 1980)	7.00

Cake Baking items

R2-D2 cake decorating kit (Wilton 1980)	15.00
Darth Vader cake decorating kit (Wilton 1980)	15.00
C-3PO cake pan (Wilton 1980)	10.00
Boba Fett cake pan (Wilton 1980)	25.00
Darth Vader cake pan (Wilton 1980)	15.00
R2-D2 and C-3PO figural CakeTops (Wilton #3607, 1979)	10.00
Darth Vader and Stormtrooper figural CakeTops (Wilton #3643, 1979)	10.00
R2-D2 and C-3PO figural PutOns (Wilton 1980)	8.00
Chewbacca Cake Candle 3½" (Wilton 1980)	5.00
Darth Vader Cake Candle 3½" (Wilton 1980)	5.00
R2-D2 Cake Candle 3½" (Wilton 1980)	5.00

Kids Mugs, 6oz Vinyl (Applause 1997)

C-3PO (#42683)	5.00
Darth Vader (#42684)	5.00
Ewok (#42685)	5.00
Stormtrooper (#42686)	5.00

Puffs Box: AT-ATs on Hoth (1981)

Star Wars *Dixie Cup: Princess Leia Box and 5 cups (1978)*

Paper Cups and Tissues
Puffs facial tissue boxes (Puffs 1981) picturing:
AT-ATs on Hoth 10.00
Darth Vader and Luke battle over Bespin 10.00
R2-D2 in Dagobah swamp 10.00

Star Wars Dixie Cups, 100 5oz. cups in assorted
styles (Dixie Cups 1978) in boxes picturing:
Darth Vader 10.00
Death Star, X-Wing and Darth Vader TIE Fighter . 10.00
Han & Chewbacca 10.00
Luke Skywalker and X-Wing 10.00
Obi-Wan Kenobi 10.00
Princess Leia 15.00
R2-D2 and C-3PO 9.00
Stormtrooper and TIE Fighter 10.00

The Empire Strikes Back Film Cup Assort-
ment, 100 .5oz. cups in assorted styles (Dixie
Cup 1980) in boxes picturing:
AT-ATs and Snowspeeder 8.00
Darth Vader 8.00
Imperial Star Destroyer 8.00
Luke on Tauntaun 9.00
Millennium Falcon 8.00
Twin-Pod Cloud Car and Cloud City 9.00
X-Wing in Swamp 8.00
Yoda 8.00

Return of the Jedi 5 oz. Kitchen Cups Dixie
Cups, 100 5oz. cups in assorted styles (Dixie
Cup 1983) in boxes picturing:
Luke Skywalker, B-Wing Fighter and Yoda 6.00
Princess Leia (prisoner) and Jabba the Hutt 8.00

Two Ewoks 5.00
Emperor Palpatine, Darth Vader and Royal Guard . 6.00

Star Wars Saga Film Cup Assortment (Dixie Cup
1984) in boxes picturing:
C-3PO and R2-D2 . . . . 10.00
Princess Leia, Han Solo and Stormtroopers 12.00
Darth Vader 10.00

OTHER ROOMS

Most *Star Wars* furniture, rugs and wastebaskets were
initially designed for kids' bedrooms or playrooms, but now
that those kids have grown up, or at least gotten older, and
have their own houses and apartments, *Star Wars* items can be
found all over the house.

Cork Bulletin Boards (Manton Cork)
Star Wars (1979) $15.00
Yoda, 16"x22" 15.00
AT-ATs, 11"x17" 12.00
Chewbacca, 11"x17" 12.00
Darth Vader, 11"x17" 12.00
Luke on Tauntaun, 11"x17" 15.00
R2-D2 and C-3PO, 11"x17" 10.00
Yoda, 11"x17" 12.00
Max Rebo Band 15.00

Drapery
Vehicle Diagram Rod Pocket Drape, 84"x84" (1997) . . 45.00
Vehicle Diagram Rod Pocket Drape, 84"x63" (1997) . . 35.00
Vehicle Diagram Rod Valance 84"x15" (1997) 20.00

Return of the Jedi *Wastepaper Basket (Chein 1983)*

Character Study Rod Pocket Drape, 84"x84" (1997) . . 45.00
Character Study Rod Pocket Drape, 84"x63" (1997) . . 35.00
Character Study Rod Valance 84"x15" (1997) 20.00

Furniture

Return of the Jedi Bookcase, 20"x18"x41", wood
  with scenes from Jedi on back panel (Am.
  Toy and Furniture Co. 1983) 150.00
Ewok and Droid Toy Chest, 32"x18"x41" (Am. Toy
  and Furniture Co. 1983) 175.00
Darth Vader Coat Rack, 47" tall, pix of Darth and Jedi
  logo on base (Am. Toy and Furniture Co. 1983) . 100.00
Desk and Chair, 32" high, movie scenes on back
  and sides (Am. Toy and Furniture Co. 1983) . . . 175.00
Return of the Jedi Nightstand, 20"x16½"x25" (Am.
  Toy and Furniture Co. 1983) 150.00
Picnic Table, 36" long, movie scenes on table top
  (Am. Toy and Furniture Co. 1983) 175.00
Return of the Jedi Table and Chair Set, 25½" round
  table with movie scenes on table top (Am. Toy
  and Furniture Co. 1983) 175.00
R2-D2 Toy Chest, 28" tall, wooden base on wheels
  with plastic lid (Am. Toy and Furniture Co. 1983) 150.00

Switcheroos

The Empire Strikes Back Switcheroos, "light switch
  cover for kids rooms" (Kenner 1980)
  Darth Vader, head 25.00
  R2-D2, figural 25.00
  C-3PO, head 25.00

Rugs

Star Wars Wool Hook Rug, 45"x69" picturing C-3PO
  and R2-D2 (1997) 200.00

Tins

Star Wars Special Edition Popcorn Tin (with three
  types of popcorn) 8 lbs. (1997) 35.00

Wastepaper Baskets

Return of the Jedi wastepaper basket, multiple
  characters pictured, with Luke at top (Chein
  Industries 1983) 25.00
Ewoks wastepaper basket (Chein Industries 1983) . . . 20.00

Outdoors

Gym Set (Gym-Dandy 1983) 1,200.00

Millennium Falcon *and Darth Vader ornaments*
(Hallmark 1996–97)

Paper Plate and Napkin (Party Express 1997)

HOLIDAY AND PARTY

Hallmark has made collectible Christmas ornaments for many years. In 1991, they discovered *Star Trek*, but they neglected to tell any *Star Trek* fans. Many of them wanted the initial ornament, but none of them had one, so the price went through the roof. Next year Hallmark actually advertised the ornament on "The Next Generation" TV show. They sold lots of ornaments and so they branched out into superheroes. In 1996, Hallmark discovered the marketing hype for the *Star Wars Trilogy Special Edition* movies and produced ... a grand total of one ornament! Five more ornaments followed in 1997. The marketing genius and business acumen of American companies is a constant source of inspiration for the world.

Christmas Ornaments (Hallmark 1996–98)
Millennium Falcon ornament (#7474, 1996) $60.00
Darth Vader hanging ornament (#17531, 1997) 25.00
Yoda hanging ornament (#16355, 1997) 30.00
C-3PO and R2-D2 set of ornaments (#14265, 1997) . . 20.00
Luke Skywalker hanging ornament (#5484, 1997) 25.00
Vehicles of *Star Wars*, 3 miniatures (#4024, 1997) . . . 40.00
X-wing Starfighter, light-up (#7596July 1998) 23.95
Boba Fett hanging ornament (#4053, July 1998) 14.95
Princess Leia hanging ornament (#4026, July 1998) . . 13.95
Ewoks, 3 miniatures (#4223, July 1998) 16.95

Party Supplies (1980–85)
Napkins 3.00
Invitations 3.00
Table covers 5.00
Other party supplies 2.50

Party Favors (1997) bagged
8 Blowouts (Party Express #04742) 3.50
8 Small Paper Plates, 7" (Party Express #05187) 2.50
8 Large Paper Plates, 9" (Party Express #05188) 3.00
8 Party Hats (Party Express #05190) 3.50
10 Small Napkins (Party Express #04756) 2.25
10 Large Napkins (Party Express #05186) 2.50
Crepe Paper Streamer 1.75
Party Game/Wall Game 2.00
X-wing/TIE Fighter/*Millennium Falcon* Decoration
  (#06461) 5.00
Stickers (#04758) 1.50
8 Treat Sacks (#05192) 2.00
Darth Vader Table Centerpiece (#05241) 3.25
C-3PO Thank You Notes (#07320) 2.00

MASKS, HELMETS AND COSTUMES

MASKS, HELMETS AND COSTUMES

Mask and Costume collecting extends far beyond *Star Wars*. Just about every famous or infamous person and fictional character has appeared on some type of Halloween costume over the years. Classic monsters, superheroes and science fiction characters have always been popular and *Star Wars* provides a host of interesting mask and costume possibilities. Both masks and costumes appeared in 1977, months before there were any *Star Wars* action figures.

MASKS AND HELMETS

Don Post Studios has always made the high-end masks — those designed for adults and for display, rather than for a child's Halloween costume. Lately they have added hands and collector helmets to their line-up. They also produce deluxe replica helmets, which are listed under STATUES.

Masks (Don Post Studios 1977–98)
C-3PO latex mask (Don Post 1977) $100.00
   reissue (1978) 75.00
   reissue (late 1980s) 50.00

reissue, 12" gold tone heavy vinyl (#82013,
   1994) 40.00
Cantina Band Member rubber mask (Don Post 1980) . 75.00
   reissue (1990s) 60.00
   reissue, 13" latex (#82005, 1994) 40.00
Chewbacca rubber mask (Don Post 1977) 250.00
   reissue (1978) 100.00
   reissue (1990) 75.00
   reissue, 11" multicolored hair (#82003, 1990s) . . . 60.00
Darth Vader Collector Helmet, plastic (1977) 200.00
   reissue (1978–82) 75.00
   reissue (1983) 50.00
   reissue (#82001, 1994) 60.00
Stormtrooper Collector Helmet, plastic (1977) 90.00
   reissue (1978) 75.00
   reissue (#82002, late 1980s) 60.00
Tusken Raider rubber mask (Don Post late 1970s) . . . 90.00
   reissue (late 1980s) 70.00
   reissue, 11" latex (#82016, 1995) 30.00
Ugnaught mask (Don Post 1980s) 75.00

Klaatu Mask (Don Post Studios 1990s)

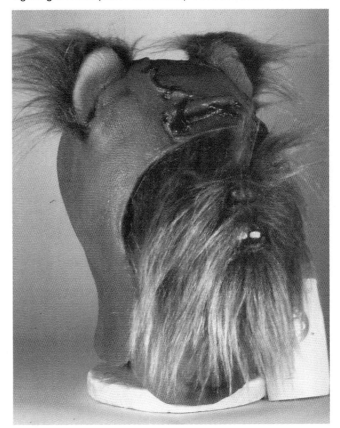

Wicket W. Warrick Mask (Don Post Studios 1994)

Yoda rubber mask (Don Post 1980s). 60.00
   reissue (1990s) 50.00
   reissue, 10" latex with hair (#82007, 1994). 30.00
Admiral Ackbar rubber mask (Don Post 1983). 75.00
   reissue (1990s) 60.00
   reissue, 13" latex (#82011, 1994). 40.00
Gamorrean Guard rubber mask (Don Post 1983) 75.00
   reissue, 11" (#82017, 1995) 25.00
Klaatu rubber mask (Don Post 1983) 75.00
   reissue (1990s) 60.00
   reissue, 12" latex with hood (#82018, 1995). . . . 35.00
Nien Nunb rubber mask, 11" (#82015, 1996). 25.00
Weequay rubber mask (Don Post 1983) 90.00
Wicket W. Warrick rubber mask (Don Post 1983) . . . 90.00
   reissue (1990) 75.00
   reissue, 10" hair and hood (#82012, 1994). 40.00
Emperor Palpatine rubber mask 80.00
   reissue, 11" latex with cloth hood (#82014,
     1994) 40.00
Greedo, 11" latex (#82027, 1997) 35.00
Prince Xizor, 12" latex and hair (#82021, 1994). 35.00

Hands

Prince Xizor's Hands, 9" latex (#82041, 1994). 25.00
Cantina Band Member's Hands, 10" latex (#82043,
   1994). 20.00
Admiral Ackbar Hands, 15" latex (#82044, 1994). . . . 25.00

Collector Helmets (Don Post 1996–98)

Boba Fett, 10" plastic with smoked viewplate and
   moveable antenna (#82019, 1996). 80.00
Darth Vader, 13" plastic faceplate and overhelmet,
   with tinted eyepieces (#82001). 50.00
Emperor's Royal Guard, 18" crimson plastic with
   smoked visor (#82020, 1996). 80.00

Stormtrooper, 11" white plastic with simulated
   breathing filters and com-link (#82002). 80.00
TIE Fighter, 11" (#82025, 1997) 90.00
Scout Trooper Helmet, 11" (#82024, 1997) 90.00
X-wing Fighter, 13" (#82026, 1997) 90.00

Classic Action Helmets (Don Post 1997)

Darth Vader Classic Action Helmet, 15" (#82108) . . . 150.00
Stormtrooper Classic Action Helmet, 13" (#82107) . . 125.00
TIE Fighter Classic Action Helmet, 15" (#82105) 125.00

RIDDELL MINI-HELMET
Collectible Mini-Helmets, 45% of scale with display base
Darth Vader Mini-Helmet, 3 pieces 95.00
X-wing (Pilot) Mini-Helmet, moveable pieces. 85.00
C-3PO Mini-Helmet, battery powered eyes 80.00
Stormtrooper Mini-Helmet, with die-cast metal parts . . 85.00
Boba Fett Mini-Helmet, die-cast metal parts 85.00

COSTUMES

Ben Cooper was the most famous maker of collectible Halloween costumes in the 1970s and 1980s. All of their product was made for kids. This means that it was made, and sold, inexpensively and was not initially designed as a collectible. This means that old costumes in prime condition are hard to find.

Rubies currently makes Halloween costumes for the same market. Their current crop of classic *Star Wars* items may never receive much collector attention, since it must compete with the Ben Cooper originals and with the Don Post Studios higher quality. This could change with the expected appearance of a large crop of new costumes based on the next

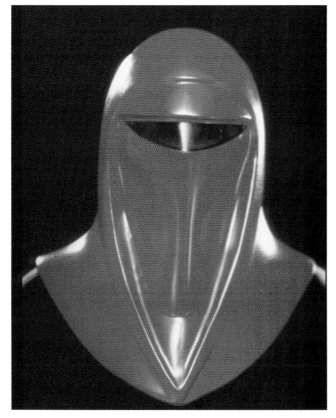

Emperor's Royal Guard Helmet and Boba Fett Helmet (Don Post Studios 1996) Photos courtesy of Don Post Studios

Chewbacca Mask (Don Post Studios 1990s)
Photo courtesy of Don Post Studios

movie. Look for these in the fall of 1999, and then do a little bargain hunting right after Halloween. There should be some excellent first character appearances available then.

Costume and Mask, boxed (Ben Cooper)
Darth Vader (#740, 1977–85)
 Star Wars $35.00
 The Empire Strikes Back 20.00
 Return of the Jedi 20.00
Luke Skywalker (#741, 1977–85)
 Star Wars 35.00
 The Empire Strikes Back 20.00
 Return of the Jedi 20.00
C-3PO (#742, 1977–85)
 Star Wars 35.00
 The Empire Strikes Back 20.00
 Return of the Jedi 20.00
Luke Skywalker, X-Wing
 Star Wars 35.00
 The Empire Strikes Back 20.00
 Return of the Jedi 20.00
R2-D2 (#744, 1977–85)
 Star Wars 35.00
 The Empire Strikes Back 20.00
 Return of the Jedi 20.00
Princess Leia (#745, 1977–85)
 Star Wars 35.00
 The Empire Strikes Back 20.00
 Return of the Jedi 20.00

Chewbacca (#746, 1977–85)
 Star Wars 35.00
 The Empire Strikes Back 20.00
 Return of the Jedi 20.00
Stormtrooper (#747, 1977–85)
 Star Wars 35.00
 The Empire Strikes Back 20.00
 Return of the Jedi 20.00
Boba Fett (#748, 1977–85)
 Star Wars 35.00
 The Empire Strikes Back 20.00
 Return of the Jedi 20.00
Yoda Costume (#749, 1980–85)
 The Empire Strikes Back 30.00
 Return of the Jedi 30.00
Wicket, *Return of the Jedi* (#735, 1983–85) 25.00
Admiral Ackbar, *Return of the Jedi* (#736, 1983–85) . . 25.00
Gamorrean Guard, *Return of the Jedi* (#737, 1983–85) 25.00
Klaatu, *Return of the Jedi* (#738, 1983–85) 25.00

Costumes and Masks (1995–97)
Darth Vader polyester jumpsuit, bootcovers, cape
 and PVC mask (J.C. Penney 1997) 25.00
Chewbacca costume, includes jumpsuit, mask and
 sash (#15242, 1996) 95.00
Chewbacca rubber mask (#C2867) 20.00
Darth Vader costume, includes jumpsuit, chest-
 piece, cape and mask (#15236, 1996) 75.00
Stormtrooper costume, includes jumpsuit, chest-
 piece and mask (#15243, 1996). 70.00
C-3PO Costume (#15237, 1997). 70.00
Yoda Costume (#15400, 1997) 50.00

Halloween Costumes (1997) Party City Catalog
Darth Vader deluxe child costume, with silkscreened jumpsuit, cape and 3/4 mask (#26)
 small medium or large sizes. 13.00
Super Deluxe Darth Vader child costume, with
 jumpsuit with boot tops, chestpiece, cape and
 mask (#27) small, medium or large sizes 30.00
Super Deluxe Princess Leia child costume, with
 dress, belt and wig (#80) small, medium or
 large sizes. 30.00
Stormtrooper deluxe child costume, with silkscreen-
 ed jumpsuit and 3/4 mask (#105) small,
 medium or large sizes 13.00
C-3PO deluxe child costume, with silkscreened
 jumpsuit and 3/4 mask (#14) small medium or
 large sizes. 13.00
Darth Vader adult costume with silkscreened jump
 suit, cape, and 2-piece PVC mask (#231)
 small, medium or large. 40.00

Rubies Costumes
Darth Vader mask (#2865) 25.00
C-3PO hard mask (#2866) 30.00
Chewbacca mask (#2867) 25.00
Stormtrooper latex mask (#2868) 25.00
Yoda mask (#2869). 30.00
Darth Vader Costume Kit, cape, chest armor, mask
 and lightsaber (#17016, 1996), boxed 15.00
Darth Vader mask (#2993) 25.00
Chewbacca mask (#2994) 30.00
C-3PO mask (#2995) 25.00
Princess Leia wig 20.00

MICRO FIGURES AND VEHICLES

MICRO FIGURES AND VEHICLES

STAR WARS MICRO COLLECTION
Kenner (1982)

Kenner's Micro Collection consists of plastic playsets and plastic vehicles for use with 1" die-cast figures. The nine playsets could be bought individually or grouped into three "Worlds:" Hoth Ice Planet, Bespin Cloud City and Death Star. With nine playsets and three worlds you might think that there would be three playsets per world, but you would be wrong. There were two Death Star playsets, three Bespin playsets, and four Hoth playsets. The Hoth Generator Attack set was omitted from the Hoth World group.

There were two ships in the original Micro Line: The X-Wing Fighter and the TIE Fighter. Each had a pilot and a crash feature so that it suffered battle damage at the push of a button along with battle damage stickers. Two exclusive ships were offered in 1983 — the *Millennium Falcon* was a Sears exclusive, while the Rebel Armored Snowspeeder was a JC Penney exclusive.

There was also two mail-in "Build Your Armies" set of six figures, offered on specially marked boxes with the usual proof of purchase. Certain Kellogg's C-3PO cereal boxes had a mail-in offer for four figures. The offer was good through August 31, 1985, and was fulfilled with existing stock.

All of the die-cast figures have product numbers on the base or body. They are given below to aid in identification of loose figures. Die-cast ships are not listed here. They are in the DIE-CAST section.

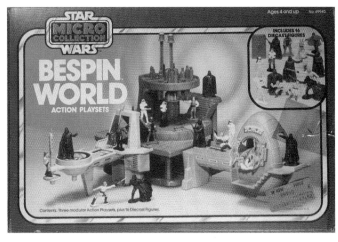

Bespin World Action Playset (Kenner 1982)

Action Playsets

Bespin Control Room (#69920) includes 2 Luke figures and 2 Darth Vader figures (#256-001–004) . $30.00

Bespin Freeze Chamber (#69930) includes 8 figures (#460-009–017) 75.00

Bespin Gantry (#69910) includes 2 Luke figures and 2 Darth Vader figures (#258-001–004) 30.00

Bespin World: Bespin Control Room, Bespin Freeze Chamber and Bespin Gantry sets, includes 16 figures in 12"x8"x7" box (#69940, 1982) 125.00

Hoth Generator Attack Action Playset (Kenner 1982)

Death Star Compactor (#93300) includes 8 figures (#517-014–021) 50.00

Death Star Escape (#69990) includes 6 figures (#583-018–023) 50.00

Death Star World: Death Star Compactor and Death Star Escape sets (#93310) includes 14 figures . . 125.00

Hoth Generator Attack (#93420) includes 6 figures (#668-001–006) 25.00

Hoth Ion Cannon (#69970) includes 8 figures (#692-001–008) 35.00

Hoth Turret Defense (#69960) includes 6 figures (#463-010–015) 25.00

Hoth Wampa Cave (#69950) includes a Wampa and 4 figures (#269-001–004 & #269-009-A) 25.00

Hoth World: Hoth Generator Attack, Hoth Ion Cannon and Hoth Wampa Cave sets, includes 19 figures.............................. 100.00

Vehicles

Imperial TIE Fighter, includes pilot figure (#270-010) . . 75.00

X-Wing Fighter (#69670) includes pilot figure (#270-014)...................................... 65.00

Millennium Falcon (#70140) includes 6 figures (#733-001–006) Sears exclusive 400.00

Rebel Armored Snowspeeder, with working harpoon (#70150) includes pilot and Harpooner figures (#261-015–016) JC Penny exclusive. . 200.00

Mail-In Figures

Build Your Armies, including 3 Rebel Soldiers (#088-001–003) and 3 Snowtroopers (#088-005–007)................................ 25.00

Star Wars: A New Hope Micro Machine Vehicles (Galoob 1994)

MICROMACHINES
Galoob (1994–98)

"Think Big, Play Small"

The Galoob *Star Wars* MicroMachines collection debuted in 1994, as part of their "Space" segment. At the time, *Star Wars* was the hottest collectible going, but very few new items had started to appear. The JustToys *Star Wars* Bend-Ems were out, but the action figures from Kenner were not. The first batch of MicroMachines contained a three figure set for each of the three movies. The earliest ones have a 1993 Lucasfilm Ltd. copyright, an individual movie logo in the front, and only list the first three series on the back (3-back). These were reissued when the next three items were released, with a generic "*Star Wars*" logo on the front, a 1994 copyright, and list all six series on the back (6-back). All were issued on rectangular header cards as part of MicroMachines "Space" series.

By April 1996, most of these were still available at KayBee stores, discounted to $3.33. They were replaced by the *Star Wars* Vehicle Collection, which also said "Space" on

its original packages, but had different figures in the numbered collections and different UPC codes. Packaging was then changed to omit "Space" and just say "*Star Wars*." Packaging was changed again in 1997 to a striped design, similar to the stripes on the Action Fleet packages.

While you can still find some early MicroMachines on store shelves, you can also find some serious collectors looking for them. All of the MicroMachines have small parts and small figures, so, even if they survive battles between the Galactic Empire and the Rebel Forces, most of them are destined to an ignominious defeat at the hands of mom's vacuum cleaner. This will make completing any loose set very difficult. The larger X-Ray fleet and the even larger Action Fleet ships are covered below. See also DIE-CAST for Galoob's MicroMachine Die-Cast ships.

SPACE SERIES VEHICLES (1993–95)

First Batch (Asst. #65860, 1993) on header card

#1 *Star Wars: Millennium Falcon*; Imperial Star-Destroyer; X-wing Starfighter (#65886) on 3-back card $15.00

    Reissue as *Star Wars: A New Hope*, 1994 copyright, generic logo, 6-back 7.00

#2 *The Empire Strikes Back*: TIE Starfighter; Imperial AT-AT; Snowspeeder (#65887) on 3-back card 15.00

    Reissue, 1994, generic logo, 6-back 7.00

#3 *Return of the Jedi*: Imperial AT-ST (Chicken Walker); Jabba's Desert Sail Barge; B-wing Starfighter (#65888) on 3-back card 15.00

    Reissue, 1994, generic logo, 6-back 7.00

#4 *Star Wars: A New Hope*: Y-wing Starfighter; Jawa Sandcrawler; Rebel Blockade Runner (#65897) 8.00

#5 *The Empire Strikes Back*: Imperial TIE Bomber, Boba Fett's *Slave I*; Bespin Twin-Pod Cloud Car (#65898) 8.00

#6 *Return of the Jedi*: Speeder Bike with Rebel Pilot; Imperial Shuttle *Tyderium*; A-wing Starfighter (#65899) 8.00

VEHICLE COLLECTION (1996–98)

First Batch (Asst. #65860, 1996)

I TIE Interceptor, Imperial Star Destroyer, Rebel Blockade Runner (#66111) 7.00

II Landspeeder, *Millennium Falcon*, Jawa Sandcrawler (#66112) 7.00

III Darth Vader's TIE Fighter, Y-wing Starfighter, X-wing Starfighter (#66113) 7.00

IV Imperial Probot, Imperial AT-AT, Snowspeeder (#66114) 7.00

V Rebel Transport, TIE Bomber, Imperial AT-ST (#66115) 7.00

VI Escort Frigate, Boba Fett's *Slave I*, Bespin Twin-Pod Cloud Car (#66116) 7.00

VII Mon Calamari Star Cruiser, Jabba's Desert Sail Barge, Speeder Bike with Rebel Pilot (#66117) 7.00

VIII Speeder Bike with Imperial Pilot, Imperial Shuttle *Tydirium*, TIE Starfighter (#66118) 7.00

IX Super Star Destroyer *Executor*, B-wing Starfighter, A-wing Starfighter (#66119) 7.00

X Incom T-16 Skyhopper, Lars Family Landspeeder, Death Star II (#66137) 7.00

XI Bespin Cloud City, Mon Calamari Rebel Cruiser, Escape Pod (#66138) 7.00

Star Wars Trilogy Gift Set, MicroMachines (Galoob 1996)

Classic Series III, Darth Vader's TIE Fighter and
  Millennium Falcon (#67088, 1996) *Star Wars*
  catalog 15.00
The Balance Of Power, X-wing Fighter and TIE
  Fighter (#66091, 1996) 15.00
Rebel Forces vs. Imperial Forces Gift Set, 8 pieces
  (#68042, 1996) Musicland exclusive 15.00
Millennium Falcon playset, opens into *Star Wars*
  command center, with Y-wing Starfighter and 7
  figures (#65878) 38.00
  In early box, with 24kt promotion offer 45.00
Master Collector's 40-vehicle set (#68048, 1997)
  Toys "R" Us exclusive 40.00

MICROMACHINE X-RAY FLEET
Galoob (1996–97)

X-Ray Fleet vehicles are the same size as Galoob's die-cast vehicles and considerably bigger than the regular MicroMachine size, but still a lot smaller than their Action Fleet ships. For me, it's a very attractive size, because I can appreciate the details without a magnifying glass.

The outer hull of each X-Ray Fleet ship is clear plastic, allowing the collector to view the inner portions of each vehicle. This only really works if the inside portions correspond to the known insides of the ship, as seen in the movies. Some of the X-Ray Fleet correspond fairly well to the movie version, notably the Imperial AT-AT and AT-ST, but most are not so successful.

The *Star Wars* Trilogy Gift Set includes only one X-Ray Fleet ship, the Shuttle *Tyderium*. The other nine ships are the same size as the X-Ray Fleet (and Die-Cast ships) but are painted. This set was originally a JC Penney exclusive, but left over sets found their way to KayBee Toys and sold for $15.00. That's where I got mine.

First Batch (Asst. #67070, 1996) "Space" packaging
I   Darth Vader's TIE Fighter and A-wing
    Starfighter (#67071) $7.00
II X-wing Starfighter and Imperial AT-AT
    (#67072) 7.00
III *Millennium Falcon* and Jawa Sandcrawler
    (#67073) 7.00
IV Boba Fett's *Slave I* and Y-wing Starfighter
    (#67074) 7.00

Second Batch (1997)
V   TIE Bomber and B-wing Starfighter 7.00
VI TIE Fighter and Landspeeder 7.00
VII Imperial AT-ST and Snowspeeder 7.00

Large Boxed Set
Star Wars Trilogy Gift Set, 10 larger, X-Ray vehicle-
  sized, ships with display stands (#67079, 1996) . . 35.00

Luke's X-wing Starfighter Action Fleet Vehicle (Galoob 1996)

Rebel Snow Speeder Action Fleet Vehicle (Galoob 1996)

MICROMACHINE ACTION FLEET
Galoob (1996–98)

VEHICLES

Action Fleet vehicles are larger than Galoob's X-Ray fleet and die-cast vehicles, but still smaller than Kenner's action figure vehicles. It has proven to be a popular size with both kids and collectors.

The first 2,500 pieces, from the production run of each of the first batch vehicles, were numbered with a special blue collector's sticker, The Rebel Snowspeeder was short packed in the assortment.

In 1997, Galoob introduced Series Alpha, which included both an original concept design vehicle and the familiar final design vehicle, along with two figures. This is one of the only ways to collect design prototypes, but some see it as just a gimmick to get them to buy another copy of the a vehicle that they already own.

Galoob has also produced a number of battle packs and playsets which include figures and accessories on the same scale as the ships.

First Batch (Spring 1996)
Luke's X-wing Starfighter, with pilot Luke Sky-
    walker and R2-D2 (#67031) $12.00
    With numbered collector sticker 20.00
Darth Vader's TIE Fighter, with Lord Darth Vader
    and Imperial Pilot (#67032) 12.00
    With numbered collector sticker 20.00
Imperial AT-AT, with Storm Trooper and Imperial
    Driver (#67033) 12.00
    With numbered collector sticker 20.00
A-wing Starfighter, with C-3PO & Rebel Pilot (#67034) 12.00
    With numbered collector sticker 20.00
Imperial Shuttle *Tydirium*, with Han Solo and
    Chewbacca (#67035) 12.00
    With numbered collector sticker 20.00
Rebel Snow Speeder, with Luke Skywalker and
    Rebel Gunner (#67036) 15.00
    With numbered collector sticker 20.00

Second Batch (Fall 1996)
Jawa Sandcrawler with Scavenger Droid and Jawa
    (#67039) 10.00
Y-wing Starfighter with Gold Leader and R2 Unit
    (#67040) 10.00
Slave I, with Boba Fett and Han Solo in carbonite
    (#67041) 10.00
TIE Interceptor, with two poseable Imperial Pilots
    (#67058) 10.00

Third Batch (Asst. #67030, Spring 1997)
Rancor, with Luke Skywalker and Gamorrean
    Guard (#66989) 10.00
Virago, with Prince Xizor and Guri (#66990) 10.00
X-wing Starfighter, with Wedge Antilles and R2
    Unit, X-wing Squadron colors (#66991) 10.00
Y-wing Starfighter, with Yellow leader and R2 Unit,
    Y-wing Squadron colors (#66992) 10.00
A-wing Starfighter, with Rebel Pilot and Mon
    Mothma, A-wing Squadron colors (#66993) 10.00
TIE Fighter, with Imperial Pilot and Grand Moff
    Tarkin (#66995) 10.00
TIE Bomber, with Imperial Pilot and Imperial Naval
    Trooper (#67059) 10.00

Fourth Batch (Asst. #67030, Fall 1997)
Bespin Twin-Pod Cloud Car, with Lobot and Cloud
    Car Pilot (#66996) 10.00

B-wing Starfighter, with Rebel Pilot and Admiral
    Ackbar (#66994) 10.00
X-wing Starfighter, with Jek Porkins and R2-Unit,
    Red Six colors (#67023) 10.00
Y-wing Starfighter, with Blue Leader and R2 Unit,
    Y-wing Squadron colors (#67024) 10.00
Rebel Snowspeeder, with Rebel Pilot and Rebel
    Gunner, Rogue Two colors (#67025) 10.00

Fifth Batch (Spring 1998)
Millennium Falcon, with Han Solo and Chewbacca . . . 10.00
Rebel Blockade Runner, with Rebel Trooper and
    Princess Leia Organa 10.00
Incom T-16 Skyhopper, with Luke Skywalker and
    Biggs Darklighter 10.00
Imperial Landing Craft, with Imperial Officer and
    Sandtrooper 10.00

*Luke's Landspeeder and Imperial AT-ST two-pack
Kay-Bee exclusive (Galoob 1995)*

Ice Planet Hoth and Death Star Action Fleet Playsets (Galoob 1997)

Sixth Batch (Fall 1998)
Jabba's Sail Barge with Saelt-Marae (Yak Face)
    and R2-D2 . . . . 10.00
TIE Defender with Imperial Pilot and Moff Jerjerrod . . . 10.00
E-wing Starfighter with Rebel Pilot and R7 Unit 10.00

TWO-PACKS, Kay Bee exclusive (1995)
Luke's Landspeeder, with Luke Skywalker and Obi
    Wan Kenobi and Imperial AT-ST with Imperial
    Driver and Stormtrooper (#67077) 20.00

SERIES ALPHA (1997–98)
Concept Design Prototype and Final Design
First Batch (Asst. 73420, Spring 1997)
1. X-wing Starfighter, with Biggs Darklighter and
    R2 Unit (#73421) 15.00
2. Imperial AT-AT, with Imperial Driver and
    Snowtrooper (#7342) 15.00
3. Imperial Shuttle, with Stormtrooper and TIE
    Fighter Pilot (#73422) 15.00
4. Rebel Snowspeeder, with Luke Skywalker
    Rebel Pilot and Rebel Gunner (#73423) 15.00

Second Batch (Spring 1998)
Twin-Pod Cloud Car, with Cloud Car Pilot and Copilot . 15.00
Y-wing Starfighter, with Y-wing Pilot and Gunner 15.00
B-wing Starfighter, with B-wing Pilot and Gunner 15.00

CLASSIC DUELS (1997–98)
Toys "R" Us special (Asst. #68300, Nov. 1997)
Millennium Falcon, with Lando Calrissian and Rebel
    Trooper vs. TIE Interceptor, with Imperial Pilot
    and Imperial Officer (#68302) 20.00
X-wing Starfighter, with Luke Skywalker and R2-D2
    vs. TIE Fighter, with Imperial Pilot and
    Stormtrooper (#68301) 20.00

FLIGHT CONTROLLERS (1997–98)
First Batch (Asst. #73416, Spring 1997)
Rebel Flight Controller, with Luke's X-wing Star-
    fighter and 2 figures (#73417) 20.00
Imperial Flight Controller, Darth Vader's TIE Fighter
    and 2 figures (#73418) 20.00

Second Batch (Spring 1998)
Rebel Flight Controller with Y-wing Starfighter and 2
    figures 20.00
Imperial Flight Controller with TIE-Interceptor and 2
    figures 20.00

BATTLE PACKS (1996–98)
First Batch (Asst. #68010, 1996)
#1 Rebel Alliance, two Speeder Bikes and 5 figure
    (#68011) 8.00
#2 Galactic Empire, Imperial AT-ST and 4 figures
    (#68012) 8.00
#3 Aliens and Creatures, Bantha and 4 figures
    (#68013) 8.00
#4 Imperial Hunters, Dewback and 4 figures (#68014) 8.00
#5 Shadows of the Empire, two Swoops and 5
    figures (#68015) 8.00

Second Batch (Spring 1997)
#6 Dune Sea, Desert Skiff and 5 figures (#68016) 8.00
#7 Droid Escape, Escape Pod and 5 figures (#68017) . 8.00
#8 Desert Palace, Jabba the Hutt and 5 figures
    (#68018) 8.00

Third Batch (Fall 1997)
#9 Endor Adventure, Hang Glider, Speeder Bike
    and 5 figures (#68019) 8.00
#10 Mos Eisley Spaceport, Ronto and 5 figures
    (#68020) 8.00
#11 Cantina Encounter, Landspeeder and 5 figures
    (#68021) 8.00

Fourth Batch (Spring 1998)
#12 Cantina Smugglers and Spies, 8 figures (#68090) . 8.00
#13 Hoth Attack, Tauntaun, Wampa and 4 figures
    (#68091) 8.00
#14 Death Star Escape, 7 figures (#68092) 8.00
#15 Endor Victory, 3 glow-in-the-dark figures and 5
    hero figures (#68093) 8.00

Fifth Batch (Fall 1998)
#16 Lars Family Homestead, Landspeeder and 5
    figures 8.00
#17 Imperial Troops, Speeder Bike and 5 figures 8.00
#18 Rebel Troops, 8 figures 8.00

PLAYSETS
Asst. #67090 in box with slant side
Ice Planet Hoth, includes 6 figures, Ralph
    McQuarrie original box art (#67091) 30.00
The Death Star, includes 6 figures, Ralph
    McQuarrie original box art (#69092) 30.00
Yavin Rebel Base, includes 6 figures, Ralph
    McQuarrie original box art (#69090) 30.00

MODEL KITS

MODEL KITS

MPC was Kenner's model kit company. Early kits have their logo. When The Ertl Company bought MPC in about 1990, the logo was changed to MPC/Ertl. Still later, the logo was changed to AMT/Ertl, which is what it is today. The original models have been reissued, and this availability has brought down the collectors' price of the originals. The most notable exception is the original *Millennium Falcon*, with lights, since the reissues are unlighted.

Star Wars Characters
The Authentic C-3PO (See-Threepio) model kit, 10"
   tall, 1/7 scale (MPC #1913, 1977) 7½"x10" *Star
   Wars* box $25.00
   Reissue, 6"x10" box 20.00
C-3PO model kit (MPC #1935, 1984) *Return of the
   Jedi* box 15.00

The Authentic R2-D2 (Artoo-Detoo) model kit 6" tall,
   1/10 scale (MPC #1912, 1977) *Star Wars* box . . . 25.00
   Reissue, 6"x10" box 20.00
R2-D2 model kit (MPC #1934, 1984) *Return of the
   Jedi* box 15.00
Darth Vader model kit, 11½" tall, 1/7 scale, black full
   figure with glow-in-the-dark lightsaber (MPC
   #1916, 1979) *Star Wars* box 45.00
Darth Vader Bust Action model kit, snap-togeth-
   er, 1/2 scale (MPC #1921, 1978) illuminated
   eyes and raspy breathing sound, *Star Wars* box. . 60.00

Space Ships
The Authentic Darth Vader TIE Fighter model kit,
   7½" wide, 1/48 scale, with Darth Vader pilot
   figure (MPC #1915, 1977) 14"x10" *Star Wars* box 35.00
   Reissue, 14"x8" *Star Wars* box 25.00
The Authentic Luke Skywalker X-Wing Fighter
   model kit, 12" long, 10" wingspan, 1/48 scale
   (MPC #1914, 1977) 14"x10" *Star Wars* box 35.00

R2-D2 (original wide box) Model Kit (MPC 1977) and C-3PO (narrow box) Model Kit (MPC 1980s)

Darth Vader TIE Fighter (narrow box) and Luke Skywalker X-Wing Fighter (narrow box) (MPC 1980s)

Reissue, 14"x8" *Star Wars* box 25.00
Han Solo's *Millennium Falcon* model kit, 18" long,
    1/72 scale, with lights (MPC #1925, 1979) *Star
    Wars* box 120.00

The Empire Strikes Back Ships
Star Destroyer model kit (15" long, MPC #1926,
    1980) *The Empire Strikes Back* box 45.00
Luke Skywalker's Snowspeeder model kit, 8" long
    (MPC #1917, 1980) *The Empire Strikes Back*
    box 40.00
AT-AT model kit (MPC #1918, 1980) *The Empire
    Strikes Back* box 40.00
Millennium Falcon model kit, no lights (MPC #1933,
    1982) *The Empire Strikes Back* box 40.00
X-Wing Fighter model kit, 12½" (MPC #1930, 1982)
    The Empire Strikes Back box 25.00
Boba Fett's *Slave I* model kit (MPC #1919, 1982)
    The Empire Strikes Back box 35.00

Return of the Jedi Ships
AT-AT model kit (MPC #1929, 1983) *Return of the
    Jedi* box 25.00
Shuttle *Tyderium* model kit, 20" wingspan (MPC
    #1920, 1983) *Return of the Jedi* box 30.00
Speeder Bike Vehicle model kit, 12" long (MPC
    #1927, 1983) *Return of the Jedi* box 22.00

Snap Kits
AT-ST model kit, 6" high, scout walker (MPC #1976,
    1983) *Return of the Jedi* box 30.00
A-Wing Fighter model kit (MPC #1973, 1983)
    Return of the Jedi box 15.00
B-Wing Fighter model kit (MPC #1974, 1983)
    Return of the Jedi box 15.00
TIE Interceptor model kit (MPC #1972, 1983)
    Return of the Jedi box 20.00
X-Wing Fighter model kit (MPC #1971, 1983)
    Return of the Jedi box 15.00
Y-Wing model kit (MPC #1975, 1983) *Return of the
    Jedi* box 15.00

Dioramas
Rebel Base Diorama Snap model kit (MPC #1924,
    1981) *The Empire Strikes Back* box 45.00
Battle on Ice Planet Hoth model diorama, snap
    together, 11¾"x17¾" (MPC #1922, 1981) *The
    Empire Strikes Back* box 35.00
Encounter With Yoda on Dagobah model kit, snap
    together, 5¾"x10" (MPC #1923, 1981) *The
    Empire Strikes Back* box 35.00
Jabba the Hutt Throne Room model kit, diorama
    (MPC #1928, 1983) *Return of the Jedi* box 40.00

Mirr-A-Kits
AT-ST model kit (MPC #1105, 1984) *Return of the
    Jedi* box 15.00
Shuttle *Tyderium* model kit (MPC #1103, 1984)
    Return of the Jedi box 15.00
Speeder Bike (MPC #1106, 1984) *Return of the Jedi*
    box 15.00

*Luke Skywalker Snowspeeder (*The Empire Strikes Back*) and Speeder Bike (*Return of the Jedi*) (MPC 1980s)*

TIE Interceptor model kit (MPC #1102, 1984) *Return of the Jedi* box........................... 15.00

Y-Wing model kit (MPC #1104, 1984) *Return of the Jedi* box.............................. 15.00

X-Wing model kit (MPC #1101, 1984) *Return of the Jedi* box............................... 15.00

Structors Action Walking models, wind-up motor
AT-AT model kit (MPC/Structors #1902, 1984) 30.00
    AT-AT (AMT/Ertl #6036, 1998) 10.00
AT-ST model kit, 4½" high (MPC/Structors #1903, 1984) *Return of the Jedi* box 25.00
    Scout AT-ST (AMT/Ertl #6029, 1998) 10.00
C-3PO model kit (MPC/Structors #1901, 1984) 25.00

Vans: Snap together, with glow-in-the-dark decals
Artoo-Detoo Van model kit, 1/32 scale (MPC #3211, 1979)................................... 30.00
Darth Vader Van model kit, 1/32 scale (MPC #3209, 1979) 35.00
Luke Skywalker Van model kit, 1/32 scale (MPC #3210, 1979)........................... 35.00

MPC/ERTL and AMT/ERTL (1990–98)
Figures
Darth Vader, stands 12" tall, glow in the dark light saber (#8154, 1992) 14"x8¼" *Star Wars* box 15.00
    Reissue: AMT/Ertl 12.50
Darth Vader Model Kit (AMT/Ertl #8784, 1996) 25.00
Luke Skywalker Model Kit (AMT/Ertl #8783, 1995) ... 25.00
Han Solo Model Kit (AMT/Ertl #8785, 1995) 25.00
Prince Xizor Model Kit (AMT/Ertl #8256, 1996) in *Shadows of the Empire* box 25.00
Emperor Palpatine (AMT/Ertl #8258, 1996) in *Shadows of the Empire* box 25.00

Action Scenes
Rebel Base Action Scene (MPC/Ertl and AMT/Ertl #8735, 1993) 18¾"x12¾" *The Empire Strikes Back* box 15.00
Jabba's Throne Room Model (AMT/Ertl #8262, 1996) . 13.50
Encounter with Yoda Model (AMT/Ertl #8263, 1996) .. 13.50
Battle on Hoth Action Scene, with 11½"x17½" vacu-formed base (AMT/Ertl #8743, 1995) 13.50

Flight Displays
TIE Fighter Flight Display (AMT/Ertl #8275, 1996).... 20.00

Jabba the Hutt Throne Room (AMT/Ertl 1990s)

Speeder Bike Flight Display (AMT/Ertl #6352, 1997).. 20.00
X-Wing Flight Display (AMT/Ertl #8788, 1995)....... 19.50

Limited Editions
X-Wing Limited Edition (AMT/Ertl #8769, 1995)...... 31.50
TIE Interceptor Limited Edition (AMT/Ertl #8770, 1995). 31.50
B-Wing Limited Edition Model (AMT/Ertl #8780, 1995) 25.00

Ships
Shuttle *Tyderium* (MPC/Ertl and AMT/Ertl #8733, 1992) 18¾"x12¾" *Return of the Jedi* box 15.00
Return of the Jedi 3-piece Gift Set: B-Wing Fighter, X-Wing Fighter, TIE Interceptor, snap together (MPC/Ertl and AMT/Ertl #8912, 1992) 14¼"x10" box 20.00
Speeder Bike (MPC/Ertl and AMT/Ertl #8928, 1990) 14"x8" *Return of the Jedi* box................ 10.00
Luke Skywalker's Snowspeeder (MPC/Ertl and AMT/Ertl #8914, 1990) 10"x7" *The Empire Strikes Back* box 15.00
Star Destroyer (MPC/Ertl and AMT/Ertl #8915, 1990) 20"x10" *The Empire Strikes Back* box 15.00
Darth Vader TIE Fighter (MPC/Ertl and AMT/Ertl #8916, 1990) 14"x10¼" *Star Wars* box......... 12.00
Millennium Falcon (MPC/Ertl and AMT/Ertl #8917, 1990) 19¾"x14½" *Return of the Jedi* box 20.00

*A-Wing Fighter and AT-ST (*Return of the Jedi*) (MPC/Ertl 1990s)*

Yoda and Boba Fett Model Kits (Screamin 1994)

X-Wing Fighter (MPC/Ertl and AMT/Ertl #8918,
  1990) 14"x8" *Return of the Jedi* box 12.00
AT-AT (MPC/Ertl and AMT/Ertl #8919, 1990) 14"x8"
  Return of the Jedi box 15.00
Star Wars Shadows of the Empire Virago Model
  (AMT/Ertl #8377, 1997) 15.00
TIE Fighter Plus Pack, with glue, paint and paint
  brush (AMT/Ertl #8432, 1997) 16.00
Slave I (AMT/Ertl #8768, 1995) 13.50
Fiber Optic Star Destroyer Model (AMT/Ertl #8782,
  1995) *Empire Strikes Back* box 50.00
Millennium Falcon Cutaway Model (AMT/Ertl
  #8789, 1996) 27.00

Snap Kits
AT-ST, Snap together (AMT/Ertl #8734, 1992)
  10"x7" *Return of the Jedi* box 9.00
TIE Interceptor, snap together (AMT/Ertl #8931,
  1990) 10"x7" *Return of the Jedi* box 10.00
X-Wing Fighter, snap together (AMT/Ertl #8932,
  1990) 10"x7" *Return of the Jedi* box 11.00
A-Wing Fighter, snap together (AMT/Ertl #8933,
  1990) 10"x7" *Return of the Jedi* box 10.00
Y-Wing Fighter, snap together (AMT/Ertl #8934,
  1990) *Return of the Jedi* box 10.00

Princess Leia and Obi-Wan Kenobi Vinyl Model Kits (Polydata 1995)

VINYL MODEL KITS

Luke Skywalker pre-painted model, 1/6 scale
(Polydata 1995) $35.00
Obi Wan Kenobi pre-painted model, 1/6 scale
(Polydata 1995) 35.00
Tusken Raider pre-painted model, 1/6 scale
(Polydata 1995) 35.00
Princess Leia pre-painted model, 1/6 scale
(Polydata 1995) 35.00
Chewbacca pre-painted model, 1/6 scale (Polydata
1996) 35.00
Lando Calrissian pre-painted model, 1/6 scale
(Polydata 1997) 35.00
Boba Fett pre-painted vinyl model kit, 13" tall,
9,000 copies, box illo by Nelson DeCastro
(Polydata1997) 35.00

Luke Skywalker Vinyl Model, 1/4 scale (Screamin
#3010, 1996) 65.00
Darth Vader Vinyl Model, 1/4 scale (Screamin
#3200, 1992) 65.00
Yoda Vinyl Model, 1/4 scale (Screamin #3300, 1992) . 60.00
Han Solo Vinyl Model, 1/4 scale (Screamin #3400,
1993) 65.00
C-3PO Vinyl Model, 1/4 scale (Screamin #3500, 1993) 65.00
Stormtrooper, 1/4 scale (Screamin #3600, 1993) 65.00
Chewbacca Vinyl Model, 1/4 scale (Screamin
#3700, 1994) 68.00
Boba Fett Vinyl Model, 1/4 scale (Screamin #3800,
1994) 70.00
Tusken Raider Vinyl Model, 1/4 scale (Screamin
#3900, 1995) 68.00

STEEL MODELS

Millennium Falcon Star Wars Steel Tec Kit (Remco
#7140, 1995) $25.00
X-Wing Fighter *Star Wars* Steel Tec Kit (Remco
#7141, 1995) 25.00

FLYING MODELS

Original Rocket Model Kits
R2-D2 Flying Rocket Kit (Estes #1298, 1979) $25.00
T.I.E. Fighter Flying Model Rocket Kit (Estes #1299,
1979) 30.00
X-Wing Fighter Flying Model Rocket Outfit Kit
(Estes #1302, 1979) 30.00
Proton Torpedo Flying Model Rocketry Outfit with
Launching Kit, Darth Vader picture box (Estes
#1420, 1979) 50.00
X-Wing Fighter Flying Model Rocket with Launching
Kit (Estes #1422, 1979) 50.00

New Starter Sets
X-wing Flying Model Rocket Starter Set (Estes
#1490, 1996) battery operated 35.00
A-wing Flying Model Rocket Starter Set (Estes
#1491, 1996) battery operated 35.00
Y-wing Flying Model Rocket Starter Set (Estes
#1492, 1996) battery operated 35.00
Death Star Flying Model Rocket Starter Set (Estes
#1493, 1996) battery operated 35.00

Luke Skywalker X-wing Fighter and Darth Vader TIE
Fighter Starter Set, with 6 launch engines, controller and parachutes (Estes #1801, 1998) 50.00

New Flying Model Rockets
R2-D2 Flying Model Rocket (Estes #2142, 1997) 15.00
Death Star Flying Model Rocket (Estes #2143, 1997) . 15.00
Darth Vader's TIE Fighter Flying Model Rocket,
16½" (Estes #2144, 1997) 15.00
Millennium Falcon Flying Model Rocket (Estes
#2146, 1997) 15.00
Star Destroyer Flying Model Rocket (Estes #2147,
1997) 15.00
Shuttle *Tyderium* Flying Model Rocket (Estes
#2148, 1997) 15.00

Flying Model Rockets with Recovery Parachute
TIE Fighter Flying Model Rocket with Recovery
Parachute 9" (Estes #2102, 1997) 24.00
X-wing Flying Model Rocket with Recovery
Parachute 10¾" (Estes #2103, 1997) 18.00
R2-D2 Flying Model Rocket with Recovery
Parachute 9" (Estes #2104, 1997) 29.00

Ready-Built Flying Model Rocket
Star Wars Flying Model Rocket, Red Squadron
X-wing Starfighter (Estes #01810, 1998) on
header card 6.00

Balsa Model Glider Kits 1995–97
Star Destroyer Flying model kit (Estes #05020) 8.00
A-wing Fighter Catapult Flying model kit (Estes
#05021) 8.00
X-wing Fighter Flying model kit (Estes #05022) 6.00
Y-wing Fighter Flying model kit (Estes #05023) 6.00

Control Line Aircraft
X-wing Control Line Fighter kit, with Cox engine
(Estes Cox #9310) 60.00
Darth Vader's TIE Fighter Control Line Fighter kit,
with Cox engine (Estes Cox #9330) 60.00
Snowspeeder Control Line Fighter kit, with Cox
engine (Estes Cox #9320) 60.00
Death Star Battle Station with X-wing Control Line
Fighter kit, with Cox engine, Radio Controlled
(Estes Cox #9420) 150.00
Landspeeder Radio Control Vehicle kit, with Cox
engine (Estes Cox #9430) 100.00
Star Wars Combat Set, flying 13.6" wingspan
X-wing Fighter and 9.5" wingspan TIE fighter
with motor and control lines (Estes #9410, 1997) 100.00
X-wing Sterling Model Kit Control Line Fighter, 13"
wingspan (Estes #6760, 1997) requires Cox
engine 25.00
Y-wing Sterling Model Kit Control Line Fighter,
10¾" wingspan (Estes #6761, 1997) requires
Cox engine 25.00

Deluxe Rocket Kits
X-wing Fighter North Coast Rocketry high powered
model rocket, 20" long, 18" wingspan, with
recovery parachute (Estes #3540, 1997) 100.00

PAPER COLLECTIBLES

PAPER COLLECTIBLES

CALENDARS — CATALOGS — MAGAZINES — POINT OF PURCHASE AND STORE DISPLAYS — PROOFS

This section includes all kinds of miscellaneous paper collectibles which don't fit in other sections; Books, Comics, Trading Cards, and Wall Art (posters, lithos, etc.) are all covered in their own sections; and Customizable Card Games can be found at the end of the GAMES section.

BOOKMARKS AND BOOKPLATES

Many bookmarks and bookplates contain attractive art work; but as collectibles, they are associated with books, and book collecting is *not* the driving force behind *Star Wars* collecting. This has kept the price of these items at, or near, original retail price.

Bookmarks
Return of the Jedi bookmarks (Random House
   1983) each $4.00
   Set, 16 bookmarks. 50.00
Star Wars 20th Anniversary tasseled bookmark
   (Antioch #KBO13986, 1997) 2.00
Return of the Jedi 20th Anniversary tasseled book
   mark (Antioch #KBO13994, 1997) 2.00

Star Wars Bookmarks, full color photographs of
   characters (Antioch 1997)
   Han Solo. 2.50
   Lando Calrissian 2.50
   Obi-Wan Kenobi 2.50
   Princess Leia. 2.50
Star Wars Bookmarks, Drew Struzan book art plus
   photo, with tassel (Antioch 1997)
   Darth Vader. 3.00
   Glove of Darth Vader 3.00
   Truce at Bakura 3.00
   Crystal Star 3.00
   Luke Skywalker 3.00
Star Wars 3-D Bookmarks, 3 piece set (A.H. Pris-
   matic #1006SW, 1997). 6.00

Star Wars Shapemarks: (Antioch 1997)
   Boba Fett. 3.00
   C-3PO. 2.00
   Tusken Raider. 2.00
   Yoda 2.00

Bookplates
Return of the Jedi bookplates (Random House
   1983) each 5.00
   Set, 4 bookplates. 20.00
Star Wars bookplates (Antioch 1997)
   C-3PO and R2-D2 photo (#01961). 3.00
   Hildebrandt poster (#02046). 3.00

CALENDARS

Calendars were only made for a few years when the movies first appeared. Since 1995, calendars have been sold every year and you can bet this will continue. Calendars appear in about July of the year before the year printed on the calendar, and by December they are available at discount and by January they are discounted heavily. If you intend to collect them, wait to get them at half price and don't unseal them.

The 1978 *Star Wars* Calendar (Ballantine Books
   #27377, 1977) originally $4.95
   Sealed. $30.00
   Open. 15.00
1979 *Star Wars* Calendar (Ballantine Books)
   Sealed. 20.00
   Open. 10.00

Star Wars *Calendar (Cedco 1990)*

1980 *Star Wars* Calendar (Ballantine Books)
 Sealed................................. 20.00
 Open.................................. 10.00
1981 *The Empire Strikes Back* Calendar (Ballantine Books)
 Sealed................................. 25.00
 Open.................................. 10.00
1984 *Return of the Jedi* Calendar (Ballantine Books)
 Sealed................................. 15.00
 Open.................................. 10.00
Return of the Jedi, The 1984 Ewok Calendar
 (Ballantine Books) with peel-off stickers
 Sealed................................. 15.00
 Open, complete with all stickers 10.00

Calendars (1990s)
Star Wars 1990 Calendar (Cedco) sealed......... 10.00
Star Wars 1991 Calendar (Cedco) sealed......... 10.00
Star Wars 1991 Lucasfilm Calendar (Abrahms) sealed 25.00
Star Wars calendars, 1995–98 (Cedco)
 Sealed............................. cover price
 Open .... half cover price
Star Wars Vehicles 1997 Calendar (Chronicle
 Books, #1246-4, 1996) with bonus poster....... 13.00
Star Wars 20th Anniversary Collector's 1997
 Calendar (Golden Turtle Press #399-1, 1996) ... 12.00
The Art of *Star Wars* Classic Characters 1998
 Calendar (Cedco #520-9)................... 13.00
Star Wars Trilogy Special Edition 1998 Calendar
 (Cedco #543-8) 13.00

CATALOGS

Kenner issued two kinds of catalogs which covered *Star Wars* toys. The best known are the small pocket or consumer catalogs included in most of the vehicle packages. They were issued for all there movies and contain interesting pictures and early information which is not always accurate to what was actually produced. The larger retailer catalogs were given to the stores to get them to order *Star Wars* toys. Catalogs such as this are issued every year or more frequently by just about every toy company and are often available at Toy Fair, at least to the press and retailers. As you might expect, the earlier catalogs sell for more than the later ones.

Every toy company with a *Star Wars* license has a cata-log, but most of the collector interest focuses on Kenner. The

Kenner Fall 1977 *Star Wars* catalog features the Early Bird Certificate Package and naturally pre-dates it, since the retail-er must buy the toy before it gets in the toy store for the con-sumer to purchase. This makes it the very first Kenner col-lectible, but hardly the first *Star Wars* collectible. After all, the paperback book and the first Marvel comics appeared *before* the movie premiere. Sears Wish Books (Christmas Catalogs) are also interesting because they feature the Sears exclusives, which are some of the most valuable collectibles.

One of Kenner's more interesting *Star Wars* catalogs is from the 1986 Toy Fair. This is the last one to contain *Star Wars* merchandise until the mid 1990s revival of the line. The 1986 catalog covers the Droids and Ewoks lines and includes pictures of a number of figures which were never actually released.

Consumer Mini Catalogs
Star Wars 1977, logo cover, list 12 figures $20.00
Star Wars, X-Wing cover, lists 8 new figures
 (1978–79) 15.00
  Variation, Burger Chef Fun 'N' Games Booklet,
  added puzzle and game pages to 1978 X-
  Wing catalog 10.00
Star Wars, Death Star and X-Wing cover (#428-063,
 1979)................................. 10.00
The Empire Strikes Back logo (#359-096, 1980) 10.00
The Empire Strikes Back, Luke and Yoda cover,
 logo back cover (1980) 10.00
The Empire Strikes Back, Luke and Yoda cover
 (#1037-144, 1981)....................... 10.00
Star Wars Collections (#236-068-00, 1982)......... 10.00
Return of the Jedi, picturing Darth Vader and Royal
 Guards (#175-017-00, 1983) 10.00
Return of the Jedi, picturing Jabba the Hutt
 (#76719000, 1984) 10.00

Retailer Catalogs (Kenner)
"*Star Wars* Toys and Games Available Fall 1977"
 featuring the Early Bird Certificate Package 75.00
Star Wars 1978 Catalog, features the first nine figures 50.00
Star Wars 1979 Catalog, features the Boba Fett
 rocket firing backpack 35.00
Star Wars Collector Series 1984 Catalog 30.00
Kenner 1986 Toy Fair Catalog.................... 25.00

Star Wars *Consumer Mini-Catalog (Kenner 1979) and* Return of the Jedi *Mini-Catalog (Kenner 1984)*

GREETING CARDS

Star Wars Birthday Card (1994) full color multiple
   fold-out $2.00
Star Wars Greeting Card 12-pack, color (1992) 21.00
Yoda Christmas Cards, art by Tsuneo Sanda, 10
   cards and envelopes (1997) 10.00
Deluxe *Star Wars* Valentine Kit (1997) 3.00

LOBBY CARDS

Lobby cards are large prints containing scenes from a movie, or pictures of the stars which, as the name implies, were designed for display in the lobby of a movie theater. They are 11"x14" in size and come in sets of eight different cards. Lobby cards are produced for every movie, just like movie posters (covered under "WALL ART") and they are standard sizes because the theater can't change its display spaces for each movie. Theaters are also sent sets of 8"x10" photo cards, and frequently star and scene photos in larger sizes.

Star Wars lobby cards, photo cards and similar items can generally be acquired from dealers who specialize in lobby cards and posters from movies generally. Since there is ongoing collector interest in movie memorabilia, these items are not thrown away. There is also no great secret to collecting them. Lobby cards from popular movies with famous stars are naturally worth more than ones from movies you refuse to watch on free television, and bigger cards are worth more than smaller ones. However, popular movies like *Star Wars* play for a long time in a lot of theaters and are re-released too, meaning that more lobby cards, photo cards and similar items are produced, and that more are saved by collectors.

Star Wars
Set of eight lobby cards, 11"x14" (1977) $125.00
Set of eight photo cards, 8"x10" (1977) 100.00

The Empire Strikes Back
Set of eight lobby cards, 11"x14" (1980) 90.00
Set of eight photo cards, 8"x10" (1980) 75.00

Lobby Card from The Empire Strikes Back *(LucasArts 1980)*

Bantha Tracks #13 (Lucasfilm 1981)

Return of the Jedi
Set of eight lobby cards, 11"x14" (1983) 75.00
Set of eight photo cards, 8"x10" (1983) 60.00

MAGAZINES

There have been several magazines devoted exclusively, or almost exclusively, to *Star Wars* — almost as many as Leonardo DiCaprio has today. The only surprising part is that some of these magazines were started more than a decade after the last movie had come and gone. Magazines covering collectibles, general interest and humor are covered immediately following those which exclusively featured *Star Wars*.

BANTHA TRACKS
Lucasfilm

#1 to #4, each $15.00
Combined reissue #1–#4 . . . . 10.00
#5 to #9 . . . . 6.00
#10 to #19 . . . . 5.00
#20 to #33 . . . . 4.00
#34 . . . . 7.50
#35 10th Anniversary, last issue 6.00

LUCASFILM FAN CLUB MAGAZINE
The Fan Club (1987–94)

1987
1 Anthony Daniels interview, 14pgs $10.00
1988
2 Star Tours, 14pgs 3.00
3 Mark Hamill interview, 14pgs. 4.00
4 14pgs 3.00
5 14pgs 3.00

Star Wars Insider #24, #29 and #35 (Star Wars Fan Club 1995–97)

1989
6 George Lucas interview 4.00
7 Harrison Ford interview. 6.00
8 Steven Spielberg interview, ... 3.00
9 Sean Connery interview 9.00
1990
#10 . . . . 3.00
#11 *The Empire Strikes Back* 10th Anniv. 8.00
#12 Maniac Mansion. 3.00
#13 . . . . 3.00
1991
#14 Billy Dee Williams interview 6.00
1992
#15 . . . . 5.00
#16 *Star Wars* comics. 6.00
#17 George Lucas Interview. 7.50
1993
#18 Art of Drew Struzan 7.50
#19 *Return of the Jedi* 10th Anniv., 30 pgs. 10.00

#20 34 pgs. 10.00
1994
#21 36pgs 10.00
#22 TIE Fighter video game 5.00
Becomes:

STAR WARS INSIDER
The *Star Wars* Fan Club (1994–98)

1994
#23 56 pages, Obi-Wan photo cover. $9.00
1995
#24 Ralph McQuarrie cover, 60 pages 10.00
#25 James Earl Jones interview, 72 pages 5.00
#26 George Lucas interview, 80 pages 6.00
1996
#27 Luke and Landspeeder cover, 80 pages. 8.00
#28 Peter Mayhew interview, 64 pages. 5.00
#29 Shadows of the Empire, 64 pages 5.00

Official Poster Monthly #1, #6 and #9 (Paradise Press 1978–79)

#30 Han and Jabba fold out cover, 64 pages 5.00
#31 Expanded *Star Wars* Universe, 68 pages 4.00
1997
#32 84 pages 5.00
#33 Wampa cover, 76 pages 4.50
#34 Mark Hamill cover, 74 pages 4.50
#35 Tusken Raider cover, 74 pages 4.50
1998
#36 Jawa cover, Liam Neeson interview 4.50
#37 Senator Palpatine, Ian McDiarmid interview 4.50

OFFICIAL POSTER MONTHLY

Star Wars
#1 Stormtrooper cover $10.00
#2 Darth Vader/Luke Skywalker cover. 5.00
#3 Han Solo cover 5.00
#4 Chewbacca/Darth Vader cover 5.00
#5 Darth Vader/C-3PO cover 5.00
#6 Droids/Sand People cover 5.00
#7 R2-D2/C-3PO cover. 5.00
#8. . . . . 5.00
#9 Luke and Leia circus cover 5.00
#10 Darth Vader cover 5.00
#11 through #18, each 10.00

The Empire Strikes Back
#1 through #5, each 5.00

Return of the Jedi
#1 through #4, each 5.00

STAR WARS GALAXY MAGAZINE
Topps (1994–97)

#1 Fall 1994, *Star Wars* Widevision SWP3 card $7.50
#2 Winter 1995 Luke Skywalker on Tatooine cover
 by Dave Dorman 5.00
#3 Spring 1995 cover by Jae Lee; All Alien issue,
 The Empire Strikes Back Widevision #0, *Star
 Wars* Cap #0, Topps Finest Chromium #3,
 SWGM3 AT-AT (McQuarrie) chromium 5.00
#4 Summer 1995, collage cover; *Star Wars Galaxy
 3* #000 Princess Leia card; *Star Wars* Galaxy
 Topps Finest SWGM4 chromium card; *Star
 Wars Galaxy Magazine* 4-card sheet; Battle of
 Hoth 4-page poster 5.00
#5 Fall 1995, Luke, Obi-Wan, Darth and Yoda
 cover, Ralph McQuarrie poster; *Star Wars*
 Mastervisions P2 large promo card; *Star Wars
 Galaxy* 3 P6 promo card; *Return of the Jedi*
 Widevision P1 promo card 5.00
#6 Winter 1996, Bounty Hunter issue, Boba Fett
 cover by Chris Moeller; *Return of the Jedi*
 Widevision promo card #0, *Star Wars* Finest
 #1 promo card 5.00
#7 Spring 1996, Shadows of the Empire cover by
 Hugh Fleming, Tim & Greg Hildebrandt poster;
 Star Wars Finest #2 promo card; *Star Wars*
 Shadows of the Empire #1 promo card;
 Company store catalog 5.00
#8 Summer 1996, The Dark Side cover by Cam
 Kennedy, Shadows of the Empire #4 promo
 card, Dark Side cover card. 5.00
#9 Fall 1996 Luke and Xizor cover by the Bros.
 Hildebrandt, with *Star Wars* 3-D promo card
 3Di #1 and *Star Wars* Galaxy Mag. promo C2 . . . . 5.00
#10 Winter 1997, Han Solo vs. a Selonian cover by

Star Wars Galaxy *Magazine #1 (Topps 1995)*

Joe Jusko, *Star Wars* Galaxy Mag. promo card
C3; *Star Wars* Trilogy Widevision promo card P2 . . 5.00
#11 1997, Darth Vader cover by Walt Simonson,
 with *Star Wars* Trilogy Hologram promo #1 of 2
 or #2 of 2; *Star Wars Galaxy* Magazine promo
 card C4; *Star Wars* Vehicles promo postcard 5.00
#12 Aug. 1997, Princess Leia cover by Dave
 Devries, with *Star Wars* Trilogy Widevision
 promo P1 and poster of cover painting. 5.00
#13 Nov. 1997, Obi Wan Kenobi, Yoda and Luke
 cover by Joe Quesada, Jimmy Palmiotti and
 Atomic Paintbrush 5.00
Becomes:
STAR WARS GALAXY COLLECTOR
Topps (1998)

#1 Feb. 1998 Drew Struzan poster, SW2 prequel card . 5.00
#2 May 1998 Flying Models poster, SW1 and SW3
 prequel cards. 5.00
Boba Fett one-shot special (April 1998) 5.00

STAR WARS: TECHNICAL JOURNAL
Starlog (1993–94)

#1 *Star Wars*: Technical Journal of the Planet
 Tatooine, holographic foil logo, 8-page gatefold
 blueprints, etc. (1993) $9.95
#2 *Star Wars*: Technical Journal of the Imperial
 Forces (1994) 6.95
#3 *Star Wars*: Technical Journal of the Rebel Forces . . 6.95

Star Wars Technical Journal #1, #2 and #3 (Starlog 1993–95)

MAGAZINES: COLLECTIBLES

Many collector magazines have run *Star Wars* covers. The prices in the listing below are for newsstand versions — those without promotional giveaways such as trading cards and posters. However, many of these collector magazines came with *Star Wars* promos polybagged with the magazine. Magazines with their original promos can be worth a lot more money, depending on the collectibility of the item, but they can often be found, bagged and complete, at reduced prices in comics shops or at shows. All known promo cards, along with their source, are listed in the TRADING CARDS section. Use this as your guide when bargain hunting.

The following is a sampling of collector and distributor magazines with *Star Wars* covers. There are undoubtedly many others. Since they are primarily sold to collectors the covers are usually pictures of *Star Wars* toys or trading cards, or art supplied by the manufacturers.

Advance Comics (Capitol City Distribution)
Issue #82 Empire's End cover. $10.00

Baby Boomer Collectibles (Antique Trader Publications)
Vol. 3, No. 4 Han, Darth, Luke, Yoda, Chewbacca,
C-3PO vinyl figures cover 3.00

Card Collector's Price Guide (Century Publishing Company)
Vol. 2, No. 5 *Star Wars* Galaxy Yoda cover 2.00

Cards Illustrated (Warrior Publications)
Issue #20 Star Destroyer and *Millennium Falcon* cover . 3.00
Issue #25 C-3PO and R2-D2 cover. 3.00

Collect! (Tuff Stuff Publications)
Jan. 1995 Issue Darth Vader (McQuarrie art) cover. . . . 7.50
Oct. 1996 Issue Shadows of the Empire, Darth
Vader cover (Hildebrandt art) 7.50
March 1997 Issue. 5.00
May 1998 Issue Jabba the Hutt and Leia cover. 5.00

Advance Comics #82 and Star Wares (Capitol City Distribution 1995–96) Previews *Nov. 1996 (Diamond Distribution 1996)*

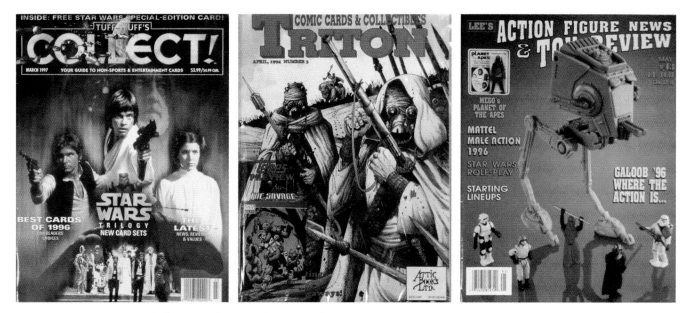

Collect! *March 1997;* Triton *#3; and* Lee's Action Figure News & Toy Review *#43*

Collectible Toys and Values (Attic Books)
Issue #15 Kenner figures cover 7.50
Issue #35 Yoda cover 5.00

Combo (Century Publishing Company)
Issue #27, Han and Jabba cover 3.00

Hero Illustrated (Warrior Publications)
Issue #26 Dave Dorman art cover 4.00
1994 Science Fiction Annual C-3PO with gun cover . . . 4.00

Lee's Action Figure News & Toy Review (Lee Publications)
Issue #6 Micro Collection cover 7.00
Issue #15 . . . . 10.00
Issue #23 R2-D2 cover 7.00
Issue #31 *Millennium Falcon* cover 7.00
Issue #32 TIE Fighter cover 7.00
Issue #43 Galoob AT-ST cover 10.00
Issue #45 Boba Fett cover 9.00
Issue #49 Luke Stormtrooper cover 9.00
Issue #50 Galoob TIE Fighter Pilot playset cover 7.00
Issue #56 Kenner Cinema Scenes Han, Luke and
    Chewbacca cover 8.00
Issue #64 Kenner: Rystall, Greeta, and LynMe cover . . 6.00

Non-Sport Update (Roxanne Toser Non-Sport Enterprises)
Volume 4, No. 2 Ken Steacy art cover 5.00

Diamond Previews (Diamond Distribution)
Aug. 95 . . . . 3.00
Nov 96 . . . . 3.00

Star Wares (Capital City Distribution)
Vol. 1 to Vol 6, each 3.00

Tomart's Action Figure Digest (Tomart Publications)
Issue #27 Chewbacca toys cover 6.00
Issue #32 Darth Vader and Obi Wan Kenobi toys 6.00
Issue #39 Luke Skywalker and Wampa toy cover 6.00
Issue #40 Han Solo and Tauntaun toy cover 6.00
Issue #45 Mos Eisley toy scene cover 6.00

ToyFare (Wizard Press)
Issue #1 AT-AT Cover 3.00

Triton (Attic Books)
Issue #3 *Star Wars* Galaxy card art cover 5.00

White's Guide to Collecting Figures (Collecting Concepts)
    "Comic Cover Version"
Issue #1 . . . . 6.00
Issue #8 . . . . 6.00
Issue #13 Boba Fett toy cover 6.00
Issue #26 Darth Vader vs. Obi Wan Kenobi F/X cover . . 6.00
Issue #30 Boba Fett sculpture cover 6.00
Issue #34 Leia prisoner cover 6.00

Wizard (Wizard Press)
Sci-Fi Invasion 1997 Boba Fett cover 3.00

MAGAZINES: GENERAL

Mass market Collectible #3 is the issue of *Time* magazine (May 30, 1977) which appeared a few days before the movie opened and featured a two-page spread praising the movie as the best picture of the year. The movie opened on a Friday and it wasn't hard to get a ticket for the first evening showing. There was a long line for the second showing and for every showing thereafter for many months.

The value of old magazines generally depends on the cover photo or painting. The *Star Wars* movies have generated hundreds, perhaps thousands, of magazine covers. When something is popular, everybody wants it on their cover. In addition to obvious magazines, like those that cover the movies generally, or science fiction movies, or special effects, magazines like *People* will tell you about the sad love life or happy home life of the stars, while financial magazines will tell you about all the money the movie is making. There is probably some *Bounty Hunter* trade magazine that elected Boba Fett their "Hunter of the Year." There may even be a health food magazine suggesting that Jabba the Hutt could slim down a bit by eating "free range" live creatures, instead of fat domestic ones as seen in the movie.

The list below includes "selections" which I forthrightly admit is merely a euphemism for "the ones that I have pho-

Starlog #7, People, *July 18, 1977;* Nickelodeon, *March 1997*

tos of" plus the original *Time* magazine issue, which I haven't yet found to photo. I wanted to include some of the photos, so I needed to have a short listing. Generally the covers are photos from the movie, or photos of the stars. Often the photos are promotional releases provided by Lucasfilms, but magazines like to get their own, exclusive, photos whenever they can.

Cinefantastique
Vol. 6 No. 4 The Making of *Star Wars* $20.00
Vol. 7 No. 1 The Making of *Star Wars* 20.00
Feb. 1997 *Star Wars* 20th Anniversary 5.00

Cinescape (MVP Entertainment)
March/April 1997 X-wing cover 5.00
Star Wars Special, March 1997. . . . . 5.00

Famous Monsters (Warren)
Issue #148 Darth Vader cover. 5.00

Nickelodeon
March 1997 Luke Skywalker and Princess Leia cover . . 4.00

People Magazine
July 18, 1977 C-3PO cover. 10.00
Aug. 14, 1978 Carrie Fisher cover 10.00

Reel Fantasy
Issue #1 . . . . 5.00

Science Fiction, Horror & Fantasy
Issue #1 Darth Vader and Stormtroopers cover. 7.00

Sci-Fi Entertainment
Feb. 1997 *Star Wars* 20th Anniversary 5.00

Starlog (Starlog Group)
Issue #7, X-Wing and TIE Fighter 35.00
Issue #13 David Prowse. 10.00
Issue #14 SF Matte painting cover 10.00
Issue #21 Mark Hammil 10.00
Issue #31 Empire Strikes Back 10.00
Issue #35 Billy Dee Williams 10.00
Issue #99 C-3PO and R2-D2 . . . . 8.00

Issue #236 *Star Wars* 20th Anniversary 6.00
Issue #237 George Lucas. 6.00
Time Magazine (Time Warner)
May 30, 1977 . . . . 20.00
May 19, 1980 Darth Vader cover. 10.00
Feb. 10, 1997. . . . . 3.00

MAGAZINES: HUMOR

Personally, I enjoy humorous take-offs of the movies and TV shows that I like. The quintessential humor magazine (of course I mean *Mad Magazine*) has done quite a few *Star Wars* issues. As with any magazine, it is the appearance of *Star Wars* on the cover that makes it a *Star Wars* collectible.

Mad Magazine
Issue #196, Jan. 1978, Alfred E. Newman as Darth
    Vader cover $10.00
Issue #203, Dec. 1978, The Mad *Star Wars* musical
    cover. 9.00
Issue #220, Jan. 1981, Alfred E. Newman as Yoda
    cover. 7.00
Issue #242, Oct. 1983, Unmasks the *Return of the
    Jedi* cover 7.00

The Empire Strikes Back *stamp, First Day Cover (March 19, 1996)*

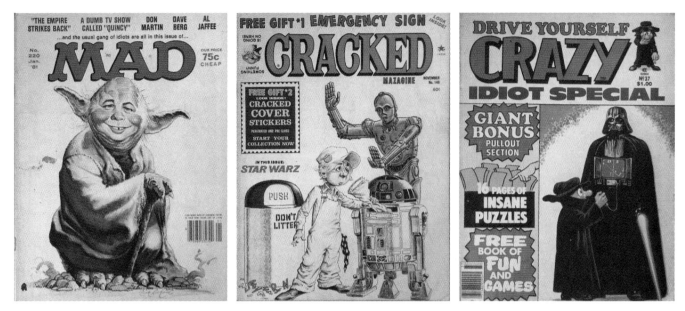

Mad Magazine #220, Cracked Magazine #146, Crazy Magazine #37

Cracked
Issue #146, Star Warz spoof cover 5.00

Crazy
Issue #37, Darth Vader cover 5.00

Comics
Adolescent Radioactive Black Belt Hampsters in
    3-D issue #2, *Star Wars* spoof cover 3.00
Samurai Cat, issue #3 (of 3) *Star Wars* spoof cover . . . 3.00
Married With Children 2099, issue #3, May the
    Farce Be With You cover 3.00

MISCELLANEOUS PAPER

Doorknob Hangers
Star Wars Doorknob Hangers (Antioch, 1997)
    Darth Vader "Your Destiny Lies with Me"
        (#61085, 1997) $1.50
    C-3PO "Signal Alliance" (#78859, 1997) 1.50

Holograms
Holograms, 2"x2", mounted on acrylic display stand
    (A.H. Prismatic 1995), 4 different, each 15.00
Star Wars Hologram stickers, large, 6"x6" sheets
    (A.H. Prismatic #1019/SW, 1997) 3.00
Star Wars 3-D small stickers 2"x2" (A.H. Prismatic
    1997) 4 different, each 1.00

Stamps
Star Wars Postage Stamps, issued by St. Vincent
    and the Grenadines
    Metallic Stamp gift pack, folder containing 9-
        stamp sheet, plus a souvenir sheet with
        three triangular stamps printed on metallic foil . 25.00
    First Day Covers stamp set, 3 covers, boxed,
        with certificate of authenticity. 15.00

Wallet Cards
Star Wars Wallet Cards (Antioch, 1997)
    6 different, each 1.00

POINT OF PURCHASE DISPLAYS

Before a *Star Wars* product gets to the consumer, it has to be designed, manufactured, packaged, shipped and displayed for purchase in your local store. Just about every part of this process produces something that could be, and frequently is, collected.

The design process yields product and packaging prototypes and proofs or samples. Prototypes are internal items, available only to company employees, LucasArts' licensing people (for approval) and possibly advertising agencies. You really have to know somebody to get them initially. Proofs

Star Wars 21-figure store display (Kenner 1979)

The Empire Strikes Back, *32-figure store display (Kenner 1981)*

and samples are often more widely available, because they often reach salesmen and store buyers. If you don't have an actual finished sample product to show to the buyers, you may, at least, have a packaging proof to convince them that the item will be a hot seller.

Shipping yields boxes, but they are usually simple light brown corrugated items with black labels, of no real visual interest. Stores throw them away, or give them away if you ask for them. A number of collectors store their *Star Wars* action figures in the original boxes, because they have been designed for this purpose and are just the right size, but they do not consider the boxes to be part of the collection and they have never attracted much of a market for themselves.

The fact that you are a collector raises enough questions about your sanity already. A large horde of empty corrugated boxes is more likely to be mentioned at your commitment hearing, than at your enshrinement in the collectors' hall of fame. Still, somebody must have boxes from the original shipments of *Star Wars* action figures in 1978, or perhaps a complete set of shipping boxes from the current figures, #69570.01 to #69570.99. Who knows? Maybe they will turn out to be quite valuable someday. Your relatives may yet regret having you locked up in that padded cell and throwing them away.

Point of Purchase displays and store signs are much more interesting. They are designed to attract your attention, so they are colorful. They display the product just as nicely in your room as they did in the store. And, best of all, they are items that were never intended to be sold to the general public in the first place, so not everybody has one.

Generally, point of purchase items are not collected so as to acquire an entire set. Rather, a few are acquired to form a backdrop or focal point for the display of ones collection.

STORE DISPLAYS

Kenner, and every other large manufacturer, makes displays to promote their products at the point of purchase. If they have a contest or giveaway promotion, they will want to let you know about it. These come in all sizes and shapes and are frequently made of cardboard. They are hanging or standing or sitting on or over the rack where the toy or other items are selected, or in the store's window. Over the years a lot of them have been produced and many more are to come. Size and art work are important components of their collectable value, along with the importance of the product they promote. Displays for Kenner's action figures rank at the top.

Since the displays go to stores, it helps to work there if you want to collect them. Undoubtedly many displays are damaged in use or simply thrown away at the end of the promotion; however, there are thousands of stores that sell action figures and each store gets a reasonable supply, so initial print runs have to be 25,000 to 50,000 minimum for ordinary items. This tends to keep the price within reason. Signs and displays that are flat look very nice when framed and make a handsome addition to your collection.

Star Wars Action Figure sign (1978–80) depending
    on size $100–250
The Empire Strikes Back Action Figure sign (1980–
    1982) depending on size 75–125
Return of the Jedi Action Figure sign (1983–
    1984) depending on size 40–90

The most valuable store display is quite recent. In the fall of 1997 many Toys "R" Us stores got a four-foot hanging *Millennium Falcon*, made in plastic and looking just like a scaled up version of the toy. Only 500 were supposed to be made and they were given away in a drawing by Rosie O'Donnell. You could enter the drawing with a one dollar contribution to her charitable foundation. I entered, but didn't win. You probably entered too. The contest entry forms estimated the value of the item at $500.00, but I would think $2,500.00 would be closer. When you entered, did you think where you would store the item if you won? Of course not, because you just wanted to win one. The store display for the contest is a nice consolation collectible. It shows the *Falcon* in a reversed picture.

The Empire Strikes Back *store display (Kenner 1979)*

Millennium Falcon *Sweepstakes store display (Kenner 1997)*

PORTFOLIOS AND BLUEPRINTS

The Empire Strikes Back promo art portfolio $40.00
Star Wars Intergalactic Passport & Stickers
  (Ballantine 1983) 10.00
Star Wars Blueprints, includes 15 prints, 13"x19" in
  vinyl pouch (Ballantine 1977) 15.00
  Reprint: $6.95 (Ballantine 1992) 7.00
Star Wars Portfolio by Ralph McQuarrie, 11"x14"
  color paintings, originally $7.95 (Ballantine
  Books #27382, 1977) 20.00
The Empire Strikes Back Portfolio by Ralph
  McQuarrie, Ballantine Books (1980) 15.00
Return of the Jedi Portfolio by Ralph McQuarrie,
  Ballantine Books (1983) 15.00
Star Wars Power of the Force Planetary Map, set,
  issued as a mail-in 20.00
Star Wars/The Empire Strikes Back Portfolio, six
  11"x14" plates (#875-007, 1994) 12.00
Star Wars Trilogy Print Portfolio set, eight 11"x14"
  moviecards (Zanart #SW-1 1996) 12.00
Star Wars Post-Art portfolio, 11"x14" (Classico
  #02762, 1995) 15.00
Star Wars Trilogy Moviecard Portfolio, eight 11"x14"
  movie cards plus 8"x10" ChromArt card of the
  Millennium Falcon (Zanart 1994) 14.00

Return of the Jedi *Portfolio (Ballantine 1983)*

POSTCARDS

Star Wars Movie Poster Postcards (#110-038,
  1992) pack of 25 . . . . $15.00
The Empire Strikes Back Movie Poster Postcards
  (#110-037, 1992) pack of 25 . . . . 15.00
The *Return of the Jedi* Movie Poster Postcards
  (#110-030, 1992) pack of 25 . . . . 15.00
Stormtroopers Postcards (#110-057, 1992) pack of 25 15.00
Luke and Han in the Garbage Chute (#110-058,
  1992) pack of 25 . . . . 15.00
Luke Climbing into X-Wing (#105-059, 1992) pack
  of 25 . . . . 15.00
Artoo-Deetoo (#105-060, 1992) pack of 25 . . . . 15.00
Leia and Darth Vader (#105-061, 1992) pack of 25 . . . 15.00
R2-D2 and C-3PO (#105-062, 1992) pack of 25 . . . . . 15.00
See-Threepio (#105-072, 1992) pack of 25 . . . . 15.00
Han Solo (#105-073, 1992) pack of 25 . . . . 15.00
Luke Skywalker (#105-074, 1992) pack of 25 . . . . 15.00
Luke, Ben and C-3PO (1992) pack of 25. . . . . 15.00
Star Wars Postcard Set, 5 full color cards (Classico
  1994). 7.50
Star Wars Special Edition postcards, 11"x14" featur-
  ing poster art from movies, 4 different, each. 3.50
Star Wars Laser Postcard Set, holographic images
  (A.H. Prismatic 1994). 6.00
  Darth Vader. 1.50
  Millennium Falcon in asteroids 1.50
  Millennium Falcon and Death Star 1.50
  X-Wing and Death Star 1.50
The Empire Strikes Back Leia 8"x10" postcard
  (#422-012, 1994). 2.50
Star Wars Circus Poster 8"x10" postcard
  (#422-013,1994) 2.50
Star Wars Movie Poster 8"x10" postcard (#422-014,
  1994). 2.50
The Empire Strikes Back Concept 8"x10" postcard
  (#422-015, 1994). 2.50
Star Wars X-Wing 8"x10" postcard, Ralph
  McQuarrie art (#422-016, 1994). 2.50
The Empire Strikes Back Romantic 8"x10" post-
  card (#422-017, 1994) 2.50
Star Wars Character Art Postcards 12-card set 10.00
Star Wars Complete Postcards 12-card set. 10.00
Star Wars Poster Art Postcards 18-card set 15.00
The Empire Strikes Back Complete Postcards 8-cards . 7.00
Return of the Jedi Complete Postcards 8-card set. . . . 7.00
Star Wars Complete Oversize Postcards 10-card set . 26.00
The Empire Strikes Back Complete Oversize Post-
  cards 8-card set. 21.00
Star Wars Lasergram Postcards (A.H. Prismatic, 1997)
  Deathstar (#2001/SS) 2.00
  Millennium Falcon & Tie Fighters (#2001/FT) 2.00
  Darth Vader (2001/DV, 1997) 2.00
  Millennium Falcon in Asteroids (#2001/FA) 2.00
Luke and Darth Flicker Motion postcard, 1983 Fan
  Club item (offered in previews for Sept. 1997) . . . 10.00

Star Wars Trilogy Postcards (1997)
Star Wars Trilogy Postcard Set #1, 8 postcards 6.00
Star Wars Trilogy Postcard Set #2, 8 postcards 6.00
Star Wars Trilogy Postcard Set #3, 8 postcards. 6.00
Star Wars Trilogy Postcard Set #4, 10 postcards 8.00

Yoda The Empire Strikes Back *card proof (Kenner 1980)*

Boba Fett Revenge of the Jedi *card proof (Kenner 1982)*

PRESS KITS

Press Kits

Original *Star Wars* kit (1977)	$150.00
Star Wars kit (1978)	100.00
Holiday special kit (1978)	175.00
NPR Presents kit (1979)	35.00
The Empire Strikes Back kit (1980)	60.00
Introducing Yoda kit (1980)	35.00
NPR Playhouse kit (1981)	30.00
Return of the Jedi kit (1983)	30.00

PROGRAMS

Star Wars Movie Program (1977) limited quantity offered in 1994	$75.00
The Empire Strikes Back Official Collector's Edition (Paradise Press)	15.00
The Return of the Jedi Official Collector's Edition (Paradise Press)	10.00

PROOFS

A few header card proofs are made for every action fig-ure, so that design personnel, company executives and others can check the graphics, weigh the sales appeal of the package and generally bless the product. Everybody wants to get into the act and justify their job, so changes are frequent and often the proof is not quite like the final package. This makes them

quite interesting collectibles. The most valuable proofs are those for products that were never made, or where the design was changed in some significant way. After that, the value of proofs varies with the value of the final figure.

ACTION FIGURE CARD PROOFS

The most famous of these changes in the *Star Wars* world was the retitling of the third movie from *Revenge of the Jedi* to *Return of the Jedi*. No product was actually released with a *Revenge of the Jedi* package, but the original name is mentioned on a number of packages, and in magazines and action figure card proofs exist which have the *Revenge of the Jedi* logo. These are the most highly sought of the card proofs.

COVER PROOFS

Cover Proofs are to books what card proofs are to action figures. They are sent to retailers, along with the publishers monthly catalog, to help solicit orders. You may not be able to "tell" a book by its cover, but you sure can "sell" a book by its cover. I have seen dust jacket proofs for hardcover books, but most cover proofs are from paperback and trade paper-back books. All of them have the corner clipped and/or a small hole punched in them to prevent them being returned for credit by the retailer as unsold copies (unsold paperbacks are not returned to the publisher — the retailer rips off the front cover and returns it instead).

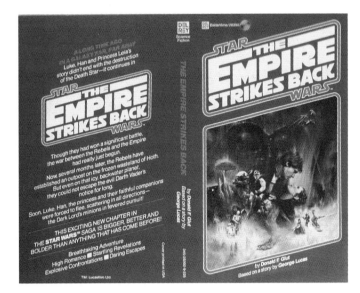

The Empire Strikes Back paperback cover proof
(Ballantine 1980)

I only know of a couple of people who actually collect cover proofs, but they do contain nice cover artwork. The cover proof for the original *Star Wars* paperback book would be the very first thing with the title *Star Wars* which was actually produced. Since I am calling the actual paperback "Collectible #1," I suppose it would be "Collectible #0."

Cover Proofs
Star Wars paperback cover proof $5.00
Star Wars paperback and trade paperback cover proofs:
    From 1977–79 . . . . 3.00
    From the 1980s 2.00
    From the 1990s 1.00

OTHER PROOFS

Just about every *Star Wars* product ever made has generated some kind of printing proof, sample, prototype or similar item. There is also an original piece of artwork or an original photo for every trading card, comic book cover, comic book interior page, paperback cover, hardcover dustjacket, poster, lobby card, video tape box, record jacket, video game box, T-shirt design, or other artistic product or product package. For every original piece of art, there is probably a concept drawing or sketch that went to the art director for approval before the artist did the actual drawing or painting.

The packaging proofs and prototypes for Kenner products, particularly action figures, command high prices today, and will probably always top the list. However, there are a very, very large number of proofs, prototypes and even originals for other products that were created and someone associated with the company has them. Maybe they even want to throw them away or give them away. Ask around in your area. Don't forget to check the local stores for signs. They won't have much use for it when the promotion is over. The right trash can make a very nice collectible.

STAND-UPS

Standees are near lifesize cardboard figures, designed as store displays and sold by Advanced Graphics. Comic shops

Emperor Palpatine Standee (Advance Graphics 1996)

and other stores buy them and some dealers get them to highlight their table at shows. Nobody seems to collect them, but if you want one, they are available for their retail price of about $25.00 (maybe a little less for smaller figures, like R2-D2 and Yoda.) The same goes for your favorite *Star Trek* figure, movie star or sports hero (maybe a little less for jockeys, girl Olympic acrobats, Danny DeVito and Mugsy Bogues.)

STANDEES
Advance Graphics (1993–98)
Admiral Ackbar $25.00
Ben Obi-Wan Kenobi (#225) 25.00
Boba Fett 25.00
C-3PO (#114) 25.00
Chewbacca (#177) 25.00
Darth Vader (#113) 25.00
Darth Vader, with lightsaber (#216) 25.00
Emperor Palpatine, on throne 25.00
Emperor's Royal Guard (#217) 25.00
Han Solo (#112) 25.00
Han Solo as Stormtrooper. 25.00
Han Solo in Carbonite (#214) 25.00
Jawa (#206) 20.00
Luke Skywalker (#110) 25.00
Princes Leia (#111) 25.00
Princess Leia, slave girl 25.00
R2-D2 (#116) 20.00
Stormtrooper (#115) 25.00
Tusken Raider 25.00
Yoda (#176) 20.00

RECORDINGS AND STILLS

RECORDINGS

AUDIO — MUSIC — VIDEO

All of the movies have been adapted as radio plays and many of the new novels and even a few of the comic books have become books on tape. There is collector interest in the former, particularly in the National Public Radio dramatizations. It is not yet clear whether books on tape are collected, in the sense that older tapes will go up in value, or whether *Star Wars* fans buy tapes to play, in which case newer formats with the next generation of sound quality enhancements will always be more desirable than older tapes.

AUDIO

Movie Adaptations

Star Wars: The Original Radio Drama, National Public Radio (Highbridge #099-4, 1993) 6 cassettes $35.00

Star Wars: The Original Radio Drama, National Public Radio (Highbridge #005-6, April 1993) 7 CDs 65.00

The Empire Strikes Back: The Original Radio Drama, National Public Radio (Highbridge #007-2, Sept. 1993) 5 CDs 55.00

The Empire Strikes Back: The Original Radio Drama, National Public Radio (Highbridge #000-5, Sept. 1993) 5 cassettes. 30.00

Star Wars/*The Empire Strikes Back* Limited Edition CD set (Highbridge #006-4, Sept. 1993) 12 CDs   125.00

Complete *Star Wars*/Empire CD set (Lucasfilm #114-1, April 1995) 12 CDs 100.00

Return of the Jedi: The Original Radio Drama, National Public Radio (Highbridge #158-3, Oct. 1996) 3 CDs 35.00

Return of the Jedi: The Original Radio Drama, George Lucas (Highbridge #157-5, Oct. 1996) 3 cassettes 25.00

Star Wars Complete Trilogy on CD, National Public Radio (Highbridge #164-8, Oct. 1996) 15 CDs . . 125.00

The *Star Wars* Limited Edition Collector's Trilogy CD, National Public Radio (Highbridge #165-6, Oct. 1996) deluxe slipcase, only 7,500 made . . . 175.00

Star Wars Trilogy CD Set (Highbridge #169-2) 9 CDs . 75.00

New Story Adaptations

Children of the Jedi, by Barbara Hambly, BDD Audio Cassette #47195-3, May 1995 . . . . 15.00

The Courtship Of Princess Leia, by Dave Wolverton, BDD Audio Cassette #47193-7, May 1994 . . . . 15.00

The Crystal Star, by Vonda N. McIntyre, BDD Audio Cassette #47194-5, Dec. 1994. . . . . 15.00

Dark Empire, by Tom Veitch, Donald I. Fine #201-6, June 1997 . . . . 15.00

Dark Empire, The Collector's Edition, by Tom Veitch, Donald I. Fine #347-4, 1995, 5 CDs, adaptation of Dark Horse Comics series. 60.00

Dark Lords of the Sith, by Tom Veitch, Donald I. Fine #199-0, July 1997 . . . . 15.00

Dark Lords of the Sith, by Kevin J. Anderson and Tom Veitch, Time Warner Audio Books 298-2, 1995, 2 cassettes. 17.00

Darksaber, by Kevin J. Anderson, BDD Audio Cassette #47423-5, Nov. 1995, 180 minutes, 2 cassettes, includes music and sound effects 15.00

I, Jedi, by Michael Stackpole, BDD Audio Cassette #47948-2, Feb. 1998 . . . . 15.00

The New Rebellion, by Kristine Kathryn Rusch, BDD Audio Cassette #47743-9, Dec. 1996. . . . . . 15.00

Nightlily, The Lovers' Tale, by Barbara Hambly, BDD Audio Cassette #45541-9, Nov. 1995. . . . . . 10.00

Nightlily, The Lover's Tale #2, by Barbara Hambly, BDD Audio Cassette #47413-8, Jan. 1996 . . . . . . 12.00

Planet of Twilight, by Barbara Hambly, BDD Audio Cassette #47196-1, May 1997 . . . . 15.00

Star Wars, *The Original Radio Drama (Highbridge 1993)*

Rebel Agent, by William C. Dietz, Highbridge Audio
#244-X, Feb. 1998 . . . . 15.00
The Rebel Dawn, by A. C. Crispin, BDD Audio
Cassette #47746-3, March 1998 . . . . 15.00
Shadows Of The Empire, by Steve Perry, BDD
Audio Cassette #47438-3, May 1996 . . . . 15.00
Soldier for the Empire, abridged ed., by William C.
Dietz, Donald I. Fine #202-4, Feb. 1997 . . . . 15.00
Specter of the Past, by Timothy Zahn, BDD Audio
Cassette #47893-1, Nov. 1997 . . . . 15.00
Tales of the Jedi, by Tom Veitch, Donald I. Fine
#198 2, June 1997 . . . . 15.00
The Truce At Bakura, by Kathleen Tyers, BDD
Audio Cassette #47197-X, Jan. 1994 . . . . 15.00

Black Fleet Crisis by Michael Kube-McDowell
Before The Storm (Black Fleet Crisis #1) BDD
Audio Cassette #47422-7, April 1996 . . . . 15.00
Shield Of Lies (Black Fleet Crisis #2) BDD Audio
Cassette #47424-3, Sept. 1996 . . . . 15.00
The Tyrant's Test (Black Fleet Crisis #3) BDD Audio
Cassette #47421-9, Jan. 1997 . . . . 15.00

Corellian Trilogy by Roger Allen
Ambush At Corellia (The Corellian Trilogy #1) BDD
Audio Cassette #47202-X, March 1995 . . . . 15.00
Assault At Selonia (The Corellian Trilogy #2) BDD
Audio Cassette #47203-8, July 1995 . . . . 15.00
Showdown At Centerpoint (The Corellian Trilogy
#3) BDD Audio Cassette #47204-6, Oct. 1995 . . . 15.00

Han Solo Trilogy by A.C. Crispin
The Paradise Snare (Han Solo Trilogy #1) BDD
Audio Cassette #47744-7, June 1997 . . . . 15.00
The Hutt Gambit (Han Solo Trilogy #2) BDD Audio
Cassette #47745-5, Sept. 1997 . . . . 15.00

Jedi Academy by Kevin J. Anderson
Jedi Search (Jedi Academy Trilogy #1) BDD Audio
Cassette #47199-6, March 1994 . . . . 15.00
Dark Apprentice (Jedi Academy Trilogy #2) BDD
Audio Cassette #47200-3, July 1994 . . . . 15.00
Champions Of The Force (Jedi Academy Trilogy
#3) BDD Audio Cassette #47201-1, Oct. 1994 . . . 15.00
Jedi Academy Omnibus, BDD Audio Cassette
#47848-6, July 1997, 6 cassettes. 35.00

Thrawn Trilogy by Timothy Zahn
Heir To The Empire (*Star Wars* #1) BDD Audio
Cassette #45296-7, June 1991 . . . . 15.00
Dark Force Rising (*Star Wars* #2) BDD Audio
Cassette #47055-8, June 1992 . . . . 15.00
The Last Command (*Star Wars* #3) BDD Audio
Cassette #47157-0, May 1993 . . . . 15.00
Star Wars Audio Boxed Set, BDD Audio Cassette
#47322-0, Oct. 1994, with exclusive collector's
cassette in a collector's case featuring a
molded *Millennium Falcon* 60.00

X-Wing by Michael Stackpole
X-Wing: Rogue Squadron, BDD Audio Cassette
#47418-9, Feb. 1996 . . . . 15.00
Wedge's Gamble (X-Wing #2) BDD Audio Cassette
#47419-7, June 1996 . . . . 15.00
The Krytos Trap (X-Wing #3) BDD Audio Cassette
#47420-0, Oct. 1996 . . . . 15.00
Bacta War (X Wing #4) BDD Audio Cassette
#47425-1, Feb. 1997 . . . . 15.00

The Empire Strikes Back *Read-Along Book and Record*
(Buena Vista 1983)

X-Wing by Aaron Alston
Wraith Squadron (X-Wing #5) BDD Audio Cassette
#47888-5, Feb. 1998 . . . . 15.00

*Star Wars: We Don't Do Weddings, The Band's
Tale* by Kathleen Tyers, BDD Audio Cassette
#47393-X, Aug. 1995, 60 minute adaptation
of story from *Tales From the Mos Eisley Cantina* . 12.00
*Star Wars: We Don't Do Weddings: The Band's
Tale* (*Star Wars*) by Kathleen Tyers, BDD
Audio CD #45540-0, Aug. 1995 . . . . 14.00

Juvenile Adaptations, Read Along Books and Records
Star Wars 24 Page Read-Along Book and Record,
33 -1/3 RPM record with color photos (Buena
Vista Records) 15.00
The Empire Strikes Back 24 Page Read-Along
Book and Record, 33-1/3 RPM record with
color photos (Buena Vista Records #451) 15.00
Return of the Jedi 24 Page Read-Along Book and
Record, 33-1/3 RPM record with color photos
(Buena Vista Records #455, 1983). 15.00
Return of the Jedi 24 Page Read-Along Book and
Record, 33-1/3 RPM record with color photos:
Ewoks Join the Fight (Buena Vista Records
#460, 1983) 25.00
Droid World (Buena Vista Records #453, 1983) . . 30.00
Planet of the Hoojibs (Buena Vista Records
#454, 1983) 30.00
*Note: The above three items were offered through Diamond
Distribution in 1997 at the prices indicated.*

Other Juvenile Adaptations
Star Wars: A New Hope, Playasound Audio, Feb.
1997 . . . . 15.00
Star Wars Playpack and book, Walt Disney Audio
#197-8, Feb. 1996 . . . . 12.00
A New Hope Read-along: with book, Walt Disney
Audio #195-1, Jan. 1997 . . . . 7.00
The Empire Strikes Back Playpack and book, Walt
Disney Audio #198-6, Feb. 1996 . . . . 12.00
The Empire Strikes Back Read-along: with book,
Walt Disney Audio #194-3, Jan. 1997 . . . . 7.00
Return of the Jedi Read-along: with book, Walt
Disney Audio #193-5, Jan. 1997 . . . . 7.00

The Empire Strikes Back *soundtrack album back (RSO 1980)*

Return of the Jedi Playpack and book, Walt Disney
      Audio #196-X, Feb. 1996 . . . . 12.00
Star Wars: The Mixed-Up Droids (#274-5, 1995) 9.00
*See also Read-Along Play Packs, with PVC figures,
      listed under DOLLS AND FIGURES*

MUSIC SOUNDTRACKS

If you can't hum the *Star Wars* theme by John Williams
you probably bought this book by mistake. While you can get
the various movie soundtracks on 8 track tape, on cassettes
and in other formats, the collectible items are the original
soundtrack LP albums. Obviously you would like to get ones
that were never played and are still in their original shrink
wrap. Of course, shrinkwraping equipment is not too expensive and so shrinkwrap on a product is not a guarantee of anything. Just about every other format and every other record,
whether performed by the Boston Pops, the Utah Symphony
Orchestra, the Biola University Symphony Band or the
Electric Moog Orchestra can be had for under $20.00. Of
course, if it has a colorful insert, it's worth a little more.

Albums and CDs
Star Wars LP Soundtrack album, Music composed
      and conducted by John Williams, Performed
      by the London Symphony Orchestra, two
      records, with two sleeves, an insert and a
      poster (20th Century Records #2T-541, 1977) . . $30.00

The Empire Strikes Back LP Soundtrack album,
      Music composed and conducted by John
      Williams, Performed by the London Symphony
      Orchestra, two records with a 12 page color
      insert (RSO Records, RS2-4201, 1980) album
      back features Han and Leia romantic art 40.00
Return of the Jedi LP Soundtrack album, London
      Symphony Orchestra, one record, with 4 page
      color insert (RSO Records, 1983). 25.00
Star Wars Trilogy Special Edition soundtrack CD
      with Bonus Darth Vader shaped single, CDs
      set laser engraved with picture, plus 20
      pages of liner notes (1997). 110.00

VIDEOTAPES

The three *Star Wars* movies are available in original and
special editions and in letterbox and pan and scan formatted
for your television set, which, as you should know, has a
much different aspect ratio than a widescreen movie. Like all
special effects movies, *Star Wars* is much better seen in a
movie theater than on TV. Video tapes were released over the
years with different box art and they can be collected for the
art, but few people do so. Collectors who have videotapes of
the movie got them to watch, not collect. Collectors who have
Droids and Ewoks video tapes got them for their kids to
watch, not themselves. Whether their kids actually watch
them is unknown.

Boxed Videotapes
Star Wars (CBS/Fox Home Video 1991) $20.00
The Empire Strikes Back (CBS/Fox Home Video 1991) 20.00
Return of the Jedi (CBS/Fox Home Video 1991) 20.00
Star Wars Trilogy (CBS/Fox Home Video 1991)
      boxed set. 60.00

From Star Wars to Jedi: The Making of a Saga
      (CBS/Fox Home Video #1479, 1992) 10.00
Star Wars Video Trilogy Letterbox Collectors
      Edition, with documentary tape *From Star
      Wars to Jedi*, abridged book *George Lucas:
      The Creative Impulse* (Fox Video #0656,
      1993) in holographic gift box 100.00
Star Wars: A New Hope Special Edition Video
      (#6097, 1997) 20.00
The Empire Strikes Back Special Edition Video
      (#6098, 1997) 20.00
Return of the Jedi Special Edition Video (#6099, 1997). 20.00
Star Wars Trilogy Special Edition Boxed Set (1997)
      Pan & Scan format (#2930) 50.00
      Widescreen (letterbox) format (#2934) 60.00

Star Wars, The Empire Strikes Back *and* Return of the Jedi *video tapes, old and new THX widescreen boxes (Fox Video)*

Droids: The Pirates and the Prince, featuring R2-D2, Jann Tosh and C-3PO plus the voice of Anthony Daniels, written by Peter Sauder (CBS/Fox Home Video #8467, 1996) 10.00
Ewoks: The Haunted Village (CBS/Fox Home Video #8466, 1996) 10.00

Star Wars *Film Frame, Han Solo Edition (Willitts Designs 1995)*

STILLS

FILM FRAMES
Willitts Designs (1995–97)

Film Frames are a full screen, letterbox movie image, with a one-of-a-kind 70mm film frame, in a 7½"x2¾" acrylic holder. They are sold by Willitts Designs, who also produced the limited edition lithographs by Ralph McQuarrie (listed under WALL ART). The retail price of these strips is $24.95, but we have seen dealers offering them for as little as $15.00. They are the only way that a collector can own an actual piece of the film. Each "edition" is numbered and limited to 9,500 sets, but each frame is unique since only a single 70mm print of the film was cut up.

Star Wars: A New Hope (1995)
Luke Skywalker Edition (#50007) $25.00
Darth Vader Edition (#50008) 25.00
Princess Leia Edition (#50009) 25.00
Ben Kenobi Edition (#50010) 25.00
Han Solo Edition (#50011) 25.00
Chewbacca Edition (#50012) 25.00
Creatures Edition (#50013) 25.00
Galactic Empire Edition (#50014) 25.00
Stormtrooper Edition (#50015) 25.00
Rebel Alliance Edition (#50016) 25.00
C-3PO Edition (#50017) 25.00
R2-D2 Edition (#50018) 25.00

The Empire Strikes Back (1996–97)
Luke Skywalker (#50031) 25.00
Rebel Alliance (#50032) 25.00
Imperial Attack (#50033) 25.00
Millennium Falcon (#50034) 25.00
Jedi Training (#50041) 25.00
Luke Skywalker on Cloud City (#50042) 25.00
Jedi Master Yoda (#50043) 25.00

Darth Vader (#50044) 25.00
Lando Calrissian (#50045) 25.00
Rebel Escape (#50046) 25.00
Han Solo and Leia (#50047) 25.00

Return of the Jedi
Jedi Emerges (#50056) 25.00
Final Confrontation (#50057) 25.00
Princess Leia (#50058) 25.00
Han Solo (#50059) 25.00
Droids (#50060) 25.00
Return of the Jedi (#50061) 25.00
Ewoks (#50062) 25.00
Emperor Palpatine (#50063) 25.00
Darth Vader (#50064) 25.00
Rebellion (#50065) 25.00
Imperial Forces (#50066) 25.00
Turning Points (#50067) 25.00
Aliens of Jabba (#50068) 25.00

PHOTOS

The best way to get a signed photograph is to find a show where your favorite star is appearing and go and get the autograph yourself. I can guarantee you that there will be someone at the show selling photos of him or her. This gives you good memories — and a genuine collectible. It won't be free, but then what is? If several stars are available, make the person you dragged to the show wait in the long line for the major stars' autograph, while you get autographs from several of the lesser stars. Their lines will be shorter, and they might even sign multiple items.

Photos of your favorite star from *Star Wars* are also available from a variety of sources. Their value on the market depends more on their movie star status as of today, than on their role in the movie. Consequently, Harrison Ford's autographed photo is expensive, but not the others. The price list below is designed to give you a baseline for evaluating any photo that you wish to purchase, or sell. They are for standard 8"x10" photos, double matted and ready for framing, with a certificate of authenticity. If the item you are considering buying at a dealer's table, or from and advertisement or cable TV show, is reasonably priced, go ahead and buy it — but don't expect to sell it later at a huge profit.

Signed Photos
Harrison Ford $150.00
Mark Hamill 50.00
Carrie Fisher 40.00
Sir Alec Guiness 50.00
David Prowse 45.00
Peter Cushing 50.00
George Lucas 95.00
Just about anyone else . . . . under $50.00
Return of the Jedi Mark Hamill autographed photo plaque (1993) 100.00
The Empire Strikes Back Anthony Daniels autographed photo plaque (1993) 80.00
Darth Vader David Prowse autographed photo plaque, limited to 2,500 pieces (1997) 70.00
Darth Vader/David Prowse signed photo collage, matted (Timeless 1993) 30.00
Star Wars Movie Photos 5.00
The Empire Strikes Back Movie Photos 4.00
Return of the Jedi Movie Photos 3.00

ROLE PLAY TOYS

ROLE PLAY TOYS

Role play toys include weapons, communicators, armor, utility belts and similar items which are full size, or sized for a kid to play with. They are hardly a new idea. Every movie serial and TV western hero, from the time of Hopalong Cassidy, Roy Rogers and the Lone Ranger onwards had cap guns, holsters, hats, boots and all manner of full-sized licensed products. It's action figures that are the new idea. Nobody figured out how to sell dolls to boys until the mid 1960s.

With all the different weapons used in the trilogy, it's a miracle there aren't a lot more *Star Wars* role play weapons. There are lightsabers, pistols and laser rifles. The first Chewbacca Bowcaster arrived in mid 1997, and there are no weapons yet for any of the bounty hunters or Mos Eisley Cantina aliens, although Boba Fett's armor should be available soon. Maybe it's just as well. I suppose we'd loose too many little sisters if Kenner made a life-size Carbon-Freezing Chamber. On the other hand, Kenner could do well in the adult market with Princess Leia bondage gear.

With so little product, collector interest in the few classic items is quite high. As yet, there has been little collector interest in the 1990s items and they can all be acquired for around their original retail prices.

Classic Lightsabers
Star Wars Light Saber, inflatable, 35" long, light-up
(Kenner #38040, 1997) boxed $90.00
Loose 40.00

Droids Battery Operated Lightsaber (Green)
(Kenner 1984) 75.00
Loose 25.00
Droids Battery Operated Lightsaber (Red) (Kenner
1984) 150.00
Loose 40.00

Classic Weapons
3 Position Laser Rifle, folding stock, secret on/off button, two-speed laser sound, battery powered (Kenner #69310, 1978) in *Star Wars* package 225.00
Loose, with *Star Wars* logo 75.00
Reissue as Electronic Laser Rifle (1980) in
The Empire Strikes Back package 100.00
Loose, with *The Empire Strikes Back* logo 40.00
Laser Pistol replica of Han Solo's laser pistol with secret on/off button, battery powered (Kenner #38110, 1978)
Original *Star Wars* package 125.00
Loose, with *Star Wars* logo 25.00
Reissue *The Empire Strikes Back* package 100.00
Loose, with *The Empire Strikes Back* logo 20.00
Reissue *Return of the Jedi* package 75.00
Loose, with *Return of the Jedi* logo 15.00
Biker Scout Laser Pistol, battery powered (Kenner #71520, 1983) original *Return of the Jedi*
package 90.00
Loose 25.00

New Lightsabers (Asst. #69600, 1995–98)
Electronic Luke Skywalker Lightsaber (Kenner #69795, March 1996) 20.00
Loose 7.00

3 Position Laser Rifle and Laser Pistol (Kenner 1978–83)

Battery Operated Water Blaster and Electronic Heavy Blaster (Kenner 1996)

Electronic Darth Vader Lightsaber (Kenner #69796,
    Sept. 1996) orange box 25.00
    Reissue, green box 20.00
    Loose 7.00

Other Lightsabers
Star Wars Lightsaber, battery operated (Rubies
    #1588, 1995)
    white 7.50
    blue. 7.50
    red. 7.50
    Loose, any color 3.00

New Weapons
Chewbacca's Bowcaster (Kenner #27734, June 1997) 18.00
    Loose 6.00
Electronic Heavy Blaster BlasTech DL-44 (Kenner
    #27737, July 1996) in orange box 15.00
    Loose 6.00
Electronic Blaster Rifle BlasTech E-11 (Kenner
    #27738, July 1996) in orange box 20.00
    Loose 7.00
Star Wars Electronic Blaster Lazer Rifle, 18fi" long,
    battery powered Stormtrooper weapon with
    lights and sounds. 17.00
    Loose 6.00
Star Wars Endor Blaster Pistol (Kenner #27737, 1998) . 14.50
Star Wars Commando Blaster Laser Rifle (Kenner
    #27738, 1998) 20.00

New Accessories
Luke Skywalker Utility Belt (Kenner #27735, Aug.
    1997) in green box. 19.00
    Loose 6.00
Star Wars Imperial Walkie-Talkie (Tiger Electronics
    #88-061, 1997) reception up to 100 feet. 13.00
Darth Vader Voice Changer Walkie Talkies (Tiger
    Electronics #88-062, 1997) reception up to 200
    feet 20.00
Star Wars Rebel Alliance Long Range Walkie
    Talkies (Tiger Electronics #88-063, 1997)
    reception over 1,500 feet 35.00

    Loose 12.00
Electronic Com-Link Communicators (Kenner #27791). . 15.00
    Loose 6.00
Darth Vader and Chewbacca Walkie Talkie Masks
    (Micro Games of America #SW-3980, 1995) 50.00
Darth Vader and Stormtrooper Walkie Talkies (Micro
    Games of America #SW-WT920M, 1995) 23.00
Boba Fett Armor Set, includes chest shield, blaster,
    two arm gauntlets and face shield (Kenner
    #27796, 1998) 16.00
    Loose 7.00

Water Pistol
Water Blaster BlasTech DL-44 (Kenner #8402-0)
    battery operated
    Silver color (March 1997). 15.00
    Black color (Fall 1997) 12.00
    Loose 5.00

SPACE SHOOTERS

    These are not replica weapons, but disk firing model spaceships. Or maybe they are games, since they come with targets you can knock down. Something tells me the targets are only used when mom is watching or when no friends, siblings, or pets are convenient targets. Anyway, I have listed them here. If you think they belong in some other section, write your own book.

Space Shooters
Star Wars Space Shooters
    Millennium Falcon Blaster (Milton Bradley
        #04622, Feb. 1997) $20.00
    Darth Vader TIE Fighter Blaster (Milton Bradley
        #04798, Feb. 1997) 20.00
    Space Shooter Battle Belt, with 32 Foam Disks
        (Milton Bradley #04777, Feb. 1997) 10.00

SCHOOL AND OFFICE SUPPLIES

SCHOOL AND OFFICE SUPPLIES

You awaken from a sound sleep on your *Star Wars* sheets, and outfit yourself from head to toe with *Star Wars* clothing. Are you ready to go forth to do battle with the faceless minions of an evil empire? Are you? Okay, well in that case you will just have to go to school, or to work and pretend that your teacher is Emperor Palpatine or your boss is Darth Vader. Actually, this may not be much of a stretch, in which case you will need to outfit yourself with an array of school and office supplies bearing *Star Wars* pictures and logos.

SCHOOL SUPPLIES

Pencils

Star Wars pencils & pens, each	$5.00
The Empire Strikes Back pencils & pens, each	4.00
Return of the Jedi pencils & pens, each	3.00
Star Wars, 6 Foil Pencils (RoseArt #1653, 1997)	2.50

Star Wars Pen, several styles (Mead 1997) each	2.00
Star Wars Millennium Falcon Pencil Sharpener (RoseArt #1658, 1997)	3.00
Lightsaber Pencil Case (Roseart #1669, 1997)	4.00
Star Wars Pencil Tins (A.H. Prismatic #1071, 1997) . . .	4.00

Star Wars/Return of the Jedi Erasers (Butterfly Originals/ Spindex 1983)

Admiral Ackbar Eraser	5.00
Baby Ewoks Eraser	5.00
Bib Fortuna Eraser (#90029)	5.00
Darth Vader Collectible Eraser	5.00
Gamorrean Guard Eraser	5.00
Jabba the Hutt Eraser	5.00
Max Rebo Eraser	5.00
Wicket the Ewok Collectible Eraser	5.00
Yoda Collectible Eraser	5.00
Return of the Jedi Glow In The Dark Erasers, *Millennium Falcon*, Darth Vader and C-3PO on 5"x7" header card (reoffered 1996)	4.00

Bib Fortuna Eraser (Butterfly 1983) and Millennium Falcon *Pencil Sharpener (Rose Art 1997)*

Notebooks

The Empire Strikes Back notebooks, each 5.00
Return of the Jedi notebooks, each. 4.00
Wookiee doodle pad. 3.00
Pencil tablet 3.00
Darth Vader Duty Roster. 4.00
Star Wars portfolio 5.00
Star Wars Fat Little Neatbook, 180 count (Mead
    #57188, 1997) 10.00
Star Wars Wirebound 60-page Notebook, 6 different
    designs (Mead #05718, 1997). 4.00

Funkit

Star Wars Funkit, with stickers, pens, scissors
    (Roseart #1649, 1997) 10.00

Lunch Boxes

Lunch boxes have their own groups of collectors, making these more valuable than other school related items.

Star Wars, space battle on front & Tatooine scene
    on reverse, *Droids* thermos (King Seeley-
    Thermos 1977)
    metal box. 55.00
    thermos 20.00
Star Wars, red with Darth and Droids pictured on
    front, *Droids* thermos (King Seeley-Thermos 1978)
    plastic box. 35.00
    thermos 15.00
The Empire Strikes Back, *Millennium Falcon* on
    front & Luke, Yoda and R2-D2 on back, Yoda
    thermos (King Seeley-Thermos 1980)
    metal box. 45.00
    thermos 15.00
The Empire Strikes Back, Dagobah scene on lid,
    Hoth battle on back, Yoda thermos (King
    Seeley-Thermos 1980)
    metal box. 45.00
    thermos 15.00
The Empire Strikes Back, red, Chewbacca, Han,
    Leia and Luke on lid, Yoda thermos (King
    Seeley-Thermos 1980)
    plastic box. 30.00
    thermos 15.00

Star Wars *Lunch Box (King Seeley-Thermos 1977)*

The Empire Strikes Back, photo cover with logo
    and inset pictures, Droids and logo on thermos
    (King Seeley-Thermos 1980)
    plastic box. 30.00
    thermos 15.00
Return of the Jedi, Luke in Jabba's Palace on lid
    and space scene on back, Ewok thermos (King
    Seeley-Thermos 1983)
    metal box. 40.00
    thermos 15.00
Return of the Jedi, red with Wicket and R2-D2 on
    front, Ewok thermos (King Seeley-Thermos
    1983)
    plastic box. 25.00
    thermos 10.00

Notebook Binders

Star Wars Zipper Binder (Mead #29254, 1996)
    Blue, with Darth Vader. 10.00
    Black/Gray with *Star Wars* logo 10.00

The Empire Strikes *Back and* Return of the Jedi *Lunch Boxes (King-Seeley-Thermos 1980–83)*

Princess Leia Portfolio (Mead 1997)

Portfolios

Star Wars Portfolio, 12 designs (Mead #33384, 1997)
Princess Leia. 3.00
Han Solo 3.00
Luke Skywalker 3.00
"A long time ago in a galaxy far, far away" 2.00
"Never underestimate the power of the Dark
  Side". 2.00
R2-D2: "General Kenobi, years ago you served
  my father". 2.00
C-3PO: "Did you hear that?" 2.00
"May the Force be with you". 2.00
"Freeze, you Rebel scum!". 2.50
Yoda: "A Jedi's strength flows from the Force" 2.00
Darth Vader: Dark Lord of the Sith 2.50
Star Wars spaceships 2.00

Star Wars Zipper Pouch (Mead (#50744, 1997)

Star Wars logo, grey and black 5.00
Yoda 5.00
Darth Vader 5.00
"*Star Wars*" in red, in circle 5.00

Backpacks

Darth Vader and Imperial Guards Backpack, red
  (Adam Joseph 1983) 30.00
R2-D2 and C-3PO Backpack, blue (Adam Joseph
  983). 30.00
Yoda Backpack, red (Adam Joseph 1983) 30.00
Return of the Jedi Backpack, blue canvas Darth
  Vader and 2 Stormtroopers on flap, Luke, Leia,
  C-3PO, and R2-D2 on front with Jedi logo 30.00

Star Wars Backpack (Pyramid Handbags #91166,
  1996)
Black, with Darth Vader pictured 25.00
Black, with C-3PO pictured 25.00
Navy Blue, with Stormtrooper pictured 25.00
Star Wars Backpacks, high tech nylon
Boba Fett (1997) 25.00
Darth Vader (1997) 25.00
Stormtrooper (1997). 25.00
Yoda (1997). 25.00
Star Wars Backpacks, Interactive, with sounds
Darth Vader/TIE-Fighter (1997) 18.00
Luke Skywalker/X-wing Fighter (1997) 18.00
Darth Vader breathing (1997). 18.00
Star Wars Backpacks (Pyramid #91066, 1996)
Black with Darth Vader. 13.00
Black with Stormtrooper. 13.00
Black, soft side, Dark Lord of the Sith 13.00

Beltbags

Darth Vader Breathing Beltbag (1997). 11.00
Luke/X-wing Light Flashing Beltbag (1997) 11.00
Star Wars Beltbags, high tech nylon (1997) picturing:
Boba Fett 10.00
Stormtrooper. 10.00
Darth Vader 10.00
Yoda. 10.00

OFFICE SUPPLIES

The only problem with *Star Wars* office supplies is that they favor the rebel alliance, while most offices resemble the galactic empire. To be true to life, they should have faceless Stormtrooper images. Why sell pens one at a time to individual rebels. I bet a carton of Gamorrean Guard pens, with a bonus Jabba the Hutt pen for the boss, would sell better — at least if the boss were doing the buying!

Pens

Star Wars Rebel Fighter Space Pen (Fisher
  #54944,1995) $15.00
Star Wars The Force Titanium Plated Space Pen
  (Fisher #86734, 1996) in plastic box. 75.00
Star Wars Rebel Pen, Fisher Space Pen (#SWR,
  1997) 20.00

Star Wars Stationery Set, 3 designs packaged as a
  paper/ envelope set (#91022, 1997). 5.00

Magnets (Applause 1996)

Imperial TIE Fighter (#42972) 3.00
Rebel Snowspeeder (#42970). 3.00
Rebel X-wing (#42971) 3.00
Millennium Falcon (#42974) 3.00
Imperial AT-AT (#42969) 3.00

3-D Magnets, 2"x2" (A.H. Prismatic #1008swx, 1997)

Darth Vader 3.00
Millennium Falcon. 3.00
R2-D2 & C-3PO 3.00
X-wing Fighter 3.00

Window Decals

Darth Vader (#SW1002, 1994) 3.50
R2-D2 and C-3PO (#SW1003, 1994) 3.50
Yoda (#SW1004, 1994). 3.50
Star Wars Space Fight (#SW1006, 1994) 3.50

STATUES

STATUES

STATUES — MAQUETTES — BUSTS — FINE REPLICAS

It would take an impressive bankroll to collect all of the items in this section, and I doubt that very many people do so. However, most collectors could afford to buy, save up for, or convince a relative to buy one (or a few) items, which then forms the centerpiece of their collection.

The prices listed here are either the full list price for the item, or a slightly lower price if I found several dealers selling the items for less. You may be able to find the one you want for even less, particularly if the dealer has had it for a long time. This does not mean that these fine collectibles will never rise in value. The first ones only came out a few years ago, so just about all of them are still available. It takes that long for expensive items to sell through to the ultimate consumer. Prices can't rise until the pieces have finally sold out. When this finally happens, future prices will depend on the statues' intrinsic artistic value.

TIE Fighter Replica (Icons 1997)
Image courtesy of Icons

Don't buy these collectibles to make money. Buy them because you want one to look at and enjoy. Although expensive collectibles hold their value, they are hard to sell quickly. Since almost no one is trying to collect all of them from a series, there is not much extra demand for the first one produced, or any particularly scarce one. A collector with a spare $500 or $1,000 to spend will usually be just as happy to buy the next one produced, and as long as there are collectors willing to buy, the companies will produce new items. This may limit your price speculation, but not your enjoyment. Invite your *Star Wars* buddies to your house to see your fine collectible and go to their house to see their different ones.

Where do I find one of these, you ask? You can't just drive to your local store and look over a large selection in order to make your choice. One place to try is your local comic shop. All these fine items are distributed to comic shops via Diamond Distribution, but most shops would have one or two, at most. If you shop at a comic store regularly, you could buy Diamond Previews and look for your favorite items as they appear. Then you can get your shop to order one for you. They may be able to get older items for you as well. Some stores, like Spencer Gifts or Sharper Image, stock these collectibles, especially around Christmas time. Check their catalogs too, because there will probably be a better selection listed there. Ask the sales staff to check with the other stores in the chain. The internet is another good place to shop, and it may be the best source price-wise. If these sources fail you, you can try calling the respective companies. Because of the difficulty that you may have finding these fairly expensive collectibles, I asked the companies for their phone numbers,

Yoda Maquette (Illusive Originals 1995)

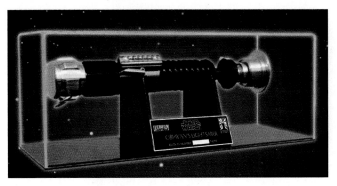

Obi-Wan Kenobi Replica Lightsaber (Icons 1997)
Image courtesy of Icons

Darth Vader Replica Lightsaber (Icons 1997)
Image courtesy of Icons

and I pass this information along to you. They are listed below. All three companies were kind enough to supply me with photos and information for this section, but I have no financial interest in, or business relationship with, any of them. Also, please understand that no company wants to undercut their dealers' prices and so they will generally be charging full list price.

Manufacturers of Fine Collectibles
Don Post Studios. (800) 874-4087
Icons . . . . (818) 982-6175
Illusive Originals: Customer Service   . (800) 278-4085 x 216

Maquettes
Yoda Maquette, 26" mounted on black wood base with1"x4" brass plate, with certificate of authenticity, limited to 9,500 (Illusive Originals #672000, 1995) listed as "sold out" by the manufacturer $600.00
Boba Fett Maquette, sculpted by Mario Chiodo, 15" tall, mounted on black wood base with 1"x4" brass plate, with certificate of authenticity, limited to 10,000 (Illusive Originals #672001) . . . 225.00
Admiral Ackbar Maquette, sculpted by Mario Chiodo,11" tall, mounted on black wood base with 1"x4"brass plate, with certificate of authenticity, limited to 10,000 (Illusive Originals #672003) listed as "retired" by the manufacturer . 125.00
Jabba the Hutt Maquette, sculpted by Mario Chiodo, 27" long, mounted on black wood base with 1"x4" brass plate, with certificate of authenticity, limited to 5,000 (Illusive Originals #672004) 250.00
Chewbacca Maquette, sculpted by Mario Chiodo, 17" tall bust, mounted on black wood base with 1"x4" brass plate, with certificate of authenticity, limited to 7,500 (Illusive Originals #672006). 250.00
Han Solo in Carbonite Prop Replica, 7' tall, cast in fiberglass from the original mold, sculpted by Mario Chiodo, with 2½"x8" brass plaque, with collector's brochure, limited to 2,500 (Illusive Originals #672008) 1,200.00
Darth Vader Reveals Anakin Skywalker Bust, 26" tall, 40" wide, 17½" deep, 3-piece mask/helmet opens to reveal life-size Anakin Skywalker sculpted head by Mario Chiodo, plus stand, limited to 9,500, with full color collector's brochure and certificate of authenticity (Illusive Originals #672009, 1998) 1,100.00
Rancor Creature Maquette, 21"x7"x24", mounted on base, with 2"x4" silver-plated brass plaque, limited to 9,500 (Illusive Originals #672011) 600.00

Han Solo Special Edition Statue, Release from Carbonite, cold-cast resin with built-in light source, 2,500 pieces (Jan. 1998) 110.00

STATUES

Boba Fett Bronze Statue, sculpted by Randy Bowen, 12½" tall, weighs 18 lbs, mounted on black Spanish marble, with certificate of authenticity (Dark Horse Comics, May 1997) . $3,000.00
Rancor Bronze Statue, sculpted by Randy Bowen, 15" tall, weighs 25 lbs, mounted on black Spanish marble, limited edition of 50 numbered copies, with certificate of authenticity (Nov. 1997) 3,000.00

REPLICAS

Icons Authentic Replicas
Authentic Darth Vader Lightsaber, die-cast metal and plastic prop replica, with numbered plaque, certificate of authenticity and plexi-glass display case, limited to 10,000 (Icons 1996) . . . $350.00
Authentic Obi Wan Kenobi Lightsaber, die-cast metal and plastic prop replica, with numbered plaque,certificate of authenticity and plexi-glass display case, limited to 10,000 (Icons) 350.00
Authentic Luke Skywalker Lightsaber, die-cast metal and plastic prop replica, with numbered plaque, certificate of authenticity and plexi-glass display case, limited to 10,000 (Icons) 350.00
TIE Fighter replica miniature, injected poly-eurethane with weathered appearances, with numbered plaque, certificate of authenticity plexi-glass and display case, limited to 1,977 (Icons) 1,500.00
X-wing Fighter replica miniature, injected poly-eurethane with weathered appearances, with numbered plaque, certificate of authenticity and plexi-glass display case, limited to 1,977 (Icons 1996) 1,500.00

DELUXE REPLICA HELMETS

Don Post Studios, cast from original movie prop
Deluxe Stormtrooper Helmet, 13" fiberglass helmet with lining (#82102) numbered edition of 1,000. $750.00
Deluxe Scout Trooper Helmet, 13" fiberglass (#82114) numbered edition of 500 . . . . 750.00
Deluxe X-wing Fighter Helmet, 13" fiberglass helmet with lining (#82116) limited edition of 750   750.00

Darth Vader Statue (Cinemacast 1995)

Deluxe TIE-Fighter Helmet, 15" fiberglass helmet
  with lining (#82116) limited edition of 500 . . . . . . 750.00
Deluxe Darth Vader Helmet, 15" black fiberglass
  (#82100) 900.00
Deluxe Boba Fett Helmet, 15" fiberglass (#82101) . . 750.00

LIFE SIZE REPLICA STATUES

Don Post Studios Statues
Boba Fett Life Size Replica Statue, 6'1½" fiberglass,
  cast from original props (#82023) $6,000.00
Stormtrooper Replica Statue, 6' fiberglass, cast
  from original props (#82022) limited to 500
  pieces. 4,500.00

Rubies Figure
Darth Vader full size Display Figure (Rubies 1997) . 4,500.00

PORCELAIN BUSTS

Cold Cast Porcelain Busts
Emperor Palpatine bust sculpture, sculpted by Greg
  Aronowitz, box art by Drew Struzan, limited to
  3,000 (Legends in Three Dimensions, 1997) . . $150.00
Greedo bust sculpture, sculpted by Greg Aronowitz,
  9½" in box with art by Drew Struzan, limited to
  3,000 (Legends in Three Dimensions, March
  1998). 160.00

Emperor Palpatine bust (Legends in Three Dimensions 1997)

Boba Fett bust sculpture, sculpted by Greg
  Aronowitz, box art by Drew Struzan, limited to
  3,000 (Legends in Three Dimensions, 1998) . . . 200.00

OTHER FINE COLLECTIBLES

Star Wars Official Pewter Chess Set, 15"x15"x3"
  board plus 32 pewter figures on bases, sold
  at $19.95 per figure (Danbury Mint 1995) $650.00
Cinemacast Darth Vader statue, 15½" cold-cast
  porcelain, limited to 10,000 (Kenner/Cinema-
  cast 1995) 250.00
Life-Size Ewok Plush figure, 30" tall in sitting
  position, 12 lbs, 3,200 made, PepsiCo promo
  (Douglas Toys 1997) 500.00

Star Wars Chess set pieces (Danbury Mint 1995)

TRADING CARDS

Star Wars, *Series 1, card and sticker (Topps 1977)*

STAR WARS
Topps (1977)

Topps was the major producer of movie tie-in cards in the 1960s, 1970s and 1980s. The standard that they created and followed with just about every movie set was 66 (or 88) cards plus 11 (or 22) stickers. If the cards were successful, a second series of "all new" cards was produced. The cards and stickers came in colorful wax wrappers, and all three came in boxes of 36 packs. In those days there were no holograms, foils, autographed cards, 3-D redemption cards and not even any promo cards, so collectors had nothing to collect except the cards, stickers, wrappers and boxes.

Star Wars was very successful, so a total of five series of cards and stickers was produced. They are numbered consecutively, so as to form one large set of 330 cards and 55 stickers. Stickers came one to a pack, making a sticker set harder to assemble than a card set. Some stickers were even rumored to have been, (gasp!), peeled off and stuck to something, further reducing the number in circulation. Consequently, stickers are worth about $2.00 each, while the cards go for less.

Series 1, blue border with stars

Set: 66 cards/11 stickers	$100.00
Pack: 7 cards + 1 sticker	7.50
Box: 36 packs	250.00
Box: Empty	15.00
Wrapper: C-3PO, black background	5.00

CARD CHECKLIST

1 Luke Skywalker	$1.00
2 See-Threepio and Artoo-Detoo	1.00
3 The little droid, Artoo-Detoo	1.00
4 Space pirate Han Solo	1.00
5 Princess Leia Organa	1.00
6 Ben (Obi-Wan) Kenobi	1.00
7 The villainous Darth Vader	1.00
8 Grand Moff Tarkin	1.00
9 Rebels defend their starship!	1.00
10 Princess Leia–captured	1.00
11 Artoo is imprisoned by the Jawas	1.00
12 The droids are reunited!	1.00
13 A sale on droids!	1.00
14 Luke checks out his new droid	1.00
15 Artoo-Detoo is left behind!	1.00
16 Jawas of Tatooine	1.00
17 Lord Vader threatens Princess Leia!	1.00
18 Artoo-Detoo is missing!	1.00
19 Searching for the little droid	1.00
20 Hunted by the Sandpeople!	1.00
21 The Tusken Raiders	1.00
22 Rescued by Ben Kenobi	1.00
23 See-Threepio is injured!	1.00
24 Stormtroopers seek the droids!	1.00
25 Luke rushes to save his loved ones	1.00
26 A horrified Luke sees his family killed	1.00
27 Some repairs for See-Threepio	1.00
28 Luke agrees to join Ben Kenobi	1.00
29 Stopped by stormtroopers	1.00
30 Han in the Millennium Falcon	1.00
31 Sighting the Death Star	1.00
32 Lord Vader's Guards	1.00
33 The droids in the Control Room	1.00
34 See-Threepio diverts the guards	1.00
35 Luke and Han as stormtroopers	1.00
36 Blast of the laser rifle!	1.00
37 Cornered in the labyrinth	1.00
38 Luke and Han in the refuse room	1.00
39 Steel walls close in on our heroes!	1.00
40 Droids rescue their masters!	1.00
41 Facing the deadly chasm	1.00
42 Stormtroopers attack!	1.00
43 Luke prepares to swing across the chasm	1.00
44 Han and Chewie shoot it out!	1.00
45 The light sabre	1.00
46 A desperate moment for Ben	1.00
47 Luke prepares for the battle	1.00
48 Artoo-Detoo is loaded aboard	1.00
49 The rebels monitor the raid	1.00
50 Rebel leaders wonder about their fate!	1.00
51 See-Threepio and Princess Leia	1.00
52 Who will win the final Star War!	1.00
53 Battle in outer space!	1.00
54 The victors receive their reward	1.00
55 Han, Chewie and Luke	1.00
56 A day of rejoicing!	1.00
57 Mark Hamill as Luke Skywalker	1.00
58 Harrison Ford as Han Solo	1.00
59 Alec Guinness as Ben Kenobi	1.00
60 Peter Cushing as Grand Moff Tarkin	1.00
61 Mark Hamill in Control Room	1.00
62 Lord Vader's stormtroopers	1.00
63 May the Force be with you!	1.00
64 Governor of Imperial Outlands	1.00
65 Carrie Fisher and Mark Hamill	1.00
66 Amazing robot See-Threepio	1.00

Stickers:

1 Luke Skywalker	2.00
2 Princess Leia Organa	2.00
3 Han Solo	2.00
4 Chewbacca the Wookiee	2.00
5 See-Threepio	2.00
6 Artoo-Detoo	2.00
7 Lord Darth Vader	2.00
8 Grand Moff Tarkin	2.00
9 Ben (Obi-Wan) Kenobi	2.00
10 Tusken Raider	2.00
11 Battle in Outer Space	2.00

Series 2, red border

Set: 66 cards/11 stickers	$75.00
Pack:	6.00
Box: 36 packs	150.00
Box: Empty	12.00
Wrapper: Darth Vader, yellow background	5.00

Star Wars, *Series 2, pack (Topps 1977)*

CARD CHECKLIST

67 See-Threepio and Luke. . . . $ .50	99 Ben with the light sabre! 50
68 The Millennium Falcon 50	100 Our heroes at the
69 Threepio's desert trek! 50	spaceport 50
70 Special mission for Artoo-	101 The Wookiee Chewbacca . . .50
Detoo! 50	102 Rebels prepare for the big
71 The incredible See-Threepio! .50	fight! 50
72 Ben Kenobi rescues Luke! . . .50	103 Stormtroopers attack our
73 The droids wait for Luke 50	heroes! 50
74 Luke Skywalker on Tatooine . .50	104 Luke's uncle and aunt 50
75 Darth Vader strangles a	105 Imperial soldiers burn
rebel! 50	through the starship! 50
76 Artoo-Detoo on the rebel	106 A message from Princess
starship! 50	Leia! 50
77 Waiting in the control room . . .50	107 The Tusken Raider 50
78 Droids to the rescue! 50	108 Princess Leia observes the
79 Preparing to board Solo's	battle! 50
spaceship! 50	109 Ben turns off the Tractor
80 "Where has R2-D2 gone?" . . .50	beam 50
81 Weapons of the Death Star! . .50	110 Threepio fools the guards! . .50
82 A daring rescue! 50	111 Chewie and Han Solo! 50
83 Aboard the Millennium	112 Threatened by Sandpeople! .50
Falcon 50	113 Ben hides from Imperial
84 Rebel pilot prepares for the	stormtroopers! 50
raid! 50	114 Planning to escape! 50
85 Luke on the sand planet 50	115 Hiding in the Millennium
86 A mighty explosion! 50	Falcon! 50
87 The droids try to rescue	116 Honored for their heroism! . .50
Luke! 50	117 Chewbacca poses as a
88 Stormtroopers guard Solo's	prisoner! 50
ship 50	118 R2-D2 and C-3PO 50
89 The imprisoned Princess	119 Threepio, Ben and Luke! 50
Leia 50	120 Luke destroys an Imperial
90 Honoring the victors! 50	ship! 50
91 Solo and Chewie prepare to	121 Han Solo and Chewbacca. . .50
leave Luke. 50	122 The Millennium Falcon
92 Advance of the Tusken	speeds through space! 50
Raider 50	123 Solo blasts a Stormtrooper! . .50
93 Stormtroopers blast the	124 Threepio searches for R2-
rebels! 50	D2 50
94 Interrogated by	125 Luke in disguise! 50
stormtroopers! 50	126 A quizzical Threepio! 50
95 Sighting Artoo-Detoo! 50	127 The Rebel Fleet 50
96 The droids on Tatooine 50	128 Roar of the Wookiee! 50
97 Meeting at the cantina 50	129 "May The Force be with
98 See-Threepio 50	you!" 50

130 Pursued by the Jawas! 50	16 Chewbacca 2.00
131 Spectacular battle! 50	17 Threatened by Sandpeople . 2.00
132 Lord Vader and a soldier. . . .50	18 The Rebel Fleet 2.00
Stickers:	19 The Wookiee Chewbacca. . . 2.00
12 Han and Chewbacca 2.00	20 R2-D2 and C-3PO 2.00
13 Alec Guinness as Ben 2.00	21 The Millennium Falcon
14 The Tusken Raider. 2.00	Speeds Through Space! . . 2.00
15 See-Threepio. 2.00	22 Spectacular Battle! 2.00

Star Wars, *Series 3, four cards and a sticker (Topps 1978)*

Series 3, yellow border
Set: 66 cards/11 stickers. $75.00
Pack: 5.50
Box: 36 packs 130.00
Box: Empty 10.00
Wrapper: R2-D2, purple background 4.00

CARD CHECKLIST

133 Ben and Luke help C-3PO	159 Luke Skywalker's home 50
to his feet. . . . . $ .50	160 Destroying a world! 50
134 Luke dreams of being a	161 Preparing for the raid! 50
star pilot 50	162 Han Solo cornered by
135 Cantina troubles! 50	Greedo! 50
136 Danger from all sides! 50	163 Caught in the tractor beam! . .50
137 Luke attacked by a strange	164 Tusken Raiders capture
creature! 50	Luke! 50
138 On the track of the droids . . .50	165 Escaping from
139 Han Solo...Hero or	stormtroopers! 50
Mercenary? 50	166 A close call for Luke and
140 "R2-D2, where are you?". . . .50	Princess Leia! 50
141 Some quick-thinking by	167 Surrounded by Lord
Luke! 50	Vader's soldiers! 50
142 Darth Vader inspects the	168 Hunting the fugitives 50
throttled ship 50	169 Meeting at the Death Star! . .50
143 Droids on the sand planet . . .50	170 Luke and the
144 Harrison Ford as Han Solo . .50	princess...trapped! 50
145 Escape from the Death	171 "The walls are moving!". 50
Star! 50	172 Droids in the Escape Pod . . .50
146 Luke Skywalker's aunt	173 The stormtroopers. 50
preparing dinner 50	174 Solo aims for trouble! 50
147 Bargaining with the Jawas! . .50	175 A closer look at a "Jawa" . . .50
148 The fearsome	176 Luke Skywalker's dream . . .50
stormtroopers! 50	177 Solo swings into action!. . . .50
149 The evil Grand Moff Tarkin . .50	178 The Star Warriors! 50
150 Shoot-out at the chasm! 50	179 Stormtroopers search the
151 Planning an escape! 50	spaceport! 50
152 Spirited Princess Leia! 50	180 Princess Leia honors the
153 The fantastic droid	victors 50
Threepio! 50	181 Peter Cushing as Grand
154 Princess Leia comforts	Moff Tarkin 50
Luke! 50	182 Deadly blasters! 50
155 The Escape Pod is	183 Dave Prowse as Darth
jettisoned! 50	Vader. 50
156 R2-D2 is lifted aboard! 50	184 Luke and his uncle 50
157 "Learn about the Force,	185 Luke on Tatooine 50
Luke!" 50	186 The Jawas 50
158 Rebel victory. 50	187 Threepio and friend. 50

188 Starship under fire! 50
189 Mark Hamill as Luke 50
190 Carrie Fisher as Princess
    Leia 50
191 Life on the desert world. 50
192 Liberated Princess! 50
193 Luke's uncle buys
    Threepio! 50
194 Stormtroopers attack! 50
195 Alec Guinness as Ben
    Kenobi. 50
196 Lord Darth Vader 50
197 Leia blasts a stormtrooper! . .50
198 Luke decides to leave
    Tatooine! 50

Stickers:
23 Dave Prowse as Darth
    Vader 2.00
24 Droids on the Sand Planet . . 2.00
25 The Escape Pod is
    Jettisoned 2.00
26 The Fantastic Droid Threepio 2.00
27 A Closer Look at a "Jawa" . . 2.00
28 Peter Cushing as Grand
    Moff Tarkin 2.00
29 Han Solo Hero or
    Mercenary?. 2.00
30 The Fearsome
    Stormtroopers. 2.00
31 Princess Leia Comforts Luke 2.00
32 Preparing for the Raid! 2.00
33 Solo Aims for Trouble! 2.00

Star Wars, Series 4, wrapper (Topps 1978)

Card #207 (in Series 4) was originally printed (intentionally or unintentionally, depending on which story you believe) with C-3PO appearing to have a large, one might even say, "presidential," but very un-droid-like male appendage. This would have been appropriate in the movie *Flesh Gordon*, but not in *Star Wars*. The card was reprinted, with the offending item removed. Collectors with warped minds have placed a high value on the card — I'm still looking for it at a better price.

Series 4, green border
Set: 66 cards/11 stickers. $65.00
Pack: 4.00
Box: 36 packs. 110.00
Box: Empty 10.00
Wrapper: Obi-Wan and Luke, green background 3.00

CARD CHECKLIST

199 The star warriors aim for
    action! . . . . $ .50
200 C-3PO searches for his
    counterpart 50
201 Raid at Mos Eisley! 50
202 Inquiring about Obi-Wan
    Kenobi. 50
203 A band of Jawas 50
204 Stalking the corridors of
    Death Star. 50

205 Desperate moments for our
    heroes! 50
206 Searching for the missing
    droid 50
207 C-3PO (Anthony Daniels) . . .50
207 C-3PO (Anthony Daniels)
    obscene variant 40.00
208 Luke Skywalker on the
    desert planet 50
209 The Rebel Troops 50

210 Princess Leia blasts the
    enemy 50
211 A proud moment for Han
    and Luke 50
212 A stormtrooper is blasted! . . .50
213 Monitoring the battle 50
214 Luke and Leia shortly
    before the raid 50
215 Han bows out of the battle . .50
216 Han and Leia quarrel about
    the escape plan 50
217 The Dark Lord of the Sith . . .50
218 Luke Skywalker's
    home...destroyed! 50
219 The swing to freedom! 50
220 "I'm going to regret this!" . . .50
221 Princess Leia (Carrie
    Fisher). 50
222 "Evacuate? In our moment
    of triumph?" 50
223 Han Solo covers his friends. .50
224 Luke's secret yen for
    action! 50
225 Aunt Beru Lars (Shelagh
    Fraser) 50
226 Portrait of a princess 50
227 Instructing the Rebel pilots . .50
228 R2-D2 is inspected by the
    Jawas 50
229 Grand Moff Tarkin (Peter
    Cushing) 50
230 Guarding the Millennium
    Falcon 50
231 Discussing the Death Star's
    future. 50
232 The Empire strikes back!. . . .50
233 Raiding the Rebel starship . .50
234 Envisioning the Rebel's
    destruction. 50
235 Luke Skywalker (Mark
    Hamill). 50
236 Readying the Rebel fleet. . . .50
237 The deadly grip of Darth
    Vader. 50
238 Uncle Owen Lars (Phil
    Brown). 50
239 The young star warrior 50
240 Artoo's desperate mission! . .50

241 The Rebel fighter ships 50
242 Death Star shootout! 50
243 Rebels in the trench! 50
244 Waiting at Mos Eisley 50
245 Member of the evil Empire . .50
246 Stormtrooper–tool of the
    Empire. 50
247 Soldier of evil! 50
248 Luke suspects the worst
    about his family 50
249 Ben Kenobi (Alec
    Guinness) 50
250 Luke and Ben on Tatooine . .50
251 An overjoyed Han Solo! 50
252 The honored heroes! 50
253 R2-D2 (Kenny Baker) 50
254 Darth Vader (David
    Prowse). 50
255 Luke poses with his
    weapon 50
256 The marvelous droid See-
    Threepio! 50
257 A pair of Jawas 50
258 Fighting impossible odds! . . .50
259 Challenging the evil
    Empire! 50
260 Han Solo (Harrison Ford) . . .50
261 Fury of the Tusken Raider. . .50
262 Creature of Tatooine 50
263 The courage of Luke
    Skywalker 50
264 Star pilot Luke Skywalker . . .50
Stickers:
34 The Star Warriors Aim for
    Action! 2.00
35 Han Solo (Harrison Ford) . . . 2.00
36 Star Pilot Luke Skywalker! . . 2.00
37 The Marvelous Droid See-
    Threepio 2.00
38 R2-D2 (Kenny Baker). 2.00
39 Creature of Tatooine 2.00
40 Darth Vader (David Prowse). 2.00
41 A Pair of Jawas 2.00
42 Luke Poses with his
    Weapon 2.00
43 Stormtrooper-Tool of the
    Empire 2.00
44 Monitoring the Battle 2.00

Series 5, brown/orange
Set: 66 cards/11 stickers. $60.00
Pack: 4.00
Box: 36 packs. 110.00
Box: Empty 10.00
Wrapper: X-wing Fighter, purple background 3.00

CARD CHECKLIST

265 Anxious moments for the
    Rebels. . . . . $ .50
266 Threepio and Leia monitor
    the battle 50
267 No-nonsense privateer Han
    Solo! 50
268 Ben prepares to turn off the
    tractor beam 50
269 Droids on the run! 50
270 Luke Skywalker: farmboy-
    turned-warrior! 50
271 "Do you think they'll melt us
    down, Artoo?" 50
272 Corridors of the Death Star . .50
273 "This is all your fault,
    Artoo!" 50
274 Droids trick the
    stormtroopers! 50
275 Guarding the Millennium
    Falcon 50
276 It's not wise to upset a
    Wookiee! 50
277 Bizarre Inhabitants of the
    cantina! 50
278 A narrow escape! 50

279 Awaiting the Imperial attack. .50
280 "Remember Luke, The
    Force will be with you". . . .50
281 A monstrous thirst! 50
282 "Hurry up, Luke–we're
    gonna have company!" . . .50
283 The Cantina musicians 50
284 Distracted by Solo's assault .50
285 Spiffed-up for the Awards
    Ceremony 50
286 Cantina denizens! 50
287 Han and Chewie ready for
    action! 50
288 Blasting the enemy! 50
289 The Rebel Fighters take off! .50
290 Chewie aims for danger! . . .50
291 Lord Vader senses The
    Force. 50
292 The stormtroopers
    assemble. 50
293 A friendly chat among alien
    friends! 50
294 Droids make their way to
    the Escape Pod 50
295 Han and the Rebel Pilots . . .50

Star Wars, *Series 5 box (Topps 1979)*

296 Artoo-Detoo is abducted by
      Jawas!. 50
297 Inside the Sandcrawler 50
298 Chewie gets riled!. 50
299 Leia wishes Luke good
      luck! 50
300 A crucial moment for Luke
      Skywalker 50
301 Luke, the Star Warrior! 50
302 Threepio and Artoo 50
303 Various droids collected by
      the Jawas 50
304 The Jawas ready their new
      merchandise 50
305 Director George Lucas and
      "Greedo". 50
306 Technicians ready C-3PO
      for the cameras 50
307 A touch-up for Chewbacca! . .50
308 Directing the Cantina
      creatures 50
309 The birthday celebration for
      Sir Alec Guinness 50
310 Filming the Awards
      Ceremony 50
311 The model builders proudly
      display their work. 50
312 Using the "blue screen"
      process for X-wings 50
313 The birth of a droid 50
314 Shooting in Tunisia 50
315 Inside the Millennium
      Falcon 50
316 Photographing the
      miniature explosions 50
317 Filming explosions on the
      Death Star. 50
318 "Make-up" for the Bantha . . .50
319 Dave Prowse and Alec
      Guinness rehearse 50

320 Flight of the Falcon 50
321 George Lucas directs his
      counterpart "Luke" 50
322 Constructing the Star
      Destroyer. 50
323 Aboard the Millennium
      Falcon 50
324 Chewie takes a breather
      between scenes. 50
325 The princess gets the
      brush! 50
326 Animating the "chessboard"
      creatures 50
327 Filming the Sandcrawler . . .50
328 X-wings positioned for the
      cameras 50
329 Sir Alec Guinness and
      George Lucas 50
330 Filming Luke and Threepio
      in Tunisia. 50
Stickers:
45 A Crucial Moment for Luke
      Skywalker. 2.00
46 Chewie Aims for Danger! . . 2.00
47 Droids on the Run!. 2.00
48 Inside the Sandcrawler. . . . 2.00
49 Luke, the Star Warrior!. . . . 2.00
50 Director George Lucas and
      "Greedo". 2.00
51 Technicians Ready C-3PO
      for the Cameras 2.00
52 The Jawas Ready Their New
      Merchandise 2.00
53 Directing the Cantina
      Creature 2.00
54 Leia Wishes Luke Good
      Luck! 2.00
55 A Touch-Up for Chewbacca!. 2.00

OTHER EARLY STAR WARS CARDS

There were several other types of *Star Wars* cards,
stickers and wrappers which appeared in the late 1970s and

early 1980s. The Wonder Bread series of 16 cards came one
per loaf of bread. General Mills cereals had two series of
stickers and Kellogg's had peel away sticker cards in its cereal. Meanwhile, Topps produced sugar-free bubble gum with
distinctive wrappers and inside photos. Burger King gave out
3-card strips, while Hershey's candy bars could be purchased
in 6-packs with a tray card.

Star Wars, *Chewbacca and Jawa cards (Wonder Bread 1977)*

STAR WARS
Wonder Bread (1977)

Set: 16 cards $25.00

CARD CHECKLIST

One: Luke Skywalker $1.50		Nine: Chewbacca 1.50	
Two: Ben (Obi-Wan) Kenobi . . . 1.50		Ten: Jawas 1.50	
Three: Princess Leia Organa . . 1.50		Eleven: Tusken Raider 1.50	
Four: Han Solo 1.50		Twelve: Stormtroopers 1.50	
Five: Darth Vader 1.50		Thirteen: Millennium Falcon . . . 1.50	
Six: Grand Moff Tarkin 1.50		Fourteen: Star Destroyer. 1.50	
Seven: See-Threepio 1.50		Fifteen: X-Wing. 1.50	
Eight: Artoo-Detoo 1.50		Sixteen: TIE, Vader's ship 1.50	

STAR WARS
SUGAR FREE GUM WRAPPERS
Topps (1978)

Set: 56 wrappers $75.00
Wrapper: each 1.25
Box: empty. 10.00

STAR WARS
General Mills Cereals (1978–79)

Set: 18 different large cards $50.00
Card: each. 3.00

STAR WARS
ALBUM STICKERS
Panini (1977)

Set: 256 stickers with album. $35.00
Single sticker 25

Star Wars/The Empire Strikes Back, *three-card strip*
(Burger King 1980)

STAR WARS AND
THE EMPIRE STRIKES BACK
"Everybody Wins Trading Cards"
Burger King (1980)

Set: 12 different strips. $30.00
Set: 36 cards, cut. 25.00
Card: cut. 75
(Cards are unnumbered)

CARD CHECKLIST

Star Wars
Space Adventurer Han Solo!;
  Raid on the Death Star!;
  R2-D2 and C-3PO $3.00
Cantina Denizens!; Han and
  Chewie Mean Business!;
  Search for the Droids 3.00
The Wonderful Droid, R2-D2;
  Han Solo in Action!; Star
  Pilots Prepare for Battle . . 3.00
Weird Cantina Patrons; Jawas
  of Tatooine; Princess Leia
  Organa 3.00
One of the Sandpeople;
  Stormtrooper Attack!; Jedi
  Warrior Ben Kenobi 3.00
Luke Disguised as a
  Stormtrooper!; Flight of the
  Millennium Falcon;
  Captured by the Jawas! . . 3.00

The Empire Strikes Back
Yoda, The Jedi Master; Darth
  Vader and Boba Fett;
  Chase Through the Aster
  oids! 3.00
The Defenders of Freedom!;
  Luke's Training; The
  Imperial Snow Walkers! . . . 3.00
Snowswept Chewbacca; Battle
  of the Lightsabers!; The
  Bounty Hunters 3.00
Seduced by the Dark Side!; The
  Dashing Han Solo; Luke
  Instructed by Yoda 3.00
Yoda on Dagobah; Pursued by
  the Empire!; Luke Astride
  his Tauntaun 3.00
The Dark Lord of the Sith;
  Imperial Stormtrooper;
  Droids Inside the Rebel
  Base 3.00

The Empire Strikes Back, *Series 1, two cards*
(Topps 1980)

THE EMPIRE STRIKES BACK
Topps (1980)

While there were only three series of *The Empire Strikes Back* cards from Topps, there were more actual cards and stickers offered than for the previous movie. As before, stickers are more valuable than cards because there was only 1 sticker per pack. The packs also contained a stick of bubble gum, which is not a collectible and no longer edible. If you open a pack, save the wrapper and throw the gum away.

Series 1, grey and red border
Set: 132 cards/33 stickers $80.00
Pack: 12 cards. 8.00
Box: 36 packs 90.00
Box: Empty 10.00
Wrapper: 2.50

CARD CHECKLIST

1 1st Series–Introduction . . . . $ .60
2 Luke Skywalker 60
3 Princess Leia. 60
4 Han Solo 60
5 Chewbacca 60
6 See-Threepio. 60
7 Artoo-Detoo. 60
8 Lando Calrissian 60
9 Yoda. .60
10 Darth Vader 60
11 Boba Fett 60
12 The Imperial Probot 60
13 Planet of Ice 60
14 "Where's Luke?" 60
15 Droids on Patrol 60
16 The Hidden Rebel Base 60
17 New Rebel Strategy 60
18 General Rieekan. 60
19 Leia's Plan 60
20 Prey of the Wampa. 60
21 Examined: Luke's Tauntaun . .60
22 "But Sir, I Mmh..Mffh.." 60
23 In Search of Luke 60
24 Frozen Death 60
25 Skywalker's Rescue 60
26 Luke's Fight for Life 60
27 Rejuvenation Chamber 60
28 Surgeon Droid 60
29 Artoo's Icy Vigil 60
30 Metal Monster. 60
31 Zeroing in on Chewie!. 60
32 Han Aims for Action! 60
33 Destroying the Probot 60
34 Death of Admiral Ozzel 60
35 The Freedom Fighters 60
36 Rebel Defenses 60
37 Armed Against the Enemy. . . .60
38 Joined by Dack. 60
39 The Sound of Terror 60
40 Suddenly...Starfire! 60
41 Rattled by the Enemy 60
42 Might of the Imperial Forces . .60
43 The Snow Walkers 60
44 Luke...Trapped!. 60
45 Escape from Icy Peril 60
46 "Retreat! Retreat!". 60
47 Headquarters in Shambles . . .60
48 Solo's Makeshift Escape. 60
49 Invaded! 60
50 Vader and the Snowtroopers. .60
51 Snowtroopers of the Empire . .60
52 Millennium Falcon: Getaway
   Ship! 60
53 Emergency Blast Off! 60
54 Battle of the Star Destroyer. . .60
55 Fix-It Man Han Solo! 60
56 A Sudden Change of Plan. . . .60
57 Misty World of Dagobah 60
58 The Creature Called Yoda. . . .60
59 "Welcome, Young Luke!" 60

60 Journey Through the Swamp . .60
61 Yoda's House 60
62 Artoo Peeking Through 60
63 The Secret of Yoda 60
64 The Princess Lends a Hand . .60
65 Repairing Hyperdrive 60
66 Star Lovers 60
67 "Pardon Me Sir, But...Ohhh!". .60
68 Mysterious and Deadly
   Chamber 60
69 Attacked by Batlike
   Creatures! 60
70 "Use the Force, Luke!" 60
71 Raising Luke's X-Wing 60
72 A Need Beyond Reason 60
73 A Gathering of Evils 60
74 The Bounty Hunters 60
75 IG-88 and Boba Fett 60
76 Enter Lando Calrissian 60
77 Warm Welcome for an Old
   Buddy 60
78 Conniving Pals 60
79 "Greetings, Sweet Lady" 60
80 Calrissian's Main Man 60
81 Pretty as a Princess!. 60
82 A Swarm of Ugnaughts 60
83 Threepio...Blasted to Bits! 60
84 A Pile of See-Threepio! 60
85 Escorted by Lando 60
86 Dinner Guests. 60
87 Host of Horror. 60
88 Deflecting Solo's Blasts. 60
89 Alas, Poor Threepio! 60
90 The Ordeal 60
91 The Prize of Boba Fett 60
92 His Day of Triumph 60
93 The Carbon-Freezing
   Chamber 60
94 End of the Star Warriors? 60
95 Pawn of the Evil One 60
96 "No! This Can't Be
   Happening!". 60
97 The Fate of Han Solo 60
98 Boba's Special Delivery 60
99 Observed by Luke. 60
100 Luke Arrives 60
101 Ready for Action! 60
102 The Search for Vader 60
103 "Where Are you,
    Skywalker?". 60
104 Dark Lord of the Sith. 60
105 Weapon of Light 60
106 The Confrontation 60
107 Duel of the Lightsabers 60
108 Escape from Their Captors . .60
109 Iando..Friend or Foe? 60
110 Leia Takes Control! 60
111 Blasting the Stormtroopers! . .60
112 Artoo to the Rescue! 60
113 Spectacular Battle! 60

114 "Embrace the Dark Side!" . . .60
115 "Hate Me, Luke! Destroy
    Me!". 60
116 Luke's Last Stand 60
117 "Do You Have a Foot in My
    Size?" 60
118 Probot 60
119 Falcon on Hoth 60
120 Snow Walkers. 60
121 The Pursued 60
122 Darth Vader 60
123 Swamps of Dagobah. 60
124 Cloud City. 60
125 Lando's Greeting 60
126 Threepio's Destruction 60
127 Luke Battling Darth 60
128 The Final Stand 60
129 Rescue. 60
130 Ion Cannon. 60
131 Checklist – 1-66 60
132 Checklist – 67-132 60
Stickers: yellow, red border
1 F O. 2.00
2 R I 2.00
3 A E. 2.00
4 B X. 2.00
5 U I 2.00
6 W U. 2.00
7 M N 2.00
8 C D. 2.00
9 O U 2.00
10 H E 2.00

11 E O 2.00
12 Y U 2.00
13 A K 2.00
14 A V 2.00
15 E S 2.00
16 Q L 2.00
17 A I 2.00
18 I O 2.00
19 Z T 2.00
20 G J 2.00
21 E I 2.00
22 A P 2.00
23 Montage–Luke Skywalker,
    Darth Vader, Luke
    Skywalker, C-3PO. 2.00
24 C-3PO 2.00
25 Luke with Yoda and Han
    Solo Tauntaun. 2.00
26 Stormtrooper and Boba Fett. 2.00
27 Trooper Luke Skywalker and
    Yoda. 2.00
28 Montage–Too-Onebee,
    Bossk and Lobot. 2.00
29 Montage–Princess Leia,
    Luke Skywalker, Han Solo,
    and Chewbacca 2.00
30 Boba Fett. 2.00
31 Stormtrooper and IG-88 . . . . 2.00
32 Montage–C-3PO, Lando
    Calrissian and R2-D2 . . . . 2.00
33 Darth Vader 2.00

Series 2, grey and blue border
Set: 132 cards/33 stickers $65.00
Pack: 7.00
Box: 36 packs 70.00
Box: Empty 7.50
Wrapper: 2.50

CARD CHECKLIST

133 2nd Series–Introduction . . $ .60
134 Millennium Falcon. 60
135 The Executor 60
136 Imperial Star Destroyer 60
137 Twin-Pod Cloud Car 60
138 Slave I 60
139 Rebel Armored Snow-
    speeder 60
140 The Avenger 60
141 Tie Fighter 60
142 Rebel Transport 60
143 Tie Bomber. 60
144 Preparing for Battle. 60
145 Seeking the Missing Luke . . .60
146 The Searcher 60
147 Star Pilot Luke Skywalker . . .60
148 Luke's Patrol. 60
149 Shelter on Icy Hoth 60
150 Imperial Spy 60
151 Tracking the Probot. 60
152 Han Solo, Rescuer 60
153 Medical Treatment 60
154 Worried Droids on Hoth. 60
155 Imperial Assault!. 60
156 Narrow Escape! 60
157 Fighting Against the Empire .60
158 Roar of the Wookiee. 60
159 Chewie's Task. 60
160 Moments Before the
    Escape 60
161 Last Stages of the Battle. . . .60
162 Gallant Warrior 60
163 "Raise Those Ships!" 60
164 The Awesome One 60
165 Vader and His Snow-
    troopers 60
166 Takeover of Rebel Base 60
167 The Man Called Han Solo. . .60
168 The Falcon in Repairs 60
169 Skills of the Star Pilot 60

170 "Sir...Wait for Me!" 60
171 Han's Desperate Plan 60
172 An Overworked Wookiee?. . .60
173 "Oh, Hello There,
    Chewbacca!" 60
174 Artoo's Bumpy Landing 60
175 Mysterious Planet 60
176 "Luke...In Trouble?". 60
177 Working Against Time 60
178 Han and the Princess 60
179 Soldiers of the Empire. 60
180 The Wookiee at Work 60
181 Vader and a Bounty Hunter. .60
182 World of Darkness 60
183 Taking no Chances! 60
184 Farewell to Yoda and
    Dagobah 60
185 Racing to the Falcon. 60
186 The Ominous Vader 60
187 The Dark Pursuer 60
188 Young Senator from
    Alderaan 60
189 Don't Fool with Han Solo. . . .60
190 Kindred Spirits 60
191 Lobot's Task 60
192 A Brave Princess. 60
193 Corridors of Bespin. 60
194 Lando's Aide, Lobot 60
195 "Get Back Quick..It's
    Vader!" 60
196 Held by the Stormtroopers . .60
197 Han's Torment. 60
198 Lando's Game 60
199 Deadly Device 60
200 In Vader's Clutches. 60
201 A Tearful Farewell 60
202 Han Faces His Fate 60
203 Into the Carbon-Freezing
    Pit!. 60
204 An Ugnaught. 60

DASHING HAN SOLO   **STAR PILOT LUKE SKYWALKER**

The Empire Strikes Back, *Series 2, two cards (Topps 1980)*

205 Tears of a Princess 60
206 Suspended in Carbon
    Freeze. 60
207 Gruesome Fate! 60
208 Evil Threatens! 60
209 "This Deal is Getting
    Worse!" 60
210 The Captor, Boba Fett. 60
211 Fear on Cloud City 60
212 A Warrior Driven 60
213 Courage of Skywalker. 60
214 The Pursuer 60
215 Stalked by Vader! 60
216 A Droid Gone to Pieces. 60
217 Threepio's Free Ride. 60
218 Stormtrooper Takeover!. 60
219 Princess Leia Under Guard! .60
220 Bounty Hunter Boba Fett. . . .60
221 Lando Covers Their
    Escape!. 60
222 Tumbling to an Unknown
    Fate. 60
223 On the Verge of Defeat! 60
224 Gifted Performer 60
225 Actress Carrie Fisher 60
226 Han Solo (Harrison Ford) . . .60
227 Anthony Daniels as C-3PO . .60
228 Our Favorite Protocol Droid. .60
229 R2-D2 (Kenny Baker) 60
230 "Mynocks Outside? Oh My!" .60
231 Actor Billy Dee Williams 60
232 Galaxy's Most Loyal Droids. .60
233 Dashing Han Solo. 60
234 The Force and the Fury 60
235 Yoda's Squabble with R2-
    D2 60
236 Blasted by Leia 60
237 The Art of Levitation 60
238 Snowswept Chewbacca 60
239 Dreamworld...or Trap? 60
240 Swampland Peril! 60
241 "Tried, Have You?" 60
242 Encounter on Dagobah 60
243 Captain Solo Senses a
    Trap. 60
244 A Test for Luke 60
245 R2-D2 on the Misty Bog 60
246 Confronting the Dark Side. . .60
247 Luke Battles...Himself?. 60
248 Blooming Romance. 60
249 Chewie Retaliates. 60
250 Stormtrooper Battle. 60
251 Director Irvin Kershner 60
252 Spiffing up a Wookiee 60
253 Filming the Falcon 60

254 Kershner Directs Mark
    Hamill 60
255 Shooting the Exciting
    Climax. 60
256 Filming Vader in His
    Chamber 60
257 Dagobah Comes to Life 60
258 Building the Falcon 60
259 Hoth Rebel Base
    Sequence 60
260 Filming an Explosion. 60
261 Spectacular Swampland
    Set 60
262 Acting Can be a Dirty Job!. . .60
263 Checklist – 133-198 60
264 Checklist – 199-264 60
Stickers
34 F O 2.00
35 R I 2.00
36 A E 2.00
37 B X 2.00
38 U I 2.00
39 W U 2.00
40 M N 2.00
41 C D 2.00
42 O U 2.00
43 H E 2.00
44 E O 2.00
45 Y U 2.00
46 A K 2.00
47 A V 2.00
48 E S 2.00
49 Q L 2.00
50 A I 2.00
51 I O 2.00
52 Z T 2.00
53 G J 2.00
54 E I 2.00
55 A P 2.00
56 Empire Forces – Darth
    Vader 2.00
57 Empire Forces – Boba Fett . 2.00
58 Empire Forces – Probot 2.00
59 Rebel Forces – Luke
    Skywalker. 2.00
60 Rebel Forces – Princess
    Leia 2.00
61 Rebel Forces – Han Solo . . . 2.00
62 Rebel Forces – Lando
    Calrissian 2.00
63 Rebel Forces – Chewbacca . 2.00
64 Rebel Forces – R2-D2 . . . . . 2.00
65 Rebel Forces – C-3PO. 2.00
66 Rebel Forces – Yoda 2.00

Series 3, green and yellow border
Set: 88 cards/22 stickers $60.00
Pack 6.00

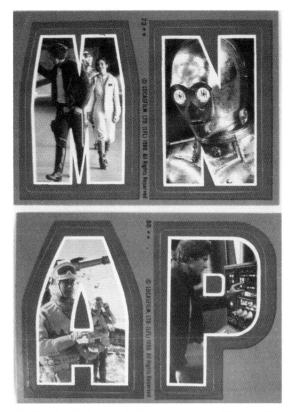

*The Empire Strikes Back, Series 3, stickers #73 and #88
(Topps 1981)*

Box: 36 packs 65.00
Box: Empty 7.50
Wrapper: 2.00

CARD CHECKLIST

265 3rd Series–Introduction . . . $ .55		299 Hostile World of Hoth	.55
266 Han Solo	.55	300 Descent into Danger!	.55
267 Princess Leia	.55	301 Luke...Long Overdue!	.55
268 Luke Skywalker.	.55	302 Toward the Unknown	.55
269 C-3PO	.55	303 In Search of Han.	.55
270 R2-D2.	.55	304 Luke's Desperate Decision .	.55
271 Darth Vader	.55	305 Emerging from the Pit	.55
272 Boba Fett	.55	306 Busy as a Wookiee!	.55
273 Probot.	.55	307 Portrait of an Ugnaught. . . .	.55
274 Dengar	.55	308 The Wizard of Dagobah . . .	.55
275 Bossk	.55	309 Emergency Repairs!	.55
276 IG-88	.55	310 Han on the Icy Wasteland . .	.55
277 FX-7	.55	311 The Walkers Close In!	.55
278 Chewbacca.	.55	312 Toward Tomorrow...	.55
279 Lando Calrisian	.55	313 In the Path of Danger!	.55
280 Stormtrooper.	.55	314 The X-Wing Cockpit	.55
281 Yoda.	.55	315 Hero of the Rebellion	.55
282 Imperial Ships		316 Vader's Private Chamber . . .	.55
Approaching!	.55	317 Aboard the Executor	.55
283 The Courageous Trench		318 The Ominous One	.55
Fighters!	.55	319 Lord Vader's Orders	.55
284 Too-Onebee	.55	320 "He's Still Alive!"	.55
285 Rebel Protocol Droids	.55	321 Lando's Warm Reception . .	.55
286 Within the Hidden Base. . . .	.55	322 The Landing	.55
287 Calrissian of Bespin	.55	323 Their Last Kiss?	.55
288 Testing the Carbon-		324 Bounty Hunter IG-88	.55
Freezing Process	.55	325 The Icy Plains of Hoth.	.55
289 Flight of the X-Wing	.55	326 Luke Astride His Tauntaun. .	.55
290 Dodging Deadly		327 Rebel Snowspeeders Zero	
Laserblasts!	.55	In!	.55
291 The Lovers Part	.55	328 Champions of Freedom. . . .	.55
292 Canyons of Death!	.55	329 Inside the Falcon	.55
293 Magnificent Rebel Starship .	.55	330 The Training of a Jedi	.55
294 Old Friends...or Foes?	.55	331 Yoda's Instruction	.55
295 Power of the Empire	.55	332 The Warrior and the Jedi	
296 Threepio in a Jam!	.55	Master.	.55
297 Swamp Plane!	.55	333 Imperial Snow Walker	
298 A Hasty Retreat!	.55	Attack!.	.55

334 The Asteroid Chase	.55	68 R I	2.00
335 Approaching Planet		69 A E	2.00
Dagobah.	.55	70 B X	2.00
336 Power Generators.	.55	71 U I	2.00
337 Beauty of Bespin.	.55	72 W U	2.00
338 Dreamlike City	.55	73 M N	2.00
339 Luke's Training	.55	74 C D	2.00
340 Snow Walker Terror.	.55	75 O U	2.00
341 Tauntaun.	.55	76 H E	2.00
342 Cloud City Reactor Shaft. . .	.55	77 E O	2.00
343 Yoda's Home	.55	78 Y U	2.00
344 Escape from Bespin	.55	79 A K	2.00
345 Deadly Stompers	.55	80 A V	2.00
346 Snow Walker Model	.55	81 E S	2.00
347 Of Helmets and Costumes .	.55	82 Q L	2.00
348 Filming the Star Destroyer. .	.55	83 A I	2.00
349 Millennium Falcon Miniature	.55	84 I O	2.00
350 Launching an X-Wing	.55	85 Z T	2.00
351 Model Star Destroyer	.55	86 G J	2.00
352 Checklist–265-352	.55	87 E I	2.00
Stickers: green, blue border		88 A P	2.00
67 F O	2.00		

THE EMPIRE STRIKES BACK GIANT PHOTO CARDS
Topps (1980)

Test Issue Set: 60 Giant cards $85.00
Test Issue, single card 2.00
Regular Set: 30 cards. 35.00
Regular Set Box. 50.00
Box: empty. 5.00

REGULAR SET CHECKLIST

1 Darth Vader	$ .75	15 AT-ATs	.75
2 Lando Calrissian	.75	16 Darth Vader	.75
3 Chewbacca	.75	17 Yoda.	.75
4 Leia and Han Solo.	.75	18 Darth Vader's Ship	.75
5 Luke and Darth	.75	19 Luke and TaunTaun	.75
6 Darth and Lando	.75	20 X-Wing and Dagobah	.75
7 Han and C-3PO.	.75	21 Luke, Leia, C-3PO & R2-D2 .	.75
8 Luke and Yoda	.75	22 Snow Speeders	.75
9 The Millennium Falcon.	.75	23 Darth Vader	.75
10 Chewbacca an Leia	.75	24 Han Solo	.75
11 Darth Vader and Bounty		25 Stormtrooper.	.75
Hunters	.75	26 Luke Skywalker	.75
12 Yoda.	.75	27 Luke and Yoda	.75
13 Luke and TaunTaun	.75	28 C-3PO and R2-D2	.75
14 Millennium Falcon and TIE-		29 Yoda.	.75
Fighter	.75	30 Luke, Leia, Han and Chewie .	.75

THE EMPIRE STRIKES BACK
Hershey's (1980)

Cards appeared on 6-pack candy bar trays
Set: 5 Trays (with uncut cards) $8.00
Set: 5 cards cut from trays 5.00

CARD CHECKLIST

Boba Fett.	$1.00	Darth Vader	1.00
Chewbacca	1.00	Luke on a Tauntaun	1.00
C-3PO and R2-D2	1.00		

RETURN OF THE JEDI
Topps (1983)

There were only two series of *Return of the Jedi* cards and only about half as many total cards as in the previous two series. Stickers are again more valuable and each comes with two different backgrounds. Topps was consistent, as usual and if consistency is a virtue, these cards are virtuous indeed. On the other hand, anyone looking for Topps to "top" itself was disappointed. They were still making cards like this in

Return of the Jedi, *Series 1, two cards (Topps 1983)*

the early 1990s, until other companies forced them to upgrade. On the other hand, while modern cards are of much higher quality than these and the previous Topps *Star Wars* cards, hardly anyone collects them! All the collecting action is in the promo cards and chase cards. At least these sets are collected.

Series 1, red border

Set: 132 cards/33 stickers	$35.00
Pack: 10 cards, 1 sticker	2.50
Box: 36 packs	55.00
Box: Empty	5.00
Wrapper:	1.00

(4 different wrappers: Luke; Jabba; Ewok; Darth Vader)

CARD CHECKLIST

1 Title Card	$ .40
2 Luke Skywalker	.40
3 Darth Vader	.40
4 Han Solo	.40
5 Princess Leia Organa	.40
6 Lando Calrissian	.40
7 Chewbacca	.40
8 C-3PO and R2-D2	.40
9 The New Death Star	.40
10 The Inspection	.40
11 Toward the Desert Palace	.40
12 Bib Fortuna	.40
13 Court of Evil	.40
14 Jabba the Hutt	.40
15 Intergalactic Gangster	.40
16 Salacious Crumb	.40
17 A Message for Jabba the Hutt	.40
18 Dungeons of Jabba the Hutt	.40
19 Beedo and a Jawa	.40
20 Sy Snootles and the Rebo Band	.40
21 Droopy McCool	.40
22 Sy Snootles	.40
23 Watched by Boba Fett	.40
24 Boushh's Captive	.40
25 The Bounty Hunter Boushh	.40
26 The Villains Confer	.40
27 Han Solo's Plight	.40
28 The Rescuer	.40
29 Decarbonized!	.40
30 Princess Leia to the Rescue!	.40
31 Heroes in Disguise	.40
32 The Princess Enslaved	.40
33 Luke Skywalker Arrives	.40
34 The Young Jedi	.40
35 The Court in Chaos!	.40
36 The Rancor Pit	.40
37 Facing Jabba the Hutt	.40

38 The Sail Barge and the Desert Skiff	.40
39 Jabba the Hutt's New Dancing Girl	.40
40 On the Sail Barge	.40
41 A Monstrous Fate!	.40
42 The Battle Begins	.40
43 Lando Calrissian's Flight for Life	.40
44 Fury of the Jedi	.40
45 Princess Leia Strikes Back!	.40
46 The Demise of Jabba the Hutt	.40
47 Boba Fett's Last Stand	.40
48 The Rescue	.40
49 Gamorrean Guard	.40
50 The Deadly cannon	.40
51 The Raging Battle	.40
52 Princess Leia Swings into Action!	.40
53 Swing to Safety	.40
54 On the Death Star	.40
55 Guards of the Emperor	.40
56 The Deciders	.40
57 The Emperor	.40
58 Yoda the Jedi Master	.40
59 A Word with Ben (Obi-Wan) Kenobi	.40
60 The Allies Meet	.40
61 A New Challenge	.40
62 Pondering the Raid	.40
63 Mission: Destroy the Death Star!	.40
64 Mon Mothma	.40
65 The Friends Depart	.40
66 Benevolent Creature	.40
67 The Plan Begins	.40
68 Forest of Endor	.40
69 Droids on the Move	.40

70 Blasting a Speeder Bike	.40
71 Approaching the Princess	.40
72 A New Found Friend	.40
73 Princess Leia's Smile	.40
74 Under Attack!	.40
75 Imperial Scout Peril!	.40
76 Entering the Throne Room	.40
77 The Skywalker Factor	.40
78 Captured by the Ewoks	.40
79 The Netted Droid	.40
80 All Hail See-Threepio!	.40
81 Royal Treatment	.40
82 Sitting with Royalty	.40
83 Levitated by Luke	.40
84 The Ewok Leaders	.40
85 Lograi and Chief Chirpa	.40
86 Help from Princess Leia	.40
87 Will Han Solo Be Dinner?	.40
88 The Baby Ewok	.40
89 The Forest Creatures	.40
90 The Droid and the Ewok	.40
91 R2-D2 Meets Wicket	.40
92 Unexpected Allies	.40
93 Serious Situation	.40
94 Luke Skywalker's Destiny	.40
95 Quiet, See-Threepio!	.40
96 Imperial Biker Scout	.40
97 Biker Scout and the Battlefield	.40
98 Han Solo's Approach	.40
99 The Ultimate Mission	.40
100 Ready for Action!	.40
101 Ambushed by the Empire	.40
102 Observed by the Ewoks	.40
103 The Courageous Ewoks	.40
104 Prisoners	.40
105 Revising Their Plan	.40
106 AT-ST (All Terrain Scout Transport)	.40
107 The Forest Fighters!	.40
108 Break for Freedom!	.40
109 Artoo-Detoo–hit!	.40
110 Chewbacca Triumphant!	.40
111 Ewoks to the Rescue!	.40
112 Battle in the Forest	.40
113 Stormtrooper Attack!	.40

114 The Victorious Rebels	.40
115 Time Out for Love	.40
116 Facing the Emperor	.40
117 Master of Terror	.40
118 The Emperor's Offer	.40
119 Battle of the Jedi	.40
120 Lightsaber Battle!	.40
121 Darth Vader is Down!	.40
122 The Confrontation	.40
123 The Death Star Raid	.40
124 Military Leader Admiral Ackbar	.40
125 Within the Death Star	.40
126 Victory Celebration!	.40
127 Congratulating Wedge	.40
128 The Triumphant Trio	.40
129 The Heroic Droids	.40
130 Toward Brighter Tomorrow	.40
131 Checklist I	.40
132 Checklist II	.40

Stickers: (untitled)
Yellow border

1 Yoda, The Jedi Master (#58)	1.25
2 Logray (#84)	1.25
3	1.25
4 Jabba the Hutt (#14)	1.25
5	1.25
6 Admiral Ackbar	1.25
7 Bounty Hunter Boushh (#25)	1.25
8 Han Solo (#4)	1.25
9 Princess Leia	1.25
10 Luke Skywalker (#2)	1.25
11 Han Solo (#100)	1.25

Red border

12 C-3PO	1.25
13 Chewbacca	1.25
14 Sy Snootles (#22)	1.25
15 The Baby Ewok (#15)	1.25
16 Nien Nunb	1.25
17 Lando Calrissian (#6)	1.25
18 R2-D2	1.25
19 Obiwan Kenobi	1.25
20 Luke Skywalker (#51)	1.25
21 Luke Skywalker (#130)	1.25
22 Gamorrean Guard (#49)	1.25

Return of the Jedi, *Series 1, pack (Topps 1983)*

Green border

23	. . . .	1.25	28 Lando Calrissian (#31)	. . . . . 1.25
24	. . . .	1.25	29 Max Rebo	. . . . 1.25
25 Boba Fett (#47)	. . . .	1.25	30 Princess Leia (#73)	. . . . 1.25
26	. . . .	1.25	31 Princess Leia	. . . . 1.25
27 Jabba the Hutt (#15)	. . . . . .	1.25	32 Han Solo	. . . . 1.25
			33 Biker Scout (#97)	. . . . 1.25

Return of the Jedi, *Series 2, seven cards (Topps 1984)*

Series Two, blue border

Set: 88 cards/22 stickers $25.00
Pack: 10 cards, 1 sticker, ... 2.50
Box: 36 packs 40.00
Box: Empty 5.00
Wrapper: 1.00
(4 different wrappers, Leia; Lando; C-3PO; Young Ewok;
all say "New Series")

CARD CHECKLIST

133 Title Card	$ .30	165 Inside Jabba the Hutt's	
134 Path to Destiny	.30	Palace.	.30
135 Captured!	.30	166 The Ewok Village	.30
136 The Courageous Jedi	.30	167 A Collection of Creatures. . .	.30
137 The Victors	.30	168 Alert to Danger!	.30
138 Wicket and Princess Leia . .	.30	169 Walking the Plank!	.30
139 The Emperor's Arrival	.30	170 A Gamorrean Guard	
140 Sail Barge Battle!	.30	Emerges	.30
141 Luke Skywalker, The Jedi . .	.30	171 The Imperial Fleet.	.30
142 The Approach of Wicket . . .	.30	172 Jabba the Hutt on the Sail	
143 A Close Call!	.30	Barge	.30
144 Above the Sarlacc Pit	.30	173 Escorted to the Ewok	
145 Admiral Ackbar's Defenders	.30	Village.	.30
146 R2-D2 on Endor	.30	174 A Monstrous Guest!.	.30
147 Boba Fett Attacks!.	.30	175 Village of the Ewoks	.30
148 Deadly Plunge!	.30	176 Aboard the Sail Barge	.30
149 Lando Calrissian's Disguise	.30	177 Confronting Their Destiny . .	.30
150 Soldiers of the Empire.	.30	178 "Where's Princess Leia?" . .	.30
151 A Curious Ewok	.30	179 Horror From the Pit.	.30
152 A Pensive Luke Skywalker .	.30	180 "Give In to Your Hate!"	.30
153 The Captive Princess	.30	181 Awaiting His Majesty	.30
154 Luke Skywalker Surrenders.	.30	182 A Mother Ewok and Child . .	.30
155 Thoughts of a Jedi	.30	183 A Concerned Princess Leia .	.30
156 The Jaws of Death	.30	184 Lead Singer Sy Snootles. . .	.30
157 Princess Leia Has the		185 The Arrival of Boushh	.30
Force!	.30	186 Master of His Court.	.30
158 Arrival of the Emperor	.30	187 Star Lovers	.30
159 Reunion on Endor.	.30	188 Luke Skywalker...Now a	
160 Toward the Sarlacc Pit	.30	Jedi!	.30
161 Sail Barge Creatures.	.30	189 Battle of the Bunker!	.30
162 Friends of the Alliance!	.30	190 Portrait of Wicket	.30
163 The Dreaded Rancor	.30	191 Trapped by the Empire	.30
164 Face of Terror.	.30	192 Their Secret Revealed	.30
		193 Rethinking the Plan.	.30

194 Snagged by the Ewoks	.30	217 The Interceptor	.30
195 Han Solo's in Trouble!.	.30	218 The Emperor's Shuttle	.30
196 Is Han Solo Giving Up?. . . .	.30	219 Portrait of Chewbacca.	.30
197 The Royal Droid	.30	220 Checklist.	.30
198 Princess Leia Intercedes. . .	.30	**Stickers:**	
199 Rescuing Han Solo	.30	34	.75
200 Father Versus Son	.30	35	.75
201 Luke Skywalker, Jedi		36	.75
Warrior	.30	37	.75
202 The Young Jedi Knight	.30	38	.75
203 Han Solo Is Alive!	.30	39	.75
204 Lando Calrissian		40	.75
Undercover	.30	41	.75
205 Horrendous Creature	.30	42	.75
206 Corridors of the Imperial		43	.75
Destroyer.	.30	44	.75
207 Surrounded by Ewoks	.30	45	.75
208 Gamorrean Guard Profile . .	.30	46 Chewbacca.	.75
209 Hulking Gamorrean Guard .	.30	47	.75
210 Guests of Jabba the Hutt . .	.30	48	.75
211 A Full-Fledged Jedi!.	.30	49	.75
212 Bizarre Alien Creatures	.30	50	.75
213 Headquarters Frigate	.30	51	.75
214 TIE Interceptor	.30	52	.75
215 The Nearly Completed		53	.75
Death Star.	.30	54	.75
216 Rebel Cruiser	.30	55	.75

Return of the Jedi *Sticker Album (Topps 1983)*

RETURN OF THE JEDI
ALBUM STICKERS
Topps (1983)

Set: 180 stickers with album $20.00
Single sticker 25
Wax Box 40.00

STAR WARS GALAXY
Topps (1993, Art)

Star Wars Galaxy cards were the first new set of *Star Wars* cards in 10 years and the first to use art rather than pictures from the movies. The first section provides an all new look at the main characters, with art by Joe Smith. Variant cards with these images were used with the Just Toys Bend-Ems figures as well. A number of them also made their way

Star Wars Galaxy (One), box (Topps 1993)

Star Wars Galaxy Cards, Millennium Falcon Factory Set (Topps 1993)

onto T-shirts. The New Visions 60-card subset features full color illustrations from top comic book artists, including Gil Kane, Sam Keith, Dale Keown, Ken Steacy, Dave Stevens and Al Williamson. In addition, there are subsets covering the design of *Star Wars* and the art of *Star Wars*.

This first *Star Wars Galaxy* set is also an important element in the *Star Wars* marketing revival. New novels and comics had started in 1991, but very few other collectibles were being produced. This card series was heavily marketed and gave a good boost to the *Star Wars* revival.

It gave a much needed boost to Topps as well. They had fallen behind their competitors in trading card quality and had only begun to catch up the previous year. Superhero trading cards were hot at this time, and Topps was in the process of was loosing their only foothold in this market, the *Batman* movie cards. They were concentrating on promoting their own comic book lines and needed to show that they were still serious about trading cards. They showed everybody, and have been producing *Star Wars* cards regularly ever since. Their *Star Wars Galaxy* magazine started the following fall.

The *Millennium Falcon* factory set was one of the best publisher/editor freebees Topps ever gave away. Thanks again, Topps, for sending me one.

Set: 140 cards $25.00
Pack: 8 cards 2.00
Box: 36 packs 50.00
Millennium Falcon factory foil stamped set, plus
    holo-foil cards, plus Darth Vader 3-D holo
    gram and #0 card and preview, in plastic ship
    model 100.00
Millennium Falcon factory set, publishers proof,
    "limited to 500 sets" on sticker 125.00
Binder, with card SWB1 . . . . 18.00
Etched-Foil cards, untitled, Walt Simonson art
1 (Darth Vader) 10.00
2 (Lando Calrissian) 10.00
3 (Luke and R2-D2) 10.00
4 (C-3PO and Chewbacca) 10.00
5 (Yoda and Obi-wan) 10.00
6 (Luke) 10.00
Autographed Cards 35.00
Six-card uncut-sheet (1:case) 50.00
Promo Cards
Boba Fett and Dengar (Cam Kennedy art) from
    Classic Star Wars #8 . . . . 15.00
Jabba the Hutt, Oola and Salacious Crumb (Sam
    Keith art) from *Starlog* #181 and *Wizard* #20 . . . . 10.00
Princess Leia (Brian Stelfreeze art) from *Non-
    Sports Update* Vol. 4 #2 and shows 10.00
Dewback/Stormtrooper (Al Williamson art) from
    Non-Sports Update Vol. 4 #2 . . . . 10.00
Princess Leia and Dewback promo sheet, from
    Advance Comics #52 . . . . 6.00
Jabba the Hutt/Oola/Salacious Crumb promo sheet,
    from *Previews*, Feb. 1993 and *Comics
    Scorecard*, Feb. 1993, 5½"x7¾" 15.00
SWB1 binder card from *Star Wars* Galaxy Binder 10.00

CARD CHECKLIST

1 Title Card	$ .25	12 R2-D2	.25
2 George Lucas	.25	13 Boba Fett	.25
Character Portraits (Joe Smith art)		14 The Emperor Palpatine	.25
3 Luke Skywalker	.25		
4 Darth Vader	.25	**The Design of Star Wars** (various	
5 Leia Organa	.25	artists)	
6 Obi-Wan "Ben" Kenobi	.25	15 Ralph McQuarrie	.25
7 Han Solo	.25	16 The Death Star Trench	.25
8 Chewbacca	.25	17 Ron Cobb's	.25
9 Lando Calrissian	.25	18 Hammerhead (Ron Cobb)	.25
10 Yoda	.25	19 "Typical Wookiee Family"	.25
11 C-3PO	.25	20 The *Star Wars* Holiday Special	.25

Star Wars Galaxy (One), 4 promo cards (Topps 1993)

Star Wars Galaxy *Bonus Cards Set (Topps 1993)*

Star Wars Galaxy *(One), six cards (Topps 1993)*

21 Too-Onebee (McQuarrie) 25
22 The All-Terrain Armored
  Transport (Joe Johnston) . . .25
23 Yoda (Joe Johnston) 25
24 A Space Slug (McQuarrie) 25
25 IG-88 (McQuarrie) 25
26 The Death Star (Joe
  Johnston) 25
27 Jabba the Hutt (Joe
  Johnston) 25
28 Costume Design (Rodis-
  Jamero) 25
29 Princess Leia (Rodis-
  Jamero) 25
30 Original Sketches (Rodis-
  Jamero) 25
31 Lando Calrissian (Rodis-
  Jamero) 25
32 Yoda as Gremlin (Joe
  Johnston) 25
33 Bad Hair Day? (Joe
  Johnston) 25
34 The Rancor (Joe Johnston) . . .25
35 Jabba's Menagerie
  (McQuarrie) 25
36 Gamorrean Guards
  (J.Johnston) 25
37 Bib Fortuna (Rodis-Jamero) . .25
38 Creature Collaboration
  (Johnston) 25
39 Princess Leia's Hair
  (LeBlanc) 25
40 Ewoks (Joe Johnston) 25
41 Leia as a Pin-up (Rodis-
  Jamero) 25
42 Ralph McQuarrie 25
43 The Max Rebo Band
  (McQuarrie) 25
44 Luke Skywalker's Confrontation (Ralph McQuarrie art) .25
45 The Speeder Bike Chase
  (Ralph McQuarrie art) 25
46 The Emperor Strikes Back
  (Ralph McQuarrie art) 25
47 Wedge Antilles (McQuarrie) . .25
The Art of Star Wars (various artists)
48 Cartoonist Howard Chaykin's .25
49 Artist John Berkey 25
50 John Berkey's Concept 25
51 A Huge Space Battle
  (Berkey) 25
52 A More Realistic
  (J.Campbell) 25

53 The Continuing Success 25
54 Foreign Movie
  Posters(T.Cantrell) 25
55 Recapturing the Style
  (C.White) 25
56 Artists' Imaginations
  (W.Siudmak) 25
57 A Highly Stylized (P.Druillet) . .25
58 Italian Poster Art (Papuzza). . .25
59 An Evil Darth Vader
  (McQuarrie) 25
60 A Close Encounter
  (McQuarrie) 25
61 If Droids Can Frolic
  (B.Carter) 25
62 The Popularity of Villains
  (Del Nichols) 25
63 Dave Dorman 25
64 Two Lukes 25
65 The Main International
  (N.Ohrai) 25
66 Once A Design Firm
  (Sanjulian) 25
67 The Mountain (Roger Kastel) .25
68 The Noble Tauntaun 25
69 A Pastiche 25
70 The Rebels Transcend
  (N.Ohrai) 25
71 Boris Vallejo 25
72 Male Bonding (Boris Vallejo) . .25
73 When George Lucas 25
74 Heat Seems to Rise
  (N.Ohrai) 25
75 "We're Moving!" (McQuarrie) . .25
76 Even Droids Celebrate
  (B.Carter) 25
77 Santa Threepio (McQuarrie) . .25
78 Strike Up The Droids
  (J.Alvin) 25
79 Thomas Blackshear 25
80 Jim Steranko 25
81 Steranko's "Empire" 25
New Visions (various artists)
82 Kyle Baker 25
83 Bret Blevins 25
84 Ted Boonthanakit 25
85 June Brigman 25
86 Paul Chadwick 25
87 Howard Chaykin 25
88 Mark Chiarello 25
89 Geof Darrow 25
90 Steve Ditko 25
91 Dave Dorman 25

92 George Evans 25
93 Fastner and Larson 25
94 Keith Giffen 25
95 Paul Gulacy 25
96 Bo Hampton 25
97 Scott Hampton 25
98 Michael Wm. Kaluta 25
99 Gil Kane (A) 25
100 Gil Kane (B) 25
101 Cam Kennedy 25
102 Dale Keown 25
103 Karl Kesel 25
104 Sam Keith (A) 25
105 Sam Keith (B) 25
106 David Lapham 25
107 Mike Lemos 25
108 Esteban Maroto 25
109 Cynthia Martin 25
110 Michel Mignola 25
111 Jean 'Moebius' Giraud 25
112 Jerome Moore 25
113 Jon J. Muth 25
114 Mark Nelson 25
115 Earl Norem 25
116 Allen Nunis 25

117 Jason Palmer 25
118 George Perez 25
119 George Pratt 25
120 Joe Quesada 25
121 P. Craig Russell 25
122 Mark Schultz 25
123 Bill Sienkiewicz 25
124 Walter Simonson 25
125 Ken Steacy 25
126 Brian Stelfreeze (A) 25
127 Brian Stelfreeze (B) 25
128 Dave Stevens 25
129 William Stout 25
130 Greg Theakston 25
131 Angelo Torres 25
132 Jim Valentino 25
133 John Van Fleet 25
134 Charles Vess 25
135 Russell Walks 25
136 Al Williamson (A) 25
137 Al Williamson (B) 25
138 Thomas Wm. Yeates II 25
139 Bruce Zick 25
140 Checklist 25

STAR WARS GALAXY TWO
Topps (1994)

The second *Star Wars Galaxy* card series continued the fine art work and great overall quality of the first series. As with the first series, most of the collecting has centered around the promo cards and chase cards. Some promo cards, such as those given away at shows, are inevitably difficult to obtain. If you didn't go to the show, you may have to pay a lot for the card. The value of other promo cards, such as those that came with magazines or comic books, can be puzzling. Often they can still be found, bagged with the magazine or comic, for a very reasonable price. I have attempted to list the sources for as many of them as possible. Don't pay a fortune for a promo card without first looking for the original comic, magazine or toy that it came with. You might save money and have another collectible in the bargain.

Set: 135 cards (#141-#275) $20.00
Pack: 8 cards 1.75

*Star Wars Galaxy Two, Biker Scout/Ewok promo card
and regular series card (Topps 1994)*

Box: 36 packs	40.00
Factory tin Set, with #00 card, Boris Vallejo holo-gram card and Galaxy III promo card	100.00

Etched-Foil cards, untitled (1:18) by Walt Simonson

#7 (Grand Moff Tarkin)	9.00
#8 (Imperial Troopers)	9.00
#9 (Emperor Palpatine)	9.00
#10 (Boba Fett)	9.00
#11 (Jabba the Hutt, Bib Fortuna & Salacious Crumb)	9.00
#12 (Slave 1)	9.00
Uncut Etched-Foil sheet	100.00
Autographed card (2000)	50.00
Six-card uncut sheet (1:case)	50.00
Album	16.00

Promo cards

P1 Rancor (Jae Lee art) from *Cards Illustrated #2*	15.00
P2 Lightsaber construction (Chris Sprouse art) from *Non-Sports Update*, Vol. 5 #2	15.00
P3 Yoda at Shrine, not released but samples exist	unknown
P4 Jawas and C-3PO (Dave Gibbons art) from *Star Wars* Galaxy I *Millennium Falcon* Factory set	15.00
P5 Chewbacca and droid (Joe Phillips art) from *Cards Illustrated #5* & Just Toys mail-in	15.00
P6 Boba Fett (Tom Taggart art) from *Hero* #12	15.00
SWG1 promo	10.00
Tusken Raiders (Tim Truman art) from *Classic Star Wars* #20 or Just Toys mail in	10.00
Biker Scout/Ewok (Jim Starlin art) from *Triton* #3 variant card #266, Ewok with knife	20.00
Promo sheet with P1 card from *Previews* Feb. 1994, 5¼"x7"	2.00

CARD CHECKLIST

141 Series 2 Title Card	$ .20	156 Marvel's Return	.20
The McQuarrie Portfolio		157 Lumiya, A Half-Human	.20
142 Ralph McQuarrie	.20	158 Darth Vader's	.20
143 A Giant Swamp Slug	.20	159 Ulic Qel-Droma	.20
144 Imperial Walkers	.20	160 Pirate Captain	.20
145 High Over Bespin	.20	161 Dark Empire	.20
146 The Entertainment	.20	162 World Devastors	.20
147 The Imperial Palace	.20	163 Princess Leia	.20
148 Santa Yoda	.20	164 Emperor Palpatine	.20
The Comic Art of Star Wars		165 As Luke Fights	.20
149 Marvel Comics	.20	**The Illustrators of Star Wars**	
150 Marvel's Series	.20	166 Boris Vallejo	.20
151 War in the Ice	.20	167 Ken Barr	.20
152 Luke Patrols	.20	168 Michael Whelan	.20
153 Danger! Ugnaughts	.20	169 Melanie Taylor Kent	.20
154 The Duel Begins	.20	170 George Gaadt	.20
155 Blasting Their Way	.20	171 Basil Gogos	.20

172 Scott Gustafson	.20	210 Dan Barry	.20
173 Sir Alec Guinness	.20	211 John Bolton	.20
174 Tony Auth	.20	212 Timothy Bradstreet	.20
175 Todd Andrews	.20	213 Dan Brereton	.20
176 Michael David Ward	.20	214 Ron Brown	.20
177 Morgan Weistling	.20	215 Frank Brunner	.20
Film Production and Poster Art		216 Rich Buckler	.20
178 Joe Johnston	.20	217 Greg Capullo	.20
179 Nilo Rodis-Jamero	.20	218 Amanda Conner	.20
180 Ewok Break Time	.20	219 Richard Delgado	.20
181 John Mollo	.20	220 Joe DeVito	.20
182 Creatures Galore	.20	221 Colleen Doran	.20
183 A Spider Bike Pilot	.20	222 Norm Dwyer	.20
184 "Assorted Aliens"	.20	223 Bob Fingerman	.20
185 Although The Ewoks	.20	224 Hugh Fleming	.20
186 The *Star Wars* Holiday	.20	225 Franchesco	.20
187 Imperial City On	.20	226 Drew Friedman	.20
188 Kazuhiko Sano	.20	227 Rick Geary	.20
189 The Characters From	.20	228 Dave Gibbons	.20
190 A More Stylized	.20	229 Mike Grell	.20
191 The *Star Wars* Concert	.20	230 Rebecca Guay	.20
192 Luke Surveys All	.20	231 Lurene Haines	.20
193 Vader is the Death Star	.20	232 Matt Haley	.20
194 Where's Luke?	.20	233 Cully Hamner	.20
195 Telling A Story	.20	234 Rich Hedden	.20
The Merchandising Art of Star Wars		235 Dave Hoover	.20
196 Merchandising	.20	236 Janine Johnston	.20
197 A Tatooine Skiff	.20	237 Jeffrey Jones	.20
198 The A-Wing Fighter	.20	238 Kelley Jones	.20
199 Boba Fett	.20	239 Miran Kim	.20
200 Anakin Skywalker	.20	240 Jack Kirby	.20
201 Pinball Wizards	.20	241 Ray Lago	.20
202 *Star Wars* Trilogy	.20	242 Zohar Lazar	.20
203 Gene Lemery	.20	243 Jae Lee	.20
204 Bill Schmidt	.20	244 Paul Lee	.20
New Visions 2		245 John Paul Lona	.20
205 Michael Allred	.20	246 David Lowery	.20
206 Karl Altstaetter	.20	247 Shawn C. Martinbrough	.20
207 Thom Ang	.20	248 Mike Mayhew	.20
208 Sergio Aragonic	.20	249 Walter McDaniel	.20
209 Marshall Arisman	.20	250 Mike McMahon	.20

Star Wars Galaxy Two, four cards (Topps 1994)

251 Linda Medley	.20	264 Zina Saunders	.20
252 David O. Miller	.20	265 Chris Sprouse	.20
253 C. Scott Morse	.20	266 Jim Starlin	.20
254 Nelson	.20	267 Arthur Suydam	.20
255 Hoang Nguyen	.20	268 Sylvain	.20
256 Kevin O'Neill	.20	269 Tom Taggart	.20
257 Mark Pacella	.20	270 Jill Thompson	.20
258 Jimmy Palmiotti	.20	271 Tim Truman	.20
259 Jason Peterson	.20	272 Keith Tucker	.20
260 Brandon Peterson	.20	273 Jeff Watts	.20
261 Joe Phillips	.20	274 Mike Zeck	.20
262 Whilce Portacio	.20	275 Checklist	.20
263 Ralph Reese	.20		

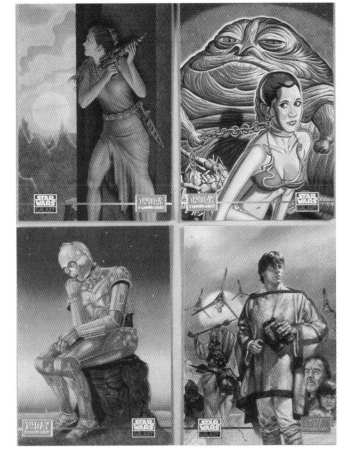

Star Wars Galaxy *Three, four first-day cards (Topps 1995)*

STAR WARS GALAXY THREE
Topps (1995)

Set: 90 cards: #276–#365 + #L1–#L12 . . . . $20.00
Pack: 5 cards + 1 1st day issue card and 1 insert card . 2.00
Box: 36 packs 40.00
First day set: 90 cards 75.00
First day card, each 1.00
Etched Foil Cards untitled (1:12) by Walt Simonson
13 Lando Calrissian 9.00
14 Millennium Falcon 9.00
15 Jawas 9.00
16 Jawas 9.00
17 Tusken Raiders 9.00
18 Jedi Spirits 9.00
Uncut Etched Foil panorama sheet 100.00
Agents of the Empire Clearzone (1:18)
E1 Brett Booth 10.00
E2 Jeff Scott Campbell 10.00
E3 Jeff Rebner 10.00
E4 Joe Chiodo 10.00

E5 Tom Rainey 10.00
E6 Brian Denham 10.00
Promo Cards
P1 promo, does not seem to exist
P2 Snowtroopers, convention give away 18.00
P3 Darth Vader (John Van Fleet art) from *Non-
    Sports Update*, Vol. 6 #4 . . . . 5.00
P4 Luke Skywalker (Arthur Suydam art) from *Combo* #7 . 5.00
P5 Snowspeeder and AT-AT (Steve Reiss art) from .
    Advance Comics #83 . . . . 5.00
P5 error promo 35.00
P6 cover of *Star Wars Galaxy Magazine* #5 (Bros.
    Hildebrandts art) from *Star Wars* Galaxy
    Magazine #5 . . . . 5.00
P7 Leia and twins (Russell Walks art) from *Wizard* #52 5.00
P8 Darth Vader and Boba Fett, from *Cards
    Illustrated* #25 . . . . 5.00
No # Boba Fett, from *Star Wars* Galaxy II factory set . 15.00
#000 Princess Leia promo (Drew Struzan art) from
    Star Wars Galaxy Magazine #4 . . . . 5.00
One-Card promo sheet, card #000, from *Previews*
    Sept. 1995 . . . . 5.00

CARD CHECKLIST

276 Title Card	$ .25	323 Dave Dorman	.25
The Struzan Portfolio		324 Hugh Fleming	.25
277 The Glove of Darth Vader	.25	325 Hugh Fleming	.25
278 The Lost City of the Jedi	.25	326 Killian Plunkett	.25
279 Mission from Mount Yoda	.25	327 June Brigman	.25
280 The Truce at Bakura	.25	328 Dave Dorman	.25
281 The Courtship of Princess		329 Mark Harrison	.25
Leia	.25	**From Camelot to Tatooine, The**	
282 The Crystal Star	.25	**Campbell Connection**	
283 Ambush at Corellia	.25	330 The Call to Adventure	.25
284 Assault at Selonia	.25	331 Supernatural Aid	.25
285 Showdown at Centerpoint	.25	332 The Road of Trials	.25
286 Children of the Jedi	.25	333 The Ultimate Boon	.25
287 We Don't Do Weddings:		334 Joseph Campbell/George	
The Band's Tale	.25	Lucas	.25
Promotional and Licensed Illust-		335 The Force	.25
ration		336 Leia	.25
288 C-3PO Thinker	.25	337 Han Solo	.25
289 C-3PO Birthday	.25	338 Skywalker/Vader	.25
290 Luke and Starfighters	.25	**Newest Visions**	
291 C-3PO and R2-D2	.25	339 Kelly Freas	.25
292 Cantina Poster	.25	340 Gene Colan	.25
293 Bounty Hunters	.25	341 Mitch O'Connell	.25
294 C-3PO Robot Book	.25	342 Mike Avon Oeming	.25
295 Luke with Gang	.25	343 Tim Eldred	.25
296 Marvel Comic	.25	344 Cathleen Thole	.25
297 The Ewok Adventure	.25	345 Don Ivan Punchatz	.25
298 Cindel and Ewok	.25	346 John Pound	.25
299 Wicket Finds a Way	.25	347 Rick Buckler	.25
300 Lando Montage	.25	**Alternate Visions**	
301 Boba Fett Cloud City	.25	348 Scott Neely	.25
302 C-3PO Director	.25	349 Joann Daley	.25
303 Mos Eisley Cantina	.25	350 Jack Davis	.25
304 Mos Eisley at Dark	.25	351 Mark "Crash" McCreery	.25
305 Christmas Card	.25	352 Mike Smithson	.25
306 Magistrates of the Empire	.25	353 John Eaves	.25
307 Grand Moff Tarkin	.25	354 Clark Schaffer	.25
308 Hand and Chewie Fight		355 Will Vinton Studios	.25
Boba Fett	.25	356 Gahan Wilson	.25
309 The Tatooine Years	.25	**The Empire Strikes Back**	
310 The Four Jedi	.25	357 Steve Reiss	.25
311 The Reluctant Jedi	.25	358 Mark Harrison	.25
The Novels		359 Campbell/Garner	.25
312 Nick Choles	.25	360 Vince Locke	.25
313 David Deitrick	.25	361 John K. Snyder	.25
314 Gary Gianni	.25	362 Therese Nielsen	.25
315 Courtney Skinner	.25	363 Chris Moeller	.25
316 Lou Harrison	.25	364 John Paul Leon	.25
317 Les Dorscheid	.25	365 Checklist	.25
318 Brian Ashmore	.25	**Lucasarts Foil Cards**	
319 Hector Gomez	.25	L1 Dark Forces Display Art	.50
320 Jae Lee	.25	L2 Dark Forces Ad Art	.50
The Comics Strike Back		L3 Dark Trooper	.50
321 Arthur Adams	.25	L4 Keith Carter	.50
322 Dave Dorman	.25	L5 TIE Fighter	.50

Star Wars Galaxy Three, one-card promo sheet (Topps 1995)

L6 Defender of the Empire.....	.50	L10 Keith Carter..............	50
L7 Keith Carter..............	.50	L11 Rebel Assault............	.50
L8 X-Wing..................	.50	L12 Keith Carter.............	.50
L9 *The Farlander Papers*......	.50		

STAR WARS
Merlin (1997)

These are a recent set of standard-sized trading cards available to comic shops through Diamond Distribution. The cards cover all three movies, plus character and vehicle profiles. Merlin is owned by Topps, which explains how they have the rights to produce *Star Wars* trading cards.

Set: 125 cards $30.00
Pack: 1.50
Box: 45.00
Chase Cards, oversize
   Three different, each 20.00

CARD CHECKLIST

Star Wars: A New Hope
1 Imperial Star Destroyer .... $ .30
2 R2-D2 and C-3PO .... .30
3 Rebel Forces.............. .30
4 Darth Vader............... .30
5 C-3PO.................... .30
6 Sandcrawler .... .30
7 Stormtrooper on Dewback ... .30
8 Luke Skywalker and Owen
   Lars.................... .30
9 Luke, C-3PO and R2-D2 .... .30
10 Tusken Raider .... .30
11 Luke Skywalker and
   Lightsaber .... .30
12 Death Star and Star
   Destroyer.............. .30
13 Landspeeder in Mos Eisley .. .30
14 Luke, Ben and C-3PO with
   Stormtroopers .... .30
15 Han Solo and Chewbacca... .30
16 Han Solo with Jabba the
   Hutt................... .30
17 The *Millennium Falcon* ..... .30
18 Princess Leia with Grand
   Moff Tarkin.............. .30
19 *Millennium Falcon* Interior... .30
20 Death Star Docking Bay .... .30
21 Luke, Han and C-3PO...... .30
22 Han Solo and Princess Leia . .30
23 Ben Kenobi .... .30
24 *Millennium Falcon*......... .30

25 *Millennium Falcon*
   approaching Yavin 4 ..... .30
26 Han Solo with Luke
   Skywalker .... .30
27 X-wing fighters .... .30
28 X-wing fighter and TIE
   fighter .... .30
29 Y-wing fighters in Death Star
   trench .... .30
30 Darth Vader/TIE fighter
   interior .... .30
31 Princess Leia and C-3PO ... .30
32 Luke Skywalker/X-wing
   Interior................ .30
33 Death Star exhaust port .... .30
34 Luke, Leia and Han .... .30
35 Han Solo winking .... .30
The Empire Strikes Back
36 Imperial Probot .... .30
37 Luke Skywalker in Wampa
   lair................... .30
38 Han Solo with Rebel
   Commander............ .30
39 Han Solo waving to
   Snowspeeder........... .30
40 Han Solo firing at Imperial
   probe droid .... .30
41 Darth Vader with General
   Veers................. .30
42 Luke Skywalker .... .30
43 Snowspeeder/AT-AT legs ... .30
44 *Millennium Falcon* leaving
   Rebel base .... .30
45 *Falcon* entering asteroid field .30
46 Exploding TIE fighter....... .30
47 Yoda.................... .30
48 Luke and Yoda .... .30
49 *Millennium Falcon* & Star
   Destroyer.............. .30
50 *Falcon* on back of Star
   Destroyer.............. .30
51 *Millennium Falcon* cockpit
   interior................ .30
52 Rebels arriving Bespin ..... .30
53 Darth Vader tortures Han
   Solo................... .30
54 Luke's X-wing approaching
   Cloud City .... .30
55 Han Solo/Carbon freezing
   chamber .... .30
56 Luke and Darth Vader duel .. .30
57 *Slave I* leaving Cloud City ... .30
58 Darth Vader .... .30
59 Luke Skywalker .... .30
60 Luke Skywalker/Reactor
   shaft .... .30
61 Luke and Vader
   dueling/Reactor shaft..... .30
62 Darth Vader reaching out to
   Luke .... .30
63 Luke Skywalker .... .30
64 *Millennium Falcon* and
   Cloud City .... .30
65 R2-D2 repairing C-3PO..... .30
66 Luke/*Millennium Falcon*
   main hold. .... .30
67 Leia/*Millennium Falcon*
   cockpit................ .30
68 Luke Skywalker's bionic
   hand .... .30
69 R2-D2 with C-3PO .... .30
70 Luke, Leia, R2-D2 and C-
   3PO .... .30

Return of the Jedi
71 Shuttle leaving Star
   Destroyer.............. .30
72 Darth Vader with Grand Moff
   Jerjerod............... .30
73 Jabba's Palace........... .30
74 Jabba the Hutt .... .30
75 Boushh the bounty hunter... .30
76 Han Solo escaping the
   carbonite .... .30
77 Luke with Bib Fortuna...... .30
78 Luke Skywalker in Rancor's
   grip .... .30
79 Luke, Han and Chewbacca.. .30
80 Luke Skywalker .... .30
81 Boba Fett .... .30
82 Han Solo reaches for Lando . .30
83 C-3PO and Salacious
   Crumb................ .30
84 Luke and Leia on Jabba's
   Sail Barge .... .30
85 The Emperor Palpatine..... .30
86 Yoda Instructing Luke ...... .30
87 Mon Mothma and Admiral
   Ackbar................ .30
88 Shuttle *Tyderium*/Cockpit ... .30
89 Luke and Leia on Speeder
   Bike.................. .30
90 Luke tackles a Scout
   Trooper .... .30
91 Luke, Han and Chewie
   surrounded .... .30
92 Luke and Leia at the Ewok
   village .... .30
93 The Rebel fleet.......... .30
94 Vader and Luke before the
   Emperor .... .30
95 Ackbar watching the Rebel
   fleet................. .30
96 Battle above the Death Star . .30
97 Han plants explosive
   charges............... .30
98 The Death Star fires on the
   Rebels................ .30
99 Lightsabers clash .... .30
100 Darth Vader is defeated ... .30
101 The Emperor/Throne room . .30
102 *Millennium Falcon*/Interior
   Death Star............. .30
103 Anakin Skywalker .... .30
104 The Death Star explodes .. .30
105 Anakin, Ben and Yoda..... .30
Character Profiles
106 Luke Skywalker.......... .30
107 Han Solo .... .30
108 Leia Organa .... .30
109 Obi-Wan Kenobi .... .30
110 Chewbacca .... .30
111 C-3PO................. .30
112 R2-D2................. .30
113 Darth Vader............ .30
114 Yoda.................. .30
115 Boba Fett.............. .30
Vehicle Profiles
116 X-wing fighter .... .30
117 Death Star............. .30
118 Sandcrawler .... .30
119 *Millennium Falcon*........ .30
120 TIE fighter.............. .30
121 Imperial Shuttle.......... .30
122 AT-AT .... .30
123 Star Destroyer .... .30
124 Vader's TIE fighter .... .30
125 Checklist............... .30

ACTION MASTERS
Kenner (1994)

Action Master die-cast figures came with trading cards that were unique to the figures, not promo cards for some card series. Because of this they are generally overlooked by trading card magazines.

Star Wars *Action Masters, Boba Fett and Han Solo cards*
(Topps 1994)

Cards come with Die Cast figures

Star Wars

C-3PO	$3.00	Han Solo (511821-00)	3.00
R2-D2	3.00	Stormtrooper (509997-00)	3.00
Darth Vader	3.00	Luke Skywalker (515860-00)	3.00
Luke Skywalker (509221-01)	3.00	Boba Fett (509998-00)	3.00
Chewbacca	3.00	Chewbacca (515859-00)	3.00
Stormtrooper	3.00	**Star Wars, from 4 pack**	
Snowtrooper	3.00	C-3P0	3.00
Star Wars, from 6 pack (different)		Princess Leia Organa	3.00
Darth Vader (509996-00)	3.00	R2-D2	3.00
		Obi-Wan Kenobi	3.00

Eight Star Wars *Galaxy Bend-Em cards (Topps 1993–95)*

STAR WARS GALAXY—BEND-EMS
Topps (1993–95, Art)

Most of JustToys' Bend-Em figures came with trading cards from 1993 to 1995. The cards are variant *Star Wars Galaxy* cards, which are lettered on the back instead of numbered. There earliest cards and figures matched, but the later ones were random, making it that much harder to complete a set of cards. Consequently, later cards are worth more than earlier cards. There are 28 cards in the set, plus three mail-in cards. The cards may very well be more collectible (and more valuable) than the figures.

Just Toys Bend-Ems variants (Joe Smith art)

0 Darth Vader mail-in card (Ken Steacy art)	$15.00
00 Darth Vader mail-in card (Ralph McQuarrie art)	15.00
Checklist card, variation of checklist card from series, mentions Series Two	15.00

Cards come with Bend-Em figures

A Darth Vader (Joe Smith)	$3.00	Q The Art of *Star Wars* (Boris Vallejo)	5.00
B C-3PO (Joe Smith)	3.00	R X-wing Pilot	5.00
C R2-D2 (Joe Smith)	3.00	S Admiral Ackbar (Michael Wm. Kaluta)	5.00
D Imperial Troopers (Al Williamson)	3.00	T Tusken Raider	5.00
E Yoda (Joe Smith)	3.00	U Emperor's Royal Guard (Jerome Moore)	5.00
F Chewbacca (Joe Smith)	3.00	V Gamorrean Guard	5.00
G Luke Skywalker (Joe Smith)	3.00	W Bib Fortuna	5.00
H Obi-Wan "Ben" Kenobi (Joe Smith)	3.50	X Darth Vader and Luke	5.00
I Han Solo	5.00	**Star Wars Galaxy Series 2 cards**	
J Princess Leia (Joe Smith)	2.00	Y The Merchandising Art of *Star Wars*	5.00
K Emperor Palpatine	5.00	Z Luke & Leia (Zina Saunders)	5.00
L (Wicket) Ewok (Wm. Stout)	3.00	AA (Luke, Vader, Han & Leia)	5.00
M Boba Fett (Joe Smith)	3.00	BB The Illustrators of Star Wars, Ken Barr	5.00
N The Design of *Star Wars*, The Death Star Trench	5.00		
O Death Star II, series 2	5.00		
P Lando Calrissian	5.00		

Star Wars *Mastervision Card (Topps 1995)*

STAR WARS MASTERVISION
Topps (1995)

Topps Mastervision cards are large enough to be called wall art and come on premium 24-point stock, UV-coated and foil-stamped. The series features full-bleed artwork by Ralph McQuarrie, Dave Dorman, The Hildebrandts, Boris Vallejo, Ken Steacy, Drew Struzan, Hugh Fleming, Michael Whelan and more.

Boxed Set: 36 cards 6¾"x10¾"	$40.00
Card:	1.25
Promos	
No #.	2.50
P2 promo (*Star Wars Galaxy Mag. #5*)	2.50

STAR WARS FINEST
Topps (1996)

This is an all-chromium set, subtitled "The character guide to the *Star Wars* universe." The cards features text written by Andy Mangels and consist of 10 nine-card subsets by different artists.

Set: 90 Chromium cards	$60.00
Pack: 5 cards	3.50
Box: 36 packs	75.00

Topps Matrix Chase Cards (1:12)

Han Solo and Chewbacca (Ray Lago)	10.00
Emperor Palpatine (Ray Lago)	10.00
C-3PO and R2-D2 (John Van Fleet)	10.00
Boba Fett (John Van Fleet)	10.00

Embossed Chase Cards (1:9) Dan Brereton art

6 different, each	10.00
Topps Matrix six-up chasecard panel (Dan Brereton art) one per case ordered by retailer	
Topps Finest Refractor (1:12) 90 different, each	15.00
Refractor Set: 90 cards	1,100.00
Mastervisions Matrix redemption (1:360)	75.00
Mastervision Matrix mail-in	75.00
Album, with card	20.00
Album card	8.00

Promos

SWF1 promo, from *Star Wars Galaxy Magazine* #6	4.00
SWF2 promo, from *Star Wars Galaxy Magazine* #7	4.00
SWF3 Luke on TaunTaun, from *Non-Sports Update* Vol. 7 #3	4.00
Refractor promo	40.00
Oversize Chromium Promo	15.00

CARD CHECKLIST

1 Credits, Hugh Fleming art	$ .65

Rebel Alliance Command by Russell Walks

2 Luke Skywalker	.65
3 Princess Leia	.65
4 Mon Mothma	.65
5 Admiral Ackbar	.65
6 Jan Dodonna	.65
7 Han Solo	.65
8 Chewbacca	.65
9 Lando Calrissian	.65

Rebels & Affiliates by Juda Tverski

10 Crix Madine	.65
11 Garm Bel Iblis	.65
12 Borsk Fey'lya	.65
13 Wedge Antilles	.65
14 Biggs Darklighter	.65
15 Nien Nunb	.65
16 Winter	.65
17 Wicket	.65
18 Owi Xux	.65

Imperial Command by Chris Moeller

19 Emperor Palpatine	.65
20 Darth Vader	.65
21 Grand Moff Tarkin	.65
22 Joruus C'Baoth	.65
23 Admiral Thrawn	.65
24 Captain Pellacon	.65
25 Admiral Piett	.65
26 Admiral Daala	.65
27 General Veers	.65

Imperials & Affiliates by Mark Harrison

28 Royal Guard	.65
29 Death Star Gunner	.65
30 Stormtrooper	.65
31 TIE Fighter Pilot	.65
32 AT-AT Walker Pilots	.65
33 Biker Scout	.65
34 Boba Fett	.65
35 Dengar	.65
36 Bossk	.65

Force Users by Joe Phillips

37 Obi-Wan Kenobi	.65
38 Yoda	.65
39 Callista	.65
40 Jacen Solo	.65
41 Anakin Solo	.65
42 Jaina Solo	.65
43 Kyp Durron	.65
44 Kirana Ti	.65
45 Tionne	.65

Spies, Smugglers & Rogues by Lou Harrison

46 Mara Jade	.65
47 Talon Karrde	.65
48 Salla Zend	.65
49 Zuckuss	.65
50 Lobot	.65
51 Galleandro	.65
52 Moruth Doole	.65
53 Garindan	.65
54 Lady Valerian	.65

Indigenous Life Forms by Mark Sasso

55 Tusken Raider	.65
56 Bantha	.65
57 Jawa	.65
58 Ugnaught	.65
59 Noghri	.65
60 Ssi-Ruuk	.65
61 Wampa	.65
62 Tauntaun	.65
63 Sarlacc	.65

Mos Eisley Cantina by Tony Harris

64 Greedo	.65
65 Cantina Band	.65
66 Labria	.65
67 Dr. Evazan	.65
68 Ponda Baba	.65
69 Feltipern Trevagg	.65
70 Kabe & Muftak	.65
71 Momaw Nadon	.65
72 Wuher & Chalmun	.65

Jabba's Palace by Joe Chiodo

73 Jabba the Hutt	.65
74 Bib Fortuna	.65
75 Salacious Crumb	.65
76 Max Rebo Band	.65
77 Oola	.65
78 Rancor	.65
79 Gamorrean Guard	.65
80 Weequay	.65
81 Tessek	.65

Droids by Den Beauvais

82 C-3PO	.65
83 R2-D2	.65
84 2-1B	.65
85 R5-D4	.65
86 4-LOM	.65
87 Blue Max & Bollux	.65
88 EV-9D9	.65
89 IG-88	.65
90 Probot/Checklist	.65

Star Wars: Shadows of the Empire,
promo cards #SOTE7 and #SOTE1 (Topps 1996)

STAR WARS: SHADOWS OF THE EMPIRE
Painted by the Greg and Tim Hildebrandt
Topps (1996)

Set: 90 cards (#1 through #72 and #82 through #100)	$15.00
Pack: 9 cards	1.50
Box: 36 packs	50.00
Etched foil, gold gilt (1:9) 6 diff., each (see checklist)	7.00
Foil Embossed (1:18) 4 diff., each (see checklist)	10.00
Redemption card (1:200)	60.00
Autographed Mastervision mail-in redemption	50.00
Four different wrappers: Luke, Xizor, Darth, Boba Fett	

Promos

One card promo sheet, SOTE#3, 5¼"x7"	5.00

Star Wars Finest, *cards #61 and #16 (Topps 1996)*

SOTE1 Prince Xizor (Bros. Hildebrandt art) from
  Star Wars Galaxy Magazine #7 . . . . 3.00
SOTE2 Darth Vader (Bros. Hildebrandt art) from
  Non-Sports Update Vol. 7 #4 . . . . 3.00
SOTE3 Luke and Lightsaber (Bros. Hildebrandt art)
  from *Star Wars* Topps Finest Series One box. 3.00
SOTE4 Dash Rendar (Bros. Hildebrandt art) *Star
  Wars Galaxy Magazine #8.* 3.00
SOTE5 Boba Fett (Bros. Hildebrandt art) from QVC
  and convention giveaway 3.00
SOTE6 Guri (Bros. Hildebrandt art) from *Fan #19*. 3.00
SOTE7 R2-D2 and C-3PO (Bros. Hildebrandt art)
  San Diego Con giveaway, *Collect* Vol. 4, #9,
  Combo #24 . . . . 3.00

CARD CHECKLIST

1 Xizor is Lurking . . . . $ .20	40 Leia and Chewie Go
2 Leia's Recurring Nightmare . . .20	Underground. 20
3 Luke Feels the Dark Side. 20	41 Leia Visits Spero's Plant Shop .20
4 Leia Defends Herself. 20	42 Vader Seethes Over Luke's
5 Reunion on Tatooine 20	Escape. 20
6 Xizor Greets Vader 20	43 Leia Arrives at Xizor's Palace . .20
7 Xizor's Dirty Handiwork 20	44 Leia Finally Meets Xizor 20
8 Ferreting Out a Traitor 20	45 Leia is Smitten 20
9 Beautiful...And Lethal. 20	46 Vader Senses His Son 20
10 Xizor Summons Jabba 20	47 Leia Prepares For Xizor 20
11 Leia Meets Dash Rendar. 20	48 Hyperspace...At Last! 20
12 Vader Stays Sharp 20	49 Xizor Prepares For Leia 20
13 Xizor Relishes the Good Life. .20	50 The Kiss. 20
14 Fancy Flying. 20	51 Take *That*, Xizor!. 20
15 Luke Scores a Tie. 20	52 Xizor Sharpens His Claws. . . .20
16 "Help Me, Obi-Wan..." 20	53 Dash Does It Again. 20
17 Boba Fett Escapes From Gall .20	54 Luke Becomes One With
18 Narrow Escape. 20	The Force. 20
19 Dealing With Dash 20	55 Xizor's Troubled World 20
20 Vader Grows Wary of Xizor. . .20	56 Vader Uncovers Xizor's
21 Xizor Wants it All. 20	Secret Past. 20
22 The Emperor Insists 20	57 Same Beast, Different Sewer . .20
23 It'th Greedo'th Uncle 20	58 Dash Fires the Guide 20
24 The Waiting Game 20	59 Artoo and Threepio Helm
25 Luke Hones His Lightsaber	the *Falcon*. 20
Skills. 20	60 Luke Blocks Xizor's Fire 20
26 Swoop Troop Attack 20	61 Will Xizor Call Luke's Bluff?>. .20
27 Luke Axes a Swooper. 20	62 Five Minutes Until Impact 20
28 Good Ol' Beggar's Canyon 20	63 Guri Goes Toe–To–Toe With
29 Vader Destroys the Rebel	Luke 20
Base. 20	64 Xizor Narrowly Escapes 20
30 Guri Does Xizor's Dirty Work. . .20	65 Xizor's Castle Blows Up 20
31 Luke and Dash's Bothan	66 Battle Over Coruscant: Part I .20
Mission. 20	67 Battle Over Coruscant: Part II .20
32 Dash's Persuasive Charm. . . .20	68 Battle Over Coruscant: Part III. .20
33 Attack on the *Subrosa*. 20	69 Good Riddance, Xizor! 20
34 Leia Meets Guri 20	70 Watch Out, Dash! 20
35 Luke and Melan Are	71 Dash's Secret Getaway. 20
Ambushed 20	72 Luke Plans Han's Rescue. . . .20
36 Luke's Taken Prisoner. 20	**Foil Chase Cards**
37 Guri Turns the Tables 20	73 Luke Skywalker 7.00
38 Boarding Guri's *Stinger*. 20	74 Leia & Chewbacca. 7.00
39 Chewbacca in Disguise. 20	75 Lando Calrissian 7.00
	76 R2-D2 & C-3PO 7.00

77 Dash & Leebo 7.00	91 4-LOM Tries His Luck Against
78 Prince Xizor. 7.00	Fett. 20
Embossed Foil Chase Cards	92 Another Narrow Escape for
79 Guri 10.00	Boba Fett 20
80 Darth Vader 10.00	93 Fett Deals with Zuckuss 20
81 Jix & Big Gizz 10.00	94 At Last, Fett Delivers Han to
82 Boba Fett. 10.00	Jabba 20
Ships	**Lucasarts**
83 *Millennium Falcon*. 20	95 Dash Battles AT-ATs on Hoth. . .20
84 *Outrider* 20	96 Dash Uncovers the Swoopers'
85 *Virago*. 20	Plot. 20
86 *Stinger*. 20	97 Dash Aboard the Suprosa 20
87 *Swoop* 20	98 Dash Attacks Xizor's Skyhook. .20
88 *Slave I* 20	99 Dash Rides Od Mantell
Dark Horse	Hovertrain. 20
89 IG-88's Bold Attack on Boba Fett .20	100 Dash Battles IF-88 on
90 Fett Fends Off Fellow Bounty	Ord Mantell. 20
Hunters. 20	

STAR WARS WIDEVISION
Topps (1995)

With Widevision cards, Topps went back to images from the movies. This time they had high quality and the same aspect ratio as the films (like the letterbox videotape version). The images were transferred directly from the original film master, not a second-generation version. Production was limited to 4,000 cases.

Widevision versions of the other two movies followed and in 1997 the Special Edition was covered in turn.

Set: 120 cards, 4½" $50.00
Pack: 10 cards 5.00
Box: packs 100.00
Topps Finest (1:11) Ralph McQuarrie art
C1 C-3PO and R2-D2 on Tatooine. 20.00
C2 Luke watches two suns setting. 20.00
C3 Pulled into the Death Star Docking Bay 20.00
C4 On the run within the Death Star 20.00
C5 Darth Vader vs. Luke 20.00
C6 Imperial TIE Fighter chases *Millennium Falcon*. . . 20.00
C7 Rebels approach the Death Star 20.00
C8 TIE Fighter chases X-wing. 20.00
C9 X-wing in the Death Star trench 20.00
C10 . . . . 20.00
Album, with #00 card 16.00
Promo Cards
SWP0 Han, Luke and Chewie enter final ceremony,
  from *Star Wars* Galaxy II factory set 15.00
SWP1 Stormtroopers stop Luke and Ben in land-
  speeder, from *Non-Sport Update* Vol. 5 #6
  and show give-away 5.00
SWP2 Interior of Millennium Falcon cockpit, from
  Advance Comics #72 . . . . 10.00
SWP3 TIE Fighters in Death Star trench, from *Star
  Wars Galaxy Magazine #1*. 10.00
SWP4 Exterior of Star Destroyer, from *Wizard #42* 5.00
SWP5 Darth Vader throttling Rebel, from *Tuff Stuff
  Collect* Jan. 1995 . . . . 10.00
SWP6 Leia & C-3PO in Yavin IV control room, from
  Cards Illustrated #14 . . . . 10.00
0 Luke outside X-wing, from *Star Wars* Widevision
  binder album. 8.00
No# promo sheet Han in gunport, from *Previews*
  Oct. 1994 . . . . 10.00
Promos from Classic Edition 4-Pack action figures
K01 Int. Rebel Blockade Runner—Corridor. 8.00
K02 Int. Millennium Falcon—Gunport 8.00
K03 Int. Millennium Falcon—Cockpit. 8.00
K04 Int. Tatooine—Mos Eisley—Cantina. 8.00

Star Wars WideVision, four promo cards (Topps 1995)

Star Wars *WideVision, four cards (Topps 1995)*

CARD CHECKLIST

1 Credits, John Berkey art . . . $ .50
2 Ext. Imperial Star Destroyer—
   Space 50
3 Ext. Spacecraft in Space 50
4 Int. Rebel Blockade Runner—
   Sub-Hallway 50
5 Int. Rebel Blockade Runner—
   Main Hallway 50
6 Int. Rebel Blockade Runner—
   Main Hallway 50
7 Int. Rebel Blockade Runner—
   Sub-Hallway 50
8 Int. Rebel Blockade Runner—
   Corridor 50
9 Int. Rebel Blockade Runner—
   Sub-Hallway 50
10 Int. Escape Pod 50
11 Ext. Tatooine—Dune Sea 50
12 Ext. Tatooine—Rock Canyon. .50
13 Ext. Tatooine—Rock Canyon—
   Sandcrawler 50
14 Int. Sandcrawler 50
15 Ext. Tatooine—Desert 50
16 Ext. Tatooine—Lars Home-
   stead 50
17 Int. Lars Homestead—
   Garage Area 50
18 Int. Lars Homestead—
   Garage Area 50
19 Int. Lars Homestead—
   Dining Area 50
20 Ext. Tatooine—Lars Home-
   stead 50
21 Ext. Tatooine—Desert
   Wasteland 50
22 Ext. Tatooine—Rock Mesa . . .50
23 Ext. Tatooine—Rock Mesa—
   Canyon. 50
24 Ext. Tatooine—Rock Canyon. .50
25 Ext. Tatooine—Rock Canyon—
   Floor. 50
26 Ext. Tatooine—Sand Pit 50
27 Int. Kenobi's Dwelling 50
28 Int. Kenobi's Dwelling 50
29 Int. Kenobi's Dwelling 50
30 Ext. Death Star—Imperial
   Cruiser—Space 50
31 Int. Death Star—Conference
   Room 50
32 Int. Death Star—Conference
   Room 50
33 Int. Death Star—Conference
   Room 50
34 Ext. Tatooine—Lars Home-
   stead 50
35 Int. Death Star—Detention Cell .50
36 Ext. Tatooine—Wasteland 50
37 Ext. Tatooine—Mos Eisley—
   Street 50
38 Int. Tatooine—Mos Eisley—
   Cantina. 50
39 Int. Tatooine—Mos Eisley—
   Cantina. 50

40 Int. Tatooine—Mos Eisley—
   Cantina. 50
41 Int. Tatooine—Mos Eisley—
   Cantina. 50
42 Int. Tatooine—Mos Eisley—
   Cantina. 50
43 Int. Tatooine—Mos Eisley—
   Cantina. 50
44 Int. Tatooine—Mos Eisley—
   Cantina. 50
45 Int. Tatooine—Mos Eisley—
   Cantina. 50
46 Ext. Tatooine—Mos Eisley—
   Street 50
47 Int. Mos Eisley— Space-port—
   Docking Bay 94 50
48 Ext. Tatooine—Mos Eisley—
   Street 50
49 Ext. Imperial Star Destroyers—
   Space. 50
50 Ext. Imperial Star Destroyer—
   Millennium Falcon—Space . .50
51 Int. *Millennium Falcon*—
   Cockpit. 50
52 Int. Death Star—Control Room .50
53 Int. Death Star—Blast
   Chamber 50
54 Ext. Death Star—Space 50
55 Ext. Alderran—Space 50
56 Int. *Millennium Falcon* Central
   Hold Area 50
57 Int. *Millennium Falcon*—
   Central Hold Area 50
58 Int. *Millennium Falcon*—
   Central Hold Area 50
59 Ext. Hyperspace 50
60 Int. *Millennium Falcon*—
   Cockpit. 50
61 Int. *Millennium Falcon*—
   Cockpit. 50
62 Ext. Death Star—Huge Port
   Doors 50
63 Int. Death Star—Hangar 2037 . .50
64 Int. Death Star—Hangar 2037 . .50
65 Int. *Millennium Falcon*—
   Hallway. 50
66 Int. Death Star—Forward
   Bay—Command Office 50
67 Int. Death Star—Forward
   Bay—Command Office 50
68 Int. Death Star—Detention
   Area Elevator Tube 50
69 Int. Death Star—Detention
   Area 50
70 Int. Death Star—
   Detention Corridor 50
71 Int. Death Star—
   Garbage Room 50
72 Int. Death Star—Power
   Generator Trench 50
73 Int. Death Star—Central
   Core Shaft 50
74 Int. Death Star—Central

Core Shaft 50
75 Int. Death Star—Hallway/
   Main Forward Bay 50
76 Int. Death Star—Main
   Forward Bay. 50
77 Ext. *Millennium Falcon*—Death
   Star—Space. 50
78 Int. *Millennium Falcon*—
   Central Hold Area 50
79 Int. *Millennium Falcon*—
   Solo's Gunport 50
80 Int. *Millennium Falcon*—
   Gunport 50
81 Ext. Space Around Fourth
   Moon of Yavin. 50
82 Ext. Fourth Moon of Yavin 50
83 Ext. Death Star—Yavin—
   Space. 50
84 Int. Massassi—War Room
   Briefing Area. 50
85 Int. Massassi Outpost—Main
   Hangar Deck 50
86 Int. Massassi Outpost—Main
   Hangar Deck 50
87 Ext. Massassi Outpost—
   Jungle 50
88 Ext. X-wing Fighters—
   Yavin—Space. 50
89 Ext. X-wing Fighters—
   Death Star—Space. 50
90 Ext. Space Around the Death
   Star 50
91 Int. Massassi Outpost—War
   Room 50
92 Ext. Space Around Death
   Star—TIE Fighters 50
93 Ext. Surface of the Death Star. .50
94 Int. Massassi Outpost—
   War Room 50
95 Int. TIE Fighter—Cockpit. 50
96 Ext. Surface of the Death Star. .50
97 Int. Massassi Outpost—
   War Room 50

98 Ext. Death Star Trench 50
99 Ext. Space—X-wing Fighters. . .50
100 Ext. Death Star Trench 50
101 Ext. Space Around Death
   Star 50
102 Int. TIE Fighter—Vader's
   Cockpit. 50
103 Int. TIE Fighter—Vader's
   Cockpit. 50
104 Int. Death Star—Control
   Room 50
105 Ext. Death Star Trench 50
106 Ext. Space Around the
   Death Star 50
107 Int. Massassi Outpost—
   War Room 50
108 Int. Luke's X-wing Fighter—
   Fighter 50
109 Ext. Surface of the Death
   Star 50
110 Ext. Space Around the
   Death Star 50
111 Int. *Millennium Falcon*—
   Cockpit. 50
112 Int. TIE Fighter—Vader's
   Cockpit. 50
113 Ext. X-wings—*Millennium
   Falcon*, Yavin—Space. 50
114 Int. Massassi Outpost— Main
   Hangar Deck 50
115 Int. Massassi Outpost—
   Great Assembly Hall 50
116 Int. Massassi Outpost—
   Great Assembly Hall 50
117 Int. Massassi Outpost—
   Great Assembly Hall 50
118 Int. Massassi Outpost—
   Great Assembly Hall 50
119 The Art of *Star Wars*,
   Tommy Jung art 50
120 The Art of *Star Wars*,
   Japanese 50

(STAR WARS WIDEVISION)
THE EMPIRE STRIKES BACK
Topps (1995)

Set: 144 cards $45.00
Pack: 9 cards. 2.75
2 diff. packs
Box: 24 packs 80.00
Chromium cards (1:12)
C1 Imperial Probot. 13.00
C2 Luke on his Tauntaun 13.00
C3 AT-ATs and Luke on Tauntaun. 13.00
C4 Snowspeeder circles AT-AT 13.00
C5 Yoda and Luke 13.00
C6 Space Slug 13.00
C7 Cloud City of Bespin 13.00
C8 Carbon-freezing Chamber, Darth vs. Luke 13.00
C9 Luke dangling. 13.00
C10 Droids replace Luke's Hand 13.00
Movie Poster Set (1:24)
1 of 6 Advance One-Sheet 8.00
2 of 6 Domestic One-Sheet 8.00
3 of 6 Style B Domestic One-Sheet 8.00
4 of 6 Australian One-Sheet 8.00
5 of 6 German One-Sheet. 8.00
6 of 6 Radio Show Poster 8.00
Promos
#0 Darth Vader, from *Star Wars Galaxy Magazine* #3 . . 3.00
P1 Han Solo, from *Advance* #79. . . . . 10.00
P2 AT-AT, from *Non-Sports Update* Vol. 6 #4 . . . . . . 10.00
P3 Luke, R2-D2 and Yoda, from *Cards Illustrated* #20   10.00
P4 Luke hanging by hands, from *Combo* #7 and
   also *Combo* #12 . . . . 12.00

EXT. HOTH — SNOW TRENCH

EXT. HOTH — ICE PLAIN — BATTLEFIELD

Star Wars: The Empire Strikes Back
WideVision, two cards (Topps 1996)

P5 Stormtroopers and Han Solo in Carbonite,
     convention giveaway 30.00
P6 Luke, Leia, C-3PO and R2-D2, from *Wizard* #48 . . 10.00
Three-card (P1, P2, P3) promo sheet, from May
     Previews 1995 . . . . 4.00

CARD CHECKLIST

1 The Empire Strikes Back
    credits. . . . . $ .35
2 Ext. Hoth—Meteorite Crater—
    Snow Plain 35
3 Ext. — Plain of Hoth 35
4 Ext. Plain of Hoth. 35
5 Ext. Plain of Hoth. 35
6 Int. Hoth—Rebel Base—
    Main Hangar Deck 35
7 Int. Ice Gorge 35
8 Ext. Hoth—Snowdrift 35
9 Ext. Hoth—Snowdrift 35
10 Int. Rebel Base—Medical
    Center 35
11 Int. Rebel Base—Medical
    Center—Recovery Room . . .35
12 Ext. Hoth—Snow Plain 35
13 Ext. Space—Imperial Fleet . . .35
14 Int. Darth Vader's Star
    Destroyer—Bridge 35
15 Ext. Space—Imperial Fleet . . .35
16 Int. Vader's Star Destroyer—
    Vader's Chamber Meditation
    Pod 35
17 Int. Rebel Base—Main
    Hangar Deck 35
18 Ext. Rebel Base Ice Cave—
    Ion Cannon. 35
19 Ext. Space—Hoth—Rebel
    Transport 35
20 Ext. Hoth—Ice Plain—Snow
    Trench 35
21 Int. Luke's Snowspeeder,
    Rogue Leader—Cockpit 35
22 Ext. Hoth—Ice Plain—
    Battlefield 35
23 Int. Luke's Snowspeeder,
    Rogue Leader—Cockpit 35

24 Ext. Hoth—Ice Plain—
    Battlefield 35
25 Int. Imperial Walker—Cockpit .35
26 Int. Imperial Walker—Cockpit .35
27 Ext. Hoth—Ice Plain—
    Battlefield 35
28 Int. Imperial Walker—Cockpit .35
29 Ext. Hoth—Battlefield 35
30 Ext. Hoth—Battlefield 35
31 Ext. Hoth—Snow Trench 35
32 Ext. Hoth—Battlefield 35
33 Ext. Luke's Snowspeeder,
    Rogue Leader—Cockpit 35
34 Ext. Hoth—Battlefield 35
35 Ext. Hoth—Battlefield—
    Ice Plain 35
36 Ext. Hoth—Battlefield—
    Ice Plain 35
37 Ext. Hoth—Battlefield—
    Ice Plain 35
38 Ext. Hoth—Battlefield 35
39 Int. Imperial Walker—Cockpit .35
40 Int. Rebel Base—Main Hangar .35
41 Ext. Space—Star
    Destroyers—Star Fighters. . .35
42 Ext. Asteroid Belt—*Millennium
    Falcon* 35
43 Int. *Millennium Falcon*—
    Cockpit. 35
44 Ext. Asteroid Belt—TIE
    Fighters 35
45 Ext. Asteroid Belt—*Millennium
    Falcon* 35
46 Ext. Asteroid Belt—TIE
    Fighters 35
47 Int.—*Millennium Falcon*
    Cockpit. 35
48 Ext. Giant Asteroid Crater—
    Millennium Falcon. 35

49 Ext. Giant Asteroid—
    Millennium Falcon. 35
50 Int. Giant Asteroid Cave 35
51 Ext. Dagobah 35
52 Ext. Dagobah 35
53 Int. Vader's Star Destroyer—
    Vader's Meditation Pod 35
54 Ext. Dagobah—Bog Clearing .35
55 Ext. Dagobah—Bog Clearing .35
56 Int. *Millennium Falcon*—
    Main Hold Area. 35
57 Int. Vader's Star Destroyer—
    Bridge. 35
58 Int. Vader's Star Destroyer—
    Vader's Chamber 35
59 Int. Vader's Star Destroyer—
    Vader's Chamber 35
60 Ext. Dagobah—Yoda's House .35
61 Int. Dagobah—Yoda's House .35
62 Ext. Giant Asteroid Crater—
    TIE Fighters 35
63 Int. Asteroid Cave—*Millennium
    Falcon* Cockpit 35
64 Int. *Millennium Falcon*—
    Space Slug Mouth 35
65 Int. Space Slug Mouth. 35
66 Ext. Cave Entrance—Giant
    Asteroid 35
67 Ext. Dagobah 35
68 Ext. Dagobah 35
69 Ext. Dagobah—Tree Cave . . .35
70 Int. Dagobah—Tree Cave 35
71 Int. Vader's Star Destroyer—
    Bridge. 35
72 Int. Vader's Star Destroyer—
    Bridge. 35
73 Ext. Star Destroyer Avenger—
    Asteroid Field 35
74 Ext. *Millennium Falcon*—
    Avenger—Asteroid Field 35
75 Ext. Space—*Millennium Falcon*—
    Asteroid Field 35
76 Ext. *Millennium Falcon*—
    Avenger—Asteroid Field 35
77 Ext. Dagobah—Bog 35
78 Ext. Dagobah—Bog 35
79 Ext. Dagobah—Bog 35
80 Int. Star Destroyer Avenger—
    Millennium Falcon. 35
81 Int. Slave I 35
82 Ext. Dagobah—Bog—Clearing .35
83 Int. —*Millennium Falcon*
    Cockpit. 35
84 Ext. Bespin—*Millennium
    Falcon*—Cloud Cars 35
85 Int. Bespin's Cloud City—*Millen-
    nium Falcon*—Cloud Cars. . .35
86 Ext. Bespin's Cloud City—
    Landing Platform—*Millennium
    Falcon* 35
87 Int. Bespin's Cloud City—
    Landing Platform—*Millennium
    Falcon* 35
88 Ext. Cloud City—Landing
    Platform 35
89 Ext. Cloud City—Landing Platform
    —Door of *Millennium Falcon* .35
90 Ext. Cloud City—Landing Plat-
    form—*Millennium Falcon*. . .35
91 Ext. Dagobah—Bog 35
92 Ext. Dagobah—Bog 35
93 Ext. Cloud City—Living
    Quarters 35
94 Int. Cloud City—Dining Room .35
95 Int. Cloud City—Dining Room .35
96 Int. Cloud City—Dining Room .35
97 Int. Cloud City—Large Cell . . .35
98 Int. Cloud City—Prison Entry
    Area. 35
99 Int. Cloud City—Holding
    Chamber 35
100 Int. Cloud City—Holding
    Area 35
101 Ext. Cloud City—Luke's
    X-wing 35

102 Int. Cloud City—Carbon-
    Freezing Chamber 35
103 Int. Cloud City—Carbon-
    Freezing Chamber 35
104 Int. Cloud City—Carbon-
    Freezing Chamber 35
105 Int. Cloud City—Carbon-
    Freezing Chamber 35
106 Int. Cloud City—Carbon-
    Freezing Chamber 35
107 Int. Cloud City—Carbon-
    Freezing Chamber 35
108 Int. Cloud City—Carbon-
    Freezing Chamber 35
109 Int. Cloud City—Carbon-
    Freezing Chamber 35
110 Int. Cloud City—Corridor 35
111 Ext. Cloud City—East Landing
    Platform—Slave I 35
112 Ext. Cloud City—East Landing
    Platform—Slave I 35
113 Ext. Cloud City—East Landing
    Platform 35
114 Int. Cloud City—Carbon-
    Freezing Chamber 35
115 Int. Cloud City—Carbon-
    Freezing Chamber 35
116 Int. Cloud City—Tunnel and
    Reactor Control Room 35
117 Int. Cloud City—Tunnel and
    Reactor Control Room 35
118 Int. Cloud City—Gantry—
    Reactor Shaft 35
119 Int. Cloud City—Corridor 35
120 Ext. Cloud City—Landing
    Platform—*Millennium Falcon* .35
121 Ext. Cloud City—Landing
    Platform—*Millennium Falcon* .35
122 Int. Cloud City—Gantry—
    Reactor Shaft 35
123 Int. Cloud City—Gantry—
    Reactor Shaft 35
124 Int. Cloud City—Gantry—
    Reactor Shaft 35
125 Int. Cloud City—Gantry—
    Reactor Shaft 35
126 Int. Cloud City—Gantry—
    Reactor Shaft 35
127 Int. Cloud City—Gantry—
    Reactor Shaft 35
128 Int. Cloud City—Gantry—
    Reactor Shaft 35
129 Int. Cloud City—Gantry—
    Reactor Shaft 35
130 Ext. Bottom of Cloud City—
    Weather Vane. 35
131 Ext. Bespin—*Millennium
    Falcon* 35
132 Ext. *Millennium Falcon*—
    Bottom of Cloud City. 35
133 Ext. Space—*Millennium
    Falcon*—TIE Fighters 35
134 Int. —*Millennium Falcon*—
    Hold 35
135 Int. —*Millennium Falcon*—
    Hold—Pit 35
136 Int. *Millennium Falcon*—
    Sleeping Quarters. 35
137 Int. *Millennium Falcon*—
    Cockpit. 35
138 Int. Vader's Star Destroyer—
    Bridge. 35
139 Int. Rebel Star Cruiser—
    Medical Center 35
140 Int. Rebel Star Cruiser—
    Medical Center 35
141 Ext. Galaxy—Space—
    Millennium Falcon. 35
142 Int. Rebel Star Cruiser—
    Medical Center 35
143 Int. Rebel Star Cruiser—
    Medical Center 35
144 Ext. Space—Rebel Star
    Cruiser—Rebel Ships 35

Star Wars: Return of the Jedi
WideVision, three cards (Topps 1996)

(STAR WARS WIDEVISION)
RETURN OF THE JEDI
Topps (1996)

Set: 144 cards $45.00
Pack: 9 cards 2.50
Box: 24 packs 60.00
Topps Finest Chromium (R. McQuarrie) (1:12)
C/1 Darth Vader arrives in style 11.00
C/2 Droids held captive 11.00
C/3 Jabba's Palace 11.00
C/4 In the Rancor Pit 11.00
C/5 Escape from the Sail Barge 11.00
C/6 Speeder Bikes 11.00
C/7 . . . . 11.00
C/8 Father vs. Son 11.00
C/9 Emperor and Luke 11.00
C/10 Inside Death Star II 11.00
Mini-Posters (1:box)
1 of 6 Advance One-Sheet 10.00
2 of 6 One-Sheet Style B 10.00
3 of 6 1985 Re-release One-Sheet 10.00
4 of 6 Japanese Poster 10.00
5 of 6 Japanese Poster 10.00
6 of 6 Polish Poster 10.00
3-Di (1:case) Admiral Ackbar 50.00
Redemption card 30.00
Promo Cards
#0 Three dead Jedi Warriors at Ewok celebration,
   from *Star Wars Galaxy Magazine* #6 . . . . 4.00
P1 Han, Luke and Lando, from *Star Wars Galaxy
   Magazine* #5 . . . . 4.00

P2 Biker Scout and Luke, from *Advance Comics* #83 . . 4.00
P3 Stormtroopers, Han and Leia, from *Non-Sports
   Update*, Vol. 7 #1 . . . . 4.00
P4 Emperor Palpatine, from *Cards Illustrated.* #27 . . . . 4.00
P5 Jabba the Hutt and Bib Fortuna, from *Wizard* #54 . . 4.00
P6 Han Solo, Luke and Chewbacca, from giveaway . . 50.00
One-card promo sheet (Card #0) from Previews, Nov. 95 . . 5.00

CARD CHECKLIST

1 *Return of the Jedi* credits . . . $ .35
2 Ext. Space—Endor, Death Star,
   Star Destroyer 35
3 Ext. Space—Endor, Shuttle,
   Star Destroyers 35
4 Int. Imperial Shuttle—Cockpit . .35
5 Ext. Death Star—Main Docking
   Bay 35
6 Ext. Death Star—Main Docking
   Bay 35
7 Int. Death Star—Main Docking
   Bay 35
8 Ext. Road to Jabba's Palace—
   Tatooine 35
9 Ext. Jabba's Palace—Gate . . .35
10 Int. Jabba's Palace—Hallway .35
11 Int. Jabba's Throne Room 35
12 Int. Jabba's Throne Room 35
13 Int. Jabba's Palace—Boiler
   Room 35
14 Int. Jabba's Palace—Boiler
   Room 35
15 Int. Jabba's Throne Room 35
16 Int. Jabba's Throne Room 35
17 Int. Jabba's Throne Room 35
18 Ext. Jabba's Palace—Tatooine .35
19 Int. Jabba's Throne Room—
   Night 35
20 Int. Jabba's Throne Room—
   Night 35
21 Int. Jabba's Throne Room—
   Night 35
22 Int. Jabba's Palace—Hall 35
23 Int. Jabba's Throne Room 35
24 Int. Jabba's Throne Room 35
25 Int. Jabba's Throne Room 35
26 Int. Rancor Pit 35
27 Int. Jabba's Throne Room 35
28 Int. Rancor Pit 35
29 Int. Rancor Pit 35
30 Int. Jabba's Throne Room 35
31 Ext. Tatooine Dune Sea—Skiff .35
32 Ext. Tatooine Dune Sea—Skiff .35
33 Ext. Sarlacc Pit 35
34 Int. Sail Barge—Observation
   Deck 35
35 Ext. Skiff—Plane 35
36 Ext. Skiff 35
37 Ext. Skiffs, Sail Barge 35
38 Ext. Skiff 35
39 Ext. Skiffs, Sail Barge 35
40 Ext. Skiffs, Sail Barge 35
41 Int. Sail Barge—Observation
   Deck 35
42 Ext. Skiff—Above Sarlacc Pit .35
43 Ext. Sarlacc Pit 35
44 Ext. Sarlacc Pit 35
45 Int. Sail Barge—Observation
   Deck 35
46 Int. Sail Barge—Observation
   Deck 35
47 Ext. Sail Barge—Upper Deck .35
48 Ext. Sail Barge—Upper Deck .35
49 Ext. Sand Dune—Tatooine . . .35
50 Ext. Dune Sea—Tatooine 35
51 Int. Docking Bay—Death Star .35
52 Int. Docking Bay—Death Star .35
53 Ext. Dagobah Swamp—
   X-wing 35
54 Int. Yoda's House 35
55 Ext. Dagobah Swamp—
   X-wing 35
56 Ext. Space—Rebel Fleet 35

57 Int. Headquarters Frigate—
   Main Briefing Room 35
58 Int. Headquarters Frigate—
   Main Briefing Room 35
59 Int. Headquarters Frigate—
   Main Briefing Room 35
60 Int. Headquarters Frigate—
   Main Briefing Room 35
61 Int. Headquarters Frigate—
   Main Briefing Room 35
62 Int. Headquarters Frigate—
   Main Briefing Room 35
63 Int. Stolen Imperial Shuttle—
   Cockpit 35
64 Ext. Endor Forest—Clearing . .35
65 Ext. Endor Forest—The Bike
   Chase 35
66 Ext. Endor Forest—The Bike
   Chase 35
67 Ext. Endor Forest—The Bike
   Chase 35
68 Ext. Endor Forest—The Bike
   Chase 35
69 Ext. Endor Forest—The Bike
   Chase 35
70 Ext. Endor Forest—The Bike
   Chase 35
71 Int. Emperor's Tower—Throne
   Room 35
72 Ext. Endor Forest—Dense
   Foliage 35
73 Ext. Endor Forest—Walkway
   to Ewok Village 35
74 Ext. Ewok Village Square 35
75 Ext. Ewok Village Square 35
76 Ext. Ewok Village Square 35
77 Int. Chief's Hut—Council of
   Elders 35
78 Int. Chief's Hut—Council of
   Elders 35
79 Ext. Ewok Village 35
80 Ext. Endor Forest—Imperial
   Landing Platform 35
81 Ext. Imperial Landing Platform .35
82 Ext. Imperial Landing
   Platform—AT-AT 35
83 Int. Imperial Landing
   Platform—Lower Deck 35
84 Ext. Space—Rebel Fleet 35
85 Ext. Space—Rebel Fleet—
   Entering Hyperspace 35
86 Int. Rebel Star Cruiser—
   Bridge 35
87 Ext. Endor Forest 35
88 Int. Emperor's Throne Room—
   Death Star 35
89 Int. Cockpit—*Millennium
   Falcon* 35
90 Int. Rebel Star Cruiser—
   Bridge 35
91 Ext. Space—Endor, Death
   Star, Rebel Fleet 35
92 Ext. Space—*Millennium
   Falcon*, Rebel Fleet 35
93 Ext. Space—Endor, Death
   Star, Rebel Fleet 35
94 Int. Cockpit—*Millennium
   Falcon* 35
95 Ext. Space—Endor, Death
   Star, Air Battle 35
96 Ext. Endor Forest 35
97 Ext. Endor Forest 35

98 Ext. Endor Forest—Generator
    Bunker 35
99 Ext. Endor Forest 35
100 Ext. Space—Air Battle. 35
101 Ext. Space—Air Battle. 35
102 Ext. Space—Death Star 35
103 Ext. Space—Rebel Fleet. . . .35
104 Ext. Space—Air Battle. 35
105 Int. *Millennium Falcon*—
    Cockpit. 35
106 Int. Emperor's Tower—
    Throne Room 35
107 Ext. Endor Forest 35
108 Ext. Endor Forest 35
109 Ext. Endor Forest 35
110 Int. Throne Room—
    Emperor's Tower. 35
111 Ext. Space—Air Battle 35
112 Ext. Endor Forest—Generator
    Bunker 35
113 Int. Generator Bunker 35
114 Int. Emperor's Tower—
    Throne Room 35
115 Int. Emperor's Tower—
    Throne Room 35
116 Ext. Forest—Shield Generator
    Dish 35
117 Int. Emperor's Tower—
    Throne Room 35
118 Int. Emperor's Tower—
    Throne Room 35
119 Int. Emperor's Tower—
    Throne Room 35
120 Int. Emperor's Tower—
    Throne Room 35
121 Int. Emperor's Tower—
    Central Core Shaft 35
122 Int. Emperor's Tower—
    Throne Room 35

123 Ext. Space—Death Star,
    Millennium Falcon. 35
124 Int. Death Star—TIE Fighter .35
125 Int. Death Star—TIE
    Interceptor 35
126 Int. Death Star—*Millennium
    Falcon* 35
127 Int. Cockpit—*Millennium
    Falcon* 35
128 Int. Vader's Star Destroyer—
    Bridge. 35
129 Int. Rebel Star Cruiser—
    Bridge. 35
130 Ext. Death Star—Vader's
    Star Destroyer 35
131 Int. Death Star—Main
    Docking Bay 35
132 Int. Death Star—X-wing . . .35
133 Int. Death Star—Main
    Reactor Shaft 35
134 Int. Death Star—Main
    Reactor Shaft 35
135 Int. Death Star—*Millennium
    Falcon* 35
136 Ext. Death Star—*Millennium
    Falcon* 35
137 Ext. Space—Death Star . . .35
138 Ext. Space—*Millennium
    Falcon* 35
139 Ext. Endor Forest 35
140 Ext. Endor Forest—Night . .35
141 Ext. Ewok Village—Night. . .35
142 Ext. Ewok Village Square—
    Night. 35
143 Ext. Ewok Village Square—
    Night. 35
144 Ext. Ewok Village Square—
    Night. 35

STAR WARS TRILOGY
WIDEVISION (RETAIL)
Topps (1997)

Set: 72 cards. $20.00
Pack: cards 2.00
Box: packs 50.00
Lasercut Set (1:9)
1 of 6 A New Customer Enjoys... . . . . 9.00
2 of 6 "It's Not My Fault"... . . . . 9.00
3 of 6 The *Tantive IV* Caught... . . . . 9.00
4 of 6 Chewbacca Led Away in Chains... . . . . 9.00
5 of 6 X-wings Approach Their Target... . . . . 9.00
6 of 6 Imperial View: X-wing Laser Fire... . . . . 9.00
Promos
P0 Lasercut 10.00
P1 Stormtroopers, San Diego Comic Con giveaway . . . 5.00
P2 Jabba the Hutt, *Star Wars Galaxy Magazine* #10. . . 5.00
P3 X-wing Fighter Squadron, magazines 5.00
P4 Sandcrawler, from *Star Wars* 3-D I packs 10.00
P5 Luke in Landspeeder, from *Star Wars* 3-D I packs . 10.00
P6 Millennium Falcon and Stormtroopers, from Star
    Wars 3-D I packs. 10.00
P7 Landspeeder in Mos Eisley, *Wizard Sci-Fi Spec-
    ial '97 Star Wars Trilogy Special Edition* promo . . 5.00
P8 Jabba's Dancing Girls (*Combo*). 5.00

CARD CHECKLIST

1 In the Belly of the Beast. . . . $ .40
2 Leia "Feeds" R2-D2 40
3 Demanding an Answer. 40
4 A Desolate Desert 40
5 "Look Sir, Droids!" 40
6 A Plea for Help 40
7 Alone in Thought 40
8 Sand People Strike 40
9 Kenobi Gets the Message 40
10 Into Mos Eisley 40
11 Greedo's Unlucky Day. 40
12 A Deal is Struck 40
13 Moff Tarkin's Surprise 40
14 Let the Wookiee Win! 40
15 Into the Enemy Lair. 40
16 A Close—and Smelly—Call. . .40
17 Fight to the End 40
18 Han Hits His Mark. 40
19 Preparing for Action 40
20 X-wings Attack 40
21 The Battle Unfolds 40
22 Into the Trench 40
23 The Dark Lord Attacks 40
24 Hitting their Target. 40
25 Imperial Snoop 40
26 Abominable Wampa 40
27 Rejuvenating Bacta Bath. 40
28 Vader's Meditation Ends 40
29 Lumbering Metal Monsters . . .40
30 Harpooning a Whale. 40
31 Fire and Ice 40
32 Han Plays Chicken 40
33 Down in Desolate Dagobah . .40
34 Luke Takes Aim 40
35 Vader and His Master 40
36 Shelter from a Storm. 40
37 Smoking Them Out. 40
38 Size Matters Not 40
39 Vader Hires Boba Fett. 40
40 Chasing after Solo 40
41 Luke's Balancing Act. 40
42 A Cloud City Welcome 40
43 Friend or Foe? 40
44 A Surprise Dinner Guest 40
45 Loved Ones Part. 40

46 Lightsaber Duel 40
47 A Terrible Blow 40
48 A Life Suspended 40
49 Under Construction. 40
50 Vader Motivates the Troops. . .40
51 A Slimy Crime Kingpin. 40
52 Han Comes to Life 40
53 A Jedi Tries to Reason 40
54 Sarlacc Sightseeing Tour?. . . .40
55 Fighting Fett 40
56 Luke and Leia Swing 40
57 The Emperor Arrives. 40
58 Visit to an Old Friend 40
59 Rebel Fleet at the Ready 40
60 Into Enemy Territory 40
61 Chase Through the Forest . . .40
62 Threepio Tells Tales 40
63 Vader Comes For Luke 40
64 Leading the Attack 40
65 Running For Cover 40
66 Fully Operational! 40
67 Crushing an Enemy 40
68 A Turn to the Dark Side?. 40
69 The Emperor's Lightning. 40
70 The Emperor Goes Soaring . .40
71 One Last Look 40
72 Checklist. 40

Star Wars Trilogy Special Edition, *Lasercut #2 (Topps 1997)*

STAR WARS TRILOGY
SPECIAL EDITION WIDEVISION
Topps (1997)

Set: 72 cards $25.00
Pack: 9 cards 3.00
Box: packs 75.00
Lasercut Set (1:9)
1 of 6 Luke Skywalker is Entranced... . . . . 9.00
2 of 6 Han Solo and Co-Pilot Chewbacca... . . . . 9.00
3 of 6 Admiral Ozzel feels Darth Vader's wrath... . . . . . . 9.00
4 of 6 A Hologram of Emperor Palpatine... . . . . 9.00
5 of 6 A Fate Much Worse... 9.00
6 of 6 Emperor Palpatine Unleashes... . . . . 9.00
Holograms (1:18)
    2 different 20.00
Spec. Ed. 3D card (1:Box) X-wings Departing 15.00
Galoob MicroMachine Promos
G1 R2-D2 on X-wing 3.00
G2 TIE Fighter and X-wing 3.00
G3 Luke in Landspeeder 3.00
G4 Mos Eisley 3.00
G5 Jawa on Ronto 3.00
Hasbro Vehicles Promos
H1 *Millennium Falcon* 5.00
H2 Massassi outpost 5.00
H3 Han and Jabba 5.00
H4 Droids and Calimari cruiser 5.00

CARD CHECKLIST

1 Ext. Two Spacecraft—
  Above Tatooine. . . . . $ .35
2 Ext. Tatooine—Desert 35
3 Ext. Tatooine—Desert 35
4 Ext. Tatooine—Dune Sea—
  Sandcrawler 35
5 Ext. Tatooine—Lars Homestead .35
6 Ext. Tatooine—Twin Sunset . . .35
7 Ext. Tatooine—Jundland
  Wastes 35
8 Ext. Tatooine—Mos Eisley
  Overlook. 35
9 Ext. Mos Eisley—Outskirts. . . .35
10 Ext. Mos Eisley—Street 35
11 Ext. Mos Eisley—Aerial View. .35
12 Ext. Mos Eisley—City Street . .35
13 Ext. Mos Eisley—Plaza. 35
14 Ext. Mos Eisley. 35
15 Ext. Mos Eisley. 35
16 Ext. Mos Eisley. 35
17 Ext. Mos Eisley. 35
18 Ext. Mos Eisley. 35
19 Ext. Mos Eisley—Cantina
  Entrance. 35
20 Ext. Mos Eisley—Cantina
  Entrance. 35
21 Ext. Mos Eisley—Outside
  Cantina. 35
22 Int. Mos Eisley—Cantina. 35
23 Int. Mos Eisley—Cantina. 35
24 Ext. Mos Eisley—Street 35
25 Ext. Mos Eisley—Street 35
26 Int. Mos Eisley—Space-port—
  Docking Bay 94 35
27 Int. Mos Eisley—Space-port—
  Docking Bay 94 35
28 Int. Mos Eisley—Space-port—
  Docking Bay 94 35
29 Int. Mos Eisley—Space-port—
  Docking Bay 94 35
30 Int. Mos Eisley—Space-port—
  Docking Bay 94 35
31 Int. Mos Eisley—Space-port—
  Docking Bay 94 35
32 Int. Mos Eisley—Space-port—
  Docking Bay 94 35
33 Ext. Mos Eisley—Spaceport . .35
34 Ext. Mos Eisley—Spaceport . .35
35 Ext. Death Star—Near
  Alderaan. 35
36 Int. Death Star—Central Core
  Shaft. 35
37 Ext. *Millennium Falcon*—
  Near Yavin 35
38 Ext. Yavin Four—Massassi
  Temple 35
39 Ext. Yavin Four—Forest 35

40 Ext. Rebel Fleet—Near Yavin .35
41 Ext. Rebel Fleet—Near Yavin .35
42 Ext. Rebel Fleet—Near Yavin .35
43 Int. X-wing Fighter Cockpit . . .35
44 Ext. Space—Approaching
  Death Star 35
45 Ext. Space—Above Death Star .35
46 Ext. Space—Around the
  Death Star 35
47 Ext. Space—Around the Death
  Star 35
48 Ext. Space—Above Death Star .35
49 Ext. Space—Above Death Star .35
50 Ext. Space—Above Death Star .35
51 Ext. Death Star. 35
52 Ext. Space—Above Death Star .35
53 Ext. Space—Death Star
  Surface. 35
54 Ext. Space—Death Star
  Trench. 35
55 Ext. Space—Death Star
  Trench 35
56 Ext. Space—Death Star
  Trench 35
57 Ext. X-wing Fighter—Death
  Star Trench. 35
58 Ext. Death Star—Thermal
  Exhaust Port. 35
59 Ext. Space—Leaving Death
  Star 35
60 Int. Massassi Outpost—Main
  Throne Room 35
61 Wampa Mask—Behind-The-
  Scenes. 35
62 Int. Ice Cave—Hoth— Behind-
  The-Scenes 35
63 Int. Ice Cave—Hoth— Behind-
  The-Scenes 35
64 Ext. Bespin—Cloud City—
  Storyboard. 35
65 Ext. Cloud City—Platform
  327—Storyboard. 35
66 Int. Bespin—Cloud City—
  Storyboard 35
67 Int. Tatooine—Jabba's Palace—
  Behind-The-Scenes 35
68 Int. Tatooine—Jabba's Palace—
  Behind-The-Scenes 35
69 Int. Tatooine—Jabba's Palace—
  Behind-The-Scenes 35
70 Int. Tatooine—Jabba's Palace—
  Behind-The-Scenes 35
71 Int. Tatooine—Jabba's Palace—
  Behind-The-Scenes 35
72 Ext. Endor's Forest Moon—
  Storyboard 35

STAR WARS WIDEVISION 3-D
Topps (Feb. 1997)

This card set contains all new images from the first movie and utilizes an exclusive, multi-level 3-D digital imagery technology. The technology is quite impressive, but also expensive. When Topps (or anybody) uses their best technology for an entire set, then the extraordinary becomes ordinary and anybody can buy some for a couple of bucks. Where's the fun in that? Maybe that's why there were supposed to be similar sets for the other two movies, but they never appeared.

Set: 63 cards $90.00
Pack: 3 cards. 4.00
Box: 36 packs 120.00
Chase Card (1:36)
1m Death Star 3-D Motion card 30.00

Promos

2m Swoops and Rontos (*Star Wars Trilogy Special
  Edition* promo 10.00
3Di 1 Darth Vader, Stormtroopers and Captain Piett. . . 10.00
3Di 2 Darth and Luke 25.00
P1 Darth Vader (*Star Wars Galaxy #9*) 10.00
P2 Luke and Darth Vader (2,500 made) 50.00
P1 AT-ATs, *The Empire Strikes Back!* promo 20.00
Dm/o Admiral Ackbar *Return of the Jedi* promo 20.00

CARD CHECKLIST

1 *Star Wars: A New Hope* . . . $2.00
2 Pursuit in Space! 2.00
3 Droids in the Crossfire! 2.00
4 A Princess Strikes Back! 2.00
5 Release of the Escape Pod! . 2.00
6 Toward Tatooine! 2.00
7 Jawas in Hiding! 2.00
8 Enter Luke Skywalker! 2.00
9 The Leia Hologram! 2.00
10 Spotting the Sand People! . . 2.00
11 Attacked by Tusken Raiders! 2.00
12 Rescued by Ben Kenobi! . . . 2.00
13 A Message for Help!. 2.00
14 Power of the Dark Side! 2.00
15 Fate of the Lars Homestead! 2.00
16 Cantina Denizens! 2.00
17 Meet Han and Chewie!. 2.00
18 Alerting the Sandtroopers! . . 2.00
19 Preparing For Space Travel!. 2.00
20 Escape from Tatooine! 2.00
21 Han Solo in Command! 2.00
22 Jumping Into Hyperspace! . . 2.00
23 Target: Alderaan! 2.00
24 Laser of Destruction! 2.00
25 Leia's Ordeal! 2.00
26 Destruction of a Planet! 2.00
27 Lightsaber Practice! 2.00
28 Approaching the Death Star! 2.00
29 Drawn into Danger! 2.00
30 Heroes in Hiding!. 2.00
31 Accessing Imperial Data! . . . 2.00
32 Luke's Rescue Plan! 2.00

33 A "Captured" Chewbacca! . . 2.00
34 Han Solo's Bluff! 2.00
35 Trapped in the Alcove! 2.00
36 Trash Compactor Peril! 2.00
37 The Power Generator
  Trench! 2.00
38 Shoot-Out in the Shaft! 2.00
39 Swinging to Safety! 2.00
40 When Jedi Clash!. 2.00
41 "Run, Luke! Run!" 2.00
42 Escaping the Death Star! . . . 2.00
43 "I Can't Believe He's Gone!". 2.00
44 Skirmish in Space! 2.00
45 "Got Him! I Got Him!" 2.00
46 Destination: Yavin! 2.00
47 The Rebel Hideout! 2.00
48 Briefing the Rebels! 2.00
49 X-wings Away! 2.00
50 Assault on the Death Star! . . 2.00
51 Monitoring the Battle!. 2.00
52 Vader in the Trench!. 2.00
53 "Targets Coming Up!". 2.00
54 Artoo Hanging On! 2.00
55 Blasted by Vader!. 2.00
56 Luke uses the Force! 2.00
57 Surprise Attack! 2.00
58 Vader's Final Stand! 2.00
59 Solo to the Rescue! 2.00
60 Death Star Departure! 2.00
61 The Victorious Rebels! 2.00
62 Honored for their Bravery! . . 2.00
63 Heroes of the Rebellion!. . . . 2.00

Star Wars *Vehicles, promo postcards (Topps 1997)*

STAR WARS VEHICLES
Topps (July 1997)

The *Star Wars* Vehicle cards are the last ones produced by Topps to date. They feature 50 comic art cards by Top Cow Studios, plus 22 cards with movie photos featuring ships. All of the cards come with back blueprints and specs by Bill Smith, author of *The Essential Guide to Star Wars Vehicles and Vessels*. All of the cards are on 20 point Mirror-bond card stock.

Set: 72 cards $25.00
Pack: 5 cards. 2.00

Box: 36 packs 50.00
Cutaway cards, (1:18)
C1 .... 15.00
C2 .... 15.00
C3 .... 15.00
C4 Lamda Shuttle 15.00
3-D cards (1:36) Chris Moeller art, 2 diff. 25.00
Redemption card (1:360) for uncut pair of 3-D cards. . 60.00
Mail-in card 50.00
Promos
P1 Speeder Bikes, refractor 50.00
P2 Shuttle *Tyderium,* refractor 85.00
Postcard, 4"x6" 2.00

CARD CHECKLIST

1 Title Card, by Marc Silvestri . $ .40		38 TIE Advanced	.40
Comic Art		39 Lambda-Class Shuttle......	.40
2 *Millennium Falcon*	.40	40 I-7 Howlrunner	.40
3 A-Wing	.40	41 Interdictor Cruiser	.40
4 B-Wing	.40	42 Lancer Frigate	.40
5 Y-Wing.................	.40	43 Imperial Star Destroyer.....	.40
6 X-95 Headhunter..........	.40	44 Victory Star Destroyer......	.40
7 X-wing.................	.40	45 Executor................	.40
8 V-Wing Airspeeder.........	.40	46 Eclipse Star Destroyer	.40
9 E-Wing Fighter	.40	47 Sun Crusher...........	.40
10 Rebel Snowspeeder	.40	48 World Devastator	.40
11 Rebel Blockade Runner	.40	49 Death Star	.40
12 Escape Pod	.40	50 Death Star II.............	.40
13 Rebel Cruiser	.40	**Battle Specs**	
14 Rebel Transport	.40	51 Battle of Yavin: Strategy	.40
15 Mon Cal Cruiser	.40	52 Battle of Yavin: Warriors	.40
16 *Nebulon Ranger*	.40	53 Battle of Yavin: Hardware ...	.40
17 T-16 Skyhopper	.40	54 Battle of Hoth: Strategy.....	.40
18 Luke's Landspeeder	.40	55 Battle of Hoth: Warriors.....	.40
19 Jawa Sandcrawler	.40	56 Battle of Hoth: Hardware....	.40
20 Jabba's Sail Barge	.40	57 Battle of Endor: Strategy....	.40
21 *Lady Luck*...............	.40	58 Battle of Endor: Warriors....	.40
22 Twin-Pod Cloud Car	.40	59 Battle of Endor: Hardware...	.40
23 *Slave 1*.................	.40	***Millennium Falcon***	
24 IG-2000	.40	60 Gun Port................	.40
25 *Hound's Tooth*	.40	61 Smuggler's Hold...........	.40
26 S-Swoop...............	.40	62 Cockpit................	.40
27 Outrider	.40	63 Hyperdrive.............	.40
28 Virago.................	.40	**Characters**	
29 *Stinger*	.40	64 Han Solo	.40
30 AT-PT	.40	65 Luke Skywalker	.40
31 AT-ST	.40	66 Darth Vader	.40
32 AT-AT	.40	67 Admiral Ackbar	.40
33 Speeder Bike	.40	68 Jabba the Hutt	.40
34 Chariot Lav.............	.40	69 Boba Fett	.40
35 TIE Fighter	.40	70 Emperor Palpatine	.40
36 TIE Bomber	.40	71 Jawas.................	.40
37 TIE Interceptor	.40	72 Checklist..............	.40

OTHER STAR WARS CARDS AND STICKERS

Trix *Star Wars* stickers, each $1.00
    set: 4 stickers 5.00
Lucky Charms *Star Wars* stickers, each 1.00
    set: 4 stickers 5.00
Monster Cereals *Star Wars* stickers, each 1.00
    set: 4 stickers 5.00
Cocoa Puffs *Star Wars* stickers, each............. 1.00
    set: 4 stickers 5.00
Big G trading cards, with *Star Wars* logo
    (General Mills 1978) each 1.00
    set: 18 photos and wallet............... 30.00

The Empire Strikes Back Sticker set and Album
    (Burger King)........................... 10.00
3-D Ewok Perk-up sticker sets, each 5.00

Star Wars Galaxy Magazine
SWGM1 promo (*Star Wars Galaxy Mag. #1*) 4.00
SWGM2 promo (*Star Wars Galaxy Mag. #2*) 4.00
SWGM3 At-At (McQuarrie) (*Star Wars Galaxy
    Mag. #3*) chromium 5.00
SWGM4 Dagobah swamp (*Star Wars Galaxy
    Mag. #4*) chromium 5.00

Dark Horse Comics
DH1 Dark Empire II promo, from Classic *Star Wars*:
    Tales of the Jedi: Dark Lords of the Sith #1...... 5.00
DH2 Dark Empire II promo, from Classic *Star Wars*
    The Early Adventures #3 .... 5.00
DH3 Dark Empire II promo, from Classic *Star Wars*:
    Return of the Jedi #1 .... 5.00

Classic Toys Trading Cards
#37 Darth Vader 12" action figure (doll) 1.00
#56 C-3PO 12" action figure (doll) 1.00

STAR WARS CAPS
Topps

Now that Milk Caps have come, and gone to their reward, you could buy up a basement full and hope that they come back some day. Just don't hold your breath!

Set: 64 caps + 2 slammers + chase caps $15.00
Pack: 3 regular caps + 1 chase cap 1.00
Box: 48 packs 30.00
Promos
0-A..................................... 2.00
0-B..................................... 2.00

Star Wars: A New Hope *Metal Cards, box
(Metallic Images 1994)*

METAL CARDS

STAR WARS: A NEW HOPE
Metallic Images (1994)

Set: 20 tin cards in tin box with certificate
    (49,900 made)......................... $40.00
Promo P1.................................. 4.00

CARD CHECKLIST

1 Luke Skywalker	$3.00	11 Tusken Raiders	3.00
2 Darth Vader	3.00	12 Jawas	3.00
3 C-3PO	3.00	13 Millennium Falcon	3.00
4 Princess Leia	3.00	14 Mos Eisley Cantina	3.00
5 Han Solo	3.00	15 Vader vs. Obi-Wan	3.00
6 R2-D2	3.00	16 X-wing Fighter	3.00
7 Obi-Wan Kenobi	3.00	17 The Jedi Knights	3.00
8 Chewbacca	3.00	18 Luke on Tatooine	3.00
9 Stormtroopers	3.00	19 R2-D2 and C-3PO	3.00
10 Grand Moff Tarkin	3.00	20 Checklist	3.00

STAR WARS: THE EMPIRE STRIKES BACK
Metallic Images (1995)

Set: 20 tin cards in tin litho box with certificate
(49,900 made) $50.00
Promo P2 . . . . 4.00

Series 2
Set: 20 tin cards in tin litho box with certificate
(49,900 made) 50.00

STAR WARS: RETURN OF THE JEDI
Metallic Images (1995)

Set: 20 tin cards in tin litho box with certificate
(49,900 made) $50.00
Promo P3 . . . . 6.00

STAR WARS: THE ART OF RALPH MCQUARRIE
Metallic Images (1996)

Set: 20 tin cards in tin litho box with certificate
(12,000 made) $60.00

Star Wars: Dark Empire Metal Cards, box
(Metallic Images 1995)

STAR WARS: DARK EMPIRE
Metallic Impressions (1995)

These metal cards reproduce cover art from the Dark Horse Comics series of the same name.

Set: 6 metal cards in tin litho box (72,000 made) . . . $15.00
Card, each 3.00

CARD CHECKLIST

1 Issue #1 The Destiny of a Jedi	$3.00	4 Issue #4 Confrontation of the Smuggler's Moon	3.00
2 Issue #2 Devastator of Worlds	3.00	5 Issue #5 Emperor Reborn	3.00
3 Issue #3 The Battle for Calamari	3.00	6 Issue #6 The Fate of a Galaxy	3.00

STAR WARS: DARK EMPIRE II
Metallic Impressions (1996)

Set: 6 metal cards in tin litho box (36,000 made) . . . $15.00
Card, each 3.00

STAR WARS: SHADOWS OF THE EMPIRE
Metallic Impressions (1997)

Set: 6 metal cards in tin litho box $20.00
Card, each 3.00

STAR WARS: JEDI KNIGHT
Metallic Impressions (1997)

Set: 6 metal cards in tin litho box $14.00
Card, each 3.00

CARD CHECKLIST

1 Luke Skywalker	$3.00	5 Anakin Skywalker	3.00
2 Obi-Wan Kenobi	3.00	6 Mos Eisley Spaceport (Special Edition)	3.00
3 Jedi Master Yoda	3.00		
4 Luke vs. Vader	3.00		

24K GOLD CARDS
Authentic Images (1997)

Gold *Star Wars* cards, limited to 1,000 units, in acrylic holder, with black vacuum-formed jewel case:

Series One: *A New Hope*
Special Edition Ingot $75.00
Han and Jabba 70.00
Luke 70.00
Leia 70.00
Darth Vader 100.00
Obi-Wan Kenobi 70.00

Series Two:
The Empire Strikes Back
Luke 75.00
Emperor 75.00
Boba Fett 100.00
Yoda 75.00
Darth Vader 75.00

Series Three: Return of the Jedi
Boba Fett/Luke 75.00
Darth Vader Unmasked 75.00
3 Spirits 75.00
C-3PO and R2-D2 . . . . 75.00
Leia & Jabba 75.00

Gold Gallery Series cards, limited to 500 units, in acrylic holder, with black vacuum formed jewel case:

Gallery Series 1: A New Hope
Jabba the Hutt & Han Solo . . 350.00
Darth Vader & Ben Kenobi . . 550.00

Gallery Series 2:
The Empire Strikes Back
Luke and Yoda 325.00
Luke and Darth Vader 400.00

24-karat gold card set, reproduction of 3 posters, each encased in a lucite block in a leatherette case, plus three 24"x36" movie posters, only 1,997 sets worldwide, JC Penney exclusive 225.00

VEHICLES AND ACCESSORIES

Millennium Falcon *loose, with figures (Kenner 1978)*

VEHICLES, CREATURES, PLAYSETS AND ACCESSORIES

Vehicles are much more important in *Star Wars* than in most other action figure lines. The 3¾" size of the figures allowed the production of vehicles which were large enough to accommodate several figures, and so the larger vehicles became virtual playsets for the figures. Actual playsets were also produced and creatures, such as the TaunTaun and Wampa, and accessories, such as the Mini-Rigs, extended this playset environment.

Today, many collectors have a large supply of loose figures which they display with the appropriate loose vehicles, creatures, playsets and accessories. This has helped to keep collector prices for these items at a high level. Vehicles, creatures and accessories from the classic movies are listed first, followed by those from the new Power of the Force series.

VEHICLES
Kenner (1978–86)

Vehicles were released over the period of all three movies and many which originally came out in "*Star Wars*" boxes can be found in boxes from one or both of the later movies. As with the figures, vehicles are listed first in their original box, followed by information and values for later issues. Usually the box logo corresponds to the vintage of the vehicle, but in 1983 Kenner released three of its original vehicles (and one creature) in the *Star Wars* Collector Series, which just meant that an orange sunburst was added to the original box design.

Star Wars Vehicles (1978–79)
Landspeeder, rolls on spring-loaded wheels, holds
    2 figures plus 2 more on rear deck (#38020, 1978)
    Original *Star Wars* box. $75.00
    Star Wars Collector's Series Land Speeder
      (1983) 35.00
    Loose 20.00
X-Wing Fighter, 14" long, electronic light and
    sound, cockpit canopy opens, wings open
    and close (#38030, 1978)
    Original *Star Wars* box. 125.00
    Reissue in *The Empire Strikes Back* box 175.00
    Loose 45.00
Imperial TIE Fighter, 12" wide, battery light and
    sound, red laser cannon, 2 "solar panels"
    can be released to simulate "battle damage,"
    escape hatch (#38040, 1978)
    Original *Star Wars* box. 135.00
    Reissue in *The Empire Strikes Back* box 175.00
    Loose 45.00
Darth Vader TIE Fighter, grey, 11" across, pop-off
    solar panels, battery light and sound in
    13"x11½"x6½" box (#39100, 1979)
    Original *Star Wars* box. 125.00
    Loose 60.00
    Original *Star Wars* box with Battle Scene
      Setting 500.00
    Loose, with Battle Scene 150.00
    Star Wars Collector's Series (1983) 60.00
    Loose 40.00
Millennium Falcon Spaceship, 21" long, 18" wide,
    with "Battle Alert Sound" in 22"x17"x6" box
    (#39110, 1979)
    Original *Star Wars* box. 325.00

Landspeeder, collector series (Kenner 1983)

Darth Vader TIE Fighter (Kenner 1979)

Reissue in *The Empire Strikes Back* box 225.00
Reissue in *Return of the Jedi* box. 150.00
Star Wars Collector Series *Millennium Falcon*
   (1983). 125.00
Loose 80.00
Radio-Controlled Jawa Sandcrawler, 17" long, in
  17½"x9"x7" box (#39270, 1979)
   Original *Star Wars* box. 550.00
   Reissue in *The Empire Strikes Back* box 650.00
   Loose 250.00
Imperial Troop Transporter, compartments for
  figures, 6 different battery operated sounds
  (#39290, 1979)
   Original *Star Wars* box. 100.00
   Reissue in *The Empire Strikes Back* box 115.00
   Loose 45.00

Exclusive Vehicles (1979–80)
Sonic-Controlled Land Speeder, battery operated,
  with mechanical clicker shaped like R2-D2,
  J.C. Penney exclusive (#38540, 1979)
   Original *Star Wars* box. 550.00
   Loose 200.00
Imperial Cruiser, similar to Imperial Troop Trans-
  porter, Sears exclusive (#93351, 1980)
   Original *The Empire Strikes Back* box 125.00
   Loose 40.00

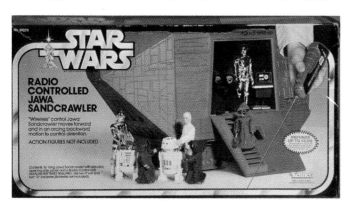

Radio Controlled Jawa Sandcrawler (Kenner 1978)

The Empire Strikes Back Vehicles (1980–82)
Darth Vader's Star Destroyer, 20" long (#39850, 1980)
   Original *The Empire Strikes Back* box 135.00
   Loose 30.00
Twin-Pod Cloud Car, 10" wide, orange plastic,
  in 11"x 9½"x4" box (#39860, 1980)
   Original *The Empire Strikes Back* box 80.00
   Reissue in *The Empire Strikes Back* box with
    Bespin Security Guard (white) figure 125.00
   Loose, no figure. 40.00
AT-AT All-Terrain Armored Transport, 17½"
  tall, posable legs, movable control center
  (#38810, 1981)
   Original *The Empire Strikes Back* box 250.00
   Reissue in *Return of the Jedi* box. 175.00
   Loose 100.00
Rebel Armored Snowspeeder, 12" long, 10¾" wide,
  battery light and sound (#39610, 1982)
   Original *The Empire Strikes Back* box 90.00
   Reissue in *The Empire Strikes Back* box with
    Rebel Soldier (Hoth Battle Gear) figure 175.00
   Loose 40.00

Slave 1, with box, packaging and contents (Kenner 1982)

Slave I, Boba Fett's Spaceship, 12" long, including
  Simulated Frozen **Han Solo** (#39690, 1982)
   Original *The Empire Strikes Back* box 90.00
   Reissue in *The Empire Strikes Back* box with
    Battle Scene Setting 275.00
   Loose 40.00
Rebel Transport, 20" long, including 5 Hoth Back-
  packs and 4 Asteroid gas masks (#69740, 1982)
   Original *The Empire Strikes Back* box 100.00
   Loose 35.00
"Battle Damaged" X-Wing Fighter, battery powered,
  "Labels Create Battle-Damaged Look" in 14"x
  12½"x4¼" box (#69780, 1981)
   Original *The Empire Strikes Back* box 150.00
   Reissue in *Return of the Jedi* box. 125.00
   Loose 35.00
Scout Walker, 10" tall, hand-operated walking
  mechanism (#69800, 1982)
   Original *The Empire Strikes Back* box 80.00
   Reissue in *Return of the Jedi* box 60.00
   Loose 25.00

AT-AT and Rebel Armored Snow Speeder (Kenner 1981 and 1982)

Imperial TIE Fighter (Battle Damaged, same mold
as original TIE but in blue with "damage"
decals) (#71490, 1983)
    Original *The Empire Strikes Back* box 150.00
    Reissue in *Return of the Jedi* box............ 125.00
    Loose 40.00

Return of the Jedi Vehicles (1983–84)
Speeder Bike 8" long (#70500, 1983)
    Original *Return of the Jedi* box.............. 30.00
    Reissue in *Power of the Force* box............ 20.00
    Loose 15.00
Y-Wing Fighter with Laser Cannon Sound in 21"x
11½"x3¾" box (#70510, 1983)
    Original *Return of the Jedi* box.............. 100.00
    Loose 50.00
B-Wing Fighter, 22" long, battery operated sound
and rotating cockpit (#71370, 1984)
    Original *Return of the Jedi* box.............. 75.00
    Loose 40.00

TIE Interceptor, with Battle Sound and Flashing
Laser Light, battery powered, 12" wide
(#71390, 1984)
    Original *Return of the Jedi* box.............. 90.00
    Loose 50.00
Imperial Shuttle, 18" tall, wings folded, battery
sound (#93650)
    Original *Return of the Jedi* box.............. 300.00
    Loose 150.00

Power of the Force Vehicles (1984–85)
Tatooine Skiff, 12" long (#71540, 1985)
    Original *Power of the Force* box.............. 600.00
    Loose 300.00

Droids Vehicles (1985)
A-Wing Fighter, 12" long, battery operated sound,
with planetary map (#93700)
    Original *Droids* box 600.00
    Loose 300.00

Twin-Pod Cloud Car and Battle Damaged X-Wing Fighter (Kenner 1980 and 1983)

A-Wing Fighter (Kenner 1984)

ATL Interceptor Vehicle (#93900)
  Original *Droids* box 35.00
  Loose 15.00
Side Gunner with *Star Wars* Planetary Map (#94010)
  Original *Droids* box 50.00
  Loose 10.00

NEW VEHICLES
Kenner (1996–98)

Power of the Force Vehicles, red boxes (1995–96)
Landspeeder (#69770, July 1995) $10.00
TIE Fighter (#69775, July 1995) 20.00
Imperial AT-ST (Scout Walker) (#69776, July 1995) . . . 25.00
Electronic X-wing Fighter (#69780, July 1995). 30.00
Electronic *Millennium Falcon* (#69785, July 1995) 50.00

Power of the Force Vehicles, green boxes (1996–98)
Luke's T-16 Skyhopper (#69663, Dec. 1996). 20.00
Cruise Missile Trooper with Twin Proton Torpedo
  Launchers (#69653, Feb. 1997) 13.00
Darth Vader's TIE Fighter with Launcher Laser
  Cannons (#69662, Feb. 1997) 20.00

Cruisemissle Trooper (Kenner 1997)

Electronic Rebel Snowspeeder with Topps "*Star
  Wars*" widevision trading card (#69585,
  July 1996) 25.00

Power of the Force Vehicles with figures (1997–98)
A-Wing Fighter with **A-Wing Pilot** figure (#69737,
  July 1997) 25.00
Electronic Imperial AT-AT Walker with exclusive
  AT-AT Commander and **AT-AT Driver** Sept.
  (#69733, 1997) [.00] sticker over bottom of
  figures' photo. 90.00
  Variation [.01] no sticker, full photo shown 75.00

Shadows of the Empire Vehicles (1996)
Boba Fett's *Slave I* (#69565, July 1996) 30.00
Boba Fett's *Slave I*, including **Han Solo in Carbon-
  ite** (#69565) reissue in Power of the Force
  green box 30.00
Dash Rendar's Outrider, with Topps "*Star Wars*"
  widevision trading card (#69593, July 1996). 35.00
Dash Rendar's Outrider (#69814) green box. 20.00

Speeder Bike Vehicles with figures (Asst. 69760)
Imperial Speeder Bike with **Biker Scout Storm-
  trooper** figure (#69765, Feb. 1996) in a red
  Power of the Force window box [none]. 20.00

Millennium Falcon and TIE Fighter (Kenner 1996)

Swoop speeder bike, with Swoop Trooper (Kenner 1996)

Swoop vehicle with **Swoop Trooper** figure
(#69591, July 1996) in a purple *Shadows of
the Empire* window box [none] 12.00
Speeder Bike with **Luke Skywalker** in Endor Gear,
with Lightsaber and Blaster, exclusive figure
(#69651, Feb. 1997) [538126.00] two white
gloves in photo 20.00
Variation [.01] wearing one black glove 12.00
Speeder Bike with **Princess Leia Organa** in Endor
Gear (#69727, July 1997) [541948.00] rocks
in side photos 20.00
Variation [.01] moss airbrushed over rocks 15.00
Power Racing Speeder Bike with **Scout Trooper**
(#60588, 1998) 12.50

Expanded Universe Vehicles (Asst. #69620, 1998)
Cloud Car with Exclusive **Cloud Car Pilot** figure,
from *The Art of Star Wars* (#69786, Feb. 1998) . . 15.00
Airspeeder with "Firing Proton Torpedo and
Exclusive **Airspeeder Pilot**" figure, from *The
Art of Star Wars* (#69774, Feb 1998) 15.00
Speeder Bike with Rebel Speeder Bike Pilot
figure (#69772, June 1998) 12.50

Electronic Power F/X Luke Skywalker Red Five
X-wing Fighter, battery operated, with 12 real

Airspeeder Vehicle (Kenner 1998)

movie sounds and phrases, plus non-remov-
able lever activated Luke Skywalker and
R2-D2 (#69784, 1998) 50.00

SHIPS
Kenner (1997–98)

Ships differ from "vehicles" because ships are not
scaled to fit action figures, but vehicles are. Obviously
Kenner can't make a Star Destroyer that is the same scale as
its other vehicles — it would be over 100 feet long!

Collector Fleet in try-me box (1997–98)
Electronic Blockade Runner (Kenner #27844, 1997) . $25.00
Electronic Star Destroyer (Kenner #27835, 1997) 25.00
Electronic Super Star Destroyer *Executor* (Kenner
#27914, 1998) 33.00

CREATURES
Kenner (1979–84)

Classic Creatures
Patrol Dewback, 10¼" long, with reins and saddle
in 11"x6"x4½" box (#39240, 1979)
Original *Star Wars* box $75.00
Reissue in *The Empire Strikes Back* box 200.00

Patrol Dewback (Kenner 1979)

Star Wars Collector Series Patrol Dewback
(1983) 50.00
Loose 25.00
Tauntaun, 8" tall, with saddle and reins in 9"x7"x4"
box (#39820, 1980)
Original *The Empire Strikes Back* box 75.00
Loose 25.00
Tauntaun, with Open Belly Rescue Feature
(#93340, 1982)
Original *The Empire Strikes Back* box 75.00
Loose 25.00
Wampa, Snow Creature from Hoth, 6¼" tall, mov-
able arms and legs (#69560, 1982)
Original *The Empire Strikes Back* box pictur-
ing Rebel Commander 60.00
Reissue as **Hoth Wampa** in *The Empire
Strikes Back* box picturing Luke Skywalker
in Hoth Gear 35.00
Reissue in *Return of the Jedi* box 40.00
Loose 15.00
Jabba the Hutt Action Playset, including Jabba and
Salacious Crumb molded figure (#70490, 1983)
Original *Return of the Jedi* box 60.00

Jabba the Hutt (Kenner 1983)

Reissue in *Return of the Jedi* box (Sears) 40.00
Loose 30.00
Rancor Monster, 10" high (1984)
Original *Return of the Jedi* box. 75.00
Reissue in *Power of the Force* box. 60.00
Loose 30.00

NEW CREATURES
Kenner (1997–98)

The first three creature and figure combination boxes arrived in August 1997. The figures are all based on the new footage from the first movie. Collectors were looking forward to the first ever version of the Bantha which arrived just at the end of May 1998.

Creature and Figure Combos (Asst. #69645, Aug. 1997)
Ronto and Jawa in green *Power of the Force* window box with exclusive **Jawa** figure (#69728) [541088.00]. $15.00
Dewback and **Sandtrooper** in green *Power of the Force* window box (#69743) [541085.00]
Galactic Empire and Unaffiliated logos on front . . 17.00
Variation, [.01] Galactic Empire logo only 15.00
Jabba the Hutt and **Han Solo** in green *Power of the Force* window box (#69742) [541082.00]

Ronto, with Jawa (Kenner 1997)

Galactic Empire and Rebel Alliance logos, Han pictured to Jabba's right 25.00
Variation [.01] Han pictured to Jabba's left in data file 15.00
Variation [.02] Unaffiliated and Rebel Alliance logos, Han pictured on left 15.00

Second Batch Scheduled, May 1998
Tauntaun and Luke Skywalker in Hoth Gear 15.00

Rancor and Luke Skywalker (Kenner 1998)

Bantha and Tusken Raider (Kenner 1978)

Death Star Playset (Kenner 1979)

Creature Cantina Action Playset (Kenner 1979)

Land of the Jawas Action Playset (#39130, 1979)
　Original *Star Wars* box.................... 150.00
　Reissue in *The Empire Strikes Back* box 200.00
　Loose 45.00
Droid Factory with 31 plastic robot parts, plastic
　base and movable crane, in 13"x11"x3" box
　(#39150, 1979)
　Original *Star Wars* box.................... 125.00
　Reissue in *The Empire Strikes Back* box 175.00
　Loose 50.00

The Empire Strikes Back Playsets (1980–82)
Imperial Attack Base, Hoth scene, in 18"x10¼"
　x3¾" box (#39830, 1980)
　Original *The Empire Strikes Back* box 125.00
　Loose 30.00
Hoth Ice Planet Adventure Set (1980, 1980)
　Original *The Empire Strikes Back* box 150.00
　Reissue in *The Empire Strikes Back* box, with
　　Imperial Stormtrooper (Hoth Battle
　　Gear) figure........................ 200.00
　Loose, no figure......................... 50.00
Dagobah Action Playset, lever-operated functions
　(#38820, 1981)
　Original *The Empire Strikes Back* box 55.00
　Loose 25.00
Turret & Probot Playset, with **Probot** figure
　(#38330, 1981)

Jabba the Hutt Dungeon Playset (Variation 1) (Kenner 1983)

Wampa and Luke Skywalker in Hoth Gear 15.00

Deluxe Creatures and Figure (Asst. #69655, May 1998)
Rancor and Luke Skywalker, with "Exclusive Battle-
　worn **Jedi Luke**" (#69771) [552624.00] 30.00
Bantha and Tusken Raider, "includes exclusive
　Tusken Raider with Gaderffii Stick" (#69769)
　[552621.00] 30.00

PLAYSETS
Kenner (1979–85)

　With all the classic playsets that Kenner produced in the
1980s, you would think that they would have reissued some
of them in 1990s. So far they have not done so.

Star Wars Playsets (1979)
Death Star Space Station, 23" high, three-story
　playset, manual elevator, exploding laser
　cannon, light bridge, trash compactor with
　garbage and Trash Monster (#38050, 1979)
　Original *Star Wars* box.................. $225.00
　Loose 60.00
Creature Cantina Action Playset, with lever-
　activated functions, no figures in 14"x8"x3½"
　box (#39120, 1979)
　Original *Star Wars* box.................... 125.00
　Loose 40.00

Turret & Probot Playset accessory (Kenner 1981)

Original *The Empire Strikes Back* box 150.00
Loose 60.00
Rebel Command Center Adventure Set, including
R2-D2, **Luke Skywalker** and **AT-AT Com-
mander** figures (#69481, 1981)
Original *The Empire Strikes Back* box 250.00
Loose 120.00

Return of the Jedi Playset (1983)
Ewok Village Action Playset, 12" high, 2-story
playset (#70520, 1983)
Original *Return of the Jedi* box. 75.00
Loose 25.00
Ewok Playset (1984)
Ewok Family Hut, 12" high, Hut plus 15 accessories
and 4 non-poseable figures (Kenner Pre-
school, 1984)
Original *Ewoks* box 50.00
Loose 15.00
Exclusive Playsets
Cantina Adventure Set (Sears' promotional set) 4
figures, including: Greedo, Hammerhead,
blue Snaggletooth and Walrus man (#38861, 1979)
Original *Star Wars* box. 650.00
Loose 250.00
Cloud City Playset (Sears' exclusive) including
4 figures: Han Solo in Bespin outfit, Ugnaught,
Lobot and Dengar, and Boba Fett (#38781, 1981)
Original *The Empire Strikes Back* box 375.00
Loose 150.00
The Jabba the Hutt Dungeon Action Playset
Variation #1, including Klaatu, Nikto and 8D8
action figures, red box, Sears exclusive
(#71381, 1983)
Original *Return of the Jedi* box. 130.00
Loose 60.00
Variation #2, including EV-9D9, Amanaman,
and Barada figures, green box, Sears
exclusive (#59262, 1984)
Original *Return of the Jedi* box. 300.00
Loose 150.00

New: None

ACCESSORIES AND MINI-RIGS
Kenner (1981–84)

Some of the accessories listed in this section were called
"playsets" or "one-figure vehicles" on their boxes. What
places them in this category is their small size.

*Radar Laser Cannon, captured intact by two Stormtroopers
(Kenner 1983)*

Accessories
Vehicle Maintenance Energizer in 6"x4½"x3¾" box
(#93430, 1983)
Original *The Empire Strikes Back* box $20.00
Reissue in *Return of the Jedi* box 15.00
Loose 9.00
Radar Laser Cannon (#93440, 1983)
Original *The Empire Strikes Back* box 20.00
Reissue in *Return of the Jedi* box 15.00
Loose 7.50
Tri-Pod Laser Cannon, 4½"x6" box (#93450, 1983)
Original *The Empire Strikes Back* box 20.00
Reissue in *Return of the Jedi* box 15.00
Loose 9.00
Ewok Assault Catapult, 4½"x6" box (#71070, 1984)
Original *Return of the Jedi* box. 18.00
Loose 8.00
Ewok Combat Glider, 4½"x6" box (#93510, 1984)
Original *Return of the Jedi* box. 18.00
Loose 8.00
Ewok Battle Wagon, 12" long with *Star Wars* Planet-
ary Map (#93690, 1984)
Original *Power of the Force* box. 100.00
Loose 40.00
Imperial Sniper Vehicle, 1-figure vehicle with over-
head wings (Asst. #93920, 1984)
Original *Power of the Force* box. 80.00
Loose 30.00
Security Scout, camouflage colored, 1-figure
vehicle (Asst. #93920, 1984)
Original *Power of the Force* box. 250.00
Loose 60.00
One-Man Sand Skimmer, small 1-figure vehicle
(Asst. #93920, 1984)
Original *Power of the Force* box. 80.00
Loose 25.00
Ewok Fire Cart, accessories plus 2 non-poseable
figures (Kenner Preschool, 1984)
Original *Ewoks* box 40.00
Loose 15.00
Ewok Woodland Wagon, covered wheel cart, horse
and accessories (Kenner Preschool, 1985)
Original *Ewoks* box 75.00
Loose 20.00

MLC-3 Mobile Laser Cannon (Kenner 1981)

Desert Sail Skiff (Kenner 1984)

MINI-RIGS

Mini-Rigs were one-man "crawling, climbing, flying" accessories for the action figures, that were too small to be part of the regular vehicle line-up. They came in a box with a hanging flap and the best graphics are on the back of the package.

None of these mini-rigs never appeared in the three movies, but a few showed up in the animated Droids series. These days Kenner packages such items with a figure and sells them as a "Deluxe" figure.

Mini Rig 1-Figure Vehicles, 6"x4½" boxes (1981-83)
MTV-7 Multi-Terrain Vehicle (#40010, 1981)
  Original *The Empire Strikes Back* box $35.00
  Reissue in *The Empire Strikes Back* box with
    AT-AT Driver figure. 60.00
  Reissue in *Return of the Jedi* box 25.00
  Loose, without figure 9.00
MLC-3 Mobile Laser Cannon, 6"x4½"x1" box + flap
  (#40020, 1981)
  Original *The Empire Strikes Back* box 25.00
  Reissue in *The Empire Strikes Back* box with
    Rebel Commander figure. 60.00
  Reissue in *Return of the Jedi* box 25.00
  Loose, without figure 9.00
PDT-8 Personnel Deployment Transport (#40070, 1981)
  Original *The Empire Strikes Back* box 30.00
  Reissue in *The Empire Strikes Back* box with
    2-1B figure 60.00
  Reissue in *Return of the Jedi* box 15.00
  Loose, without figure 9.00
INT-4 Interceptor (#69750, 1982)
  Original *The Empire Strikes Back* box 30.00
  Reissue in *The Empire Strikes Back* box with
    AT-AT Commander figure. 60.00
  Reissue in *Return of the Jedi* box 15.00
  Loose, without figure 9.00
CAP-2 Captivator (#69760, 1982)
  Original *The Empire Strikes Back* box 20.00
  Reissue in *The Empire Strikes Back* box with
    Bossk figure. 60.00
  Reissue in *Return of the Jedi* box 20.00
  Loose 9.00
AST-5 Armored Sentinel Transport (#70880, 1983)
  Original *Return of the Jedi* box 15.00
  Loose 7.00

ISP-6 (Imperial Shuttle Pod) (#70890, 1983)
  Original *Return of the Jedi* box. 20.00
  Loose 9.00
Desert Sail Skiff (#93520, 1984) mini rig
  Original *Return of the Jedi* box. 15.00
  Loose 10.00
Endor Forest Ranger (#93610, 1984) mini rig
  Original *Return of the Jedi* box. 15.00
  Loose 10.00

NEW ACCESSORIES
Kenner (1996–98)

First Batch (Asst. #27597, Oct. 1996)
Detention Block Rescue (#27598). $15.00
Death Star Escape with Firing Cannon and Remov-
  able Bridge (#27599) 15.00

Second Batch (Asst. #27857, Aug. 1997)
Hoth Battle with Rotating Gun Turret and Shooting
  Laser (#27858, Aug. 1997). 18.00
Endor Attack with Swinging Tree Branch and Rock
  Launcher (#27859, Aug. 1997). 18.00

VANS AND RACERS
Various (1978–80)

A less authentic toy than a *Star Wars* van would be hard to design. Not only are there no cars or vans in the movies, there aren't even any roads. However, there actually is a guy who has a real *Star Wars* van which I see driving on the highway in southern Connecticut from time to time. Anyway, I suppose it could have been a lot worse. Kenner might have made a Superman and Darth Vader motorcycle set? After all, they both wear capes! I guess we were lucky.

Star Wars Van Set, 2 toy vans, 7" in length, black
  van with Darth Vader picture; white van with
  good guys, plus 12 barrels, 4 pylons and
  2 T-Sticks (Kenner #90170, 1978) $150.00
Darth Vader SSP (Super Sonic Power) Van, black,
  with Blazin' Action, gyro powered (Kenner
  #90160, 1978) 50.00
Star Wars Heroes SSP (Super Sonic Power) Van,
  white, with Blazin' Action, gyro powered
  (Kenner #90160, 1978) 50.00
Star Wars Duel at Death Star Racing Set, 19"x20"
  box (Fundimensions 1978). 200.00

WALL ART

WALL ART

Wall art includes just about every kind of picture, poster or other item that is designed to be framed and/or hung on a wall. Calendars are covered under PAPER.

ANIMATION CELS
Royal Animation (1995–97)

Royal Animation makes sericels from the "Droids and Ewoks" animated TV series. Sericels are silk-screened from the original cel, with an added lithograph background. Each comes with a certificate of authenticity and a Lucas Films seal. The sericels are double-matted and 14"x18" in size.

Droids Sericels

R2-D2 & C-3PO, Best Friends (DR-1)	$90.00
Battle Cruiser (DR-2)	90.00
R2-D2 & C-3PO Stranded (DR-3)	90.00
Bounty Hunter, Boba Fett and Stormtroopers (DR-4)	90.00

Ewoks Sericels

The Big Hug (EW-1)	90.00
Celebration (EW-2)	90.00

CHROMART

ChromArt prints are 8"x10" in an 11"x14" matte. They are made with acrylic, foil and etching to give an illusion of depth. The images come from CD-ROM game boxes and Video Tape Boxes, but the enhancements make them quite striking.

ChromArt Prints (Zanart Entertainment)

SW-C *Return of the Jedi*	$12.00
SW-C2 Darth Vader (1994)	12.00
SW-C3 C-3PO and R2-D2 (1994)	12.00
SW-C4 Star Destroyer	12.00
SW-C5 AT-ATs	12.00
SW-C6 Darth Vader Gold, artistic head	12.00
SW-C7 B-Wing Fight (1995)	12.00
SW-C8 Bounty Hunters (1995)	12.00
SW-C9 Asteroid Chase (1995)	12.00
SW-C10 *Star Wars* One-Sheet poster	12.00
SW-C11 *The Empire Strikes Back* One-Sheet poster	12.00
SW-C12 *Return of the Jedi* One-Sheet poster	12.00
SW-C13 Rebel Assault (CD-ROM game cover)	12.00
SW-C14 Dark Forces (CD-ROM game cover)	12.00
SW-C15 TIE Fighter (CD-ROM game cover)	12.00

SW-C16 TIE Fighter: Defender of the Empire (CD-ROM game cover)	12.00
SW-C17 X-Wing (CD-ROM game cover)	12.00
SW-C18 *Star Wars* (video box cover)	12.00
SW-C19 *The Empire Strikes Back* (video box cover)	12.00
SW-C20 *Return of the Jedi* (video box cover)	12.00

Second Series

Bounty Hunters	13.00
AT-ATs	13.00
Darth Vader	13.00
Darth Vader	13.00
R2-D2	13.00
Space Battle	13.00
Star Destroyer	13.00
Millennium Falcon	13.00
B-Wings	13.00
Star Wars Trilogy Movie Cards	14.00

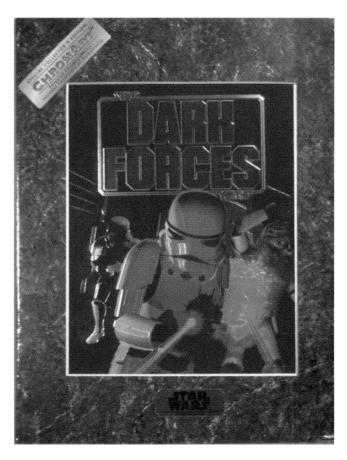

Dark Forces *Chromart Print (Zanart 1995)*

Star Wars One-Sheet Poster Chromart (Zanart)

Third Series

X-Wing Starfighter Blueprint Chromium Print
　(#SWPB-C1) 12.00
Imperial TIE Fighter Blueprint Chromium Print
　(#SWPB-C2) 12.00
B-Wing Starfighter Blueprint Chromium Print
　(#SWPB-C3) 12.00
Imperial Star Destroyer Blueprint Chromium Print . . . 12.00
AT-AT Walker Blueprint Chromium Print 12.00
Y-Wing Blueprint Chromium Print 12.00
A-Wing Blueprint Chromium Print 12.00
AT-ST Walker Blueprint Chromium Print 12.00

Fourth Series

Star Wars Bounty Hunters Framed Chromart,
　11"x14" (44-113, 1997) 20.00
Star Wars Droids Framed Chromart, 11"x14"
　(44-114, 1997) 20.00
Star Wars Heir to the Empire Framed Chromart,
　11"x14" (44-127, 1997) 20.00
Star Wars Splinter of the Mind's Eye Framed
　Chromart, 12"x15" (44-128, 1997) 20.00
Star Wars Shadows of the Empire Framed Chrom-
　art, 12"x15" (44-125, 1997) 20.00
Star Wars Xizor Framed Chromart, 12"x15"
　(44-126, 1997) 20.00

Star Wars Trilogy International Release ChromArt
　print, John Alvin art, three prints, matted in
　wood frame (SWI-3W, 1996) limited to 2,500
　copies 250.00

Star Wars International Video Chromium Print
　(#SWI-C1) 12.00
The Empire Strikes Back International Video
　Chromium Print (#SWI-C2) 12.00
Return of the Jedi International Video Chromium
　Print (#SWI-C3) 12.00

LITHOGRAPHS

　Many *Star Wars* limited edition lithographs were created by well-known science fiction and *Star Wars* artist Ralph McQuarrie. They are 18"x12" in size, framed and matted, and each comes with an Illuminated 70mm Film Frame. They were issued by Willitts Designs, which is not surprising, since they also produced the many series of 70mm Film Frames covered under STILLS.

　Many other prominent *Star Wars* artists have also produced lithographs, including Boris Valejo, Drew Struzan, the Bros. Hildebrandt and Dave Dorman. Lithographs fall in the realm of fine art and the high prices that they command are based on this, rather than being driven up by collector demand. They make excellent gifts.

Star Wars, A New Hope (Ralph McQuarrie art)
The Cantina on Mos Eisley (Willitts Designs
　#50002) limited to 2,500 copies, framed $150.00
Millennium Falcon (Willitts Designs #50004) limited
　to 2,500 copies, framed 180.00
Rebel Attack on the Death Star (Willitts Designs
　#50005) limited to 2,500 copies, framed 200.00
Rebel Ceremony (Willitts Designs #50006) limited
　to 2,500 copies, framed 150.00

The Empire Strikes Back (Ralph McQuarrie art)
Rebel Patrol of Echo Base (Willitts Designs
　#50036) limited to 2,500 copies, framed 150.00
Luke Skywalker and Darth Vader Duel (Willitts
　Designs #50037) limited to 2,500 copies,
　framed 150.00
Battle of Hoth (Willitts Designs #50038) limited to
　2,500 copies, framed 150.00
Cloud City of Bespin (Willitts Designs #50039)
　limited to 2,500 copies, framed 150.00

Return of the Jedi (Ralph McQuarrie art)
Jabba the Hutt (Willitts Designs #50050) limited to
　2,500 copies, framed 175.00
The Rancor Pit (Willitts Designs #50051) limited to
　2,500 copies, framed 175.00
Speeder Bike (Willitts Designs #50052) limited to
　2,500 copies, framed 175.00
Death Star Generator (Willitts Designs #50053)
　limited to 2,500 copies, framed 175.00

Other Lithographs (Various artists)
Star Wars 15th Anniversary Serigraph, by Melanie
　Taylor Kent, 20¼"x30½" limited to 1,100
　copies (1992) 1,750.00
Star Wars Lithograph by Ken Steacy, 17"x24"
　signed and numbered, limited to 500 copies,
　Darth Vader image from *The Art of Star Wars
　Galaxy Cards* (Gifted Images 1994) 600.00
In a Galaxy Far, Far Away, limited, signed litho-
　graph by Michael David Ward, 20"x30", sign-
　ed by Anthony Daniels and Kenny Baker,
　limited to 1,000 copies 175.00

The Empire Strikes Back*: Domestic One-Sheet Poster; Style B Domestic One-Sheet Poster; Radio Show Poster (Lucasfilm 1980s)*

Luke Skywalker Limited Edition Lithograph by Al
  Williamson, limited to 500 copies, 22½"x23" in
  29"x29" frame (1996) 300.00
Darth Vader Limited Edition Lithograph by Al
  Williamson, limited to 500 copies, 24"x24" in
  30fi"x30fi" frame (1996) 300.00
Star Wars R2-D2 Remarked Lithograph by the
  Bros. Hildebrandt, signed, 24"x18" 175.00
Star Wars Luke and Yoda Lithograph by Boris
  Vallejo, signed and numbered, 30"x36" limited
  to 500 copies 600.00

Star Wars, Special Edition Lithographs by Dave Dorman
Star Wars Dewback Patrol Lithograph by Dave
  Dorman, 34"x16", limited to 1,500 copies (1997) . 45.00
Star Wars Battle of Hoth Lithograph by Dave Dor-
  man, 34"x16", limited to 1,500 copies (1997) 45.00
Star Wars Tales of the Jedi, Freedon Nadd Uprising
  Lithograph by Dave Dorman, 18"x22", limited
  to 1,500 copies (1997) 45.00
Star Wars Star's End Lithograph by Dave Dorman,
  18"x22", limited to 1,500 copies (1997) 45.00
Star Wars Princess Leia (Boushh outfit) Lithograph
  by Dave Dorman, 16"x22", limited to 1,500
  copies (1997). 45.00
Star Wars Throne Room of Jabba Lithograph by
  Dave Dorman, 32"x14", limited to 1,500
  copies (1997). 45.00

Gallery Pieces
Star Wars: A New Hope 24k gold Gallery Pieces
  (1997) limited to 500 pieces, engraved with
  limited edition number, with certificate of
  authenticity:
Han Solo & Jabba the Hutt 10"x5" . . . . unknown
Darth Vader and Obi-Wan Kenobi 10"x9" . . . . unknown

POSTERS

There are many types of posters, from those sold in toy stores to those that come in magazines and as fast food give-aways, but the most valuable by far at the theatrical posters that were issued to promote the movie. These had no initial price — they were sent to movie theaters or given away at shows. Their value is entirely collector driven. There are a considerable number of general movie poster collectors who compete with *Star Wars* collectors for these posters, keeping the prices high. Posters are most valuable when they are rolled, not folded, and should never be put on your wall using thumb tacks. As a practical matter, this will make it hard to show it to your friends in order to impress them. If your poster is worth $150 or more, you should probably have it professionally framed, which will cost you close to $100, but at least you can then hang it on your wall and show it off.

Unfortunately, valuable posters can be reproduced and sold as if they were the original. These bootlegs are worth a lot less money — and less than nothing to a collector. It's not easy to tell a fake unless you have a real one for comparison and if you have a real one, why are you looking for another one? Naturally the most expensive and most popular posters were the first ones to be counterfeited. Collectors are advised to buy with care, from reputable dealers.

POSTERS — THEATRICAL

Star Wars
Advance A One-sheet, "A long time ago in a galaxy
  far far away..." $250.00
Star Wars advance, 2nd version 150.00
Style A One-sheet, Tommy Jung art 175.00
Star Wars, style A, with record promo 175.00
Star Wars advance, style B. 150.00
Star Wars, style C. 150.00
Style D One-sheet (Circus poster) Drew Struzan
  and Charles White III art 325.00

Revenge of the Jedi *Advance One-Sheet Poster;* Return of the Jedi: *One-Sheet Style B Poster; 1985 Re-Release One-Sheet (Lucasfilm 1980s)*

Anniversary One-sheet (1978) theater give-away . . . 600.00
'79 Re-release One-sheet, "It's Back!" 100.00
'81 Re-release One-sheet. 60.00
'82 Re-release One-Sheet 50.00

The Empire Strikes Back
Advance One-sheet 200.00
Style 'A' One-sheet (Love Story) Rodger Kastel art . . 200.00
Style 'B' One-sheet Tommy Jung art 75.00
'81 Re-release One-sheet, Tommy Jung art 50.00
'82 Re-release One-sheet, Tommy Jung art 40.00

Revenge of the Jedi
Advance Revenge of the Jedi One-sheet, 41"x27"
   with release date 350.00
Variation, no release date 400.00

Return of the Jedi
Style 'A' One-sheet. 35.00
Style 'B' One-sheet. 40.00
Return of the Jedi, 1985 reissue 25-70

Special Edition
Star Wars Trilogy Special Edition Advance One-sheet . 30.00
Version 'B' *Star Wars: A New Hope* One-sheet,
   Drew Struzan art 30.00
Version 'C' *The Empire Strikes Back* One-sheet,
   Drew Struzan art 30.00
Version 'D' *Return of the Jedi* One-sheet, Drew
   Struzan art. 30.00

POSTERS–SPECIAL EVENTS

The Art of *Star Wars*, Center for the Arts $50.00
Caravan of Courage 60.00
Immunization Poster. 10.00
Star Tours Poster 5.00
Public Radio Drama poster 150.00
Vintage Action Figures Photo poster 15.00

POSTERS–COMMERCIAL

Star Wars 10th Anniversary Poster, 27"x41" (1987)
   by Drew Struzan $10.00
Star Wars 10th Anniversary Poster, 27"x41" (1987)
   signed by Drew Struzan, limited to 200 copies
   (1992) 100.00
Star Wars 15th Anniversary poster by Melanie Tay-
   lor Kent, 20"x30" (1992). 25.00
Star Wars 15th Anniversary Movie Poster, by Greg
   and Tim Hildebrandt, limited to 5,000 copies,
   27"x 41" (Collector's Warehouse 1992) 15.00
   Deluxe, signed edition of 1,000 . . . . 50.00
   Star Wars "A New Hope" variation 15.00
Style D One-sheet (Circus poster) Drew Struzan
   and Charles White III art, reprint, 27"x41"
   (Collector's Warehouse 1993) 15.00
Star Wars Space Battle Poster (1995). 5.00
Star Wars Movie poster reproduction, 24"x36" 5.00
The Empire Strikes Back 10th Anniversary Poster,
   by Larry Noble, 27"x41" (1990) 15.00
The Empire Strikes Back Movie poster repro-
   duction, 24"x36". 5.00
Return of the Jedi 10th Anniversary Advance
   Poster, 27"x40" (1993) 15.00
   Deluxe version, gold foil border 50.00
Return of the Jedi 10th Anniversary Style A poster,
   27"x40" by Kazo Sano (1994) 15.00
Star Wars Checklist Poster, 27"x40" (Killian Enter-
   prises 1995) full color reproductions of all
   movie one-sheet posters and variants 15.00
Star Wars: A New Hope movie poster, 27"x40" 15.00
Heir to the Empire poster, from book cover, 22"x28"
   (1992) Tom Jung art. 12.00
Jabba's Palace Poster, 24"x36". 6.00
Darth Vader Photomosaic Poster 24"x36" (PHL
   #568, 1998) 10.50
Yoda Photomosaic Poster 24"x36" (PHL #567, 1998) . 10.50
Wisdom of Yoda Poster 24"x36" 6.00

Star Wars Radio Poster, advertising that the shows are "Now Available on Cassettes and Compact Discs" (1993) 15.00
Return of the Jedi Collector's Poster (#2909) 5.00
Star Wars: A New Hope Collector's Poster (#2910) 5.00
The Empire Strikes Back Collector's Poster (#2911) . . . 5.00
Return of the Jedi Collector's Poster (#2909) 5.00
Star Wars Space Battle Poster (PTW #651) 5.00
Star Wars Movie Poster, 24"x36" (PTW #531) 5.00
The Empire Strikes Back Movie Poster, 24"x36"
    (PTW #532) 5.00
Star Wars: A New Hope Video Poster, 24"x36"
    (PTW #740) 5.00
The Empire Strikes Back Video Poster, 24"x36"
    (PTW #741) 5.00
Return of the Jedi Video Poster, 24"x36" (PTW #742) . . 5.00
Star Wars: "All I Need to Know About Life I Learned
    From *Star Wars*" Poster, 24"x36" (PTW #743) 5.00
Star Wars: X-Wing Fighters Poster, 24"x36" (PTW
    #744) 5.00
Return of the Jedi–Rancor Poster, 24"x36" (PTW
    #745) 5.00
Star Wars: Star Destroyer Poster, 24"x36" (PTW #748) . 5.00
The Art of *Star Wars*: Luke Battles Darth Vader
    poster, Ralph McQuarrie art, 24"x36" (PTW #767) . 5.00
Star Wars Special Edition Gold Ingot poster, 24"x36"
    (#789) 5.50
Star Wars Special Edition Movie Poster, 24"x36"
    (#795) 5.50
Star Wars Special Edition *The Empire Strikes Back*
    Movie Poster, 24"x36" (#796) 5.50
Star Wars Special Edition *Return of the Jedi* Movie
    Poster, 24"x36" (#797) 5.50
Death Star Trench Poster, 24"x36" (#3166, 1997) 5.00
Star Wars Cantina Poster, 23"x35" (#3173, 1997) 5.00
Star Wars Darth Vader Poster (#2905, 1997) 5.00
Star Wars Cutaway *Millennium Falcon* Poster (1997) . 20.00
Star Wars Cutaway *Millennium Falcon* deluxe
    poster, signed and numbered, certificate of
    authenticity (1997) 40.00
Star Wars Cutaway X-Wing/TIE Fighter poster (1997) . 20.00
Star Wars Cutaway X-Wing/TIE Fighter deluxe
    poster, signed and numbered, certificate of
    authenticity (1997) 40.00
AT-AT and Snowspeeder Cutaway Poster, 36"x24"
    black and white 20.00
    Deluxe, signed and numbered 40.00
Boba Fett Poster, smoking gun, 24"x36" (1997) 10.00
Star Wars Cantina denizens poster print 17"x36" by
    Tsuneo Sanda (1997) 15.00
Yoda, 24"x36" by Tsuneo Sanda (1997) 15.00
George Lucas: The Creative Impulse by Drew
    Struzan, 24"x36" (1997) 15.00
Slave I by Tsuneo Sands, 24"x36" (1997) 15.00
Millennium Falcon pursued by the Empire, 24"x36"
    (1997) 15.00
Star Wars: A New Hope Special Edition One-
    Sheets by Drew Struzan, 27"x40" (1997) 20.00
The Empire Strikes Back Special Edition One-
    Sheets by Drew Struzan, 27"x40" (1997) 20.00
The *Return of the Jedi* Special Edition One-
    Sheets by Drew Struzan, 27"x40" (1997) 20.00

Food Premiums
Burger Chef Premium posters (1978)
    Luke Skywalker 5.00
    R2-D2 . . . . 5.00

    Chewbacca 5.00
    Darth Vader 5.00
General Mills Premium posters (1978)
    Star Wars montage 5.00
    TIE Fighter & X-Wing 5.00
    Star Destroyer 5.00
    R2-D2 & C-3PO 5.00
Proctor and Gamble Premium posters (1978)
    Ben Kenobi & Darth Vader 5.00
    R2-D2 & C-3PO 5.00
    Death Star 5.00
Nestea Premium poster (1980)
    Luke Skywalker 4.00
    Darth Vader 4.00
Burger King Premium poster (1980)
    Hoth 3.00
    Dagobah 3.00
    Bespin 3.00
The Empire Strikes Back montage by Boris Vallejo
    (Coca Cola 1980) 15.00
Proctor and Gamble Premium Poster (1980)
    Luke Skywalker 3.00
    R2-D2 & C-3PO 3.00
    Darth Vader 3.00
    Bespin Scenes 3.00
Dixie Cups Story card poster (1981) 10.00
Hi-C *Return of the Jedi* poster (1983) 5.00
Oral-B *Return of the Jedi* poster (1983) 5.00

Star Wars Trilogy Special Edition Pepsi mail-in
    posters, 24"x36" originally sold as a set for
    $9.99 and proof of purchase, set 15.00
    Star Wars, picturing Darth Vader 5.00
    The Empire Strikes Back, picturing C-3PO 5.00
    Return of the Jedi, picturing Yoda 5.00

Retail Posters
Star Wars
    Sword montage 20.00
    R2-D2 & C-3PO 15.00
    Luke Skywalker 20.00
    Princess Leia 25.00
Star Wars concert 30.00
Star Wars radio program 30.00
The Empire Strikes Back
    The Empire Strikes Back 5.00
    Boba Fett 10.00
    Darth Vader & Stormtroopers 5.00
The Empire Strikes Back Fan club montage poster . . . 5.00
Vehicle scene 7.00
Darth Vader montage 5.00
Read and the Force is With You (Yoda) 10.00
The Empire Strikes Back radio program 15.00
Darth Vader, life size 10.00
Return of the Jedi Space Battle (fan club) 10.00
Return of the Jedi poster album 10.00
The Ewok Adventure 5.00
Caravan of Courage, style A 5.00
Caravan of Courage, style B 5.00
Star Tours posters, 8 different, each 3.00
First Ten Years poster 7.00
First Ten Years mural poster 10.00
Star Wars Movie one-sheet poster, 24"x36" (Portal
    PTW #531, 1992) 5.00
The Empire Strikes Back Movie one-sheet poster,
    24"x36" (Portal PTW#532, 1992) 5.00

Return of the Jedi Movie one-sheet poster, 24"x36" (Portal PTW#533, 1992) 5.00
Star Wars: Space Battle Poster one-sheet poster, 24"x36" (Portal PTW#651, 1991) 5.00

PRINTS

Shadows of the Empire signed print, 24"x36" by Dave Dorman (1996) $30.00
Boba Fett: Bounty Hunter Print, by Dave Dorman, 15"x20" on 19"x24" paper, limited to 1,500 copies, signed and numbered (Rolling Thunder Graphics 1995) 45.00
Star Wars: Smuggler's Moon Print, by Dave Dorman 15"x21" on 19"x24" paper, limited to 1,500 copies, signed and numbered (Rolling Thunder Graphics 1995) 45.00
Star Wars: Dark Empire II Print, by Dave Dorman 16"x21" on 19"x24" paper, limited to 1,500 copies, signed and numbered (Rolling Thunder Graphics 1995) 45.00
Obi-Wan Kenobi Art Print, by Dave Dorman 12"x 15½" on 16"x20" paper, limited to 1,500 copies, signed and numbered (Rolling Thunder Graphics 1996) 45.00

TIN SIGNS
Tin Signs International

Embossed Movie Posters
Star Wars, tin litho, 15"x24". $25.00
The Empire Strikes Back, tin litho, 15"x24" 25.00
Return of the Jedi, tin litho, 15"x24" 25.00

1997 Batch
Star Wars: A New Hope, tin litho, 12"x17". 13.00

Star Wars: A New Hope, tin litho, horizontal poster 17"x12" 13.00
The Empire Strikes Back, tin litho, 12"x17" 13.00
Return of the Jedi, tin litho, 12"x17" 13.00

HOLOGRAMS

Darth Vader Hologram Picture, 5"x3" in 8"x10" matte (A.H. Prismatic #1021/99, 1994) $30.00
Millennium Falcon Hologram Picture, 3"x2" in 5"x7" matt (A.H. Prismatic #1020/33, 1994) 15.00
Mounted on Acrylic display stand (A.H. Prismatic #1020/33AS, 1994) 15.00
Star Wars Deluxe Fight Scene Limited Edition 3-D Hologram (Fantasma 90MT-MLF, 1993) in deluxe 8"x10" Black Matte 30.00
Millennium Falcon Deluxe Hologram Picture 3½"x5" in a 8"x10" matte (90MT-MLF, 1994) 25.00

Star Wars Holograms (A.H. Prismatic, 1997)
Darth Vader matted (#1021-99PM, 1997) 30.00
Millennium Falcon on Acrylic Stand (#1020-33AS, 1997) 17.00
Millennium Falcon matted (#1020-33PM, 1997) . . 17.00

LIGHTED POSTERS

Star Wars Neon Movie Poster (Neonetics 1993) framed $200.00
Darth Vader Neon Framed Picture (Neonetics 1995) . 225.00
Star Wars Millennium Falcon Neon Framed Picture (Neonetics 1994) 225.00
Star Wars Millennium Falcon LED Framed Picture (Neonetics 1994) 140.00

Trading Cards 210
Shampoo 150
Ships 223
Shoelaces 89
Shoes and Footwear 89
Side Gunner 222
Silkscreened T-shirts 87
Silver-colored Coins 94
Slave I 220, 222
Sleeping Bags 152
Sleepwear 88
Snaggletooth 60
Snaggletooth figure, blue 225
Snap Kits Model Kits 166
Snowtrooper 60
Soaps 151
Socks 88
Soda Containers 137
Sonic Controlled Land Speeder . . . 220
Soundtracks 185
Sourcebooks 141
Space Ships Model Kits 165
Space Shooters 188
Special Event Posters 231
Speeder Bike Vehicles 223
Splinter Of The Mind's Eye comics . 110
Squawk Boxes 133
Squid Head 60
Stamp Collecting 116
Stamping 116
Stand-ups 182
Standees 182
Star Destroyer Commander
    (Death Squad Commander) 38
Star Destroyer ship 223
Star Wars
    Action figures 3
    Action figure three-packs 13
    Album Stickers 198
    Caps 217
    CCGs 145
    Comics 101
    Dolls 121
    Model Kits 165
    Playsets 225
    Topps trading cards 195
    Vehicles 219
Star Wars Finest trading cards 210
Star Wars Galaxy
    Bend-ems trading cards 209
    Card T-shirts 85
    Magazine 174
    Trading cards 203
Star Wars Galaxy Two trading cards . . 205
Star Wars Galaxy Three trading cards . 207
Star Wars General Mills Cereals
    trading cards 198
Star Wars In 3-D comics 103
Star Wars Insider Magazine 173
Star Wars Mastervision trading cards . 209
Star Wars Merlin trading cards 208
Star Wars Sugar Free Gum Wrappers . 198
Star Wars Technical Journal 174
Star Wars/The Empire Strikes Back
    Burger King trading cards 198
Star Wars Trilogy
    Special Edition trading cards 216
    Widevision trading cards 215
Star Wars Unlimited CCG 146
Star Wars Vehicles trading cards . . . 216

Star Wars Widevision
    3-D trading cards 216
Star Wars Widevision trading cards . . 211
Star Wars Wonder Bread trading cards 198
Star Wars: A New Hope comics 103
Star Wars: Crimson Empire comics . . 105
Star Wars: Dark Empire
    Comics 105
    Metal trading cards 218
Star Wars: Dark Force Rising comics . 106
Star Wars: Dark Forces comics 106
Star Wars: Droids comics 107
Star Wars: Empire's End comics 107
Star Wars: Heir To The Empire comics 107
Star Wars: River Of Chaos comics . . . 108
Star Wars: Shadow Stalker comics . . . 110
Star Wars: Shadows Of The Empire . . 109
    Metal trading cards 218
    Trading cards 210
Star Wars: Splinter Of The Mind's Eye
    comics 110
Star Wars: Tales From Mos Eisley
    comics 110
Star Wars: Tales Of The Jedi comics . . 110
Star Wars: The Last Command comics 108
Star Wars: The Protocol Offensive
    comics 108
Statues 192
Steel Models 169
Steins 83
Sticking 117
Sticking: Magnetic 117
Stickpins 90
Stills 186
Store Displays 179
Stormtroopers 60
Structors Model Kits 167
Sugar Free Gum Wrappers 198
Suncatchers 117
Super Star Destroyer Executor ship . . 223
Supplements 144
Suspenders 89
Sweatshirts 85
Switcheroos 154
Swoop Trooper figure 223
Swoop vehicle 223
Sy Snootles 13
T-16 Skyhopper 222
T-shirts 85
Tales From Mos Eisley comics 110
Tales Of The Jedi comics 110
Tales Of The Jedi: Dark Lords Of
    The Sith comics 111
Tales Of The Jedi: The Sith
    War comics 111
Talking Toys 133
Tankards 83
Tatooine Skiff 222
Tauntaun 223
Tauntaun and Luke Skywalker
    In Hoth Gear 224
Teebo 61
The Empire Strikes Back
    Action figures 3
    Dolls 122
    Hershey's trading cards 201
    Playsets 225
    Model Kits 166
    Topps trading cards 199
    Vehicles 220

Widevision trading cards 212
The Last Command comics 108
The Protocol Offensive comics 108
Theatrical Posters 230
Three Packs 26
TIE Fighter 219, 222
TIE Fighter Pilot 61
TIE Interceptor 221
Tie-dye T-shirts 87
Ties — Poly 88
Ties — Silk 88
Toothbrushes 150
Tote Bags 92
Towels 151
Trading Cards 195
Transforming Action Sets
    MicroMachines 160
Transition — Red "Collection" Cards . . 19
Tri-logo "Series" action figures 7
Tri-pod Laser Cannon 226
Turret and Probot Playset 225
Tusken Raider (Sand People) 62, 224
20/21 Back Cards 3
24K Gold Cards 218
12-back Cards 3
Twin-Pod Cloud Car 220
2-1B 62, 227
Two-packs 18, 27
Ugnaughts figure 62, 225
Umbrellas 89
Underwear 88
Valentine Cards 172
Vans and Racers 227
Vehicle Maintenance Energizer 226
Vehicles 219
Vehicles, Creatures, Playsets
    and Accessories 219
Vests 85
Video Board Game 132
Video Tapes 185
Vinyl Dioramas 129
Vinyl Figures 128
Vinyl Keychains 93
Vinyl Model Kits 168
Wall Art 228
Wallet Cards 178
Wallets 91
Walrus Man: (Ponda Baba) 53, 225
Wampa 223
Wampa and Luke Skywalker In
    Hoth Gear 224
Warok 63
Wastepaper Baskets 154
Watches 91
Weapons 187
Weequay 63
Wholesale Club Three-packs 26
Wicket The Ewok Jewelry 91
Wicket W. Warrick 63
Window Decals 191
Wonder Bread trading cards 198
X-Ray Fleet MicroMachines 162
X-wing Fighter 219, 221, 222
X-wing Rogue Squadron comics . . . 112
X-wing Series 71
Y-wing Fighter 221
Yoda 63
Young Adult Novels 71
Zuckuss (classic) 64
Zuckuss (formerly 4-LOM) 54